Christ Has

A Biblical Case for Relational Unity in the Seventh-day Adventist Church

Gregory J. Allen & Carol Easley Allen

Unity Publishers

Huntsville, Alabama

Unity Publishers
Huntsville, Alabama

Edited by
Gatsinzi Ezra Basaninyenzi
Cover design by
Barbara Upshaw – Aura Graphics and Design
Book illustrations by
Lance Brazelton
Typeface
Garamond 11/9

ISBN 978-0-9994615-0-1 (print)
ISBN 978-0-9994615-1-8 (digital)

Printed in the United States of America

With praise to God in Christ

And in memory of our parents

William Anthony Allen
Mary Elizabeth Bell Allen

Paul Allen Easley
Koneta Seona Phillips Easley

Acknowledgments

This book is the culmination of a journey of over twelve years that we have shared with many family members and friends. We studied Paul's letter to the Romans for two and a half years with a multicultural group that included William and Terri Mitchell and Deora and Arlene LuValle Johnson, who are African American; Sifa and Alisi Uaine from Tonga; Desiree McGann, a Canadian Jamaican; and Israel Mutema from Zimbabwe. Dwayne and Eunice Duncombe and Marlon and Valerie Reid read an early manuscript and advised us on making the document more readable. Craig and Janis Newborn read the book with us, chapter by chapter, and provided invaluable editorial and substantive comments. Gatsinzi Ezra Basaninyenzi meticulously edited the final copy. We received insights from a Pauline specialist, Rollin Ramsaran, who reviewed the manuscript. He would not agree with everything in this book, and yet his contributions have made this book better than it would be otherwise. Any shortcomings in the book are ours alone.

A community of believers also gave us important feedback on our work; they include Elliott Osborne, James Kyle, Cheryl Easley, Junie Saint-Clair, Kristopher Hicks, and Anthony Krones. We thank God for Lance Brazelton who created the illustrations and gave us significant help in the mechanics of publishing, Barbara Upshaw who designed the cover, Sandra Burton who prepared the manuscript for publication, and Clara Ramirez-Johnson for the forthcoming Spanish translation of this volume. We also thank those who supported our efforts and loved us through this process over the years, our families, and most significantly our siblings and their spouses: Lois Jean Speaks, Fern Maxine Ross, Barbara Martin, Theresa Allen, Cheryl Easley, Jean and Victor Wallen, William and Andralyn Allen, and Brenda and Drake Barber. Many friends also shared our journey including T. Marshall Kelly, Ephraim and Keratiloe Gwebu, Barry and Nancy Levy, Prentice and Carol Sorrells, and the Harvest Seventh-day Adventist Church family.

Finally, we thank Jesus Christ for trusting us with this important task in His service. We continue to be amazed that He chose us to write this book. Our hope is that it will be the blessing to you that it has been to us.

Contents

Preface

There was excitement, a palpable sense of expectancy, in the air. It was inspection day. After many months of work, developing the plans, raising funds, and clearing the land, the first stage of our church building project had been completed. We stood on the church foundation with its anchor bolts, wire mesh, and exposed rebar, waiting until the building inspector from Monrovia Public Works arrived.

As we walked along the building site, discussing its readiness for construction, the inspector raised a question, completely off topic. Why are you building this church? Puzzled by the question, we reminded him that the city of Monrovia had taken our church building by right of eminent domain. Dismissing the response, the inspector reminded us of the existing *white Adventist church* just a few miles away.

We will never forget his next cutting, pointed words, "You Adventists believe that you have *the truth,* but at least we Jehovah's Witnesses know how to worship and witness together." We were left silent; no appeal to the Sabbath or sanctuary doctrines would suffice. The foundation was approved that day, yet, we had been inspected at a level we had not anticipated and we failed!

At this very moment, the whole world, both secular and religious, is characterized by hatred, alienation, and division. This animosity is played out especially along ethnic, racial, caste, and tribal lines. Based on long-standing grievances, either real or perceived, open ethnic and racial enmity exists between Ukrainians and Russians, Palestinians and Israelis, Tamil and Sinhalese, Kurds and Iraqis, Ethiopians and Eritreans, Chinese and Japanese, Mexicans and native Indians, Australians and the so-called Aboriginal people, and East Indians and Guyanese of African descent, to name a few.

In the wake of the very divisive presidential campaign of 2016, there exists in the United States, as we write, a state of thinly veiled racial intolerance, especially among whites and people of color. Interestingly, these ethnic and racial divisions are not mitigated by religious affiliation whether Protestant, Catholic, Jewish, Muslim, or Hindu. A sobering reality is that being Seventh-day Adventist makes no difference in this regard.

In His Farewell Discourse, spoken some two thousand years ago, Jesus gives His disciples a command and closes His remarks with an end-time prayer for all who would believe in Him in response to the gospel proclamation. As Jesus prepares to die on behalf of sinful humanity, He gives the eleven remaining apostles a decree that is to form the bedrock of their life and ministry. Jesus states, "A new commandment I give to you, that you love one another: just as I have loved you, you also are to love one another." (Jn. 13:34 ESV; cf. 15:12, 17).

With stirring simplicity, Jesus heightens a directive given by Moses to Israel (Lev. 19:18). His disciples are to demonstrate more than love for neighbor. They are to receive and extend a mutual love that mirrors His own self-sacrificing love: a love that is willing to lay down life for a friend (Jn. 15:13). *The disciples of Jesus are to love one another just as He loves.* Yet, Jesus goes further. He says, "By this all people will know that you are My disciples, if you have love for one another" (Jn. 13:35).

Jesus establishes His own brand of love as the mark of authentic discipleship. In fact, He identifies self-sacrificing love among believers as the second of the two essential commands (Mt. 22:36-40). As important as is the fourth commandment, Jesus does not say that unbelievers will be convinced by our Sabbath profession.

No! Jesus maintains that all people will be able to spot His genuine followers by their unconditional love one for another: sacrificial love with no regard for ethnicity, race, tribe, or caste. Why is not this command at the heart of Adventist faith and practice? How can those who have not been reconciled to each other through love be ambassadors of reconciliation for God?

Jesus not only commands mutual love among his disciples, He prays for their unity. Jesus entreats:

> I ask not only on behalf of these, but also on behalf of those who will believe in me through their word, *that they may all be one.* As you, Father, are in me and I am in you, may they also be in us, so that the world may believe that you have sent me. The glory that you have given me I have given them, *so that they may be one,* as we are one, I in them and you in me, *that they may become completely one,* so that the world may know that you have sent me and have loved them even as you have loved me (Jn. 17:20-23).

Having prayed for Himself and for His eleven disciples, Jesus prays to His Father for all who would come to believe in Him based on the word of the apostles: those who would believe in Him between His resurrection and second coming. What is the focus of the end-time prayer of Christ? In this concise plea, Jesus prays three times for oneness, indeed, perfect unity among His future disciples (cf. Jn. 17:11). Yet, Jesus does not pray for ordinary unity, a unity created by believers. He prays for an intimacy analogous to the eternal oneness experienced between the Father and the Son. Jesus is asking the Father to produce a divine oneness among all end-time believers. He envisions a unity among believers that becomes caught up in the oneness that is God.

And what is the purpose of this complete unity among the disciples of Jesus Christ? Jesus says with breath-taking clarity, "So that the world may know that you have sent me and have loved them even as you have loved me." According to Jesus, unbelievers will only come to accept Him as their Savior and Lord sent by God the Father, if there is a manifestation of divine love and oneness among genuine believers.

If God-produced oneness is what Jesus prays for to convince the world of His saving mission, then no amount of doctrine, health care, education, or evangelism will suffice. There is no doubt that Christ Himself called the Seventh-day Adventist Church into existence and gifted it for the glory of the Father. Yet, we as a church are deficient in mutual love and oneness across ethnic, racial, caste, and tribal lines. Adventism has much to give to the world. However, the authenticity of our witness is deficient, in the absence of a relational oneness produced by Christ's Spirit.

Most Christians, including most Adventists, are unaware that the apostle Paul writes his letter to the Romans to echo Jesus' call for reconciliation and unity among believers. *Christ Has Welcomed You* is a Christ-commissioned call to both corporate and individual repentance and confession in the Seventh-day Adventist Church worldwide. We believe that at this moment in salvation history, Jesus desires a unity in Adventism that only He can produce for the sake of the world. Will we yield to His love?

Introduction

If we were to ask you what the Seventh-day Adventist Fundamental Belief #14 teaches, could you give the answer?[1] We have asked this question as we traveled teaching church members around the world—in South Africa, India, the Philippines, Kenya, Ukraine, and Malawi, to name a few spots—and have always received a blank stare. As you probably know, Adventists have 28 fundamental beliefs. Some are popular and well-known, for example, the Sabbath, the sanctuary, and the state of the dead. But #14 is unknown to most Adventists. Why is this so? Why is this doctrine rarely preached, taught, or practiced?

Perhaps the answer to these questions lies in our denominational emphasis on doctrinal unity. As a church, we are careful to translate the same Sabbath School Lesson Study for members around the world in order to maintain uniformity of doctrinal belief. While doctrinal unity is important, it is not primary, according to Scripture (Mt. 23:23; Jn. 13:34-35). It is not as important as relational unity in the body of Christ. This disjunction is evidenced by our willingness to live with relational disunity among races, ethnicities, tribes, and castes. We as Adventists seem to have an uncanny ability to isolate, separate, and elevate doctrinal "truth" from Christ and the community. The resulting relational disunity is often accepted among us as a given.

So, you have probably guessed that Fundamental Belief #14 has something to do with relationships. And you are right. It is entitled "Unity in the Body of Christ." Here it is:

> The church is one body with many members, called from every nation, kindred, tongue, and people. In Christ we are a new creation; distinctions of race, culture, learning, and nationality, and differences between high and low, rich and poor, male and female, must not be divisive among us. We are all equal in Christ, who by one Spirit has bonded us into one fellowship with Him and with one another; we are to serve and be served without partiality or reservation. Through the revelation of Jesus Christ in the Scriptures we share the same faith and hope, and reach out in one witness to all. This unity has its source in the oneness of the triune God, who has adopted us as His children (Rom. 12:4, 5; 1 Cor. 12:12-14; Mt. 28:19, 20; Ps. 133:1; 2 Cor. 5:16, 17; Acts 17:26, 27; Gal. 3:27, 29; Col. 3:10-15; Eph. 4:14-16; 4:1-6; John 17:20-23).[2]

One may question the meaning of the statement, "distinctions of race, culture, learning, and nationality . . . must not be divisive among us." Should not these distinctions be rejected? It could be argued from the statement as it stands, that these distinctions are in some way acceptable in the culture and the church, and that even though they exist, they should not divide us. According to Ellen White,

> No distinction on account of nationality, race, or caste, *is recognized by God.* He is the Maker of all mankind. All men are of one family by creation, and all are one through redemption. Christ came to demolish every wall of partition, to throw open every compartment of the temple, that every soul may have free access to God. His love is so broad, so deep, so full, that it penetrates everywhere. It lifts out of Satan's circle the poor souls who have been deluded by his deceptions.[3]

Is not Ellen White suggesting that the recognition of such distinctions is sin? She maintains that these distinctions are not recognized by God, and thus should be rejected. Yet, nowhere in Adventist official statements is ethnocentrism, racism, tribalism, or caste called sin.[4] What is more disturbing, unlike many Christian denominations around the world who have attempted to confront this problem, Adventism is generally comfortable with ethnocentrism, the relational status quo, especially most church leaders. This is our proverbial elephant in the room, our acceptable sin.

Description of the Problem

Although as Seventh-day Adventists we tout our doctrinal unity and structural diversity, global Adventism, in most cases, mirrors the ethnocentrism of the societies in which it resides. Unfortunately, the values, attitudes, and practices in this area of Adventist life resemble the world.

We must begin to address this problem with definitions and clarifications. How is ethnocentrism defined? Where did it start? Are ethnocentrism and racism synonymous? How has ethnocentrism affected human relations globally, especially in the Seventh-day Adventist church, i.e., what are its consequences? We can give brief answers here, and more comprehensive answers as we journey through this book.

Ethnocentrism as defined by anthropologists combines a belief in the superiority of one's own culture with using one's culture as a standard to judge other cultures. "Ethnocentrism is also defined as a feeling that one's own group has a mode of living, values and patterns of adaptation that are superior to other groups."[5] For the purposes of this book ethnocentrism, defined loosely, is an inclusive term that embodies the idea of a personal or collective sense of superiority based on ethnicity or nationality, race, tribe, or caste.

From the Greek root *ethnos*, "a people or group," ethnocentrism refers to the belief that one's own culture is better than that of others; thus one's worldview is centered in his or her own way of life. Ethnocentrism, to the extent that it posits a particular culture as normative, regards as outsiders those who differ. Because the "standard" culture is perceived as natural, beautiful, right, and important, those cultures that differ are viewed conversely as inhuman, irrational, unnatural, and simply wrong.

Ethnocentrism is a prevailing part of the human condition; it is learned through the process of socialization and it persists because it fulfills the important psychological needs for power and a sense of belonging. Ethnocentrism is the basis for the ways people feel about themselves in contrast to others, and everyone is ethnocentric regardless of how open-minded they claim to be.[6]

> Ethnocentric cultures consider their own achievements, worldviews, social and political customs and practices, as well as their religious and theoretical beliefs and traditions as something good and special. In most cases, ethnocentric cultures base their self-understanding on shared customs and values, on a common language and history, and mainly on ethnic concepts of kinship and consanguinity.[7]

Ethnocentrism as a construct started with the ancient Greeks who, around the fifth century B.C., began to use the term "Hellenes" to denote all Greek-speaking people. The Greek historian Herodotus was the first to define "Greeks as a whole" based on shared blood, language, religious practices, and way of life. The Greeks created the concept of the barbarian as the "other": a pejorative term from the Greek "bar-bar," that was the sound a dog made, like the English "bow-wow." To the Greeks, the speech of barbarians, those who did not speak the Greek language, sounded like the barking of dogs; barbarians spoke gibberish.[8]

This derogatory term, "barbarian," represented the differences between ethnic Greeks and all others. The Greeks considered their culture superior to all others and looked down upon foreigners. The fact that most of the slaves held by the Greeks of the fifth century were not Greek contributed to the perception of barbarians (non-Greeks) as slavish and inferior by nature.[9] It is important to note, however, that the negative distinctions that the ancient Greeks made between themselves and others were not based on color-prejudice.[10]

Ethnocentric Greeks portrayed themselves as civilized, free, self-controlled, intelligent, democratic, egalitarian, and moral. Barbarians, on the other hand, were slavish, immoral, stupid, tyrannical, hierarchical, lazy, cruel, and uncivilized. The Greeks held that barbarians were incapable of self-government, and therefore, for their own good, should be dominated by the Greeks. This position formed the basis for the more modern notion that people of color were, like the barbarians, incapable of self-rule and therefore open to colonization and enslavement by Europeans who were said to inherit the characteristics of the ancient Greeks. "With the spread of Christianity, Greek views about the inferiority of barbarians were overlaid with a further sense of their religious and moral shortcomings"[11]

Unfortunately, the Romans adopted not only the word "barbarian," but also Greek ethnocentric attitudes that over time came to characterize European and American prejudices against non-Western peoples.[12] But contemporary ethnocentrism is not limited to invidious distinctions between European and American prejudice against non-Westerners. Ethnocentrism, as a pervasive human attitude, manifests itself wherever a person or group can engage in self-definition over and against another person or group. So we see tribalism in Africa, caste in India, nationalism in Europe and South America, and racism in America.

Despite the fact that there are negative consequences to ethnocentrism, as we shall see, all of the major religions—Christianity, Judaism, Islam, and Hinduism—accept division among people based on ethnicity as a cultural given. There are many examples of these consequences in the post-modern world; one of the most recent is the divisive reaction to the presidency of Barack Obama, the first black person to hold this position in a predominantly white America.

Ethnocentrism and racism, although related, are not identical. Racism is the belief that some races are inherently superior or inferior. Ethnocentrism, the belief in the superiority of one's own group, becomes racism when that belief is transformed into an ideology of power that serves the vested interests of one's own group at all costs and in any circumstances. Race is a fairly recent concept; it is only 500 years old, and the word was first recorded in the Oxford English Dictionary in 1902.[13] One author has attributed it to the discovery of the Americas and the establishment of trade routes to India, the rise of the African slave trade, the increased wealth and prestige of white people as a result of the Industrial Revolution, and Darwin's theory of evolution that posited the survival of the fittest. White people, of course, considered themselves to be the fittest.[14]

A Biblical View of Ethnicity

The Bible's treatment of the subject of ethnicity is incidental. Ethnicity has significance for believers only to the extent that it fits into God's saving plan through Jesus Christ. Thus, Paul in two passages of Scripture states,

> Therefore remember that formerly you, the Gentiles in the flesh, who are called "Uncircumcision" by the so-called "Circumcision," which is performed in the flesh by human hands . . . But now in Christ Jesus you who formerly were far off have been brought near by the blood of Christ. For He Himself is our peace, who made both *groups into one* and broke down the barrier of the dividing wall, by abolishing in His flesh the enmity, which is the Law of commandments contained in ordinances, so that in Himself He might make the two into one new man, *thus* establishing peace, and might reconcile them both in one body to God through the cross, by it having put to death the enmity (Eph. 2:11, 13-16).

> "There is neither Jew nor Gentile . . . for you are all one in Christ" (Gal. 3:28).

Scripture assumes that all humanity has a single origin. Paul makes this claim in his address to the Athenians at the Areopagus.

> The God who made the world and everything in it is the Lord of heaven and earth and does not live in temples built by human hands. And he is not served by human hands, as if he needed anything. Rather, he himself gives everyone life and breath and everything else. *From one man he made all the nations, that they should inhabit the whole earth; and he marked out their appointed times in history and the boundaries of their lands* (Acts 17:24-26 NIV).

In the hearing of pagan Greeks, who held a very different understanding of human origins, Paul echoes the Genesis assertion of a common human ancestry. He establishes that Adam is the father of all humankind and argues for the sovereignty of the Creator over the nations, including their time in history and the territories in which they would reside (cf. Dan. 2:31-45; Gen. 10:1-32).

In the Old Testament Genesis narrative, to which Paul refers, Adam and Eve are created by God in God's image: two persons yet possessing one nature. Together they paradoxically reflect the divine image: Father, Son, and Spirit—a unity in diversity (Gen. 1:26-27; 2:21-24). Yet, God's essential nature of selfless love and holiness provides the essence of human identity (Ex. 34:6-7). Adam and Eve are commanded to populate the earth as bearers of the image of God (Gen. 1:28). From the perspective of Genesis, God's ideal for humanity is corrupted by human pride and disobedience: a rejection of God's image. Consequentially, alienation from God results in human estrangement one from another. Cain's resentment of, enmity against, and murder of his brother Abel provide the prototypical example. Thus, from the beginning, Scripture depicts two families on the earth: those who would respond to God's promise of salvation through the Seed and those who would not (Gen. 3:1-7, 15; 4:1-11).

According to Scripture, where does ethnicity begin? Some would start with the table of nations, which describes human descent through the sons of Noah—Shem, Ham, and Japheth—after the flood (Gen. 10:1-32). However, this genealogy and its description of the dispersion of humanity assumes God's command in Genesis 9 and human rebellion in Genesis 11.

Genesis 9 establishes that before God makes a covenant with Noah and his sons, God twice reiterates the command first given to Adam and Eve; "Be fruitful and multiply; populate the earth abundantly and multiply in it" (Gen. 9:1, 7 NIV; cf. 1:28). As one human family in covenant relationship with God, all humanity was to spread out across the earth. Shem, Ham, and Japheth, three sons with one language, were to cover the earth as one family subject to the sovereignty of God.

In chapter 11, Genesis tells the story of humanity's post-flood disobedience and pride. It is in this context that ethnic identity is first introduced.

> Now the whole earth had one language and the same words. And as they migrated from the east, they came upon a plain in the land of Shinar and settled there. And they said to one another, "Come, let us make bricks, and burn them thoroughly." And they had brick for stone, and bitumen for mortar. Then they said, "Come, let us build ourselves a city, and a tower with its top in the heavens, and let us make a name for ourselves; otherwise we shall be scattered abroad upon the face of the whole earth." The Lord came down to see the city and the tower, which mortals had built. And the Lord said, "Look, *they are one people, and they have all one language;* and this is only the beginning of what they will do; nothing that they propose to do will now be impossible for them. Come, let us go down, and *confuse their language* there, so that they will not understand one another's speech." So the Lord scattered them abroad from there over the face of all the earth, and they left off building the city. Therefore it was called Babel, because there the Lord confused the language of all the earth; and from there the Lord scattered them abroad over the face of all the earth (11:1-9).

The Tower of Babel narrative reveals three critical truths related to the origin of ethnicity. First, when the story begins, humanity is composed of one people sharing one language. There is no ethnic distinction as they migrated east. Second, when this homogenous people settle on the plain of Shinar, they do so in direct opposition to God's covenant and the command given to Noah and his sons. Humanity was to spread throughout the earth as those in covenant relationship with God (Gen. 9:7, 9-17). Moreover, their reason for settling in the land of Shinar, building a city and a tower, is clear: "Let us make a name for ourselves; otherwise we shall be scattered abroad upon the face of the whole earth." These actions are taken in conscious opposition to God. Third, God responds to the hubris of this united people with an act that includes evaluation and judgment.

God acknowledges their sinful unity and its potential for evil. God confuses their language to diminish their ability to act against the divine intent. It is at this point that distinct ethnic identity is introduced. God creates ethnicity as Plan B. Ethnicity is created through the confusion of human language within the context of human rebellion against God. Ethnic diversity was not God's original intent. In its essence, it stands in opposition to the image of God: the unity in diversity of God. Ethnicity is created by God in response to human disobedience and pride. From this point in human history, distinct ethnic identity is used to dominate and oppress those who are considered the other. In fact, Scripture seems to indicate that, ultimately, ethnocentrism reflects Lucifer's prideful attitude towards God, especially the second person of the Godhead (Is. 14:12-20; Ezek. 28:11-19; Rev. 12:1-17). It is on this basis that one may conclude that all "isms" (race, tribe, sex, class, and age) originate with Satan (Rom. 16:17-20).

In response to pervasive human disobedience, God, based on sovereign choice, chooses Abram.

Genesis suggests that God's choice of Abram has little to do with his ethnicity. There is no indication that the descendants of Shem as a whole honor God's covenant (Gen. 11:10-32). On the contrary, Terah the father of Abram, a direct descendant of Shem, and his household worship idols (Josh. 24:2; cf. Gen. 35:1-4).[15] God calls Abram out of the land of his birth, Ur of the Chaldees, away from his kindred, and even his father's house, to a land chosen by God. Abram's response of relational faith in God's person and promise becomes the sole criterion for right relationship with God (Gen. 12:1-9). Covenant fidelity was to be maintained, not for the sake of ethnic exclusivity, e.g., prohibition against intermarriage, but rather to avoid the idolatry that characterized the nations (Dt. 7:3-4). In fact, Abraham and his progeny are called to covenant faithfulness for the sake of the nations (Gen. 12:3).

The prophetic image of Daniel 2 chronicles the rise and fall of ethnic powers throughout human history (2:31-45). From Nebuchadnezzar—the Chaldean—to the ten European nations, humans exercise dominion until the second coming of Christ. It is important to note that beginning with Greek rule ethnocentrism became normative. Persons of European descent, especially males, have exercised power and privilege that challenge God's dominion and will do so until the eschatological reign of Christ. Even Adventist leadership, once characterized as "kingly power," is affected by this idolatry and attempted usurpation of Christ's Lordship.[16]

In the New Testament, ethnicity becomes a matter of indifference in light of the life, death, and resurrection of Jesus Christ and an avenue through which the gospel is communicated (Gal. 3:27-28; 1 Cor. 9:19-23). Jesus violates ethnic boundaries for the sake of His saving mission in Samaria (Jn. 4:19-23; cf. Mt. 15:21-28). More important, Christ's death and resurrection puts an end to separation based on ethnicity. Indeed, Christ died so that He might create one new humanity; ethnocentrism is rejected (Eph. 2:11-22). By faith in God's saving provision through Christ, believers are brothers and sisters, members of one family (Gal. 4:4-7; 1 Jn. 3:1-2).

A Brief History of Ethnocentrism in the Seventh-day Adventist Church

Ethnocentrism has been, and is now, pervasive in the Seventh-day Adventist Church. Adventist ethnocentrism is but a more specific example of global ethnocentrism. The Seventh-day Adventist Church that emerged in the cradle of American democracy is characterized by ethnocentrism in every aspect of church life: the choice of church leaders; the formulation of church policy; the distribution of resources; where, how, and with whom we worship; and the definition and implementation of church mission. A brief look at how ethnocentrism has affected the Adventist church historically will illustrate this point.

Adventism was called into existence by God in the context of the juxtaposition of what Richard Hughes calls the American Creed and several American myths. The American Creed is encapsulated in the words of the Declaration of Independence, "We hold these Truths to be self-evident, that all Men are created equal, that they are endowed by their Creator with certain unalienable Rights, that among these are Life, Liberty, and the Pursuit of Happiness." American myths are not fairy tales, instead they are narratives, stories that convey shared convictions related to the meaning and purpose of the nation. Such stories provide the lens through which Americans see reality and allow them to create community based on a shared faith in the imaginative ordering of a common experience. In this sense, the American Creed is the nation's primal myth, but there are other secondary myths, rooted in a religious understanding, which also function in American life.

While each of these secondary myths hold potential for good, they can be absolutized in ways that undermine the virtues on which they were founded. Reinhold Niebuhr holds that such virtues can become vices when they are relied upon too completely.[17] Hughes argues that when the virtues of the rich and powerful become absolutized, those who are poor and marginalized in society are placed at great risk. He identifies five secondary myths; we will discuss only two: the myth of a Chosen Nation and the myth of a Christian Nation.[18] These two myths are related to the rise of Seventh-day Adventism in the nineteenth century and its ongoing development.

The myth of a Chosen Nation, that America is a chosen nation and its citizens chosen people, finds its roots in the history of the children of Israel in the Old Testament. The story of how America was able to appropriate this designation begins with William Tyndale who, in sixteenth-century England, promoted the idea that England stood in covenant relationship with God and had been chosen for a special purpose. Perpetuated through several monarchs and various religious interpretations, this myth migrated to the American colonies with the Puritans. They drew many parallels between the experience of Israel as it came out of Egyptian bondage into the Promised Land with the Puritan flight from England into the new Promised Land, the American wilderness. Puritans, such as John Winthrop, in the seventeenth century, expanded the motif of covenant to a concern for the neighbor, a community knit together by love for one another in order to do the work of the Lord.[19]

Unfortunately, according to this understanding, if the Puritans were the children of Israel, then those who were not Puritans, i.e., Native Americans, were the heathen tribes of Canaan, the agents of Satan. This notion explains the Puritan willingness to dispossess and destroy Native Americans in spite of their hospitality that saved the lives of the Puritans during the first few arduous winters in the New World. Native hospitality was not a sign of their inherent goodness, but rather an indication of God's power to use what the Puritans considered a depraved people to God's own ends. The myth of a Chosen Nation persisted, so that during the Civil War both North and South appealed to this powerful conception.[20]

American success in the Spanish-American War and the colonization of the Philippines further fueled the notion of American people as the chosen people, so that Albert Beveridge, senator from Illinois, could say in Congress that English-speaking and Teutonic peoples, as the master organizers of the world, were "so adept in government that we may administer government among savage and senile peoples. Were it not for such a force as this, the world would relapse into barbarism and night. And of all our race He [God] has marked the American people as His chosen nation to finally lead in the redemption of the world."[21]

Beveridge explicitly excluded people of color from the chosen. He and other white Americans by this time had discarded the notion of covenant responsibility for the neighbor, replacing it with an appeal to power, domination, and control. So it is not surprising that by 1937, H. Richard Niebuhr could assert that as the nineteenth century went on, the notion of America as the nation chosen to do a particular work for the Lord had morphed into the increasingly sounded myth of America as the Chosen Nation that was divinely favored.[22] "In this sense, the American people absolutized the myth of the Chosen Nation."[23]

In reaction to the white American myth of white America as the Chosen Nation, non-white peoples created alternate myths that allowed them to survive in a hostile environment. Using the same basic metaphor of the children of Israel and Egyptian bondage, black slaves cast themselves as the new Israel longing for liberation from the bondage of American slavery. Leaders of slave revolts, such as Nat Turner and Denmark Vesey, and conductors on the Underground Railroad, such as Harriet Tubman, were cast as "Black Moses." The Negro spiritual was born to express the slaves' yearning for freedom, while simultaneously providing a code for escape. This imagery is nowhere more eloquently expressed than in the sermons and speeches of Martin Luther King, Jr.[24]

Despite its shortcomings, the myth of America as a Chosen Nation has persisted. In his second inaugural address, Abraham Lincoln makes clear that the claim to divine favor can lead to presumptuous actions that ignore the fact that God stands in judgment over such claims. The Civil War was such a judgment, and "if God will it continues until all the wealth piled by the bondsman's two hundred and fifty years of unrequited toil shall be sunk, and until every drop of blood drawn with the lash shall be paid by another drawn with the sword, as was said three thousand years ago, so still it must be said 'the judgments of the Lord are true and righteous altogether.'"[25] Hughes concludes, "In spite of Lincoln's warnings, many Americans over the years have failed to see the liabilities inherent in the Chosen Nation mythology. Indeed, the notion that God chose America for power and privilege has often seemed altogether obvious and beyond dispute."[26]

The myth of a Christian Nation arose during the Second Great Awakening as an attempt to call the nation to embrace the teachings of Jesus as a model for behavior, notwithstanding the fact that the nation was founded on its *not* being a Christian nation. The Constitution is firmly in favor of the separation of church and state;

America was founded as a secular republic. But, paradoxically, the new nation as it emerged was in several cases decidedly Christian. Hughes suggests a few reasons. First, the Deism professed by the founding fathers, who resisted the notion of a Christian state, can only be understood in light of biblical faith. It can be demonstrated that the basis for American political institutions can be found in Jewish and Christian presuppositions. And second, the myth of a Christian Nation arose in the context of the objective reality of the Protestant revivalism of the Second Great Awakening. It is critical to understand that the Millerite Movement and Adventism were born during this era.

The Second Great Awakening was an attempt to create America as a Protestant nation responsive to the will of God, as envisioned by John Calvin, and to transform the republic into the Kingdom of God through the reformation of the social order in line with biblical principles. Several factors fueled the revivalism of the Awakening. Many Americans still held to the European model of a state church. The secularism upheld by the Constitution was thought to encourage heresy, skepticism, and irreligion. Many in the country were horrified by the excesses of the French Revolution, including its attacks on religion. This was especially alarming in light of the similarities between the ideas that spawned the French Revolution and those that bred the American Revolution. Finally, the westward expansion of the nation fostered the fear that the settlers were not sufficiently Christianized. Many in the east "imagined that the frontier threatened to overwhelm the entire nation with barbarism."[27]

Revival broke out spontaneously in several locations as early as the late eighteenth century. Large meetings, held in rough outdoor clearings with enthusiastic preaching from makeshift pulpits, were characterized by emotional dancing and singing, barking, jerky movements, rolling in the mud, and solemn rapture. The primary message of the preaching was God's love for sinners. The various phases of the Awakening spread not only to the western frontier, but all the way to New England, where under the leadership of Charles Finney, it took the form of a movement to alleviate social ills. The success of the Awakening is seen in statements by the federal government that designated America as a Christian nation as late as 1931.[28]

Hughes harks back to the sixteenth-century Anabaptist notion of the separation of church and state for his critique of the myth of a Christian Nation. The Anabaptists urged such separation as a means of protecting not the state, but the church. They recognized the danger that the church would adapt to the values and perspectives of the larger society in order to be acceptable. This is exactly what happened in America. The secular value of freedom to pursue self-interest was substituted for the Christian value of freedom *from* self-interest in order to serve one's neighbor. In essence, white Christians "stripped the Christian faith of much of the ability it might otherwise have had to stand in judgment on ethnocentric cultural norms. It therefore became easy to speak of 'unalienable rights' for 'all men,' but to mean by that rhetoric 'unalienable rights' for all *white* men."[29]

By the time it had done its work, the myth of a Christian Nation had become absolutized to the point that the Christianity it espoused had little resemblance to the radical demands of the ethical teachings of Jesus. Instead, the faith of white American Christianity was hardly distinguishable from the secular values of the culture of the time.

In spite of critique by those groups disenfranchised in American society, the myth of a Christian Nation has persisted, bolstered by televised proponents of the Christian Right, the so-called "moral majority," that seeks to usher in the Kingdom of God through the introduction of conservative religious ideals in American politics. The Christian Right continues to be a powerful voice even in the twenty-first century, perpetuating the myth.[30]

Early Adventism

The Adventist pioneers had a notably excellent history in their understanding and practice of biblical principles regarding ethnicity and divine justice. Several of the early leaders were strongly identified with the Abolitionist movement prior to the Civil War. Among such advocates were the former sea captain, Joseph Bates, who helped found an Abolitionist group in his home. John Preston Kellogg, the father of Dr. John Harvey and William K. Kellogg, sheltered fugitive slaves on his farm in Michigan.[31] John Byington, the first president of the General Conference, maintained a station of the Underground Railroad at his home in Buck's Bridge, New York, where he assisted the illegal transportation of fugitives to Canadian freedom. Early Adventist leaders were closely associated with Sojourner Truth, the famous anti-slavery orator; it is disputed that she was baptized by Uriah Smith. Rosetta Douglass Sprague, the daughter of noted black leader Frederick Douglass, was member of the First Seventh-day Adventist Church in Washington, DC.[32]

Erin Reid argues that while Adventist pioneers mirrored other Northern evangelical Christians of the time in their rebuke of slavery, the "national sin," Adventists did not prescribe particular political loyalties as if from God. Instead, the pre-war writers in the *Advent Review and Sabbath Herald* "applied an apolitical, apocalyptic theology to the United States and its institution of slavery and developed a distinctive ethical imperative. While the essential dynamic bore resemblance to the motivational development of other evangelical abolitionists, Adventist abolitionism differed fundamentally in principle, precept, and practice."[33]

Evangelical abolitionists were of three types: conservatives, who believed in the moral neutrality of slavery and thought that any action regarding it was solely a secular concern; moderates, who, while believing that slavery was evil, favored gradual emancipation and viewed antislavery agitation with disfavor; and radicals, who believed that slavery was a sin that must be repented of immediately and eradicated. Radicals disdained the moderate notion that a sin, such as slavery, could be gradually repented of and forsaken.

Most early Adventists were radical abolitionists, but unlike other evangelicals who were working toward the establishment of a 1000-year kingdom of God on earth prior to the second coming, Adventists believed that world conditions would deteriorate progressively until Christ came to bring in a heavenly millennium. They did not believe that the earthly situation could be perfected prior to Christ's coming. Instead, they held that America was in a state of un-repented sin because of slavery and they did not expect the nation to do better with the passage of time.

The early writers in the *Review* "taught that the proper ethical response was to prepare themselves and others for Christ's return, which meant disassociating themselves from fallen civil and ecclesiastical power structures, exercising private conscience in legal matters, and publicly proclaiming the sin of slavery."[34] Adventists, unlike other abolitionists, avoided political involvement while advocating active engagement in personal transformation and church reformation and vocal evaluation of social conditions. Thus, while they were similar to evangelical abolitionists in their criticism of slavery and of churches that were complicit, Adventists differed in their theological understandings, and therefore, in their precept and practice.[35]

Early Seventh-day Adventists viewed slavery as a sin and a crime.[36] America for them was the lamb-like two-horned beast of Revelation 13:11 that spoke as a dragon, a view that was promulgated between 1854 and 1865. Uriah Smith, the first editor of the *Review*, was one of the major proponents of this position. He condemned slavery in the strongest terms, indicting not only this practice in the South, but also the poor treatment of blacks in the North. He wrote in 1859: "Slavery is a sin we have never ceased to abhor."[37] Smith gave poetic voice to his views in the pages of the *Review*. Here is an excerpt from his poem:

> With two horns like a lamb a beast arose–
> So with two leading forms a power has risen,
> Two fundamental principles, than which
> in all the earth none can be found more mild,
> More lamb-like in their outward form and name.
> A land of freedom, pillared on the broad
> And open basis of equality;
> A land reposing 'neath the gentle sway
> of civil and religious liberty.
> Lamb-like in form, is there no dragon-voice
> Heard in our land? No notes that harshly grate
> Upon the ear of mercy, love and truth?
> And put humanity to open shame?
> Let the united cry of millions tell–
> Millions that groan beneath oppression's rod,
> Beneath the sin-forged chains of slavery,
> Robbed of their rights, to brutes degraded down,
> And soul and body bound to other's will

Let their united cries, and tears, and groans,
That daily rise, and call aloud on Heaven
For vengeance, answer; let the slave reply.
O land of boasted freedom! Thou hast given
The lie to all thy loud professions, first,
of justice, liberty and equal rights.
And thou hast set a foul and heinous blot
upon the sacred page of liberty;
And whilst thou traffickest in souls of men,
Thou hurl'st defiance, proud, in face of Heaven
Soon to be answered with avenging doom.[38]

James White, one of the founders of the Seventh-day Adventist Church, was among the many Adventist pioneers who spoke out against slavery. White held that slavery was the cause of the Civil War, viewing it as God's chastisement upon the North for its complicity in slavery. While defending Adventists who as noncombatants resisted the draft, White characterized slavery as "the darkest and most damning sin upon the nation."[39] He promised that the nation would drink God's wrath to the very dregs as a punishment for this sin.

There are numerous statements against slavery in the writings of Ellen White. Like her husband, James White, she viewed the Civil War as God's punishment upon the nation for slavery.[40] The following is among her many statements on this topic:

> God is punishing the nation for the high crime of slavery. He has the destiny of the nation in his hands. He will punish the South for the sin of slavery, and the North for so long suffering its overreaching and overbearing influences . . . . [P]rofessed Christians read of the sufferings of the martyrs, and tears course down their cheeks. They wonder that men could ever possess hearts so hardened as to practice such inhuman cruelties toward their fellow-men, but at the same time they hold their fellow-men in slavery.[41]

Adventist opposition to slavery was unique when compared to the humanistic notions that motivated the Abolitionist movement. Instead of the typical Abolitionist rationalizations rooted in concepts such as equality and the dignity of humankind, the Adventist position rested on five distinctive characteristics. (1) It was rooted in Scripture. All humankind, including those who are enslaved, are created in the image of God. (2) It was rooted in Scripture's Christ. Ellen White held that in Christ blacks and whites were equal. (3) It was a prophetic voice. The Adventist position was counter-cultural; the pioneers were unwilling to accommodate to the prevailing cultural prejudices. (4) It exhibited moral clarity. Slavery was clearly named as sin by the pioneers. (5) It was politically non-aligned. The Adventist position was moral and not political.

Opposition to slavery, however, was not universal among Adventists. There were some pro-slavery Adventists, and some who argued for cultural accommodation—a position that would later become institutionalized in church policy and exported around the world.

The Turning Point

The pattern of Southern postbellum race relations grew out of the context of antebellum slavery. The social subjugation of blacks, with its paradoxical distance and yet intimacy, was well established during slavery. The equality of blacks enforced by the Northern military occupation of the South during Reconstruction was a cataclysmic disruption of the Southern way of life. As one embittered Southern woman complained:

> It is hard to have to lay our loved ones in the grave, to have them fall by the thousands on the battlefield, to be stripped of everything, but the hardest of all is nigger equality, and I won't submit to it.[42]

The radical Reconstruction of the South (1865-1877) was a racially and politically charged era that saw significant gains for blacks under the aegis of Northern military presence. Blacks were reluctantly given some degree of education, enfranchisement, and social privilege, all constrained by black poverty and illiteracy and the resistance of white Southerners. The legal restrictions of the Black Codes of 1865 to 1866 sought to nullify the rights given blacks in the Thirteenth, Fourteenth, and Fifteenth Amendments, while the pernicious system of sharecropping plunged many blacks into virtual slavery.[43] Convict lease laws allowed blacks to be arrested for petty crimes and subjected to forced labor that some did not survive.[44]

A steep decline in the rights of post-Civil War black Americans began with the Compromise of 1877. In a complicated legal maneuver that landed Rutherford B. Hayes in the White House, the nation agreed to allow the South to work out its racial problems without interference from the federal government. The constitutional rights of blacks, now left in the hands of white Southerners, were soon violated. At the same time, public opinion in the North shifted to the right, so that it more closely reflected the Southern view of race relations.

The years that followed witnessed the rise of Jim Crow, with its forced segregation, disenfranchisement, lynchings, race riots, and racial violence. Fueled by the nation's conquests in the Caribbean and the Philippines that began in 1898, the racist doctrines of white superiority and white supremacy were crystalized in Rudyard Kipling's famous poem, "The White Man's Burden." Written in 1899 to celebrate the United States annexation and colonization of the Philippines, the poem justifies imperialism based on the inherent inferiority of non-whites.[45]

Take up the White Man's burden—
Send forth the best ye breed—
Go bind your sons to exile—
To serve your captives' need—
To wait in heavy harness,
On fluttered folk and wild—
Your new-caught, sullen peoples,
Half-devil and half-child.[46]

Ellen White was vocal during the post-Reconstruction period about the failed responsibilities of the nation, the Christian church, and the Seventh-day Adventist Church in particular, with regard to the newly freed black people.[47] By 1910, segregation was accepted by white Americans in the North as well as the South as the American way, endorsed by the leaders of government, the President, the Supreme Court, and even the most influential black leader of the time, Booker T. Washington. The "betrayal of the Negro" was firmly in place.[48]

Seventh-day Adventists were well aware of the racial mood of the nation and the problems posed to evangelism among black Americans. In 1907, the Pacific Press Publishing Association produced a pamphlet entitled, *An Agitation and an Opportunity*.[49] A collection of editorials and articles from Southern newspapers, the thrust of the pamphlet was that God was holding back the winds of racial strife in order to allow the third angel's message to be proclaimed among blacks in the South, but that the time was short for this effort. Ellen White echoed this warning[50] and predicted that soon opportunities for whites to work among blacks in the South would be restricted.[51] The history of the failure of the Adventist church to seize these opportunities is probably best exemplified by the church's lack of support for the work of James Edson White among black people on the riverboat *Morning Star* in the Mississippi Delta.[52]

After the Civil War, Adventists, who had been in the forefront of the abolition movement, were strangely silent, not venturing for decades into the American South for the purpose of evangelizing the newly freed blacks. When the first Adventist missionaries arrived in the South they encountered an often violent white supremacist culture that oppressed the black population. The missionaries' history is one of accommodation to the unbiblical social situation in which they found themselves. Kessia Bennett describes the changes in their relationship with the culture of racism over time as resistance-accommodation-institutionalization.[53]

> Early Adventist missionaries first resisted the racist beliefs and practices of the South. Then, pressured by custom and escalating violence, they began to accommodate the racism by racially segregating, yet continuing to resist the oppression of Blacks. Over time, however, the segregation which began as accommodation was normalized and institutionalized. In effect, it became part of the Adventist culture in America.[54]

The late nineteenth and early twentieth centuries witnessed an unprecedented wave of violence against Southern blacks who were forced and intimidated to adhere to a rigid racial etiquette that promised abuse for such violations as touching the elbow of a white person or a prolonged look by a black man in the direction of a white woman.[55] White Northerners who came to the South as teachers were also constrained to follow this racial etiquette by force of "social ostracism, persecution, and physical assault."[56] Lynchings, often associated with torture of black men, women, and children, were a means of punishment, terrorism, and social control. Segregation and social exclusion in the public sphere were a means of negotiating the racial tensions of the time. Segregation in religious life, which was a part of the antebellum South, now characterized the post-Reconstruction Christian church. This was the social situation that the Adventist missionaries to blacks in the South encountered.[57]

The most active years for Adventist mission work in the South were 1891 to 1903. The significant name during this period was that of James Edson White who, with his wife Etta and other colleagues, initiated the first systematic work among Southern blacks.[58] Ellen White's sermon, *"Our Duty to the Colored People,"* to the General Conference Session of 1891 was the catalyst for organized work in the South. She urged the Adventist church to reject the color line and emphasized the church's responsibility to serve the freed black people of the Southern states. Here is an excerpt from her courageous message:

> I know that which I now speak will bring me into conflict. This I do not covet, for the conflict has seemed to be continuous of late years; but I do not mean to live a coward or die a coward, leaving my work undone.
>
> I must follow in my Master's footsteps. It has become fashionable to look down upon the poor, and upon the colored race in particular. But Jesus, the Master, was poor, and He sympathizes with the poor, the discarded, the oppressed, and declares that every insult shown to them is as if shown to Himself. I am more and more surprised as I see those who claim to be children of God possessing so little of the sympathy, tenderness, and love which actuated Christ. Would that every church, North and South, were imbued with the spirit of our Lord's teaching.[59]

Published as a pamphlet, the sermon was discarded in an attic at church headquarters. Edson White found the leaflet in 1893, and with Will O. Palmer, launched the *Morning Star* in 1894. The work was not only religious; a health ministry was included. Oakwood Industrial School, the forerunner of Oakwood University, was opened in Huntsville, Alabama, in 1896.

The abolitionist sympathy that moved the early Adventists, and their primarily Northern perspective, informed the Adventist missionaries' perception of the

Southern culture of racism and their initially countercultural reaction. Their ministry was marked by positive evaluations of blacks and efforts to assist them in ways that were not normative. Interracial cooperation and social interaction were often characterized by loving personal relationships. While not ideal, the behavior of many Adventist missionaries in the early part of their work was in opposition to the racist social system they encountered. This was the stage of resistance.[60]

Gradually, however, in the face of persecution, the attitudes of the missionaries toward racism softened and their practices began to change from resistance to accommodation to the host culture. Over several decades, church policy came to adopt segregation, ostensibly motivated primarily by concern for the safety of workers and the viability of the work. Bennett maintains, "The missionary accommodation to racism was meant to keep the prejudice of Whites from jeopardizing the work for Blacks."[61]

Escalating violence and threats of violence against black converts and the missionaries, including shootings, beatings, forced expulsion, and arson, led to accommodating adaptations in policy and practice. Ellen White advised workers to avoid criticism of Southern whites with regard to their treatment of blacks.[62] Accommodation took the form of progressively segregated worship services and education.

Bennett contends that the missionaries were naïve in their belief that the accommodations in their work were apolitical.

> Tied together with this belief in apoliticism is a sense of futility to change the racist conventions of the South, though they were reprehensible . . . . The thinking that resistance and accommodation were apolitical acts contributed to the later institutionalization of racism in the denomination because it allowed Adventists to believe that their race relations were distinct from their theology and yet also distinct from political implications.[63]

Bennett also attributes to Adventist eschatology a role in their ostensibly apolitical approach. The belief in a just God who would solve all presently unsolvable problems in the end justified the focus on the dissemination of "present truth" rather than on the amelioration of social and political ills. The view that a challenge to the racist customs of the larger society would be a political act and the tendency to avoid political questions left Adventists vulnerable to the prejudice and racism of the culture. A commitment to the separation of church and state led to reluctance to address issues of social injustice.

Ellen White issued a number of statements in this regard, some seemingly in contradiction to her earlier position on the equality of the races and the importance of interracial worship. Much has been made of her counsel in volume nine of her

Testimonies for the Church. This statement has implications for the institutionalization of racism in her day and its perpetuation to this day. Here is what she wrote:

> In a council meeting held in 1895 at Armadale, a suburb of Melbourne, Victoria, I spoke of these matters, in answer to the inquiries of my brethren, and urged the necessity of caution. I said that perilous times were coming, and that the sentiments that could then be expressed in regard to *what should be done along missionary lines for the colored people could not be expressed in the future without imperiling lives.* I said plainly that the work done for the colored people would have to be carried on along lines different from those followed in some sections of the country in former years.
>
> Let as little as possible be said about the color line, and let the colored people work chiefly for those of their own race.
>
> In regard to white and colored people worshiping in the same building, this cannot be followed as a general custom with profit to either party—especially in the South. The best thing will be to provide the colored people who accept the truth, with places of worship of their own, in which they can carry on their services by themselves. This is particularly necessary in the South in order that the work for the white people may be carried on without serious hindrance.
>
> Let the colored believers be provided with neat, tasteful houses of worship. *Let them be shown that this is done not to exclude them from worshiping with white people, because they are black, but in order that the progress of the truth may be advanced.* Let them understand that *this plan is to be followed until the Lord shows us a better way.*
>
> The colored members of ability and experience should be encouraged to lead the services of their own people; and their voices are to be heard in the representative assemblies.[64]

Several points are of note. First, the accommodation urged was to avoid imperiling the lives of believers and to aid in the advance of the gospel. Second, the separation of races was not designed to exclude blacks from white worship because they were black. Third, as Ellen White's words make clear, the accommodation was only for the South at that time, not a general policy for the Adventist church as a whole and for all times. Fourth, the work among blacks should be guided by black leadership whose voices should be heard in representative assemblies. Finally, the accommodation should only prevail "until the Lord shows us a better way." The accommodation at no time represented God's ideal; it was a temporary plan based on the exigence of the time.

Adventist policy, practice, and justification for the institutionalization and perpetuation of racial discrimination and segregation have strayed from Ellen White's counsel in every particular. Our position, both in the United States and abroad, has rested on a belief in the inherent inferiority of non-white peoples. The accommodation to racist culture was enshrined as universal church policy. We have adopted and transported institutionalized racism far beyond the Southern American boundaries that Ellen White envisioned. Black leadership of the black work was long in coming, and as we shall see, the voices of black leadership when they were appointed were not heard in "the representative assemblies." Finally, and most important, the Lord has long ago showed us a better way and yet we persist in a pattern of interaction, policy, and worship that is an affront to the gospel of Christ. If the Lord has seen fit to show Christians of other denominations that racial separation is not God's way, why has God not shown it to the "remnant church"? Or is it simply that we will not submit to God's way?

Over time the accommodations that the missionaries made became policy. Racism in the form of discriminatory hiring, underrepresentation in leadership, unequal treatment of workers, unfair financial practices, and segregation in all areas of church life was institutionalized. What began as accommodation to protect lives and to facilitate the spread of the gospel became the institutionalized racism that has plagued Adventism from that time to the present.

Although it can be argued that the accommodation allowed the work to grow among black Americans, it was at the cost of ongoing problems, including the loss or silencing of some of the most promising black leaders, e.g., John Ragland, Lewis Sheafe, John Manus, and J. K. Humphrey. In the years following the death of Ellen White in 1915, these and many other black ministers and members severed their affiliation with the church. Some Adventists began to consider the notion of creating separate black conferences. Richard Schwarz notes that during the General Conference sessions of 1877 and 1885,

> the question of whether or not to bow to Southern prejudices by establishing separate work and separate churches for blacks was debated. Most speakers believed that to do so would be a denial of true Christianity since God was no respecter of persons. In 1890, however, R. M. Kilgore, the Adventist leader with the most experience relative to the South, argued for separate churches. D. M. Canright had urged this policy as early as 1876 during a brief period of labor in Texas. Eventually their recommendation prevailed, but the policy was never defended on grounds other than those of expediency.[65]

But the catalyst for the separation into black and white conferences was the death of Mrs. Lucille (Lucy) Byard in October 1943, after she was denied medical treatment at the Washington Sanitarium in Takoma Park, Maryland, simply because she was black. This terrible incident so stirred black Adventists that they demanded that the

General Conference act to ensure that there was no repetition, citing many other areas of racial discrimination in the church.

On the Sabbath following Mrs. Byard's death the president of the North American Division preached at the black Ephesus Seventh-day Adventist Church in Washington, DC, in an effort to calm the situation. Instead, in response to a strong declaration by James O. Montgomery, a group formed around him that eventually became the National Association for the Advancement of Worldwide Work Among Colored Seventh-day Adventists. Using telephone and print media, black members across the country were mobilized. The General Conference president, J. Lamar McElhany, agreed to meet with the group on October 17, 1943.[66]

The National Association for the Advancement of Worldwide Work Among Colored Seventh-day Adventists produced a pamphlet, "Shall the Four Freedoms Function Among Seventh-day Adventists?", that summarized the grievances of black Adventists related to their treatment by the church and presented ways in which the church could begin to redress the problem. Contrary to misconceptions on the part of both black and white Adventists, the Association did not ask for black conferences either in their original presentation or in their agenda; instead they called for complete integration.[67]

McElhaney brought the issue to the Spring Council, April 8-19, 1944. The notion of separate black conferences was brought to the floor. Although there were both advocates and detractors of this plan, after a lengthy debate, on April 10, 1944, the motion to establish black conferences was accepted. After the decision was reached, Joseph T. Dodson, chairman of the Association, stated, "They gave us our conferences instead of integration. We didn't have a choice. In the end it was better to have segregation with power, than segregation without power."[68]

Ricardo Graham notes that the proposal to form racially segregated conferences was imposed on blacks by white church leadership. Failing to achieve their goal of complete integration, due to resistance from white leaders and members, many black Adventists accepted the separation as the best means to further the work among their own people. He stresses that the formation of black conferences was a proposal from white church leaders in response to the request for integration. He concludes:

> In the main, African-American Adventists have always desired to follow what they consider to be the model of the Bible when it related to race relations among Christians. However, lacking full and complete inclusion, Black SDA leadership has made the best of the situation. They settled for "self-determination" and have opted to take full advantage of the separation that was foisted upon them by White leadership.[69]

Nowhere was racial discrimination more evident than in the leadership of the black work. While organized church departments for identified ethnic groups, such as Germans and Scandinavians, were led by their own people, the North American Negro Department was led by a white man for its first nine years (1909-1918). Oakwood College was led by white presidents from 1896 to 1932, and the editor of *Message* magazine was white for thirteen years (1932-1945). In addition, denominational employment at all levels displayed the underrepresentation of blacks.

Adventists excluded blacks from white schools, churches, and hospitals. Blacks could not eat in the Review and Herald Publishing House cafeteria. It was not until demonstrations by blacks at the 1962 General Conference session in San Francisco, that the church was compelled to desegregate.[70]

Bennett's analysis informs not only the pattern of race relations in the Adventist church in America following the Reconstruction, but also the larger issue of how the same pattern of accommodation to unbiblical social situations has characterized Adventist missionary enterprises around the world.

> Afro-Americans were not the only group to be treated for years in a paternal, patronizing way. Adventist missionaries going to Africa, Asia, and Latin America in the early years of the twentieth century did not escape the general Western imperialistic attitude practiced by the colonial powers. In general this attitude tended to equate European culture, education, and technology with progress. The more another culture varied from the European or North American model, the more backward it was assumed to be. It was easy to conclude that nationals from non-Western areas could not be trusted in leadership roles until they had absorbed Western ways as well as Adventist doctrines [71]

Thus, the ethnocentrism, expressed as racism in the United States, migrated with Adventist missionaries around the world, where it was strengthened by the ethnocentric bias of the cultures it encountered. There was nothing in institutionalized Adventist attitude and practice to resist this process, quite the contrary. However, it is critical to note that all Adventist missionaries did not exemplify this problem. The Lord has always reserved a remnant to Himself who refuse to yield to the prevailing wrongs of the society.

There are many examples of the institutionalization of ethnocentrism in the Adventist church, but we will examine only one: Adventist involvement in apartheid in South Africa. The sad history of racial discrimination, described and condemned by the Truth and Reconciliation Commission hearings in South Africa (1995-1998) at the end of apartheid, revealed that many faith communities were complicit in their support of and participation in the racist policies of the violent state machine. Unfortunately, the Seventh-day Adventist Church in South Africa was among them;

its participation was not difficult due to the long history of racial separation and discrimination already present in the church.[72]

As early as 1893, Philip Wessels, a member of a prominent South African Adventist family, was writing to Ellen White to register his refusal to allow his children to mix with people of color or to think that there was no difference between them. His children were in no case to consider marriage with colored people. Wessels considered association with colored people to be detrimental to the "moral welfare" of his children. He found support in the racial discrimination that characterized the South African culture of his day and justified his failure to take a moral stand against racism with the need to reach nonbelievers who held racist attitudes.[73] There can be little doubt that the racially prejudiced position of a family, who were primary benefactors of the South African Adventist church, was both influential in the early church as well as reflective of the pervasive attitude among church members.

In 1948, the policy of apartheid, "apartness," which mandated segregation and racial inequality, led to the complete social, political, economic, residential, and educational separation of ethnic groups in South Africa. This policy was not ended until the multi-racial elections of 1994. But the Seventh-day Adventist Church was separated along ethnic lines well before 1948. In fact, church institutions—medical, educational, and administrative structures—were "racially segregated from the beginning of the church's work in South Africa."[74] By the time that apartheid was introduced in 1948, the Adventist church had already been practicing segregation for more than sixty years. Moreover, the church lagged behind the government in abandoning it.[75]

The 1931 Working Policy of the General Conference of Seventh-day Adventists [Southern African Division] provides the following "Hints to Our Missionaries":

> It is not customary for Europeans to entertain [African] natives at meals, and the native does not expect it. If you wish to give one a meal, let him eat it outside from a plate kept especially for natives.
>
> Teach your mission students to shake hands only when you, or any white, makes an advance. It is most embarrassing to have a native come up to you in the streets of a city and offer to shake hands. You may not mind, but others will look askance at you and it will bring discredit to your work.[76]

Three years after the convening of the Truth and Reconciliation Commission, the South African Seventh-day Adventist Church issued a lengthy statement of confession and apology. It stated in part:

> In the face of the heresy of apartheid, we confess that we have failed by our sins of omission and commission to properly evidence the endurance of the saints, keep the commandments of

> God, or hold fast to the faith of Jesus, thereby misrepresenting the eternal gospel of Jesus Christ (Rev 14:6,7). This has been hurtful to our society, to the identity and mission of our corporate church, and to the lives of its individual members. Therefore, in deep repentance we seek for forgiveness from God and our fellow citizens, and commit ourselves to reformation, justice and reconciliation.[77]

The ensuing years have witnessed a number of structural rearrangements that coupled and uncoupled ethnic groups in the South African Adventist church. But in every case, there were ethnic disparities in remuneration and leadership. At present the church in South Africa continues to be plagued with the attitudes that fueled apartheid in its search for a structure that reflects the gospel of Christ in spirit as well as in organization. Jeff Crocombe could assert, as late as 2007, "To date, the Seventh-day Adventist Church in South Africa has yet to undertake appropriate initiatives of healing and reconciliation."[78]

Ethnocentrism is reflected in Adventist policy and practice around the world: in the assignment of leadership, in remuneration, and in the selection of those who manage church finances. The policy of paying so-called American and European "expatriates" a higher wage than national church workers in two-thirds world countries is a blot on church policy. When we were in India in 1995, Indian pastors questioned this policy to a group of General Conference representatives. The Indian pastors were responsible for multi-church districts with significant distances between churches. The salaries they were paid did not comprise a living wage, so they had to take on a second job to feed their families. The chilling answer they were given by one of the General Conference leaders was, "It's none of your business." The fact that this sentiment was shared by the other members of the delegation was made very clear to us in private after that disturbing meeting.

Cultural accommodation to ethnocentrism has resulted in the loss of the five unique characteristics of the Adventist pioneers' response to slavery. We have become comfortable with both social and structural ethnocentrism, often supported with political, sociological, and economic justifications that cannot be supported with Scripture. Although many Adventists in North America view women's ordination as the moral issue of our time, others have used the issue as a proxy for ethnocentrism. For example, a California Adventist blogger, critical of the "African" treatment of women during the height of the conflict in 2015 stated, "North America should not be ruled by primitives." Although this statement is extreme, the argument that North America needs to be independent has been voiced by prominent Adventist leaders. Yet, no such argument was made in Adventism when the Northern hemisphere dominated the Southern hemisphere politically.

Contrary to the belief of some Adventists, ethnocentrism is not just a problem for people of European descent. It is encountered wherever Adventists of different ethnic groups encounter each other. Despite our rhetoric to the contrary, ethnocentrism is the norm everywhere Adventism is named.

God's Solution

What is God's answer for ethnocentrism in the Seventh-day Adventist Church? Succinctly put, God's answer is Jesus Christ. In a compelling statement, Paul establishes the necessity of Christ:

> But now in Christ Jesus you who once were far off have been brought near by the blood of Christ. For he is our peace; in his flesh he has made both groups into one and has broken down the dividing wall, that is, the hostility between us. He has abolished the law with its commandments and ordinances, that he might create in himself one new humanity in place of the two, thus making peace, and might reconcile both groups to God in one body through the cross, thus putting to death that hostility through it (Eph. 2:13-16).

Although this passage is persuasive, in his letter to the Romans, Paul provides a manual on relational unity in Christ. *He writes Romans to challenge ethnocentrism.* In an attempt to foster reconciliation and unity, Paul explains God's good news in Christ in response to virulent ethnic enmity among Gentile and Jewish believers in Rome.

Each chapter of this book is designed to trace a section of Paul's argument as he explains the gospel of Jesus Christ in an attempt to unify the Roman house churches. Chapter one introduces the thesis of Paul's argument: holistic sanctification through the gospel of Jesus Christ. Although Paul affirms that believers in Rome are justified and have a renowned faith, he hints that they are in need of spiritual growth: both corporate and individual sanctification. He signals that sanctification is only possible through a more complete explanation and experience of the person and work of Jesus Christ.

Chapter two addresses Paul's exposition of the gospel of Christ and the issue of corporate sin. Paul describes both Gentile and Jewish separation from God; Gentiles and Jews share a common heritage of sin. He contends that Jews, in particular, although they possess God's law, have sinned through their hypocritical judgment of Gentiles and stand under God's wrath. Paul exposes God's present and future judgment of those who persist in ethnic sin. He makes clear that God will finally judge all sin through Jesus Christ.

Following Paul's demonstration that all humanity has sinned, chapter three develops his argument that the substitutionary death of Jesus Christ is God's solution to the problem of Jewish and Gentile sin in all its manifestations. Paul explains that faith in God's saving provision through Jesus Christ is how both Gentiles and Jews are declared righteous. They now share a common salvation. Abraham, the Father of all believers was declared righteous in the same manner: by trusting in God.

In chapter four we address Paul's claim that justified Gentile and Jewish believers now enjoy peace with God through Christ. Believers have been reconciled to God and, by extension, to one another. Through Christ's work the reign of sin and death has been broken. Believing Gentiles and Jews experience corporate salvation through participation in the death and life of Christ. Together they now live by the power of God's Spirit; they are members of God's family and co-heirs with Christ. Indeed, through Christ's love they are more than conquerors.

Chapter five reveals the fact that the gospel is not new. God's plan for the inclusion of Gentiles as a part of God's people is rooted in the Old Testament. Paul explains how God can extend mercy to the elect, both Gentiles and Jews, in anticipation of Christ's sacrifice. Gentiles must recognize that they are part of faithful Israel. As such, Gentiles are to reject ethnocentric attitudes and behaviors towards Jews.

In chapter six, disputed matters that are being used to justify ethnic division between Gentiles and Jews are identified. Paul argues that ethnic theology or ritual preferences should not be obstacles to unity. Paul offers the example of Jesus Christ to make an appeal for unity among Gentile and Jewish believers in Rome. Paul commands mutual acceptance based on Christ's acceptance of both groups, all for the glory of God.

Finally, in chapter seven, we see how Paul concludes his letter by asking the divided community to unite in prayer for his mission to Jerusalem. He also indicates that he hopes that a united Roman community will serve as a base for his anticipated mission to Spain. He enjoins believers to greet one another and shares the greetings of his diverse group of workers with the community in Rome. Paul warns the Roman churches against those who promote ethnocentrism, emphasizing that those who foster ethnic division are proxies for Satan, the one who has already been defeated by Christ. Using the language of corporate sanctification, Paul's benediction celebrates God's ability to strengthen Roman believers to live out the gospel, which is God's mystery revealed in Jesus Christ.

Christ has Welcomed You is a Christ-centered, biblically-based challenge to ethnocentrism in the Seventh-day Adventist Church. God has given this church an end-time message. God has revealed the final work of Christ in the heavenly sanctuary in preparation for His second coming. All the signs indicate that Jesus is about to culminate His work. Yet, without the love of Christ manifested in relational unity—notwithstanding ethnicity, race, tribe, or caste—Adventism has no authenticity; our profession is hollow. Jesus says that the world needs a demonstration of unconditional love and unity among believers in order to believe in Him. Will Adventists become His living epistle?

[1] From 1980 until the revision of the fundamental doctrines of the Seventh-day Adventist Church in 2015, this was Fundamental Belief #13.

[2] General Conference of Seventh-day Adventists. *28 Fundamental Beliefs: 2015 Edition.* www.adventist.org.

[3] Ellen G. White. *Christ's Object Lessons.* Hagerstown, MD: Review and Herald, 1941.

[4] This public statement was released by the General Conference president, Neal C. Wilson, after consultation with the 16 world vice-presidents of the Seventh-day Adventist Church, on June 27, 1985, at the General Conference session in New Orleans, Louisiana. The statement was issued in the context of the anti-apartheid movement in America and among some in the Adventist church. Pressure was applied during the General Conference Session for the church to voice opposition to apartheid and to endorse disinvestment in South Africa. It is notable that this was a personal statement by the General Conference president and not a voted policy of the church. There were no substantive changes in Adventist policy and practice in South Africa as a result of this statement. The statement reads:

> *One of the odious evils of our day is racism, the belief or practice that views or treats certain racial groups as inferior and therefore justifiably the object of domination, discrimination, and segregation. While the sin of racism is an age-old phenomenon based on ignorance, fear, estrangement, and false pride, some of its ugliest manifestations have taken place in our time. Racism and irrational prejudices operate in a vicious circle. Racism is among the worst of ingrained prejudices that characterize sinful human beings. Its consequences are generally more devastating because racism easily becomes permanently institutionalized and legalized and in its extreme manifestations can lead to systematic persecution and even genocide. The Seventh-day Adventist Church deplores all forms of racism, including the political policy of apartheid with its enforced segregation and legalized discrimination. Seventh-day Adventists want to be faithful to the reconciling ministry assigned to the Christian church. As a worldwide community of faith, the Seventh-day Adventist Church wishes to witness to and exhibit in her own ranks the unity and love that transcend racial differences and overcome past alienation between races. Scripture plainly teaches that every person was created in the image of God, who "made of one blood all nations of men for to dwell on all the face of the earth" (Acts 17:26). Racial discrimination is an offense against our fellow human beings, who were created in God's image. In Christ "there is neither Jew nor Greek" (Gal. 3:28). Therefore, racism is really a heresy and in essence a form of idolatry, for it limits the fatherhood of God by denying the brotherhood of all mankind and by exalting the superiority of one's own race. The standard for Seventh-day Adventist Christians is acknowledged in the church's Bible-based Fundamental Belief No. 13, "Unity in the Body of Christ." Here it is pointed out: "In Christ we are a new creation; distinctions of race, culture, learning, and nationality, and differences between high and low, rich and poor, male and female, must not be divisive among us. We are all equal in Christ, who by one Spirit has bonded us into one fellowship with Him and with one another; we are to serve and be served without partiality or reservation." Any other approach destroys the heart of the Christian gospel.*

[5] Daniel Kasomo. Historical Manifestation of Ethnocentrism and Its Challenges Today. ***International Journal of Applied Sociology***; 1(1): 8-14. 2011.

[6] Jonathan M. Hall. *Ethnic Identity in Greek Antiquity.* New York, NY: Cambridge University Press, 1994; Ethnic Identity in the Greco-Roman World: Greek representations of foreigners as 'polar-opposites' to define a sense of self. Posted by tarynpollock on May 5, 2010; Edith Hall. *Inventing the Barbarian. Greek Self-Definition through Tragedy.* Clarendon Press: Oxford, UK: 1985; K. E. Carr Barbarians. *Quatr.us.* February 2017; John E. Coleman. *Greeks and Barbarians: Essays on the Interactions Between Greeks and Non-Greeks in Antiquity and the Consequences for Eurocentrism.* Mid Devon, UK: Southgate Publishers, 1997.

[7] Helmut Heit. Western Identity, Barbarians and the inheritance of Greek Universalism. *The European Legacy* 2005; 10 (7): 727.

[8] Jonathan Hall; *Ethnic Identity in the Greco-Roman World*; Edith Hall.

[9] Aristotle. *Nicomachean Ethics*; Lewis, Bernard. *Race and Slavery in the Middle East: An Historical Enquiry*. New York, NY: Oxford University Press. 1992.

[10] Frank M. Snowden, *Before Color Prejudice: The Ancient View of Blacks*. Cambridge, MA: Harvard University Press, 1983.

[11] John E. Coleman. *Greeks and Barbarians: Essays on the Interactions Between Greeks and Non-Greeks in Antiquity and the Consequences for Eurocentrism*. Mid Devon, UK: Southgate Publishers, 1997, p. xii; see also Jonathan M. Hall. *Hellenicity: Between Ethnicity and Culture*. Chicago, IL: University of Chicago Press, 2002.

[12] Ibid.

[13] Dante A. Puzzo. Racism and the Western Tradition. *Journal of the History of Ideas*. 25(4): 579-586; Gene Demby. The Ugly, Fascinating History of the Word "Racism." *Code Switch: Race and Identity, Remixed*. January 6, 2014.

[14] Ibld.

[15] Ellen White maintains that Abraham was never an idolater. She writes: "Abraham had grown up in the midst of superstition and heathenism. Even his father's household, by whom the knowledge of God had been preserved, were yielding to the seductive influences surrounding them, and they 'served other gods' than Jehovah. But the true faith was not to become extinct. God has ever preserved a remnant to serve Him. Adam, Seth, Enoch, Methuselah, Noah, Shem, in unbroken line, had preserved from age to age the precious revealings of His will. The son of Terah became the inheritor of this holy trust. Idolatry invited him on every side, but in vain. Faithful among the faithless, uncorrupted by the prevailing apostasy, he steadfastly adhered to the worship of the one true God." Ellen G. White. *Patriarchs and Prophets*. Washington, DC: Review and Herald Publishing Association, 1890, p. 125.

[16] Ellen, G. White. *The General Conference Bulletin*, April 3, 1901, pp. 25-26; White. *Testimonies for the Church*, vol. 8. Mountain View, CA: Pacific Press Publishing Association, 1904.

[17] Reinhold Niebuhr. *The Irony of American History*. Chicago, IL: University of Chicago Press, 1952.

[18] Richard T. Hughes. *Myths America Lives By*. Urbana, IL: University of Illinois Press, 2003.

[19] John Winthrop. A Modell of Christian Charity. In Conrad Cherry (ed.). *God's New Israel: Religious Interpretations of American Destiny* (rev. ed.). Chapel Hill, NC: University of North Carolina Press, 1998.

[20] See Henry Ward Beecher. The Battle Set in Array, in Cherry; Palmer, Benjamin. National Responsibility Before God, in Cherry.

[21] *Congressional Record*, 33. Washington, DC: Government Printing Office, 711.

[22] H. Richard Niebuhr. *The Kingdom of God in America*. [reprint]. New York, NY: Harper & Row, 1959.

[23] Hughes, p. 18.

[24] James Melvin Washington (ed.). *A Testament of Hope: The Essential Writings and Speeches of Martin Luther King, Jr.* San Francisco, CA: HarperSanFrancisco, 1986.

[25] Abraham Lincoln. Second Inaugural Address. March 4, 1865. Inaugural Addresses of the Presidents of the United States. *Great Books Online.* Bartleby.com.

[26] Hughes, p. 43.

[27] Ibid., p. 71.

[28] *United States v. Macintosh.* In Robert T. Miller and Ronald B. Flowers (eds.). *Towards Benevolent Neutrality: Church, State, and the Supreme Court.* Waco, TX: Baylor University Press, 1977, p. 161.

[29] Hughes, p. 78.

[30] Hughes.

[31] *Seventh-day Adventist Encyclopedia* (2nd rev. ed.). Washington, DC: Review and Herald, 1995.

[32] *Seventh-day Adventist Encyclopedia*; First Church History. *The First Church of Seventh-day Adventists.* firstsdachurch.org.

[33] Erin Reid. *"The Army of the Lord": Principle, Precept, and Practice in Antebellum Adventist Abolition, 1856-1861.* Electronic Journal of Adventist History, 2001. http://www.oakwood.edu/historyportal/Ejah/Ereid.htm.

[34] Ibid.

[35] Ibid.

[36] Anne C. Loveland. Evangelicalism and Immediate Emancipation in American Antislavery Thought. *Journal of Southern History* 1966; 32(5): 176-177, 181, 182.

[37] Uriah Smith. Letters and Responses. *Advent Review and Sabbath Herald,* 13, no. 16, March 10, 1859, p. 124.

[38] ________. The Warning Voice of Time and Prophecy. *Advent Review and Sabbath Herald,* June 23, 1853, p. 8. Quoted in Trevor O'Reggio. Slavery, Prophecy and the American Nation as seen by the Adventist Pioneers, 1854-1865. *Faculty Publications,* Paper 23, 2006. http://digitalcommons.andrews.edu/church-history-pubs/23.

[39] James White. The Nation. *Advent Review and Sabbath Herald* 13, no. 16, August 12, 1862.

[40] See *Slavery.* blacksdahistory.org.

[41] Ellen G. White. Slavery and the War. *Advent Review and Sabbath Herald,* 13, no. 16, August 27, 1861, p. 101.

[42] "Carleton" to *Boston Journal,* February 13, 1865, reprinted in *National Freedman* 1 (April 1, 1865): 83, quoted in Jennifer Ritterhouse, *Growing Up Jim Crow: How Black and White Southern Children Learned Race.* Chapel Hill, NC: The University of North Carolina, 2006, page 28. Cited in Kessia Reyne Bennett. Resistance and Accommodation to Racism Among Early Seventh-day Adventist Missionaries in the American South: A Case Study on Relating to Oppressive Cultural Practices in Mission. *Master's Theses.* Andrews University. Paper 29, 2011.

[43] Bennett.

[44] Douglas A. Blackmon. *Slavery by Another Name: The Re-Enslavement of Black Americans from the Civil War to World War II.* New York, NY: Anchor Books, 2008; Bennett.

[45] Ronald D. Graybill. *E. G. White and Church Race Relations.* Washington, DC: Review and Herald, 1970.

[46] Rudyard Kipling. The White Man's Burden: The United States and the Philippine Islands. *New York Sun*, February 10, 1899.

[47] Ellen G. White. *Testimonies for the Church*, vol. 9. Washington, DC: Ellen G. White Estate, 1909, p. 205; *The Southern Work.* Washington, DC: Review and Herald, [1901] 2004, pp. 4-44; _____. Letter 5, 1895 (to "My Brethren in Responsible Positions in America," July 24, 1895); _____. Letter 37½, 1900 (to "Board Managers of the Review and Herald Office," February 26, 1900). Cited in Bennett.

[48] Graybill.

[49] *An Agitation and an Opportunity.* Ellen G. White Publications Office, Document File, No. 42.

[50] See for example the following works of Ellen G. White: Manuscript 15, 1909 ("Words of Encouragement to Self-Supporting Workers," April 26, 1900); Remarks on "The Work in the South," *General Conference Bulletin* IV (April 25, 1901), p. 482; Remarks on "The Southern Work," *General Conference Bulletin* V (April 14, 1903), p. 202; Letter 99, 1904 (to "James Edson White," February 23, 1904); Testimonies for the Church, vol. 9, p. 214; Manuscript 24, 1891 ("The Work in the Southern Field,"). Cited in Bennett.

[51] Graybill.

[52] See Ellen G. White. Letter 136, 1898 (to "J. E. White," August 14, 1898); also Letter 5, 1895 (to "My Brethren in Responsible Positions in America," July 24, 1895). Cited in Bennett.

[53] Bennett.

[54] Ibid, Abstract.

[55] Arthur Sheps. New introduction to *The Etiquette of Race Relations in the South: A Study in Social Control*, by Bertram Wilbur Doyle. New York: Schocken Books, 1971, p. xi; see also John Dollard. *Caste and Class in a Southern Town.* (3rd ed.). Garden City, NY: Doubleday Anchor Books, 1957. Cited in Bennett.

[56] Henry Lee Swint. *The Northern Teacher in the South, 1862-1870.* Nashville, TN: Vanderbilt University Press, 1941, p. v.

[57] Bennett; see also C. Vann Woodward. *The Strange Career of Jim Crow.* New York: Oxford University Press, 1955.

[58] There were several instances of Adventist missions to the South, but they were sporadic. See Bennett.

[59] White. Our Duty to the Colored People. Sermon to the General Conference Constituency, March 21, 1891, Battle Creek, Michigan. In Ellen G. White. *The Southern Work.* Washington, DC: Review and Herald, [1901] 2004.

[60] Bennett.

[61] Ibid., p. 54.

[62] White, *The Southern Work*; see also Graybill.

[63] Bennett, pp. 61-61.

[64] Ellen G. White. *Testimonies for the Church*, vol. 9, pp. 206-207.

[65] Richard W. Schwartz. *Light Bearers to the Remnant.* Mountain View, CA: Pacific Press, 1979, p. 234.

[66] See varying accounts of the events that led to the establishment of Regional Conferences in Louis B. Reynolds. *We Have Tomorrow: The Story of Seventh-day Adventists With an African Heritage.* Washington, DC: Review and Herald, 1984; W. W. Fordham. *Righteous Rebel.* Washington, DC: Review and Herald, 1990; Jacob Justiss. *Angels in Ebony.* Jacob Justiss (publisher), 1975.

[67] Justiss.

[68] Alexandra Yerboah. NAD Defends Racially Segregated Conferences. *ADVindicate.* April 2. 2015. advindicate.org

[69] Ricardo B. Graham. Black Seventh-day Adventists and Racial Reconciliation. In Calvin B. Rock (ed.). *Black Seventh-day Adventists Face the Twenty-first Century.* Hagerstown, MD: Review and Herald, 1996, p. 136.

[70] Bennett.

[71]Schwartz, pp. 571-572.

[72] Jeff Crocombe. The Seventh-day Adventist Church in Southern Africa—Race Relations and Apartheid. Conference Paper presented at the Association of Seventh-day Adventist Historians meetings, April 19-22, 2007, Oakwood College, Huntsville, Alabama.

[73] Phillip Wessels to Ellen G. White, January 14, 1893.

[74] Crocombe, p. 2.

[75] I. F. du Preez and Roy H. du Pre. *A Century of Good Hope: A History of the Good Hope Conference, its Educational Institutions and Early Workers, 1893-1993.* East London: Western Research Group/Southern History Association, 1994.

[76] See, Constitution, By-laws, Working Policy of the General Conference of Seventh-day Adventists [Southern African Division, 1931], p. 139.

[77] Seventh-day Adventist Church. Document to the Truth and Reconciliation Commission: Statement of Confession.
www.religion.uct.ac.za/.../DOCUMENT_TO_THE_TRUTH_AND_RECONCILIATION_COMMISSION.

[78] Crocombe, p. 7.

Prologue

In his second epistle, Peter makes a statement about the letters of Paul that provides a caution as we prepare to investigate Paul's letter to the Romans. Peter states:

> Therefore, dear friends, while you wait for these things, make every effort to be found at peace with Him without spot or blemish. Also, regard the patience of our Lord as an opportunity for salvation, just as our dear brother Paul has written to you according to the wisdom given to him. *He speaks about these things in all his letters in which there are some matters that are hard to understand. The untaught and unstable twist them to their own destruction, as they also do with the rest of the Scriptures* (2 Pet. 3:14-16 HCSB).

How Not to Read Romans

Because we take Peter's warning seriously, this prologue is designed to supply the reader with some important information for reading Paul's letter to the Romans. To begin, the much-debated question that must be addressed is: Why was Romans written? Until the nineteenth century, it was believed, according to the reformer Philip Melanchthon, that Paul wrote Romans as a "compendium of Christian theology."[1] In other words, Paul, as the apostle to the Gentiles, wrote to explain his universal gospel to believers in the capital city of the Roman Empire. In keeping with this understanding, it was generally assumed that justification by faith is the letter's major theme, and therefore, Romans should be read thematically.[2] This understanding of Paul's reason for writing Romans builds on the assumption that Paul was unaware of the social situation in Rome.

Most Christians, even Seventh-day Adventists, are familiar with this traditional way of reading Romans because it was made popular by the reformer Martin Luther in the sixteenth century. In fact, it is not an exaggeration to say that Luther's understanding of Paul's letter to the Romans was largely responsible for the Protestant Reformation. In his *Preface to the Letter of St. Paul to the Romans*, Luther describes Romans as the "purest Gospel," "the most important piece in the New Testament," "a bright light, almost bright enough to illumine the entire Scripture."[3] In the preface, Luther identifies what for him are the important themes of law, sin, grace, faith, flesh, and spirit. Then he establishes the binary tension between righteousness based on works of the law and being justified through faith. Luther ends his preface with the summary:

> We find in this letter, then, the richest possible teaching about what a Christian should know: the meaning of law, Gospel, sin, punishment, grace, faith, justice, Christ, God, good works, love, hope and the cross. We learn how we are to act toward everyone, toward the virtuous and sinful, toward the strong and the weak, friend and foe, and toward ourselves. Paul bases everything firmly

> on Scripture and proves his points with examples from his own experience and from the Prophets, so that nothing more could be desired. *Therefore it seems that St. Paul, in writing this letter, wanted to compose a summary of the whole of Christian and evangelical teaching which would also be an introduction to the whole Old Testament.* Without doubt, whoever takes this letter to heart possesses the light and power of the Old Testament. Therefore each and every Christian should make this letter the habitual and constant object of his study.[4]

When reading Luther's interpretation of Romans, it is essential that his historical context be kept in mind. Simply put, Luther read Romans against the backdrop of sixteenth-century Catholicism. Luther was reared in a Catholic family. At the age of 21 he chose to enter a monastery primarily because he lived in fear of God's judgment.

Luther was born into a religiously conservative German family in a remote village in Thuringia. His belief system was a mixture of old German paganism and the Christian mythology of Roman Catholicism. His schooling and university education instilled in him the fear of God and reverence for the church. The Catholic church used the terrors of hell and purgatory, relieved with the hope of heaven and dependence on indulgences, to ensure submission.[5]

God was alternately portrayed as a loving Father and as a frightening Deity. Christ was an implacable Judge who could only be importuned by His mother, Mary. These religious themes were graphically illustrated in handbooks that were popular during the Renaissance. One, entitled *On the Art of Dying*, includes a woodcut that depicts Christ on the day of judgment. Seated on a rainbow as Judge, Christ has a lily extending from His right ear that signifies the redeemed who are being led into paradise by angels, while from his left ear protrudes a sword that symbolizes the damned who are being hauled from their graves and cast into the fires of hell. It is little wonder that Luther suffered from bouts of depression fueled by the alternations of hope and fear in medieval religion.[6]

It is in this context that Luther sees Romans as literally, "good news." Not only does he experience personal freedom from guilt and the threat of hell, but he is also able to articulate a new understanding of truth that rocks the medieval Catholic Church. Luther makes this very point at the end of his preface.

> Paul also includes a salutary warning against human doctrines which are preached alongside the Gospel and which do a great deal of harm. It's as though he had clearly seen that out of Rome and through the Romans would come the deceitful, harmful Canons and Decretals [a papal decree concerning a point of canon law] along with the entire brood and swarm of human laws and commands that is now drowning the whole world and has blotted out this letter and the whole of the Scriptures, along with the Spirit

> and faith. Nothing remains but the idol Belly, and St. Paul depicts those people here as its servants. God deliver us from them. Amen.[7]

Yes, Luther's reading of Paul's letter to the Romans changed the course of human history. Yes, his emphasis on justification by faith alone changed the paradigm of religious discourse forever. And no doubt God used Martin Luther to arrest the dark night of Roman Catholic heresy, both its beliefs and practices. Using Adventist jargon, it may be said that Luther announced "present truth" to his generation. Yet for all its accomplishments,[8] Luther's reading of Romans is deeply problematic for several reasons.

As we will demonstrate shortly, Luther's reading of Romans has almost nothing to do with why Paul originally wrote the letter. Like most interpreters of his time, Luther read Paul's letters, including Romans, through the eyes of Augustine. The medieval theologians that were influential in Luther's thinking, e.g., Abelard, Anselm, and Aquinas derived their doctrinal understanding of the nature of humankind and of the universe from Paul, as interpreted by Augustine. Augustine was an early Christian writer who by explaining and expanding Paul's use of literal interpretation, allegory, typology, and Greco-Roman rhetorical devices laid the foundation of the rhetoric of the medieval period.[9]

Possibly based on his own struggle with guilt and a sense of damnation, Luther's reading of Romans accentuates personal salvation, i.e., grace received rather than grace extended to others. Augustine, writing three hundred years after Paul, identified justification as Paul's theological center of gravity. Although the early church understood that the relationship between Jews and Gentiles was what Paul was addressing in the letter to the Romans, for several reasons the church neglected to address this issue in any serious way. Instead, Augustine, in a self-centered approach, applied Paul's doctrine of justification to the "problem of introspective conscience, to the question: 'On what basis does a person find salvation?' And with Augustine, Western Christianity, with its emphasis on introspective achievements, began."[10] As an Augustinian monk, Luther, grappling with his conscience, found in Paul's writings, as read through the eyes of Augustine, the answer to his problem.

Most disturbing, and possibly to avoid "works righteousness," Luther's reading of Romans places emphasis on propositional truth or knowledge about Scripture—mere mental assent—while deemphasizing relational transformation of one's life through the Spirit. For example, Luther compares the letter of James with the "pure Gospel" derived from sources like Romans and concludes that James' letter is an "epistle of straw." Luther writes:

> In a word St. John's Gospel and his first epistle, St. Paul's epistles, especially Romans, Galatians, and Ephesians, and St. Peter's first epistle are the books that show you Christ and teach you all that is necessary and salvatory [salvific] for you to know, even if you were

> never to see or hear any other book or doctrine. Therefore St. James' epistle is really an epistle of straw, compared to these others, for it has nothing of the nature of the gospel about it.[11]

With these words, Luther reveals a lack of understanding of both Paul and James, and to some extent, the gospel itself. James simply emphasizes the necessity of fruit as evidence of genuine faith that is consistent with Paul's admonition to walk in the Spirit, thus rejecting the works of the flesh (Jam. 2:14-26; Rom. 8:3-11; cf. 1 Cor. 6:9-10). In fact, fearing a new type of righteousness by works, Luther advances no developed doctrine of sanctification.

Luther's misunderstanding of the implications of the gospel is more than theoretical. His ability to compartmentalize truth from lived experience had real world consequences. In 1543, just three years before his death, Luther wrote an infamous book entitled, *On the Jews and Their Lies*. In this book, he provides advice to the German authorities and people on how to deal with the Jewish populace of Germany. Luther makes seven recommendations.

> First to set fire to their synagogues or schools and to bury and cover with dirt whatever will not burn, so that no man will ever again see a stone or cinder of them. This is to be done in honor of our Lord and of Christendom. Second, I advise that their houses also be razed and destroyed. Third, I advise that all their prayer books and Talmudic writings, in which such idolatry, lies, cursing and blasphemy are taught, be taken from them. Fourth, I advise that their rabbis be forbidden to teach henceforth on pain of loss of life and limb. Fifth, I advise that safe-conduct on the highways be abolished completely for the Jews . . . . Let them stay at home. Sixth, I advise that usury be prohibited to them, and that all cash and treasure of silver and gold be taken from them and put aside for safekeeping. Seventh, I commend putting a flail, an ax, a hoe, a spade, a distaff, or a spindle into the hands of young, strong Jews and Jewesses and letting them earn their bread in the sweat of their brow, as was imposed on the children of Adam (Gen. 3:19).[12]

Luther goes so far as to claim that "We are at fault in not slaying them [thus] avenging the death of Jesus Christ."[13] Luther then makes these final recommendations.

> I wish and I ask that our rulers who have Jewish subjects exercise a sharp mercy toward these wretched people, as suggested above, to see whether this might not help (though it is doubtful). They must act like a good physician who, when gangrene has set in, proceeds without mercy to cut, saw, and burn flesh, veins, bone, and marrow. Such a procedure must also be followed in this instance.

> Burn down their synagogues, forbid all that I enumerated earlier, force them to work, and deal harshly with them, as Moses did in the wilderness, slaying three thousand lest the whole people perish. They surely do not know what they are doing; moreover, as people possessed, they do not wish to know it, hear it, or learn it. There it would be wrong to be merciful and confirm them in their conduct. If this does not help we must drive them out like mad dogs, so that we do not become partakers of their abominable blasphemy and all their other vices and thus merit God's wrath and be damned with them. I have done my duty. Now let everyone see to his. I am exonerated.
>
> My essay, I hope, will furnish a Christian (who in any case has no desire to become a Jew) with enough material not only to defend himself against the blind, venomous Jews, but also to become the foe of the Jews' malice, lying, and cursing, and to understand not only that their belief is false but that they are surely possessed by all devils. May Christ, our dear Lord, convert them mercifully and preserve us steadfastly and immovably in the knowledge of him, which is eternal life. Amen.[14]

Although some apologists may argue that *On the Jews and Their Lies* represents a "dark period" in the reformer's life, recent scholarship demonstrates that the views expressed in this book are attitudes towards Jews held by Luther throughout his life. Eric Gritsch states,

> Given Luther's consistent rejection of the Jews, ranging from theological polemics to political persecution, he is not just "anti-Judaic" (as some Luther researchers label him), but genuinely "anti-Semitic" in accordance with the broad, contemporary definition of anti-Semitism as "hostile to or prejudice against the Jews." There is even a hint of racism in Luther when he commented on the unsubstantiated rumor that Jews killed Christian children. This crime "still shines forth from their eyes and their skin. We are at fault in not slaying them [the Jews]." Such a declaration cannot be limited to a specific historical context. It is timeless and means "death to the Jews," whether it is uttered by Luther or Adolf Hitler.[15]

Granted, medieval Christianity in Europe was characterized by anti-Semitism. Catholic clerics and reformers generally viewed the Jews as Jesus killers, who without accepting Christianity were destined for destruction. They interpreted Paul's letters through an anti-Jewish cultural lens. While at the same time, they ignored Paul's seemingly enigmatic statements, "all Israel will be saved" and "from the standpoint of the gospel they [Israel] are enemies for your sake, but from the standpoint of *God's* choice they are beloved for the sake of the fathers; for the gifts and the calling of God are irrevocable" (Rom. 11:26, 28-29 NASB).[16] Luther's reading of Paul's letter to the Romans raises several questions. How do we account for the gap between Luther's gospel knowledge and his attitude and practices? Is there a fatal flaw in Luther's understanding of Romans and thus of the gospel? Was Luther's gospel compromised by cultural accommodation? More important, by creating in Luther a larger than life figure, have we obscured essential aspects of the gospel of Christ in Paul's letter to the Romans?[17]

How to Read Romans

Although the nineteenth-century scholar Ferdinand Baur was the first to challenge Luther's way of reading of Romans, the Swedish theologian, Krister Stendahl is the first (1960) interpreter to suggest that Paul wrote Romans as a pastoral letter designed to address Jews and Gentiles in Rome. Stendahl confronts the old way of interpreting Romans directly. He writes,

> Pauline interpretation—and hence both conscious and unconscious reading and quoting of Paul by scholars and lay people alike—have for many centuries been out of touch with one of the most basic of the questions and concerns that shaped Paul's thinking in the first place: the relation between Jews and Gentiles . . . . We think that Paul spoke about justification by faith, using the Jewish-Gentile situation . . . as an example. But Paul was chiefly concerned about the relation between Jews and Gentiles—and in the development of *this* concern he used as one of his arguments the idea of justification by faith . . . . The lost centrality of 'Jews and Gentiles' is most clearly to be felt in the study of Romans . . . . What is Romans about? To me the climax of Romans is actually chapters 9-11 . . . . The question is the relations between two communities and their coexistence in the mysterious plan of God.[18]

Scott Hafemann summarizes Stendhal's position as follows:

> Stendhal's reinterpretation of Paul's theology grew out of his conviction that, due to Reformation theology and the grid of Luther's own conversion experience, Paul's teaching concerning justification by faith had been removed from its original setting and transposed into the very center of his teaching about salvation. Rather than addressing the status of Gentiles within God's plan for the world, as it does in Paul's writings, the doctrine of justification by faith was now seen to be the abstract doctrinal response to the despair and failure of humanity brought about by the attempt to live up to the moral demands of the Law or by the pride caused by humanity's attempt to justify itself by the Law.

> The ultimate result of this loss of the original focus of justification is that the Pauline problem of the relationship between Jews and Gentiles becomes captive to the Western problem of the introspective conscience.[19]

Building on the work of Stendahl, many interpreters of Romans now agree that *a primary reason* for Paul's writing of Romans is the ethnic tension between Christian Gentiles and Jews living in Rome.[20] In other words, Paul writes Romans to address an actual situation. On what evidence is this new consensus based? What is known about the historical background of Roman Christianity?

Paul, the author of Romans, is a Diaspora Jew born in Tarsus. He is a moderate Pharisee of the school of Hillel, called by Christ as the apostle to the Gentiles. Paul is conversant with the three cultural influences of his day: Jewish, Greek, and Roman. He spoke the Greek language and was familiar with Greek philosophy and poetry. Although a Roman citizen who was conversant with Roman governance and rhetoric, Paul was steeped in the Jewish religion of his ancestors (Phil. 3:1-4; Acts 21:39; 22:28).[21]

When Paul dictates his letter to Tertius in Corinth and sends it, possibly by Phoebe, to the house churches in Rome (ca. 57-58 A.D.), important historical factors have shaped the situation to which he writes (Rom. 16:1, 22-23, 1 Cor. 1:14). There is evidence of a Jewish community dating back to the second century B.C. In official sources, Jews in Rome are first mentioned in 139 B.C., when they were expelled from Rome by Praetor Hispaius. Evidently, they were considered a cult by the Roman authorities. Yet, this expulsion apparently was not motivated by anti-Semitism, because other "oriental religions" were also expelled. After the annexation of Palestine in 63 A.D., Pompey brought to Rome many Jewish captives who were subsequently freed.[22] By the early first century, Cicero reports that Jews represented a large segment of the population of Rome, possibly as many as 50,000.[23]

Considerable evidence also supports the fact that Roman attitudes towards Jewish residents of Rome were negative. Although there are positive comments about Jewish people in Roman literature, most classical writers, such as Cicero, Tacitus, Horace, and Juvenal stereotyped Jews and Jewish religion. It is believed that Roman authorities, from Tiberius to Claudius, viewed Jews as a threat to Roman values. Romans were specially offended by Jewish proselytizing and the insinuation of Jewish customs into Roman society.[24] In fact, Tiberius Caesar expelled Jews from Rome in 19 A.D., "because a Roman lady [upper strata] who inclined toward Judaism had been deceived by Jewish swindlers. The synagogues were closed, the vessels burned, and 4,000 Jewish youths were sent upon military service to Sardinia."[25]

While the origins of Christianity in Rome are unknown, there is general agreement that Jewish converts to Christianity introduced the new religion to Roman synagogues in the mid-40s A.D. (cf. Acts 13:42-47; 14:1-6; 17:1-5; 18:4; 19:8-10). There can be little doubt that early Christianity in Rome had a decidedly Jewish character. This is possibly why Paul's letter to the Romans assumes knowledge of the Old Testament. Jewish converts and Gentile proselytes worshipped within the shadow of Jewish synagogues. There is no indication that in this period Roman authorities saw a distinction between Judaism and Jewish Christianity.[26]

The Roman historian Gaius Suetonius in *The Lives of the Twelve Caesars* makes the following statement. "Since the Jews constantly made disturbances at the instigation of Chrestus, he [Claudius] expelled Jews from Rome."[27] Interpreters agree that Suetonius' misspelling of the name Christ (*Christus*) was a common error. He wrote 72 years after the fact (121 A.D.). More importantly, it seems that Suetonius mistakenly believed that Christ was present, in person, causing the disturbances in the synagogues, rather than teachings about Christ.[28]

Modern commentators dispute whether the expulsion of Jews from Rome was total or partial. However, Luke indicates that the expulsion was total. He states, "After this Paul left Athens and went to Corinth. There he found a Jew named Aquila, a native of Pontus, who had recently come from Italy with his wife Priscilla, *because Claudius had ordered all Jews to leave Rome*" (Acts 18:1-2). Claudius' expulsion of Jews from Rome in 49 A.D. marks a turning point in the history of Roman Christianity. In the years after the expulsion, without Jewish leadership, Gentile Christians most likely organized into several house-churches because the use of synagogues was prohibited.[29] It is reasonable to assume that these churches, over time, became Gentile in orientation, especially as related to Jewish ritual practices (cf. Rom. 14:1-12).

After the death of Claudius in 54 A.D. and the ascension of Nero, the anti-Jewish edict was either repealed or fell into disuse. Under Nero, who was more favorable to Jews than his predecessors, Jews began to return to Rome in large numbers. Among those who returned were Prisca and Aquila, who found that their status in the Christian house churches had changed dramatically. Gentiles now held the ascendancy in numbers, power, and influence.

> It is likely that the separation from the synagogues during the years of the edict had exacerbated the tendency toward non-Jewish patterns of religious life, while the addition of new converts who were never associated with the synagogues attenuated the prominence of traditional Jewish beliefs and practices. It is also likely that the vulnerable status of the Jews and the prevailing anti-Semitism of the time were important factors in the reception the returning Jewish Christians encountered. With the Jewish Christians' return to Rome . . . there was increased potential for conflict based on the growing independence of the Roman house churches from the synagogues and the concomitant increasing of autonomy from Christianity's Jewish roots.[30]

The returning Jews were not restored to positions of leadership in the Christian assemblies and it is likely that resistance would have met any attempts to re-establish distinctively Jewish traditions. "The fact that Prisca and Aquila established a new house church may be an indication of the problem of integrating Jewish and gentile Christians and the questions of leadership raised by the return of the Jewish Christians to Rome."[31]

In light of this situation, J. Paul Sampley succinctly describes Paul's purpose for writing to believers in Rome.

> All of Romans, from beginning to end, is an apostolic intervention, pastoral in style, in an intramural, ethnically-grounded struggle over leadership and position in the Roman house churches. The entire letter is directed towards helping all of Paul's readers and hearers to recognize and affirm their unity in the powerful gospel of God"[32]

Christ Has Welcomed You is not a commentary. However, we will trace Paul's sometimes repetitious argument almost paragraph by paragraph, sometimes sentence by sentence, to demonstrate that Paul used his letter to believers in Rome to promote reconciliation and unity. Many readers of Romans find Paul's argument difficult to follow, because he introduces ideas in one place and develops them later in the letter. His use of communication devices that are unfamiliar to the modern reader also may render his prose obscure. We have attempted to address these issues while maintaining the substance and flow of Paul's argument.

Again, how should Romans be read? Romans should be read as Paul's explanation of the gospel, i.e., the person and work of Jesus Christ. Through a sustained argument using a variety of literary and rhetorical devices, the letter assumes the justification of believers. It focuses on corporate sanctification, and is written to foster reconciliation and unity among ethnically divided Gentile and Jewish Christians in Rome. Paul hopes that a united community would pray for his mission to the Jews in Jerusalem and provide a base of support for his anticipated mission to the Gentiles in Spain.

---

[1] Philip Melanchthon. *The Loci Communes of Philip Melanchthon.* Translated by C. L. Hill. Boston, MA: Meador Publishing Company, 1944, p. 69.

[2] Gregory J. Allen. *Reconciliation in the Pauline Tradition: Its Occasions, Meanings, and Functions.* Doctoral Dissertation. Boston University, School of Theology, 1995.

[3] Martin Luther. Vorrede auff die Epistel S. Paul: an die Romer. In Hans Volz and Heinz Blanke (eds.). *D. Martin Luther: Die gantze Heilige Schrifft Deudsch 1545 aufs new zurericht*, vol. 2. Translated by Andrew Thornton. Munich: Roger & Bernhard, 1972, pp. 2254-2268.

[4] Ibid.

[5] Roland H. Bainton, *Here I Stand – A Life of Martin Luther.* Nashville, TN: Abington Press, [1950] 2013.

[6] Ibid.

[7] Luther.

[8] Luther, along with other reformers, produced five principles, the so-called "five solas of the Reformation," in response to medieval Catholicism: *Sola Scriptura* (Scripture alone); *Sola Fide* (faith alone); *Sola Gratia* (grace alone); *Solus Christus* (Christ alone); *Soli Deo Gloria* (to the glory of God alone). See Terry L. Johnson. *The Case for Traditional Protestantism: The Solas of the Reformation.* Edinburgh, UK: The Banner of Truth Trust, 2004.

[9] Robert Paul Seesengood. *Paul: A Brief History.* Chichester, UK: Wiley-Blackwell, 2010.

[10] Krister Stendhal. *Paul Among Jews and Gentiles.* Philadelphia, PA: Fortress Press, 1976, p. 16.

[11] *D. Martin Luther Werke.* Kritische Gesamtausgabe. [Schriften] ("Writings"). 69 vols. plus. Weimar: Bohlaus, 1883-, 35:362.

[12] Martin Luther. *On the Jews and Their Lies.* Lexington, KY: Coleman Rydie, 2009. Summary produced by Councils of Centers on Jewish-Christian Relations. ccjr.us/dialogika-resources. See also Eric Gritsch. *Martin Luther's Anti-Semitism: Against His Better Judgment.* Grand Rapids, MI: William B. Eerdmans, 2012, p. ix; Gritsch cites *D. Martin Luther Werke.* 53, 523:1, 24, 30, 32; 524:16, 18; 525:31; 536:34-37; Jaroslav Pelikan and Martin Lehmann (eds.). *Luther's Works,* 55 vols. Philadelphia: Fortress Press; St. Louis: Concordia, 1955-1986, pp. 47, 268-272.

[13] Gritsch, p. ix, quotes, Pelikan and Lehmann, pp. 47, 267.

[14] *Luther's Works,* Volume 47: The Christian in Society IV, Philadelphia, PA: Fortress Press, 1971, pp. 268-293. Jewish Virtual Library. jewishvirtuallibrary.org.

[15] Gritsch, p. xi. Gritsch quotes Erin McKean (ed.). *The New Oxford American Dictionary* (2nd ed.). Oxford, UK: Oxford University Press, 2005; *D. Martin Luther Werke,* 53, 552:9-12; Pelikan and Lehmann, pp. 47, 267. See also Robert Michael. *Holy Hatred: Christianity, Antisemitism, and the Holocaust.* New York, NY: Palgrave McMillan, 2006. Critics of a benign view of Martin Luther cite his involvement in the Peasants War (1524-1526) that spread across the Germanic regions of the Holy Roman Empire in response to a number of social and economic changes that accompanied the death of feudalism and the rise of a new social order. Peasants revolted against high taxes, arduous labor, and starvation. The notions of freedom, the right to reject authority, and the doctrine of *Sola Scriptura,* espoused by Luther encouraged the peasants in their revolt. The peasants issued *The Twelve Articles of the Christian Union of Upper Swabia* (*The Twelve Articles of the Black Forest*), which outlined their grievances and supported them with biblical texts. Luther's *Admonition to Peace* refuted the biblical justifications of the peasants while at the same time urged the princes to recognize the peasants' demands as reasonable. Luther encouraged peaceful protest. After receiving a shock from the peasants' actions during a tour of the areas in revolt in May 1525, Luther condemned the peasants in *Against the Murderous, Thieving Hordes of Peasants,* and maintained the right of the princes to suppress them with violence. He wrote, "It is right and lawful to slay at the first opportunity a public rebel . . . . whosoever can, should smite, strangle, and stab, secretly or publicly . . . a rebellious man . . . . Just as one must slay a mad dog." (See James Harvey Robinson. Luther Against the Peasants (1525). *Readings in European History,* 2 vols. Boston, MA: Ginn & Company, 1906, pp. 2:106-108. The History Guide, Lectures on Early Modern European History. historyguide.org.) When the peasants were crushed in 1525, they felt that Luther had betrayed them. The Catholic Church took this occasion to upbraid Luther for siding with the peasants at first and then deserting them when it was clear that they would lose. Luther was even stoned in Orlamunde for his role in the conflict. It is estimated that 100,000 combatants and civilians had died in the revolt by the end of 1525, and the authorities carried out

murderous reprisals for two additional years. (Frederick Engels. *The Peasants War in Germany.* Moscow: Foreign Languages Publishing House, 1956; See Martin Luther. *Admonition to Peace* (1525); _____. *Against the Murderous, Thieving Hordes of Peasants*; Theodore G. Tappert. *Selected Writings of Martin Luther, 1523-1526.* Philadelphia, PA: Fortress Press, 2007; Peasants War. Encyclopedia.com.)

[16] Seesengood.

[17] A new history of the life of Luther, "Martin Luther: The Idea That Changed the World," that aired on PBS, September 12, 2017, identifies his many accomplishments but also seeks to rationalize his coarse language and boorish behavior. Most disturbingly, this seeks to apologize his egregious offenses against German peasants and the Jews. It is noteworthy that in Scripture no such excuses are made for "heroes," such as King David. His sins are named, and, more significantly, his repentance and confession are recorded as well his obedience to God.

[18] Stendhal, pp. 1-4.

[19] Scott J. Hafemann. Paul and His Interpreters. In G. F. Hawthorne, R. P. Martin and D. G. Reid (eds.). *Dictionary of Paul and His Letters.* Downers Grove, IL: InterVarsity Press, 1993, pp. 675.

[20] Karl P. Donfried. Introduction 1991: The Romans Debate Since 1977. In Karl P. Donfried (ed.). *The Romans Debate.* Grand Rapids, MI: Baker Academic, 1991.

[21] Richard Wallace and Wynne Williams *The Three Worlds of Paul of Tarsus.* New York, NY: Routledge, 1998.

[22] Wolfgang Wiefel. The Jewish Community in Ancient Rome and the Origins of Roman Christianity. In Donfried.

[23] Cicero, *Pro Flacco* 28. pp. 66-67.

[24] James C. Walters. *Ethnic Issues in Paul's Letter to the Romans: Changing Self-Definitions in Earliest Roman Christianity.* Valley Forge, PA: Trinity Press International, 1993.

[25] The unedited full-text of the 1906 *Jewish Encyclopedia.* JewishEncyclopedia.com.

[26] Wiefel; James D. G. Dunn. *Word Commentary, vol. 38a, Romans 1-8.* Dallas, TX: Word Books, 1988.

[27] Gaius Suetonius Tranquillus. Divus Claudius 25.4. In *The Lives of the Twelve Caesars.* (rev. ed.). Translated by Robert Graves. New York, NY: Penguin Books, 1979, pp. 200-201.

[28] F. F. Bruce. The Romans Debate—Continued. In Donfried.

[29] Ibid.

[30] Allen, p. 28.

[31] Ibid, p. 29.

[32] J. Paul Sampley. The Weak and the Strong: Paul's Careful and Crafty Rhetorical Strategy in Romans 14 – 15:13. In L. Michael White and O. Larry Yarbrough (eds.). *The Social World of the First Christians: Essays in Honor of Wayne A. Meeks.* Minneapolis, MN: Fortress Press, 1995, p. 49.

CHAPTER ONE
The Gospel

Romans 1:1-17

A thoughtful Apostle Paul sits down to compose the longest, and perhaps the most nuanced, letter of his ministry. Aware of the schism that separates the Gentile and Jewish house assemblies in Rome's Christian community, Paul invokes the apostolic authority given him by the Risen Christ to challenge the primary identity and practices of both groups. His purpose is to present Jesus Christ as the solution to their ethnic division. Paul must be cautious in his approach; he is not well known to all of his audience. Although he is acquainted with some of the Jews in Rome, he is not known to many in the Gentile majority. He did not found the assemblies in Rome, but he asserts his commission as the apostle to the Gentiles to seek some credibility among this segment of his audience. Paul uses his opening remarks to signal the need for holistic sanctification among Roman believers.

An Urgent Letter

Paul uses a pastoral technique that he has used in some of his other letters: he *commends* before he *corrects*. For example, in writing to Corinth, Paul commends the community for following the tradition of women covering their heads in worship before condemning wealthy believers for their behavior towards the poor at the Lord's Supper (1 Cor. 11:2-33). In his letter to the Romans, Paul acknowledges the faith of the Roman assemblies before he reminds them "boldly on some points" in need of rectification (15:15). In other words, he affirms the Roman believers before he corrects them.

Ever mindful of his virtual anonymity to the Gentile majority in Rome, Paul moves from veiled criticism back to affirmation. He states, "I am a debtor both to Greeks and to barbarians, both to the wise and to the foolish—hence my eagerness to proclaim the gospel to you also who are in Rome" (1:14-15). Notice that in verse 14, Paul employs the customary categories "Greek and barbarian" used in Hellenistic culture to describe all of humankind.

As we have seen, Greek thought divided all humanity into two categories. There were the "civilized" Greeks who were viewed as honorable and the "uncivilized" barbarians who were viewed as shameful.[1] Greeks considered all ethnic groups who did not speak the Greek language to be barbarians. While Paul later undermines these cultural categories for those in Christ, he nevertheless commends Gentile believers with this description to emphasize his obligation to the non-Jew.

Paul has learned his lesson; he will not attempt to persuade his Roman audience to reconcile using philosophy or rhetorical eloquence. He will use the gospel of God (1 Cor. 2:1-5; cf. Acts 17:16-34). Paul accomplishes this purpose by building his argument throughout the letter with a variety of appeals to his audience based on the compelling power of the gospel. We will consider a few examples of Paul's skillful methods.

As we already noted, Paul was not the founder of the Christian assemblies in Rome. This is possibly the reason for his diplomatic style (cf. 1 Cor. 4:14-21). He goes out of his way to affirm both Gentiles and Jews in Rome. In the salutation of his letter, Paul recognizes the Jewish minority. "For example, in 1:1-3 Paul refers to a gospel of God that is promised in the Old Testament and locates the lineage of God's Son within the descent of King David, thus acknowledging the Jewish community."[2] Paul explains that in the "history of salvation," the gospel was given first to the Jews and then the Greeks, or Gentiles (1:16). Then in his thanksgiving, Paul affirms the Gentile majority (1:14).

Paul attempts to be tactful by using a rhetorical device called *correctio* to take the edge off the delicate admonition to his audience: "For I am longing to see you so that I may share with you some spiritual gift to strengthen you—or rather so that we may be mutually encouraged by each other's faith, both yours and mine" (1:11-12). With these words, Paul acknowledges that both he and the Roman believers are in need of growth in Christ. Paul is not specific as to the spiritual gift he intends to share with them; yet, if his letter is any indication, then his gift is that of exhortation to unity (12:8a). Throughout the letter, Paul exhorts the believers in Rome to become one body in Christ (12:1-8).

Paul uses cryptic language to expand his reason for wanting to visit the Roman believers, especially the Gentiles. He says, "I want you to know, brothers and sisters, that I have often intended to come to you (but thus far have been prevented), in order that I may reap some harvest among you as I have among the rest of the Gentiles" (1:13). Paul uses the language of family, "brothers and sisters," to address the Gentile majority (cf. 11:25). He couples his address with what is known as a disclosure formula, literally, "I do not want you to be unaware," to reiterate his intense desire to visit the Roman believers and to highlight the necessity of his visit (cf. 1 Thess. 4:13).

Here, for the first time, Paul discloses *one of the primary goals* for his anticipated visit, literally, "that I may obtain some fruit among you also, even as among the rest of the Gentiles" (1:13b NASB). Paul signals specifically that Gentile believers in Rome are in need of spiritual growth. Yet, his language raises several questions. Why does Paul use evangelistic language to refer to Gentile believers in Rome? Why does he use language that seems to be drawn from his mission to the unbelieving Gentile world? Could it be that Paul uses evangelistic language, literally "to have some fruit," to signal both the urgency of his projected visit and a forthcoming appeal to the Gentile majority to promote unity? (15:1-13; 17-20).

Paul believes that his God-given work is to communicate the gospel; this is what provides the urgency for his visit to the divided church assemblies in Rome and his appeal for unity among them. Therefore, it is important for us to gain some clarity with regard to what Paul means by "the gospel of God."

Paul uses the variations, "the gospel of God," "the gospel of His Son," "the gospel," and "my gospel" throughout the letter (1:1, 9, 16; 2:16). In verses 1b-4, Paul discloses his seminal understanding of the gospel. Later in his "thesis statement," he will describe the function of the gospel (1:16-17). Now, Paul unveils the essence of the message. He states, "God's good news—which He promised long ago through His prophets in the Holy Scriptures—*concerning His Son, Jesus Christ our Lord,* who was a descendant of David according to the flesh and who has been declared to be the powerful Son of God by the resurrection from the dead according to the Spirit of holiness" (HCSB).

Paul makes three foundational claims about the gospel. First, with the expression "the gospel of God," Paul identifies God the Father as the source or originator of the gospel (cf. 15:16; 2 Cor. 11:7). He uses the term gospel to assert that God is the author of genuine good news.

Second, Paul explains that God's gospel is not a first century novelty. The good news was first announced long ago in the Old Testament. Throughout the letter, Paul uses primarily the Septuagint (LXX), the Greek translation of the Old Testament, which is familiar to both Hellenized Jews and Gentile proselytes in his audience.

Third, and most important, Paul establishes the fact that Jesus Christ is the content of God's good news with the words, "the gospel concerning his Son, who was descended from David according to the flesh and was declared to be Son of God with power according to the spirit of holiness by resurrection from the dead, Jesus Christ our Lord" (1:3-4). Christ as the content of the gospel is precisely what Paul means when he uses the expressions "the gospel of his Son" and "the gospel of Christ" (1:9; 15:19; cf. 1 Cor. 9:12).

References to a person as Savior and his story as the gospel, or good news, were not first applied to Jesus in the Greco-Roman world. First century believing communities developed in the social context of a myth that dominated most of the Mediterranean world and beyond: the myth that Caesar Augustus was the divine harbinger of peace and salvation for the world. Born in 63 B.C., Caesar Augustus was the emperor at the time of Jesus' birth. Augustus came to power in 31 B.C., during a period of civil unrest that followed the assassination of Julius Caesar. Augustus' military conquest of the enemies of Rome, and the peace (*pax Romana*) that resulted, led to his celebration as a "savior" to his people. His great deeds were described in terms of freedom, justice, peace, and salvation, and his birth was proclaimed with the Greek term *euangelion*, "good news" or "gospel." His birthday came to be celebrated as the first day of the new year. The so-called "emperor cult" that emerged was promulgated through poems, inscriptions, coins, and images.[3]

In this politically-charged environment, a world awash with a "gospel" associated with emperor worship, Paul in the opening verses of his letter to the Romans boldly asserts that Jesus Christ, Savior and Risen Lord, is the good news of God. Stated succinctly, the gospel is *not just about* Christ, Jesus Christ *is* the gospel of God. In 2 Corinthians, Paul puts it this way:

> And even if our gospel is veiled, it is veiled to those who are perishing. *In their case the god of this world has blinded the minds of the unbelievers, to keep them from seeing the light of the gospel of the glory of Christ, who is the image of God* (2 Cor. 4:3-4 HCSB).

With the words, "Jesus Christ our Lord" (1:4), Paul indicates that the historical person, Jesus of Nazareth, is the Messiah or Christ, God's anointed One, the Savior predicted in Scriptures (cf. 3:21). Paul uses the title, "Lord," to describe the reality of Christ's authority over all believers. Paul will later refer to the Lordship of Christ as the *sine qua non* for sanctification (6:15-23). Indeed, submission to Christ's lordship is at the heart of the Great Controversy. The question of who merits worship, will be answered when history culminates with the universal reenactment of the words, "every knee will bow, and every tongue will confess that Jesus Christ is Lord to the glory of God" (Phil. 2:9-11; cf. 14:11).

In addition, Paul bolsters his claim that the historical Jesus is the predicted Messiah by asserting that Jesus "was of the seed of David according to the flesh" (1:3; 2 Tim. 2:8-9; cf. Ps. 89:3). The Son of God has come as a human being to fulfill God's promise to David of an eternal throne (2 Sam. 7:12-16). The idea of a Davidic Messiah who would save the nation was known both in Judaism and in the early church. Here Paul sets forth Jesus as the royal Messiah, come to assume His throne.[4]

By establishing Jesus as the seed of David, Paul affirms that salvation is of the Jews (cf. Jn. 4:22). Later he confirms this point by arguing that Jewish believers in Rome, as well as himself, are the seed of Abraham (11:1; cf. 4:1). Although establishing here the Jewish descent of Jesus, Paul will later deconstruct the priority of Jewish descent from Abraham in order to establish the priority of faith for all who believe, both Jew and Gentile (4:16; 9:7-8). This important point serves Paul's purpose of establishing the common situation of Gentiles and Jews in Rome and appealing for reconciliation and unity between them.

Next, Paul uses the archaic expression "according to Spirit of holiness" to confirm that the Holy Spirit resurrected Christ from the dead (8:11). It is on the basis of His resurrection that Paul says Christ "was declared to be Son of God in power." Here, Paul refers to Christ's ascension and enthronement as the Risen Lord, both made possible through His resurrection from the dead (1:16; cf. Mt. 28:19). Paul emphasizes the role of the Holy Spirit in the resurrection of Jesus Christ because Paul will later argue that the same power that raised Jesus, i.e., the Holy Spirit, is needed for the ongoing sanctification of the believers in Rome (8:1-17; cf. Gal. 5:16-26).[5]

Thus according to Paul, Jesus Christ is the human descendant of David, but more important, He is the divine Son of God (1 Tim. 3:16). With these initial claims, Paul lays the foundation for a sweeping explanation of Christ as God's gospel and the solution to the ethnic division in Rome.

Notice that in these opening verses, the roles of Father, Son, and Spirit are addressed. It is generally recognized that Romans is the most "Trinitarian" of all the Pauline letters. Could it be that from the beginning Paul is recommending to the divided community in Rome the unified community that is the Godhead? Throughout the letter, Paul describes the Father, Son, and Spirit as cooperating in the work of salvation. Being of one nature, their roles are different, yet they act as one. Nevertheless, Paul focuses on the saving activity of the Son as God's good news.

Paul discloses his gospel in a nutshell in writing to Corinth.

> Now I would remind you, brothers and sisters, of the good news that I proclaimed to you, which you in turn received, in which also you stand, through which also you are being saved, if you hold firmly to the message that I proclaimed to you—unless you have come to believe in vain. *For I handed on to you as of first importance what I in turn had received: that Christ died for our sins in accordance with the scriptures, and that he was buried, and that he was raised on the third day in accordance with the scriptures* (1 Cor. 15:1-4).

Paul, in this text, stresses the idea that Christ died to pay the penalty for sin so that those who believe might be saved (1:16-17; 3:21-26; 2 Cor. 5:21). Yet, in Romans and in other letters, Paul conflates Christ's nature with His work. Paul explains that the death of Christ was motivated by His love for sinners, a love that reveals the very nature of God (5:5-8; 8:35-39; Eph. 5:2; 2 Cor. 5:14-15).

In fact, Paul prays that the Ephesians will know the immensity of the love of Christ.

> For this reason I bow my knees before the Father from whom every family in heaven and on earth takes its name . . . . I pray that you may have the power to comprehend, with all the saints, what is the breadth and length and height and depth and to know the love of Christ that surpasses knowledge, so that you may be filled with all the fullness of God (Eph. 3:14-15, 18-19).

For Paul, the gospel is Jesus Christ—loving, condescending, teaching, serving, finally dying and being raised in order to rescue sinners (2 Cor. 5:21).

How do we as Adventists understand the gospel? Is our good news primarily a set of propositions or doctrines, or is the gospel a Person? Is our gospel focus fundamental "truths" or is it the "Truth" embodied in God's Son? For Paul, the good news *is* Christ Himself, not just a correct understanding *about* Him, or biblical principles, or church doctrines, or any other person or thing. Indeed, doctrines, rightly understood, are only valid as they are viewed and interpreted through the person and work of Christ. In point of fact, the messages of the three angels in Revelation 14, especially the message of the third angel, correctly interpreted, proclaim God's final self-revelation and appeal in Jesus Christ (14:6-12; cf. Rev. 1:1; Heb. 1:1-4). Paul makes it clear in one concise statement, encapsulating salvation, that "God was in Christ reconciling the world to himself" (2 Cor. 5:19).

Note Ellen White's consistency with Paul's emphasis on the primacy of Christ.

> The sacrifice of Christ as an atonement for sin is the great truth around which *all other truths cluster*. In order to be rightly understood and appreciated, every truth in the Word of God, from Genesis to Revelation, must be studied in the light that streams from the *cross of Calvary*.[6]
>
> Let the science of salvation be the burden of every sermon. Let it be the theme of every song of praise. Let it be poured forth in every supplication. *Let nothing be brought into the preaching to supplement Jesus Christ, the wisdom and power of God.*
>
> Let his name, the only name given under heaven whereby we may be saved, be exalted in every discourse. From Sabbath to Sabbath let the trumpet of the watchmen give a certain sound. Let them hold forth the word of life, presenting hope to the penitent, and Christ as the stronghold to the believer. Let them reveal the way of peace to the troubled and despondent; let them show forth the grace and completeness of Christ as their living Saviour.[7]

Did Ellen White understand the gospel in a way that we as Adventists have lost sight of today? In light of Adventism's traditional interpretive emphasis, what do we make of her Christ-centered focus?

It is critical to observe that Paul, from the beginning to the end of his letter to the Romans, establishes Christ and Scripture's revelation of Him as the authoritative basis for faith and practice. Paul does not appeal to Scripture alone, but to God's self-revelation in Christ. For Paul, as for all other New Testament authors, Jesus Christ is the "key to knowledge," the interpretive lens through which all Christian experience is perceived and lived (1:1-4, 16-17; 15:3-7; 16:25-27; cf. Mt. 5:38-39; Lk. 24:27, 44-45; Heb. 1:1-3). Later, Paul will criticize first century Pharisaic Judaism and the so-called Judaizers for a misunderstanding of Torah (God's law)—Pharisaic

Judaism rejected the person and work of Jesus Christ, while the Judaizers rejected His priority (2:17-29; 3:19-20; 7:7-23; 10:1-21; cf. Jn. 9:40-41).

Although Paul further exposes his understanding of the gospel in his thesis statement (1:16-17) and throughout the letter, it is important to establish that Paul's treatment of the gospel of God in Romans is not abstract or theoretical. For Paul, the gospel as explained in this letter is a word on target. He explicates God's good news in Christ to the believers in Rome in order to promote reconciliation and unity. In other words, Christ Himself is the remedy for this ethnically and theologically divided community.[8]

Identity Matters

Now we come to an important consideration. What are the real-world implications of Paul's explanation of the gospel for himself as an individual and for the divided church assemblies in Rome? In short, how does Paul use the gospel to show the Romans the means and necessity of unity? As we will see, the answer turns on the question of identity. We will argue that Paul ties his own identity and that of the Roman believers to the person and work of Christ. In fact, Paul even reimages, or reshapes, his own primary identity and that of the Roman believers in light of the gospel; believers are no longer to view themselves primarily through an ethnic lens (Gal. 3:28; Col. 3:11). Believers are a new creation in Christ (2 Cor. 5:14-16).

As in all of his letters, Paul uses his Gentile name, *Paulos,* which means "small," rather than his Hebrew name, *Shaul,* which meant "desired." Paul's Gentile name connects him with his mission as apostle to the Gentiles, while his Hebrew name connects him with his ethnic heritage, the first king of Israel, and the tribe of Benjamin. According to Luke's history of the early church, Paul abandons his Hebrew name as he begins his priestly service to God on behalf of the Gentiles (Acts 9:1-8; 13:9-12; 15:16).

Why is he willing to do this? Paul provides the answer in one of his letters to the Gentile believers in Corinth. He describes his evangelistic strategy with the words,

> To the Jews I became as a Jew, in order to win Jews. To those under the law I became as one under the law (though I myself am not under the law) so that I might win those under the law. To those outside the law I became as one outside the law (though I am not free from God's law but am under Christ's law) so that I might win those outside the law. To the weak I became weak, so that I might win the weak. *I have become all things to all people, that I might by all means save some.* I do it all for the sake of the gospel, so that I may share in its blessings (1 Cor. 9:20-23).

Attention should be paid to the fact that although ethnically a Jew, Paul asserts, "To the Jews, I became as a Jew." Paul makes it clear that fundamental to his evangelistic strategy is a willingness to set aside his ethnicity in order to win people to Christ. It is telling that Paul's approach contradicts the so-called "homogeneous unit principle" that was championed and taught by evangelical and Seventh-day Adventist church mission specialists and church growth proponents beginning in the late 70s. Central to this idea of evangelism and church growth is the belief that "men like to become Christians without crossing racial, linguistic, or class barriers."[9] In fact, Donald McGavran, the father of the Church Growth Movement argued, "The normal clannishness of the new group being discipled must be cheerfully accepted and, indeed, encouraged."[10]

Although the homogeneous unit principle is demonstrably anti-Christ, has no legitimate biblical basis, and promotes ethnocentrism, many Adventist leaders still maintain its necessity. For example, there is a proliferation of ethnic churches being planted in the United States, especially by Adventist leaders of African descent. We have moved beyond African churches, to national churches, and have now embarked upon tribal churches. Although based on the homogeneous unit principle, these church plants in reality seek only to maintain tribal identity and culture. By contrast, Jesus never appealed to ethnic sameness as a means of attracting people to His kingdom. He established His self-sacrificing love for humanity experienced in the believing community without regard for ethnicity, gender, or class as the basis for evangelism (e.g., Jn. 4:1-42; 13:34-35).

It should be noted that in his introduction to the mixed Christian community, Paul does not refer to his ethnicity. He will later acknowledge that he is an ethnic Jew, but at the outset he wants to emphasize his shared identity with believers in Rome (11:1-2). In other words, Paul has subjugated his Jewish ethnic identity to his new primary identity in Christ (8:1; cf. Phil. 3:3-11; 2 Cor. 5:16-17). He is now able to identify with people of any ethnicity in order to win them to Christ. Ask yourself this question: would you as a Christian Adventist be willing to subjugate your ethnic identity as a German, a Mexican, a Haitian, a Serbian, a Jamaican, a Brahmin, or an Ashanti to a new primary identity in Christ in order to facilitate the salvation of people different from you?

In addition to describing himself using his Gentile name, Paul uses the expression, "a slave of Christ," to identify himself (Phil. 1:1; Tit. 1:1; Gal. 1:10). This self-introduction is vital to his goal of fostering unity among believers in Rome. Often, the meaning and significance of Paul's self-description are missed, because most English translations of the Bible improperly translate the Greek noun *doulos*, "slave," as either "servant" or "bondservant" (cf. ESV, NASB). In Paul's world, a servant, while a person of low status, was not owned by another. Servants were hired workers, paid for their services; they could quit at will. Although the term "bondservant" is a possible translation, its use misses the force of the metaphor.[11] Paul's use of the term *doulos* and the associated word group from which "slave" is derived depicts the status of being owned by, having dependence on, and owing obedience to a single master.[12]

This word "slave" is problematic for many people, especially in the United States. For some whites, it raises uncomfortable feelings of guilt related to the European and American practice of man-stealing, the horrors of the Middle Passage, the "peculiar institution" of chattel slavery, and the undeniable legacy of present racial inequities. The current unequal distribution of wealth in the United States and Europe is based on four centuries of unpaid labor by people of African descent. For many blacks, the word "slave" is a bitter reminder of the anguish, humiliation, and injustice that leads to anger and a fierce desire for vengeance and restitution. The uneasiness with the idea of slavery is no less true for professed Christians than for society in general.

Paul's use of the word "slave" would also have raised eyebrows in the first century Greco-Roman world, but not for the same reasons as for our modern discomfort with the term. To understand why the ancients had a problem with Paul's metaphor, we must take a brief look at first century slavery and how it differed from America's "peculiar institution."

There were many "slaveries" in the ancient world. Some were as harsh and brutal as the slavery on the plantations of the antebellum South, but on the other hand, some were relatively benign. While agricultural slaves, galley slaves, and slaves in the mines of the Greco-Roman world lived under bitter conditions, many slaves, especially in the cities, lived somewhat "normal" lives. Skilled or educated slaves could receive wages and were able to amass wealth. Some were even able to own slaves themselves and could purchase their freedom. First century slavery was more akin to what we now know as indentured servitude. A large number of slaves served as doctors, professors, administrators, and civil servants.[13]

A person could be enslaved for a number of reasons, mostly by being captured in military conflict. But slavery could result from many causes: punishment for crimes, being born to an enslaved mother, capture by pirates, or enslavement for the repayment of debt. In any event, slaves were the lowest class of society, were considered the property of their owners, and had no legal personhood. Slaves could be subject to corporal punishment, sexual exploitation, torture, and summary execution; crucifixion was the capital punishment of choice for a slave. In Paul's day, as many as one in three persons in Italy or one in five across the empire were slaves, i.e., overall, approximately 35-40% of the total population, or two to three million persons, were enslaved by the end of the first century.[14]

The Greco-Roman economy was built on the foundation of slavery and no one, even slaves themselves, could conceive of a system of labor without it. Slavery was taken as a given, and our modern notion of abolition of the system of slavery was not a part of the first-century thought world; slavery was a necessity, not an evil. Freedom was considered a privilege and not a right, available to a select group because others were enslaved. That many were slaves because they were the losers in battle justified Rome's perception of its cultural and military superiority and confirmed its divine right to rule and exploit others.[15]

Often, our negative reaction to the slave metaphor is rooted in a comparison of first-century Greco-Roman slavery and the European and American slavery of the fifteenth through the nineteenth centuries. These were not identical institutions. The major difference is that first century slavery was not based on race or skin color.[16] In fact, the notion of race was non-existent in the Greco-Roman world. The concept of race based on distinct physical characteristics did not come into being until the seventeenth century, and the use of race to distinguish genetic differences only began in the nineteenth century to justify the institution of African slavery.

Because most Roman slaves were the victims of military expansion, slaves came from every ethnic group conquered by Rome. Slaves came from all over "Europe and the Mediterranean, including Gaul, Hispania, Germany, Britannia, the Balkans, [and] Greece."[17] So slaves could be of any ethnicity or skin color, in stark contrast to American slavery in the antebellum South where most blacks, and usually, only blacks, were slaves.

There were other differences between first-century Greco-Roman slavery and American and European slavery. Greco-Roman slavery was seldom lifelong; most slaves could hope to be emancipated after ten to twenty years of enslavement. Slaves were not denied the right of public assembly, were not socially segregated in urban settings, and could hold any position except elected office. They could not be distinguished from free people by their dress or speech and were often more highly educated than their owners. Many people sold themselves into slavery for economic or social advantage. Most significantly, there was no notion of the natural inferiority of the slave; enslavement was a circumstance, not an innate condition.[18]

Why then does Paul use the ironic metaphor of slave as part of his self-description? Clearly, Jewish believers in Rome, who are acquainted with Paul, would know that not only is he *not* a slave, he is freeborn and in fact a citizen of Rome—a status that is not enjoyed by most first-century Jews (16:3-15; Phil. 3:4-6; Acts 21:39; 22:22-29). Why then this designation? There are at least two reasons.

Paul views his life as a model for believers, because it is a life that is being conformed to both the death and life of Christ (6:3-4; Gal. 3:20). Thus, he can say to believers in Corinth, "follow me as I follow Christ, to the glory of God" (1 Cor. 11:1). In other words, Paul does not reject what would be viewed in Greco-Roman society as a shameful designation, "slave," because he believes that Christ assumed the same role in His incarnation, embracing downward mobility for the sake of others (Phil. 2:5-8; cf. Gal 1:10; Phil. 1:1; 1 Cor. 9:15-19). Paul has allowed the Spirit to establish Christ as Lord of his life (1 Cor. 12:3).

Paul will use his own identity as a "slave of Christ," to shape the identity of the believing communities in Rome. Paul's solution to ethnic division in Rome rests on a radical change of believers' understanding of their *primary identity* (1:6-7). He will demonstrate in his letter that any believer who lives based on cultural values lives "according to the flesh," and therefore lives in opposition to God, or to "life in the Spirit" (8:3-11).

Through the growing influence of the mystery cults, the idea of a person being the slave of a deity was familiar in the Greco-Roman world. This was the only way that such a notion would be acceptable to the cultured Greek thought of the first century that emphasized the dignity of the free man. Paul would have also been aware of the fundamental Roman distinction between slaves and free persons, and thus would have known the conflicting images this metaphor would arouse in his audience, especially as he identified himself as a slave to the One who had suffered a slave's punishment. So, Paul's self-introduction to the Roman capital is not as a proud, freeborn Roman citizen, but as the slave of a crucified Jewish Messiah.[19]

What then is the critical importance of this precise metaphor, "slave," as used by Paul? In chapter six of his letter, Paul uses the language of enslavement to describe the very essence of what it means to experience a new life in Christ. Paul actually employs three images to depict this new life: baptism or burial, crucifixion, and enslavement. All three are used to underscore the assertion of Christ's lordship over believers' lives. For Paul, at some point in the process of sanctification, Jesus must become more than Savior—*He must also become Lord.* Paul argues that freedom from sin will result in enslavement to God, Christ, or righteousness (6:5-6, 15-23; cf. 7:6, 25).[20]

Central to Paul's purpose of ending ethnic division among Gentile and Jewish believers in Rome, the metaphor of slavery points the path to reconciliation and unity. As believers realize their common identity as slaves, they are called to model Christ's way of humility (Phil. 2:5-8). As they perceive their slavery to Christ, the One willing to become a slave for the sake of others, it becomes obvious as to how they are to treat one another. Christ's example of taking the role of a slave in washing the disciples' feet implies the sacrificial service and love for one another that all believers should demonstrate, regardless of their ethnic differences (Eph. 5:21; Jn. 13:1-17, 34-35).

Thus, believers' common identity as slaves of Christ puts an end to ethnic prejudice.[21] Paul makes this very claim to those in Colossae. "Do not lie to one another, seeing that you have put off the old self with its practices and have put on the new self, which is being renewed in knowledge after the image of its creator. *Here there is not Greek and Jew, circumcised and uncircumcised, barbarian, Scythian, slave, free; but Christ is all, and in all*" (Col. 3:9-11 ESV).

One wonders how post-modern Christians in general, and Seventh-day Adventists in particular, would respond to Paul's emphasis on slavery to Christ. Perhaps John MacArthur's comments are instructive.

> Being a slave of Christ may be the best way to define a Christian. We are, as believers, slaves of Christ. You would never suspect

> that, however, from the language of Christianity. In contemporary Christianity the language is anything but slave language. It is about freedom. It is about liberation. It is about health, wealth, and prosperity, finding your own fulfillment, fulfilling your own dream, finding your own purpose. We often hear that God loves you unconditionally and wants you to be all you want to be. He wants to fulfill every ambition, every desire, every hope, and every dream. In fact, there are books being written about dreams as if they are gifts from God, which God then having given them, is bound to fulfill. Personal fulfillment, personal liberation, personal satisfaction, all bound up in an old term in evangelical Christianity, a personal relationship. How many times have we heard that the gospel offers people a personal relationship with Jesus Christ? . . . . When you give somebody the gospel, you are saying to them, "I would like to invite you to become a slave of Jesus Christ. I would like to invite you to give up your independence, give up your freedom, submit yourself to an alien will, abandon all your rights, be owned by, controlled by the Lord." That's really the gospel. We're asking people to become slaves. I don't hear a lot of that slave talk today, do you?[22]

Yet, there is a paradox in Paul's slavery metaphor. Paul says that although he is a slave, he is the freest of men; primarily because his slavery to Christ is voluntary (1 Cor. 9:19). Paul has chosen enslavement. Slavery to Christ, for Paul, means that he has chosen through the power of the Spirit to relinquish control to Christ; it is not based on coercion (8:5-11). Paul is constrained by love (2 Cor. 5:14). For Paul, enslavement to God in Christ is central to sanctification (6:15-23). Moreover, Paul will expand the identity of those in Christ; believers are more than slaves. Ultimately, believers have received a "spirit of sonship" (8:15). They are co-heirs with Christ (8:12-17, 21-23; cf. Gal. 4:1-9).

Next, Paul identifies himself as a "called apostle." This is his typical self-designation (e.g., 1 Cor. 1:1; 2 Cor. 1:1). Thus, like the other apostles, Paul asserts that he is "selected, and sent" by Christ Himself (1:5; 15:15-16; cf. 1 Cor. 9:1; Acts 9:15; 13:47). Paul will explain to the believers in Rome, especially the Gentile majority, that Christ has commissioned him to be the apostle to the Gentiles with its authority and responsibilities (1:5; 11:13-14). While Paul will seek to correct the attitudes and behaviors of both groups in Rome, he will assert his authority as an apostle of Christ to issue a scathing rebuke to the Gentiles for their blatant ethnocentrism (15:15; cf. 2:17-24; 14:1-23; 11:13-36).

Yet, because Paul's authority is delegated from Christ, he will not use it arbitrarily or coercively; rather he will assert his authority to encourage the growth of all believers (1:11-12; 15:14-16; cf. Mt. 28:18). Therefore, Gentile believers in Rome can have confidence in Paul's ministry even though he is an ethnic Jew. It is worth noting that Paul creates a tension by identifying himself as both slave and apostle. Is he attempting to communicate both weakness and authority to introduce himself to the Roman believers in keeping with the ethos of Christ? (1 Cor. 2:3).

Finally, with the expression, "singled out for God's good news" (HCSB), or as one translation puts it, "set apart for the gospel of God" (NASB), Paul links his identity to his vocation. Paul establishes that he has been separated to the gospel by a sovereign act of God based on divine foreknowledge (cf. Gal. 1:15; Acts 9:15; 13:2). God knew Paul's future in advance and designated him as a preacher of the gospel (cf. Jer. 1:4-5). Paul believes that his God-given purpose in life is to communicate, through word and deed, God's good news concerning God's Son.

Paul ends his self-description by tying his apostleship to his mission. "We have received grace and apostleship through Him to bring about the obedience of faith among all the nations, on behalf of His name" (1:5 HCSB). Paul links his apostleship to a specific mission. Yet, he adds a critical dimension to his description of his apostleship and introduces a term that is central to his articulation of the gospel. Throughout his letter, Paul uses the term *charis,* "grace, unmerited favor," both to describe God's gift of salvation through Christ whereby believers are made right with God, and as power from God whereby believers are able to reject the reign of sin (3:24; 5:20-21).

Thus, grace is the means by which believing sinners, covered with Christ's righteousness, are declared not guilty before God (5:15; Eph. 2:4-5, 8-10). This we call justification: the process by which those who have faith in Christ are freed from the penalty of sin. But there is still the need for believers to become like Christ. The means for this transformation is also grace. Through the work of the Holy Spirit, the carnal nature of the believer is put to death and the life of Christ is implanted. We call this process sanctification: the process by which those who have faith in Christ are freed from the power of sin and made like Christ (Col. 1:27; Gal. 4:19; 5:22-24). At this point, it should be emphasized that for Paul, Spirit-enabled sanctification occurs not only in the life of the individual believer, it is to be realized within the believing community. Indeed, communal growth is in fact the goal of the letter (1:11-13, 17).

As it relates to his apostleship, Paul never forgets that the call of Christ is an act of unilateral favor. Indeed, he knows himself as one who persecuted the church of God, who rejected Christ as Israel's Messiah, and who was "the chief of sinners" (1 Cor. 15:9; 1 Tim. 1:15). Paul's profound sense of himself as a sinner, saved without any merit on his part, informs his overall understanding of salvation as an undeserved gift from God through Christ (3:21-26).

In addition, Paul's reception of grace from Christ included a missionary necessity. Paul asserts that his apostleship received from Christ is designed to bring about the "obedience of faith" among the Gentiles (1:5; cf. 15:18; 16:26). Here, Paul's language requires two clarifications. First, when Paul uses the term translated "Gentiles," which can also be translated "nations," he is using a strictly Jewish designation for non-Jews. In the first century, non-Jews would never use the term Gentiles to describe themselves. They would "have defined themselves as Greeks, Romans, Phrygians, Galatians, Cappadocians, and members of other various ethnic populations."[23] Like Jews, Gentiles would emphasize their ethnic identity. Also, Paul, an ethnic Jew, uses subtle language to explain that he has been delegated both the authority and responsibility to call unbelieving Gentiles to faith in Christ.

What Paul calls the obedience of faith, like faith itself, finds its object in God's saving ability through Christ. For Paul, *pistis*, "faith," a term that he uses liberally in his letter, means trusting God's complete salvation through Christ alone. It is a gift equally available to Gentile and Jewish believers (1:16-17; 3:22-26). Yet, this faith is not passive but active. It is a Spirit-enabled, ongoing response of submission to God's grace in Christ (8:1-11; cf. Phil. 2:12-13).

So, genuine faith issues in faithfulness, a life yielded to the love of Christ (1:17). Paul describes it to the Corinthians as being constrained, or compelled, by love (2 Cor. 5:14). For Paul, the obedience of faith is relational obedience in response to God's supreme demonstration of love revealed in the cross of Christ (5:6-8). What does this mean? In short, true obedience *to* God is based on a relationship *with* God through Christ. The love of God that motivated the cross of Christ is answered by the believer's love for God—a love that craves a relationship with God. This Spirit-enabled relationship provides the motivation and the power for the believer to obey God. This is the obedience of faith (8:1-17).

Paul assumes that all believers are granted a measure of faith that increases based on surrender to God (4:20-21; 12:3, 6). Paul later portrays Abraham as the father of faith, whose faith grew strong as it fed on the glory of God, that is, the goodness of God revealed in Christ (4:20). Faith in Christ, i.e., the obedience of faith or relational obedience, is decidedly different from legal obedience (works of the law) that attempts to adhere to the letter of the law. Paul views this type of non-relational obedience as the Achilles heel of first-century Pharisaic Judaism's understanding of righteousness. He emphatically denounces the influence of this type of obedience on his Jewish audience throughout the letter (e.g., 2:17-24; 3:19-20; 7:7-23).

What are the implications of the difference between relational obedience and non-relational obedience for contemporary Adventism? Is the traditional emphasis among many Adventists on keeping the letter of the law, largely in our own strength, blinding us to the relationship that God desires: a continuous, intimate knowing that leads to an obedience based on faith and love? Is our confusion on this matter the basis of our readiness to judge and condemn those who do not measure up, particularly the ethnic other? What impact does such a view of obedience have on the young people who are leaving North American and European Adventism in record numbers? What would change in our lives if we truly understood the obedience of faith in Christ?

Paul's self-description, his depiction of his identity, raises questions. Why this particular description? Is Paul simply concerned with introducing himself to believing Gentiles in Rome, most of whom he has never met, or is there more? It has already been observed that Paul's description of himself as a slave of Christ serves to foreshadow his discussion of the necessity of submission to Christ's lordship as the essence of sanctification. Paul subtly presents himself as a model of submission to be followed. Yet, a slave of Christ is only one element of his self-description. When Paul describes himself as a slave and apostle of Christ, as one set apart to the gospel, and sent to call unbelieving Gentiles to Christ, Paul offers his composite identity as a person in Christ (6:11; 8:1).

Therefore, beyond a mere introduction, Paul at this early stage in the letter begins shaping the ethos or character of his Roman audience by disclosing his *primary identity in Christ.* Like the moral philosophers of his day, Paul seeks to shape the character of his audience by sharing his own ethos.[24] In other words, Paul's goal is formative; he intends to reshape the primary identity of both Gentile and Jewish believers in Rome.

What does Paul seek to achieve with the introduction of his letter? Simply put, Paul signals to his audience that his primary identity is not ethnic. Yes, he is of Jewish ancestry, according to the flesh (11:1). Yet, with his self-description, Paul affirms that he is first and foremost a person abandoned to the Lord, Jesus Christ. With his self-identification, Paul begins to establish the fact that identity in Christ trumps all other secondary identities. It is on this basis that Paul says in his letter to the believers in Galatia: "For as many of you as were baptized into Christ have put on Christ. *There is neither Jew nor Greek, there is neither slave nor free, there is no male and female, for you are all one in Christ Jesus* (Gal. 3:27-28 ESV).

Paul turns from his identity as sender of the letter to its recipients. He writes, "among whom you also are the called of Jesus Christ; to all who are beloved of God in Rome, called *as* saints" (1:6-7a NASB). With these words, Paul, for the first time, makes direct reference to his audience in Rome. He has spoken of his commission to evangelize the unbelieving Gentile world (1:4b-5). Now, he addresses believing Gentiles in Rome with the words, "among whom you also" (cf. 1:13, 14-15; 11:13-24; 15:15-18). Yet, Paul immediately draws a distinction between pagan Gentiles and his Gentile Christian recipients. He describes Gentile believers as "you who are also called of Jesus Christ."

Many English translations render this expression "called to belong to Jesus Christ," which is a possible translation (NRSV, ESV). However, Paul's emphasis is on the fact that Gentile believers are *called.* He has just used this term to refer to his own apostleship. Paul is a called apostle. Here, the term can be understood in the sense of "election" (8:28, 30; cf. 1 Cor. 1:24). He signals to the believing Gentile majority that they have been chosen from among unbelieving Gentiles, and like believing Jews, they too belong to Jesus Christ. It should be noted that this language echoes Paul's self-description as a slave of Christ.

With the phrase, literally, "to all the ones being in Rome," Paul enlarges the makeup of his audience. He now acknowledges the presence of the Jewish minority (2:17; 10:1; 16:3-16). Yet, instead of focusing on ethnic difference, Paul uses language of *common identity*. He describes all believers in two ways. He depicts Roman believers as those "loved of God." By using this descriptor, Paul indicates that believing Gentiles and Jews share in the reality of God's love. Later in the letter, Paul asserts that all believers are beloved of God, not in a sentimental manner, but in view of God's demonstration of love in the death of Christ for sinners. God has shown love for all humanity, especially believers, in the substitutionary death of God's Son (5:6-8; 9:25; cf. 3:21-26).

Paul portrays Roman believers as "called saints." Again, Paul uses the language of invitation and election, but now couples it with the term *hagios*, "saint, holy, consecrated, set apart." For Paul, the term saint as applied to believers suggests two realities. (1) A saint is one who has been set apart to another. This sense represents the reality of the new standing of believers based on justification. Believers belong to Christ (1:6, 5:1). (2) Paul uses the word saint as goal language. Thus, the translation "called *to be* saints" is likely. The emphasis is on the ongoing process of sanctification, the process of being made holy. Throughout the letter, Paul emphasizes the necessity of spiritual growth among the mixed community in Rome (1:11-12, 17; 6:1 - 8:39; 15:15-16). Significantly, Paul uses the term "saint," a word originally used to describe Jews as the chosen people of God. Here he uses it to designate both Gentiles and Jews in Christ (15:25-26; cf. 1 Cor. 1:2; Acts 9:13, 32, 41).[25]

Why this description of the believers in Rome? In what way do these depictions of the Roman believers enhance Paul's formational intent? Before answering these questions, an appreciation of Greco-Roman self-identification is in order. As was noted in the introduction to this book, Greek identity in the first century was rooted in their self-designation as Hellenes over and against all others who were looked upon as barbarians. Greek identity was based on a sense of Greek superiority to all other groups.

First-century Roman males, on the other hand, found their identity in the confirmation of others. In this patriarchal, honor-shame culture, a Roman man sought the affirmation of the elders of his family, his patrons or clients, army comrades, or even the people of Rome in an election that he was a man of honor. Glory and honor could only be measured by others; no one was his own judge.[26]

For Pharisaic Jews, identity was grounded in the belief that they were exclusively the "people of God," heirs of the covenant made with Abraham. They "sought a new, communal commitment to a strict Jewish way of life based on adherence to the covenant."[27] Their separate status from Gentiles, based on their particular religious practices, was recognized by the Roman authorities in a number of concessions, e.g., allowing Jews to send a temple tax to Jerusalem rather than paying it to Rome.[28] By the first century, Jewish identity was further informed by their reactionary hatred of Gentiles based on centuries of domination.

So, when Paul describes the believing Gentiles and Jews as "called of Jesus Christ," "loved of God," and, "called as saints," he continues to shape their character by introducing a vocabulary of *common identity*. Throughout his argument, Paul expands this description. He describes the Roman believers, both Gentiles and Jews, as justified, reconciled, debtors, adopted sons (and daughters), children of God—heirs of God and fellow heirs with Christ, the elect, brothers and sisters, the body of Christ, and those welcomed by Christ (1:17; 5:1, 11; 8:12, 14, 16-17, 28; 12:1, 5; 15:7). For Paul, all these descriptors may be subsumed under the inclusive primary identity marker, *"in Christ."* Paul argues that all believers, both Gentiles and Jews, *are to live in view of their new life in Christ Jesus* (6:11; 8:1; cf. 2 Cor. 5:14-17). To live based on any other criteria—ethnicity, gender, or class—is to live "according to the flesh" (8:5:11; Gal. 3:28). It is to live a life dominated by sin (6:15-23; 14:23).

But Paul's formative strategy does not end with the language of common identity. He also will later assert a shared heritage, present and future, for those in Christ. According to Paul, all believers share a present heritage. They now possess peace with God through Christ, access into grace, hope, and most important, God's love through the gift of the Spirit (5:1-5). Moreover, Paul shows that believers share a future heritage. Being conformed to the image of Christ, they all will experience glorification—the third and final step in the process of salvation where through the work of grace the believer is finally freed from the presence of sin in the earth made new (8:28-30).

With his vocabulary of common identity and the depiction of a shared heritage, Paul deconstructs the primacy of all cultural identities and values contrary to life in the Spirit. Therefore, he views "ethnocentrism" as life lived "according to the flesh" (8:1-11). Paul thus rejects the socially constructed identities of his hearers, and by the same token would reject our modern socially constructed identities of race and class. In addition, he subordinates all secondary identities, such as ethnicity and gender. For Paul, conversion to Christ alters all relations in the body of Christ (Gal. 3:27-28; Phm. 16). Paul asserts the priority of believers' common identity in Christ. Do we as Adventists really appreciate the fact that if our primary identity, which supersedes all other identites, is not in Christ we will not see Him in peace?

Paul's greeting, "Grace to you and peace from God our Father and the Lord Jesus Christ" (1:7b; cf. 1 Cor. 1:3), reflects his awareness of the common identity of his divided audience. In the first century, writers used the formulaic greeting *chairein,* variously translated "greetings" or "best wishes."[29] Paul modifies this Hellenistic greeting possibly because of its connection to pagan religious cosmology. Both Greeks and Romans believed that their gods were capricious. Humans were subject to an uncertain fate, thus, the greeting, best wishes.

Paul's modification is significant. Contrary to the fatalistic world of the pagan, all believers, through the Father and the Son, have received grace and peace. As mentioned above, Paul develops the import of this shared heritage throughout the letter (e.g., 3:21-26; 5:1-2; 14:19; 15:13; 16:20). In addition, Paul may have wanted to include both Hellenistic and Jewish elements in his greeting with the phrase grace (Greek) and peace (Hebrew), thus emphasizing his gospel understanding of the equal status of Gentiles and Jews before God.[30]

Needed Growth

Paul, as a Greco-Roman letter writer, often uses what is called the thanksgiving to signal major themes that will be addressed throughout the letter. As demonstrated earlier, Paul employs the gospel to reshape the identity of the divided Christian community in Rome. Now he begins to use the gospel to establish unity between his Gentile and Jewish audiences.

Paul shares his reasons for wanting to visit Rome and hints that there is a problem among the believers there. "For I am longing to see you so that I may share with you some spiritual gift to strengthen you—or rather so that we may be mutually encouraged by each other's faith, both yours and mine" (1:11-12). Paul uses the infinitive form of the verb "strengthen" meaning, "to establish, make firm," to drive home the need for growth in the believers' faith (cf. 1 Thess. 3:2). Paul subtly suggests that the Roman believers need to increase their faithfulness to Christ. Paul's motive for the visit, stated literally, is that he "might impart some spiritual gift to strengthen you" (1:11; cf. 16:25). It should be noted that his emphasis here is not on individual growth among the believers. The sense is the need for corporate or communal growth.

This statement leaves no doubt that Paul signals here the necessity for *corporate sanctification* of the believers in Rome (1:17; 6:1-11; cf. Ex. 19:6; 1 Pet. 2:9). He emphasizes the need for future maturation. Paul demonstrates in the rest of the letter that justified believers have been reckoned righteous by God, but are now in the process of receiving sanctification through the Spirit, i.e., the imparted righteousness of Christ. *Believers must grow in Christlikeness* (4:11; 6:1 – 8:30). Paul argues that corporate as well as individual growth in Christ is antithetical to division based on ethnicity and to practices resulting from an exclusive identity (14:1 – 15:13). Gentile and Jewish Christians, both individually and in their church assemblies, cannot continue to remain divided if they are truly growing in Christ.

Using metaphorical language, "that I may reap some harvest among you" (1:13), Paul suggests that the Gentile majority, no doubt in control in Rome, is in need of group sanctification (11:13-24; cf. 1:5; 15:15-18). He stresses in the letter that through the Spirit, Gentile and Jewish believers alike are to embrace a radical reorientation of thought and practice that is consistent with their new life in Christ. Yet, Paul begins by placing the onus on the majority (8:5-11; Gal. 5:22-23).

Given the fact that Paul can view spiritual growth communally, why do most Christians in the Western world reject the notion of corporate sanctification? Do we as Adventists recognize that sanctification is both corporate and individual? We should remember that the Protestant reformers who shaped the Western concept of salvation characterized it as a relationship between only the individual believer and God. Yet this notion flies in the face of God's commandment for Israel to "be holy, for I am holy." Israel has been corporately set apart to Yahweh (Lev. 11:44; 19:2; 20:7, 26; 1 Pet. 1:14-16; 2:4-10). Paul echoes this understanding. We have already noted that Paul's references to the primary identity of the divided assemblies in Rome are always cast in corporate language, e.g., "you [plural] who are called to belong to Jesus Christ," and "all those in Rome who are loved of God," (1:6-7; cf. 1:17; 5:1, 11; 8:12, 14, 16-17, 28; 12:1-2, 4-5).

Our unfortunate modern dichotomy between the individual and the community, with priority given to the individual, masks Paul's emphasis on the primacy of the community as necessary to the spiritual well-being of the individual. Sampley notes,

> Paul's commitment to community may rest in and be explained by the ways the fellowship serves and assists the individual. Community is the locale of the life of faith . . . . Community is the nurturing context within which the individual is expected to live. There the individual is encouraged to grow, is edified by the love of others, is shored up in weakness, is consoled upon straying, and is called to account when behaving inappropriately. Just as surely as one does not snub the working of the Spirit, one does not disregard the community in one's life of faith . . . . For Paul the life of faith cannot be imagined apart from community. Yet belonging to community in Christ does not shackle individuation. Rather the distinctive marks of the individual find proper expression within the community of believers. [31]

The Gospel Thesis

We should recall that early in this chapter we addressed Paul's understanding of Jesus as the meaning of the gospel. Now we move to Paul's understanding of the function of the gospel: Jesus as the solution to the division in Rome. Here, Paul introduces a thesis statement that establishes the basis for his formal argument in the letter (1:18 - 15:13). He states, "For I am not ashamed of the gospel; it is the power of God for salvation to everyone who has faith, to the Jew first and also to the Greek. For in it the righteousness of God is revealed through faith for faith; as it is written, 'The one who is righteous will live by faith'" (1:16-17).

Unique to his letter to the Romans, Paul uses a gospel thesis to signal what will be developed into a sustained argument. Throughout his discussion, Paul explains God's good news in Christ to make a case for reconciliation and unity among divided believers. Moving from a definition of the gospel earlier (1:1b-4), to its function now (1:16-17), Paul's thesis makes four Christ-centered assertions about the gospel.

First, Paul states that he is "not ashamed of the gospel [of Christ]" (1:3, 9; 15:19; cf. 2 Tim. 1:8, 12, 16).[32] Paul's assertion is no idle boast. With these words, he exposes and critiques the cultural prism of his time: the Greco-Roman honor-shame system. Throughout the letter Paul modifies and at times criticizes Greco-Roman social and cultural conventions and their implied values.

The core value in the Mediterranean world of the first century was the quest for honor and the avoidance of shame. Americans are familiar with our contemporary values of freedom, democracy, and capitalism. Honor functioned in the same way in Greco-Roman society. There are several modern societies where honor is a core value, e.g., Japanese and other Asian cultures, and Iraqi and other Middle Eastern cultures. Bruce Malina provides the classic definition of the ancient view of honor: "the value of a person in the eyes of his or her social group. Honor is a claim to worth along with the social acknowledgement of worth."[33]

For the Romans, honor was viewed as a scarce commodity that was acquired through competition in almost every social arena: education, oratory, politics, poetry, music, athletics, and war. Formal competitions in these areas resulted in the award of prizes for superior performance. Among the Romans "'honor' and 'shame' referred primarily not to feelings of honor or shame, but rather to being either honored or disgraced in public."[34] In this patriarchal culture, honor was a male virtue closely aligned with public life. The responsibility of females, on the other hand, was to protect the family honor by avoiding shame, especially sexual shame. Important for Paul's unifying purpose, it should be understood that honor could be accrued by heaping shame on others.[35]

First-century Jews participated in the competition for honor as well. For them status markers included an honorable pedigree demonstrated by circumcision as required by the law and an impeccably honorable tribal identity with pure blood lines not tainted by assimilation to Gentile customs and culture.[36]

As we will see, Roman believers had embraced competition for honor by engaging in judgment of one another over disputed theological issues. Some Jewish believers based their theology on strict adherence to rules such as dietary restrictions, while Gentiles prided themselves in the claim that such things did not matter. Both groups were striving to gain the mastery rather than pursuing peace and mutual upbuilding (14:1-23).

Honor-shame was used by the Romans to undergird ethnic prejudice. Especially for the power elite in Imperial Rome, other ethnic groups by definition were considered shameful.[37] In fact, to be an ethnic Italian, i.e., of Roman birth, was one of the status indicators or criteria for inclusion in the upper strata of the Roman social system.[38] This system was also associated with hatred and fear of the Jews.[39] It is also noteworthy that bias that benefited the honorable in Greco-Roman society was normative.

Given this background, Paul's assertion "I am not ashamed of the gospel," subtly establishes the "honorable" nature of God's good news concerning Christ. Why is this a necessity? In one of his letters to Corinth, Paul describes humanity's assessment of the idea of a crucified Savior. He writes,

> For since, in the wisdom of God, the world did not know God through wisdom, God decided, through the foolishness of our proclamation, to save those who believe. *For Jews demand signs and Greeks desire wisdom, but we proclaim Christ crucified, a stumbling block to Jews and foolishness to Gentiles, but to those who are the called, both Jews and Greeks, Christ the power of God and the wisdom of God.* For God's foolishness is wiser than human wisdom, and God's weakness is stronger than human strength (1 Cor. 1:21-25).

According to Paul, both Jewish and Greek wisdoms and cultures reject the gospel proclamation of a crucified Jewish Messiah. In fact, because Jesus of Nazareth was crucified by the state, Romans would have viewed Him as exceedingly shameful.

So, with the assertion "I am not ashamed of the gospel," Paul eviscerates the central value of Greco-Roman culture, an ideal that extolled hierarchy, power, domination, and partiality. In its place, he exalts God's wisdom in Christ and in so doing inverts the reality of sinful humanity, especially the Roman honor-shame system (5:12-21). For Paul, the life, death, and resurrection of Christ embody the divine ideal that is most honorable.

Christ modeled a reality that moves from weakness to strength, from death to life, from a cross to a crown (cf. Phil. 2:5-11; Gen. 3:14-15). Thus, Paul rejects the most important value of his culture. Are Seventh-day Adventists obliged to reject values embedded in their cultures that are opposed to the gospel of Jesus Christ? For example, are we called in Europe and the United States to reject capitalism with its profit motive and implied Social Darwinism? Are Adventists in India called to reject the caste system, which in reality is rooted in Hinduism and its devaluation of human beings based on the circumstances of their birth or occupation?

Paul's second assertion provides the reason for his shameless exaltation of the gospel of Christ. He says, "for it is the power of God for salvation to everyone who believes, to the Jew first and also to the Greek" (ESV). Before fully analyzing the elements of this claim, we must understand that for Paul, Jesus Christ Himself, both in His person and work, is God's power for salvation. Paul makes this precise claim when he conflates the gospel and Christ, again speaking to the Corinthians:

> For the *message* about the cross is foolishness to those who are perishing, but to us who are being saved *it is the power of God* . . . we

> proclaim Christ crucified, a stumbling block to Jews and foolishness to Gentiles, but to those who are the called, both Jews and Greeks, *Christ the power of God and the wisdom of God* (1 Cor. 1:18, 23-24).

This point cannot be overstated. For Paul, the gospel is not just propositions about the person, it is the person Himself. Norman Geisler states,

> The purpose of the propositional revelation of the Scripture is to present the person of the Saviour; the Bible is the instrument of God to convey the message of Christ and, therefore, the Bible should not be sought so much for its own sake, but should be searched for the purpose of finding Christ, for "to him all the prophets bear witness (Acts 10:43)."[40]

In writing to the Corinthians and now to the Romans, Paul makes the same claim. Christ is God's *dynamis*, "power," that is, His saving ability: past, present, and future. Christ is God's only means of deliverance. In addition, Paul reiterates the means of appropriating God's saving ability in Christ and its scope. He again maintains that salvation is available to all those believing, literally, to "the trusting ones" (1:5, 8). Moreover, Paul uses Hebraic categories for all humanity to establish that Jews and Gentiles have access to Christ by the same means, thereby establishing God's impartiality (2:9, 11; 10:12). Yet, with the delineation "first the Jew, then the Greek," he also establishes the priority of Jews in salvation history (cf. 2:9-10; 3:1-2). Paul builds on this fact in his correction of the Gentile majority later in the letter (11:13-32).

Central to his formal argument, Paul's third assertion enhances his reason for extolling the gospel of Christ. He declares, "For in it the righteousness of God is revealed through faith for faith." What Paul means by the expression "the righteousness of God" is debated, because the phrase can mean either God is righteous, referring to the character of God, or God bestows righteousness, signifying the ability of God to make right.

Yet, the debate misses the intent of Paul's assertion. What is Paul's intent? Simply stated, Jesus Christ, who is the gospel, discloses the divine nature of God, i.e., righteousness from God. Rightly understood, Paul intends both meanings of "the righteousness of God," but, most important, *God's righteousness is Jesus Christ Himself* (1 Cor. 1:30).

Through His incarnation, Christ by word and deed disclosed the character of God. The divine nature has been made visible through creation, yet God's nature is definitively revealed in the person of Christ (1:20; cf. Col. 2:9-10). In addition, Christ is the righteousness from God made available to faith. This is true because through the death of Christ, God is able not only to declare a sinner "righteous,"—justification—but through the work of the Spirit, God is able to impart the life of

Christ to those who believe—sanctification (3:21-26; 4:4-5; 6:1- 8:39); thus, Paul's formative assertion, *"Christ in you, the hope of glory"* (Col. 1:27; Gal. 5:22-23).

It is important to observe that for Paul, God's righteousness in Christ, mediated through the Spirit, is received by faith from beginning to end (1:5; 16:26). In fact, Paul maintains that faith in God's saving ability through His Son is the only hope for both Jews and Gentiles. Paul's goal of reconciliation and unity throughout the letter turns on this point. When will we as Seventh-day Adventists come to realize that all strategies for "success" in the church, whether religio-political, cultural, or pragmatic, that do not emanate from God's saving power in Christ are doomed and stand under divine judgment? When will Adventism move from God's righteousness in Christ as a proposition to God's righteousness as a Person to be received?

Two recent examples of Adventist responses to racism in North America serve to illustrate this distinction. During the Black History Month celebration at Southern Adventist University in 2016, an African American minister was delivering a sermon at an evening meeting. While he was speaking, white students began to text each other on the social media app Yik Yak, making racially denigrating characterizations of the speaker, e.g., "The niggertry is real tonight" and "Actually, the Africans are still quite barbaric compared to europeans [sic]." Black students picked up the conversation when it hit Facebook. In response to the uproar that ensued, Southern's administration issued an apology and a plan to address the racial situation on the campus that this incident revealed.

Unfortunately, according to black faculty, actual progress was minimal. We would argue that the response by university administration exemplifies what Adventist institutions often do in response to ethnocentric issues: a good public relations statement is offered that may invoke the proper biblical position. But there is little or no appeal to the reception of Christ in the life as the motivating power to change. Usually, there is no attempt to develop an approach that leads to a relationship with Christ; only this produces lasting transformation.

The second, more recent example comes from Andrews University. Again, during Black History Month 2017, white students were offended, this time by the political nature of the remarks of a black speaker. When white parental complaints reached the administration, an apology to the white community was issued within a week. Black students, outraged by this action, created a video that cited the long history of racially-motivated offenses against blacks on the campus, and demanded an apology within "one week."

Within a week the university responded, again with a carefully crafted public relations video, mirroring the students' video, that offered an apology for past and present wrongs and a plan to redress the grievances of the black community. Again, while commendable, the institutional response tacked on a brief appeal for the help of the Lord in dealing with the crisis without any real acknowledgment that only a reception of the life of Christ among both whites and blacks could provide the transformation necessary for a successful outcome. Good public relations is never enough in Christian community.

Paul realized that only the reception of Christ as person, not merely as a set of doctrines about Him, could reconcile the divided Roman Christian community. When will Adventists come to the same realization? Until we do, we will reel from one unfortunate ethnic or racial incident to another without any permanent resolution.

Finally, with his fourth assertion, Paul uses prophetic Scripture to apply the implications of the gospel of Christ to the believers in Rome. "As it is written, 'The righteous will live by faith'" (1:17b NIV). Here, Paul quotes God's words to the prophet Habakkuk (Hab. 2:4; cf. Gal. 3:11). In context, God responds to Habakkuk's complaint about the mysterious nature of divine justice. Habakkuk points out the apostasy of Israel, and God reveals that Babylon will be used to punish Israel's unfaithfulness.

Appalled that God will use a singularly wicked nation to chastise Israel, Habakkuk queries God about what God proposes to do. After providing Habakkuk with assurance about the future fate of Babylon, God corrects the prophet with the words, "But the righteous will live by his faith" (NASB). God reveals to Habakkuk that right relation with God is maintained by trusting God's sovereign goodness in spite of contrary temporal evidence.

Paul appropriates and modifies this quotation as a critical part of his thesis.[41] Why does Paul assert, "The righteous shall live by faith"? Contrary to the traditional idea, with the word "the righteous" or "just," Paul does not signal an emphasis on justification in his letter. *He assumes the justification of believers in Rome.* They have been declared righteous through faith in Christ (5:1; cf. 3:21-22). This fact is not in question; their faith is renowned (1:8; cf. 15:14). Paul's appropriation of the expression "the righteous shall live by faith" is designed to emphasize the ongoing need for corporate and individual sanctification among the Roman believers, a theme that he will develop throughout the letter (e.g., 1:7, 11-12, 17; 6:1 - 8:39; 12:1 - 15:13; cf. 1 Pet. 2:9).

Paul uses a literary device, *synecdoche*, that was common in his day and used extensively throughout the New Testament.[42] It entails using an individual or thing to represent a group, or a part to represent the whole. For example, Paul uses Jacob to represent all of his descendants, or the Israelites (11:26), and the law to represent all of the Old Testament (3:19). Paul later uses Adam in this way (5:12-21).

In this passage, Paul uses the justified believer to represent the justified body or community. This is critical because in modern Christianity, justification has been thought of as exclusive to the individual. In Romans, Paul's emphasis is how justification is lived in community. This is not to say that Paul is not concerned with the salvation of the individual, but Paul's Semitic background provides the understanding that community is the primary context for the sanctification of the individual. It is not either/or but both/and. Sampley observes, "We have no evidence that Paul ever conceived of a solitary, isolated believer. In his letters, admittedly written to communities of the faithful, he thinks of believers as called together in Christ."[43]

Believers will *live* by faith in Jesus Christ. For Paul, it is through faith in God's ability announced in the gospel of Christ that the Romans, both Jews and Gentiles, who have been *declared* right with God (justification) are *made* right with God (sanctification). From beginning to end, Paul subtly addresses the question: will ethnically divided believers allow the Spirit of God to produce reconciliation and unity through faith in Christ?

The same question confronts the Seventh-day Adventist Church worldwide. For example, will Russian Adventists repent of and confess their participation in cultural imperialism against Ukrainians in general and their Ukrainian Adventist brothers and sisters in particular? Will Ukrainian Adventists come to the point where they can forgive Russian Adventists in spite of their history of oppression? Can both groups learn through faith in Christ to love and serve one another? These questions must be answered anywhere Adventism is found: in North America, Africa, Asia, Europe, Australia, South and Central America, and the islands of the sea.

In his letter, Paul demonstrates to the immature saints in Rome that Christ is the answer to the problem of ethnic and religious division among them. In fact, he closes his formal argument by extolling the example of Christ.

> Each of us must please our neighbor for the good purpose of building up the neighbor. For Christ did not please himself . . . . Welcome one another, therefore, *just as Christ has welcomed you*, for the glory of God. For I tell you that Christ has become a servant of *the circumcised* on behalf of the truth of God in order that he might confirm the promises given to the patriarchs, and in order that *the Gentiles* might glorify God for his mercy (15:2-3a, 5-7).

Thus, with the words, "The righteous shall live by faith," Paul establishes his thematic indicative, or statement of fact, as the foundation on which his argument will rest. Believers, both Gentiles and Jews, are called to grow by trusting God's complete salvation (justification, sanctification, and glorification) in Jesus Christ. Paul believes that mature faith in Christ among believers in Rome will create a united people, prepared to assist in outreach to the world (15:22-29).

So What? Genocide in Rwanda[44]

Beginning on April 7, 1994, for one hundred days, an estimated one million Rwandans, most from the Tutsi tribe, were slaughtered. Extremist elements among the Hutu majority were responsible for most of the killings. Surprisingly, Adventist leaders and regular members participated in the genocide. Two questions demand an answer. First, how is it possible that Seventh-day Adventists, members of the "remnant church," participated in such a vicious act? More important, what "gospel" were Rwandans taught by missionaries that made their participation possible?

To answer these questions, a brief survey of Rwandan history is in order. In pre-colonial Rwanda, there were three tribes, Tutsi, Hutu, and Twa. Although Hutus made up the vast majority of the population, by some estimates eighty-four percent, the Tutsi minority, fourteen percent of the population, comprised the ruling class. The Twa were only one percent of the population.

The historical record of Rwanda before colonization relies on oral tradition because there was no written history prior to the coming of Europeans. The three tribes shared the same culture and language (Kinyarwanda). During the fifteenth century the Tutsi established a monarchy, based on feudalism, which subordinated the Hutu. This form of government held sway for hundreds of years. Tutsis comprised the higher strata of the social system, while Hutus were in the lower strata. Upward social mobility was possible for Hutu who acquired cows; impoverished Tutsi who did not have cows could be regarded as Hutu.

Rwanda was among the last regions of Africa to be entered by Europeans. In 1885, Rwanda and Burundi were declared a German sphere of influence by the conference of Berlin. After WWI, Belgium was given the mandate to govern Rwanda-Burundi by the League of Nations. Like the Germans before them, the Belgians relied on the existing Tutsi organization to govern Rwanda, although Belgium did attempt to limit the arbitrary powers of the king. The mandate ended on December 3, 1949 when the newly organized United Nations approved a Trusteeship Agreement that placed Rwanda and Burundi under the charge of Belgium.

During the period between the world wars, the Belgians, with the support of the Catholic Church, embraced the superiority of the Tutsi and their ascendency over the Hutu. This led to growing tension between these tribes. The Hutu began to favor revolutionary notions that challenged Tutsi supremacy. As social conflict increased, the Catholic Church began to favor the growth of a Hutu counter elite.

Before European missionaries arrived in Rwanda, the people engaged in animistic worship of a creator being, "Imana," and the veneration of ancestral spirits. German Catholic missionaries, the so-called White Fathers, who arrived in 1900, considered the religion of the Rwandans to be pagan and evil. Suspicious of the potential threat of the White Fathers to their form of government, the Tutsi chiefs restricted the missionaries' access to the ruling class until the mid-1920s. The missionaries gained early converts among the Hutu peasants. The White Fathers won out by replacing the king with another who accepted a nominal Christian conversion while retaining his traditional pattern of worship. As a result, thousands were baptized into the Catholic Church.

Protestant missionary efforts in Rwanda began with the Lutherans in 1907. They were followed by Seventh-day Adventists in 1919. Eventually, missionaries from a number of denominations came to evangelize Rwandans: Baptists, Anglicans, Pentecostals, and Methodists. It is notable that Christian missionaries to Rwanda went beyond respect for the Belgian government; they became purveyors of colonial attitudes and practices. This was true even of Adventist missionaries. The spread of Protestantism in Rwanda, even among the ruling class, led to conflict. When the missionaries returned to their homelands, local Rwandan leaders were left in charge. Lacking the pastoral training and maturity to challenge the evils of government politics or Hutu extremists, many of these local church leaders became partisans of the Hutu government ideology after independence and eventually participated in the genocide of 1994.

The Seventh-day Adventist mission to Rwanda began after WWI with the arrival of David Elie Delhove, a Belgian soldier, and Henri Monnier, a Swiss. They at first occupied mission stations that had been abandoned by Germans during the war, which Adventists had to relinquish when the owners returned. Subsequently, the Adventists were able to secure three mission stations: Gitwe, Rwankeri, and Ngoma. These sites were strategically located in the east, west, and center of the county, a fact that facilitated church outreach efforts. Adventist missionaries began their work among Rwandan Christians with the proclamation of distinctive Adventist doctrines: prophecies, judgment, the Second Advent, and the Sabbath. Later, missionaries, accompanied by converted Rwandans, moved inland to work among non-Christians, combining the doctrine of Christ as Savior with the distinctive Adventist message.

The close integration of the traditional religion with the lifestyle of the people led Rwandan converts to blend the traditional religion with Christianity. The Adventist emphasis on Sabbath worship and eliminating the use of alcohol and tobacco made the Adventist message hard to accept. However, Adventism increased rapidly in spite of the difficulties, spreading from the three mission stations to other parts of the country. In general, missionaries found that Hutus were more receptive to the gospel than Tutsis. In Rwankeri, Adventists discovered that whole families and even whole villages followed the example of one family member to either accept or reject the message. This type of acceptance, based on following the example of a relative rather than on personal conviction, had a negative impact on the Christian life of the so-called believer

The strategies of the missionaries for the development of new members were somewhat troubling. After baptism, new converts were visited by older members to help them understand the Bible and the Adventist lifestyle. Local churches divided members into small groups to care for new members in their vicinity. Books were kept to record the attendance of new members at prayer meetings and other worship services. Those who were absent three times were whipped. Some attended the meetings from fear of whipping. Eventually, some of the early converts came to enjoy the meetings, especially as they developed an affection for Henri Monnier. Others apparently pretended to worship, but in reality they did not. Churches in Rwanda were still checking members' attendance once a quarter as late as the early years of the twenty-first century.

New converts in Rwanda had no problem with the doctrine of tithing because they were accustomed to pacifying their traditional gods with offerings. Converts tended to copy the Europeans in dress and other areas. Rwandans copied traditional western forms of worship; they were not allowed to use traditional African musical instruments, which were considered pagan. Rwandan names were also thought to be pagan; so, upon baptism, the convert usually chose a Hebrew name from the Bible. This was a cause of alienation for the new believers who suffered from the overall problem that Christianity was not rendered indigenous to the culture. Instead, Rwandans mixed their culture with European culture, thus becoming "cultural half castes." While professing to be Christians, many continued to practice the traditional religion in secret. Nevertheless, the Adventist church grew, so that in 1990, the Rwanda Union Mission could report 209,316 members. Of course, membership dropped after the genocide due to death and exile.

Rwandan Adventism progressed in spite of the persisting ethnic division between Tutsis and Hutus. Factors that contributed to the growth of the Adventist church in Rwanda included the witnessing of lay members, the establishing of a pervasive educational system, the combination of health services with evangelism, and the distribution of Adventist literature. Adventists as well as members of other denominations collaborated with the government in treating Rwandans as two tribal groups. The Adventist church did little to limit the increasing ethnic conflict.

When tribal violence erupted in 1959, the Belgian authorities showed partiality towards Hutus who were killing Tutsis and burning their houses. Independence for Rwanda was granted in 1962, and a government controlled by the Hutu elite was formed. From the outset, the Hutu ruling ideology as it related to the Tutsi was genocidal, with official threats that began with the first speech of the new Hutu president in 1964.

Belgians had introduced an ethnic identity card system in 1933 that was continued after independence was granted in 1962. A quota was established that limited Tutsis to ten percent in any sector of the country. The ethnic card system enabled discrimination against and social control of Tutsi. The card system made it possible for Hutu killers to identity Tutsi during the genocide. This would have been difficult without the card system because of intermarriage between the tribes.

The Hutu government used newspapers, radio, and television to mount an extremely successful campaign against the Tutsi. Young Hutus began to believe that killing Tutsis was a civic obligation. Christian churches participated in advocating propaganda that called for the "final solution" for the Tutsi who were characterized as snakes without any human value. Bible verses were used by some Adventist pastors who said that Tutsi should be killed because God had abandoned them.

The death of Rwandan president Habyarimana Juvenal in a plane struck by two missiles on April 6, 1994, sparked the genocide. The Rwandan government in 2007 implicated the former first lady and her brother as responsible for the assassination.[45] Immediately after the crash, the killing of Tutsis, and Hutus who were seen as non-supportive to the government began. Women and girls were sexually abused by their killers. The use of machetes prolonged the death agonies of the victims. Entire families were completely destroyed, and many people fled the country. The resulting psychological problems persist to this day.

The fact that Rwanda was primarily a Christian nation makes genocide a matter of wonder. Despite a few examples of individual courage among ordinary Christians, church leaders were either bystanders or complicit in the killings. No one spoke out against the genocide. Although not the only denomination to join in the massacre, many Adventist pastors and members participated in one way or another.

At least 3000 people were killed at the Adventist Mugonero Hospital (formerly Ngoma) where Field president Ntakirutimana Elisaphan was responsible for the mission station and his son Ntakirutimana Gerard, a physician, was responsible for the hospital. Pastor Ntakirutimana and his son ensured that the victims were assembled at the hospital where they had been promised safety. The Ntakirutimanas then called the soldiers and militias for the massacre.

At Gitwe and at the Adventist University of Central Africa, people who sought refuge there were killed. Adventists killed other Adventists. Some, on the counsel of their pastor that killing was only wrong if perpetrated on the Sabbath, did not kill on the Sabbath. However, the massacre at Mugonero Hospital took place on the Sabbath. The exact number of Adventists who died in the genocide is not known.

Many people left Christian churches after the genocide, and some lost faith in the goodness of God. Some Christians became Muslim, because the Muslims protected their adherents and did not participate in the killings. The Ntakirutimanas, father and son, who had fled Rwanda to escape justice, were extradited from the United States by the International Court of Justice at The Hague. They were tried, convicted, and imprisoned for their crimes. The Seventh-day Adventist Church in Rwanda was reorganized and new leaders were appointed.

How could Christian participation in genocide have happened? Ngabo Birikunzira Jerome contends that the majority of Christians in Rwanda were, and are, half converted; conversions were motivated by selfish interests. So-called Christians still held to their tribal identity, cultural values, and traditional religion.

The "gospel" that Adventists taught Rwandans did not challenge the culture that allowed ethnocentric hatred between the two major tribes. Emphasis on lifestyle adherence to our distinctive doctrines, such as Sabbath-keeping, tithing, and abstaining from alcohol and tobacco, did not replace the practice of the traditional religion, much less the transformation of hearts that would engender genuine love across tribal lines. The "gospel" that was taught allowed church leaders to share, advocate, and implement the ethnocentrism embedded in the culture and supported by a genocidal government.

Jerome describes Seventh-day Adventist Rwandans as being nominally Christian. In light of Adventism's gospel emphasis, could his assertion serve as a general description of our condition? Is it easier than we care to admit to engage in unthinkable behavior when our primary identity is other than that in Christ?

Is a "gospel" that does not oppose ethnocentrism in any of its forms—tribalism, racism, nationalism, or caste—truly the gospel of Christ? How can the gospel of God become so distorted that it becomes an ethnocentric "gospel" that allows Hutus to murder Tutsis so long as it is not done on the Sabbath? One wonders, would things have been different if the gospel of Jesus Christ had been taught and lived in Rwanda? When will we as Adventists acknowledge that doctrines and understanding prophecy and even the third angel's message, as valuable as they are, will not reproduce the character of Christ? And without Christlikeness, there can be no reconciliation or unity among believers, moreover, no authentic witness to the world.

---

[1] Robert Paul Jewett. Shame, and Honor. In J. Paul Sampley, *Paul in the Greco-Roman World: A Handbook*. Harrisburg, PA: Trinity Press International, 2003.

[2] Gregory J. Allen. *Reconciliation in the Pauline Tradition: Its Occasions, Meanings, and Functions.* Doctoral Dissertation. Boston University, School of Theology, 1995, p. 64.

[3] Patheos: Hosting the Conversation on Faith, Behind Luke's Gospel: The Roman Empire During the Time of Jesus. *patheos.org*. Priene 105.30-56=OGIS 458.30-56. Accessed September 16, 2015.

[4] Grant R. Osborne. *Romans.* The IVP New Testament Commentary Series. Downers Grove, IL: InterVarsity Press, 2004.

[5] Paul's emphasis on the role of the Holy Spirit in the resurrection of Jesus is rhetorical. The New Testament makes it clear that God—Father, Son, and Spirit—were all involved in the resurrection of Christ: God the Father (Rom. 4:24; 6:4; 1 Cor. 6:14; Acts 2:24, 32); God the Son (Jn. 10:17-18); God the Spirit (Rom. 1:4; 8:11).

[6] Ellen Gould White. *Gospel Workers.* Washington, DC: Review and Herald Publishing Association, 1915, p. 315.

[7] ______. *Review & Herald,* March 24, 1896.

[8] Francis Watson. The Two Roman Congregations: Romans 14:1 – 15:13. In Karl. P. Donfried (ed.). *The Romans Debate.* Grand Rapids, MI: Baker Academic, 1991.

[9] Donald A. McGavran, *Understanding Church Growth* (rev. ed.). Grand Rapids: Eerdmans, 1980, p. 223. Quoted in David Rogers. A Biblical Evaluation of the Homogeneous Unit Principle, December 29, 2013. sbcvoices.com/a-biblical-evaluation-of-the-homogeneous-unit-principle. Accessed September 7, 2016. See also Peter C. Wagner. *Our Kind of People.* Atlanta: GA: John Knox Press, 1969. For a critique of the homogeneous unit principle, see Antonio Carlos Barro. Unity and Diversity in the Family of God. eDiaspora Network. eDiaspora.net. Accessed October 1, 2016.

[10] Donald A. McGavran, *The Bridges of God* (rev.). New York, NY: Friendship Press, 1981, p. 130. Quoted in Rogers.

[11] John MacArthur. *Slave: The Hidden Truth About Your Identity in Christ.* Nashville, TN: Thomas Nelson, 2010, pp. 15-19.

[12] For example, see Rom. 3:24; 6:6-23; 7:14; 8:12-23; 12:11; 13:4; 14:4, 18; 16:18; cf. 1 Cor. 7:22-23; Gal. 5:13.

[13] Keith Bradley. *Slavery and Society at Rome.* Cambridge: Cambridge University Press, 1994; Richard Gamauf. Slaves doing business: the role of Roman law in the economy of a Roman household. *European Review of History* 2009; 16(3) 331–346. doi:10.1080/13507480902916837. Accessed September 7, 2016; Dennis P. Kehoe. Law and Social Function in the Roman Empire. *The Oxford Handbook of Social Relations in the Roman World.* Oxford University Press, 2011; Andy Naselli. Keller and Carson: Greco-Roman Slavery ≠ Race-Based Slavery. January 1, 2013. andynaselli.com. Accessed September 7, 2016.

[14] Naselli; Mark Cartwright. Slavery in the Roman World. *Ancient History Encyclopedia.* Last modified November 01, 2013. http://www.ancient.eu /article/629/. Accessed September 7, 2016; Barry Strauss. *The Spartacus War.* New York: Simon & Schuster, 2010; David J. Williams. *Paul's Metaphors: Their Context and Character.* Peabody, MA: Hendrickson Publishers, 1999.

[15] Cartwright; Naselli.

[16] Frank M. Snowden. *Before Color Prejudice: The Ancient View of Blacks.* Cambridge, MA: Harvard University Press, 1983; Bruce W. Frier and Thomas A. J. McGinn. *A Casebook on Roman Family Law.* Oxford University Press: American Philological Association, 2004; Stefan Goodwin. *Africa in Europe: Antiquity into the Age of Global Expansion* (vol. 1). Lanham, MD: Lexington Books, 2009.

[17] Antonio Santosuosso. *Storming the Heavens.* Boulder, CO: Westview Press, 2001.

[18] Murray J. Harris. *Slave of Christ: A New Testament Metaphor for Total Devotion to Christ.* Downers Grove, IL: InterVarsity, 1999.

[19] James D. G. Dunn. *Word Commentary, vol. 38a, Romans 1-8.* Dallas, TX: Word Books, 1988.

[20] Some would argue that Paul's use of slavery as a metaphor for life in Christ is in direct contradiction to his language of freedom and sonship (Rom. 8:15; 15:21; Gal. 5:1, 13). The Pauline metaphor can be used in a variety of ways: as in deliverance from sin, as the sacrifice of self-interest to the interests of another, or as Christian leadership or salvation. See Dale B. Martin. *Slavery as Salvation: The Metaphor of Slavery in Pauline Christianity.* New Haven, CT: Yale University Press, 1990.

[21] MacArthur, John. *Slaves for Christ.* August 5, 2007. Retrieved from Grace to You, www.gty.org, August 21, 2016, pp. 203-204.
[22] MacArthur.

[23] Christopher D. Stanley. Neither Jew nor Greek: Ethnic Conflict in Greco-Roman Society. *JSNT* 1966; 64: 101-24.

[24] A. J. Malherbe. *Paul and the Popular Philosophers.* Minneapolis, MN: Fortress Press, 1989.

[25] O. Procksch. *The Theological Dictionary of the New Testament.* Grand Rapids, MI: Eerdmans, 1984. See also Douglas J. Moo *The Epistle to the Romans.* Grand Rapids, MI: Eerdmans, 1996.

[26] Illustrated History of the Roman Empire. Roman Society, Roman Life. roman-empire.net. Accessed September 12, 2016.

[27] Anthony J. Saldarini. *Pharisees, Scribes and Sadducees in Palestinian Society: A Sociological Approach.* Wilmington, DE: Michael Glazier, 1988.

[28] Dunn.

[29] Peter T. O'Brien. Letters, Letter Forms. In Gerald F. Hawthorn and Ralph P. Martin (eds). *Dictionary of Paul and His Letters.* Downers Grove, IL: InterVarsity Press, 1993.

[30] Osborne.

[31] J. Paul Sampley. *Walking Between the Times: Paul's Moral Reasoning.* Minneapolis, MN: Fortress Press, 1991, p. 43.

[32] No modern translation says "of Christ"; however, other manuscripts add "of Christ." The context supports this rendering.

[33] Bruce J. Malina. *Christian Origins and Cultural Anthropology: Practical Models for Biblical Interpretation.* Atlanta, GA: John Knox, 1986.

[34] Ben Witherington. Honor and Shame and the Apostolic Life. April 30, 2011. Patheos: Hosting the Conversation on Faith. www.patheos.com/.../honor-and-shame-and-the-apostolic-life/. Accessed September 1, 2016.

[35] Patheos.

[36] Jewett, p. 559.

[37] A. N. Sherwin-White. *Racial Prejudice in Imperial Rome.* Cambridge: Cambridge University Press 1967.

[38] James S. Jeffers. *The Greco-Roman World of the New Testament Era: Exploring the Background of Early Christianity.* Downers Grove, IL: InterVarsity Press, 1999.

[39]Peter Schafer. *Judeophobia: Attitudes Toward the Jews in the Ancient World.* Cambridge, MA: Harvard University Press, 1997.

[40] Norman Geisler. *To Understand the Bible Look for Jesus: The Bible Student's Guide to the Bible's Central Theme.* Eugene, OR: Wipf and Stock Publishers, 1979, p. 8.

[41] Paul's quotation, "the righteous shall live by faith," omits the pronoun "his" based on the Hebrew text and the pronoun "my" used in the Septuagint. Paul's omission makes the statement more inclusive of all believers. Ross argues that Paul's modification of Habakkuk 2:4 serves to emphasize his

"eagerness" to proclaim the gospel in Rome (1:15). William A. Ross. Paul's Use of Habakkuk 2:4 in Romans 1:17. Westminster Theological Seminary, Thomas E. Welmers Memorial Prize Paper Competition in the Biblical Languages and Exegesis, 2013.

[42] See Aida Besancon Spencer. *Paul's Literary Style: A Stylistic and Historical Comparison of II Corinthians 11:16 – 12:13, Romans 8:9-39, and Philippians 3:2 – 4:13.* Lanham, MD: University Press of America, 1998; Carl D. DuBois. Metonymy and Synecdoche in the New Testament: A Revision and Augmentation (1999) of John Beckman's "Metonymy and Synecdoche, in *Notes on Translation* 23 (1967).

[43] Sampley. *Walking Between the Times: Paul's Moral Reasoning*, p. 37. See also H. Wheeler Robinson. *Corporate Personality in Ancient Israel.* Philadelphia, PA: Fortress Press, 1980.

[44] The sources for this section are as follows: Ngabo Birikunzira Jerome. Implantation and Growth of the Seventh-day Adventist Church in Rwanda (1919-2000). Master of Theology Thesis. University of South Africa, 2008; Rwanda: A Brief History of the Country. Outreach Programme on the Rwanda Genocide and the United Nations. un.org ; Rory Carroll. Pastor who led Tutsis to slaughter is jailed. *The Guardian* February 19, 2003.

[45] Ex-first Lady of Rwanda Seeks Shelter in Canada. *National Post*, January 16, 2007. http://www.canada.com/nationalpost/story.

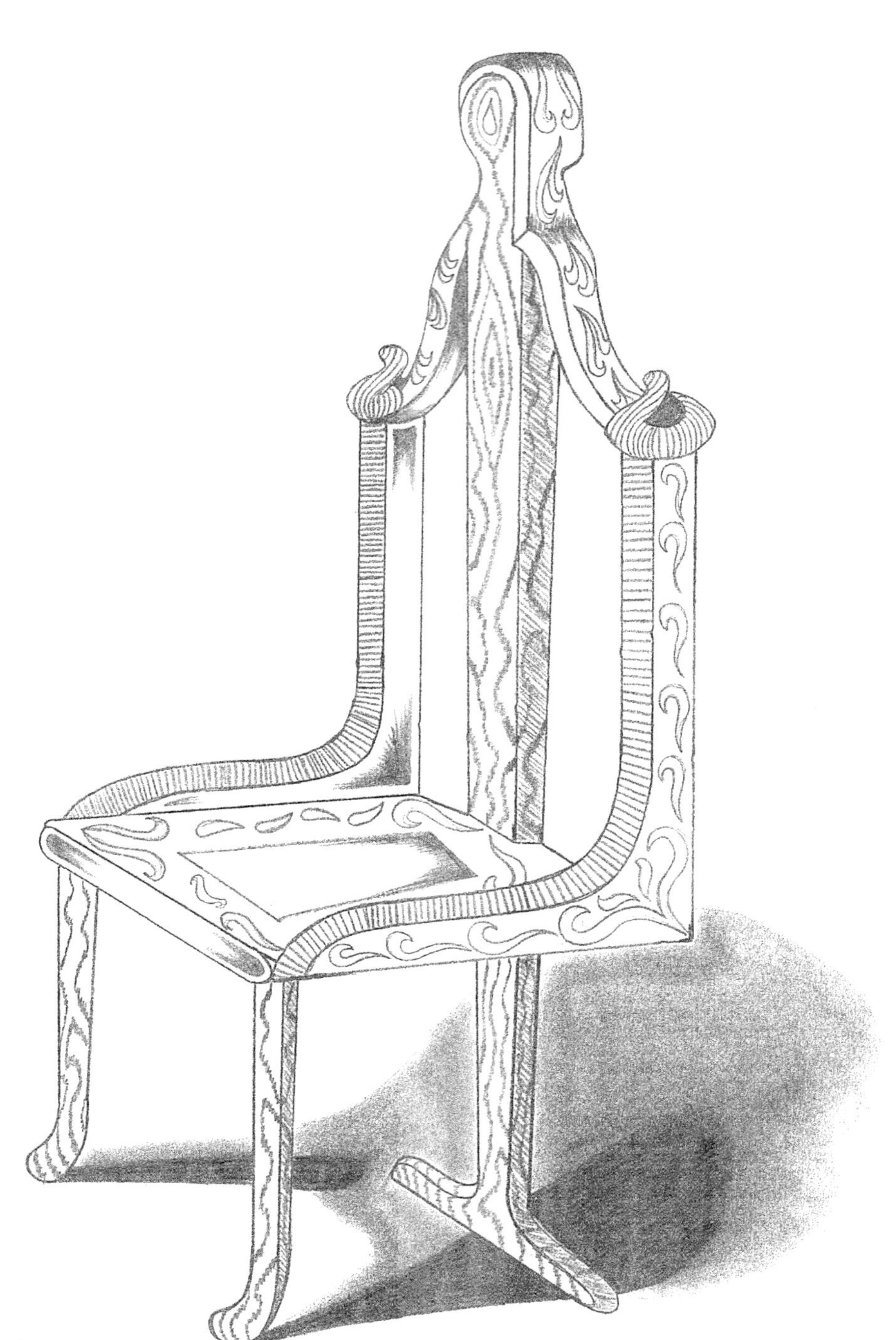

CHAPTER TWO
The Judge

Romans 1:18 - 3:20

Paul reminds Gentiles and Jews in Rome of their lives before their acceptance of the gospel of God. He rehearses their pre-justification story before faith in Jesus Christ. In his argument, Paul demonstrates that all humanity, both Gentiles and Jews, have sinned before God. Both have rejected God's sovereignty. This is the common condition of humankind, and therefore all stand under present and future divine judgment that has been given to Christ. Why does Paul begin his quest for reconciliation and unity among the Roman believers with a scathing critique of the human condition and its consequences? Paul employs the gospel of Christ to deconstruct *the cultural pride*, i.e., ethnic sin, of both Gentiles and Jews. He uses the description of Gentile and Jewish rebellion against God to level the playing field. He reminds both communities that before hearing and receiving God's good news in Christ, they shared the same sin story, a common rebellious heritage. Paul provides two profiles, but one conclusion: "all have sinned and come short of the glory of God" (3:23). Paul recognizes that life according to the flesh is a continuous threat for those in Christ. Therefore, sin—both corporate and individual—must be named in order to understand the ongoing need of Christ.

Gentile Arrogance

With the words, "For the wrath of God is revealed from heaven against all ungodliness and unrighteousness of men who suppress the truth in unrighteousness" (1:18 NASB), Paul begins his description of Gentile rejection of God and their accountability to God. Paul critiques the values, attitudes, and practices embedded in Gentile culture that still influence the worldview of Gentile believers in Rome. Paul sets the stage for criticizing Gentile arrogance towards Jews based on a sense of socio-religious superiority; Gentile Christians are discounting Jewish Christians as part of the people of God (11:13-32; 14:1-4). Before examining Paul's argument and how it is used to foster reconciliation and unity in Rome (1:19-32), we should note that this verse functions as a "hinge" in his argument, tying together what he has just said with what he is about to say. The gospel communicates not only God's righteousness; it also announces God's wrath (1:17-18).

For many contemporary Christians, the notion of the wrath of God is a bit disturbing. We like to think of God as a Father, tender and compassionate. The idea of a God of wrath must be discussed at this point. The gospel of Christ announces not only divine righteousness for those who trust God's saving work in Christ, but also reveals God's revulsion against, and judgment of, sin. In this passage, Paul demonstrates that God is against Gentiles who reject God's self-revelation in creation. In other words, in the person of Jesus Christ, as articulated in the gospel, the two dimensions of God's nature—love and justice—are maintained.[1]

In Paul's letter to the Romans, the application of God's wrath may be understood in two ways: first, as God's future judgment for the sins of the world (2:5, 8, 16; 5:9); and second, as God's wrath revealed in the present (cf. 3:5; 4:15; 9:22). Paul most likely has this second understanding of God's wrath in mind when he says, "The wrath of God is being revealed from heaven" against Gentile sin (1:18 NIV). The consequences of this present wrath are the inevitable result of being outside the will of God, i.e., the debasement of Gentiles when living in violation of God's created order.[2]

Paul begins his description of the cultural heritage of sin among Gentiles in Rome with two interlocking terms, "ungodliness," no reverence for God, and "unrighteousness," wrongness of life in relation to God. We should note that from the outset, Paul describes corporate sin, not just individual sin. Paul's language suggests a group rejection of God and the pattern of living that results. In Paul's thinking, these two descriptors, ungodliness and unrighteousness, indicate the essence of *Gentile sin.*

Paul understands sin as a power that animates human nature (7:14-23). At root, sin is the consequence of the fall, a posture of heart, mind, and body bequeathed to all humankind through Adam's sin (5:12-21; Gen. 3:1-24). In his letter to Gentile believers in Ephesus, Paul describes their former way of life as being "dead . . . in trespasses and sins." Furthermore, he argues that formerly, Gentiles were "separated from the life of God" (Eph. 2:1; 4:18). Later, in this letter, Paul makes the inextricable connection between sin and death (6:23). At present, Paul describes the Gentile world apart from God as spiritually dead. In fact, Paul accuses Gentile pagans of *intentionally* suppressing or holding down the truth about God in the way they live. Next, Paul uses two lines of argument to bolster his general assessment of Gentile guilt and the divine response.

Paul describes Gentile rejection of God and the resulting idolatry using a so-called "natural revelation" argument. He states, "For what can be known about God is plain to them, because God has shown it to them. Ever since the creation of the world his eternal power and divine nature, invisible though they are, have been understood and seen through the things he has made. So they are without excuse" (1:19-20). Paul argues that Gentiles have had access to a knowledge of the true God through creation, and that this knowledge included an understanding of God's eternal power and deity.

What is Paul saying about Gentile guilt? Paul's assertion must be understood in light of his claims about Christ as Creator. In his first doxology in this letter, in praise of God's redemptive plan, Paul makes a subtle reference to the creative role of Christ (11:33-36). However, he is more explicit on this point in his letter to

Colossae. In an attempt to refute the "Jesus plus" heresy, which argued that Christ is insufficient for salvation, Paul writes,

> He is the image of the invisible God, the firstborn over all creation. For everything was created by Him, in heaven and on earth, the visible and the invisible, whether thrones or dominions or rulers or authorities—all things have been created through Him and for Him. He is before all things, and by Him all things hold together (Col. 1:15-17 HCSB; cf. 1 Cor. 8:6; 11:12; Jn. 1:1-3; 1 Jn. 1:1; Heb. 1:2; 2:10).

In light of this description of Christ as being preeminent over creation, the agent of creation, and the conserving cause of all creation, is Paul indirectly charging the Gentile world with unwittingly rejecting their Creator, the Second Person of the Godhead?

In context, with the assertion "they are without excuse," there can be no doubt that Paul argues that Gentiles are culpable before God even though they did not have access to written revelation as did Jews (2:17; 3:2). Why? Because all creation, both animate and inanimate, bears witness to God's power and divinity, God's essential goodness (cf. Ps. 19:1-6). Rightly understood, Paul suggests that Christ as the Creator has embedded in every aspect of the natural world the reality of God's fundamental nature: God's steadfast love (Gen. 1:1 - 2:24; Ex. 33:18-23; 34:5-7). Creation reveals God's invisible nature, God's deity, which would become visible in the incarnation of Christ (cf. Col. 2:9).

Paul intensifies his depiction of Gentile responsibility. "For even though they knew God, they did not honor Him as God or give thanks to Him" (1:21a). Paul not only accuses Gentiles of an intentional rejection of God, he suggests an unmitigated arrogance. Gentiles have willfully chosen to deny what could be known about God through the natural world.

Having established the fact that Gentiles have been given a knowledge of the true God through creation, Paul now describes Gentile dismissal of God and the resulting downward progression. He explains that the Gentile decline into moral depravity begins with an intentional rejection of God's self-revelation. Paul makes two related claims about Gentiles' denial of God that identify the essence of pagan sin. Gentiles "did not glorify God as God." They willfully refuse to acknowledge God's power and divine nature as revealed in creation, i.e., they fail to worship God. They reject God's glory and, therefore, God's right to their worship. In addition, Gentiles do not "give thanks." With this allegation, Paul seems to describe pagan ingratitude towards the divine generosity manifested in the natural world. In sum, Paul charges the Gentile world with a type of atheism, a willful dismissal of the true God. The Roman myth of origin illustrates Paul's charge.

Romans traced their origin to the legend of Romulus and Remus. Romulus and Remus were infant twin brothers who were abandoned by their parents. Placed in a basket that was floated on the River Tiber, the twins ran aground and were discovered by a female wolf. The wolf nursed the babies for a short time before they were found by a shepherd who reared them to adulthood. The brothers decided to establish a city where the wolf had found them. When they quarreled over the site for the city, Romulus killed Remus. Romulus founded the new city to which he gave his name—Rome.[3]

It is on the basis of this type of Gentile flight from God that Paul now identifies the necessary interlocking consequences. He states, "But their thinking became futile and their foolish hearts were darkened. Although they claimed to be wise, they became fools and exchanged the glory of the immortal God for images made to look like a mortal human being and birds and animals and reptiles" (1:21b-23 NIV).

It should be noticed that Paul establishes a cause and effect relationship between Gentile rejection of God's self-revelation through nature and their three-fold descent into idolatry. Paul argues that Gentiles "became futile in their thinking, and their foolish hearts were darkened." Echoing the moral philosophers of his day, Paul draws a direct connection between thought and action. But unlike his contemporaries, who believed that wrong action was the result of living contrary to nature, Paul argues that the Gentiles have developed diseased thought, a mental futility or rational darkness, as a direct consequence of their denunciation of the true God. It is this denial that leads inevitably to foolish hearts, or moral corruption.

Paul next asserts that based on mental and moral darkness, Gentiles profess themselves to be wise. In other words, they construct their own system of wisdom antagonistic to the wisdom of God, which Paul describes as a foolish act of self-deception. Again, Paul suggests a deluded arrogance based on mental acuity. Through pride in a faulty assumption of their own intelligence, Gentiles have rejected the wisdom of God ultimately revealed in the person and work of Christ (cf. 1 Cor. 1:18-25). It is this arrogant elevation of human wisdom that causes Gentiles, especially Greeks and Romans, to view others, including Jews, as inferior.

Paul's claim is best illustrated by Greek philosophical tradition. Beginning with the Pre-Socratics, through Socrates, Plato, and Aristotle, Greeks established a system of wisdom that in many ways served as the foundation of Greco-Roman culture, the culture of Paul's day. The teaching of the Greek philosopher Protagoras demonstrates this point.

Greco-Roman thought of the first century and, in fact, Western humanistic thought today, are both based on the assumption of the priority of human wisdom. This type of thought finds its roots in the claims of Protagoras of Abdera, a Greek Sophist philosopher who lived approximately 500 to 411 B.C.[4] Protagoras represents a shift in Greek philosophy from an interest in the natural world to an interest in human understanding of the world. This new emphasis on human beings' subjective perception, or construction, of their world is even today an essential part of philosophy.[5]

Protagoras made three important claims that had a profound influence on Greco-Roman thought and on Western thinking today, even among Adventists. The first claim is that man is the measure of all things. In other words, everything is subject to the relativity of human thought and experience. He purported, "Of all things the measure is Man, of the things that are, that they are, and of the things that are not, that they are not."[6] This thoroughgoing, and considered by some as radically relativistic, humanism is one of the major contributions of the revival of Greek thinking that the Enlightenment brought to modern Western thought.[7]

Protagoras' second claim, "There are two sides to every question,"[8] found its corollary in the notion that he could make the worse, or weaker, argument appear the better, or stronger one. The decisive nature of human argument placed emphasis on the power of human reason, or rationalism.

Protagoras' atheism, or agnosticism, is found in his third assertion, "About the gods, I am not able to know whether they exist or do not exist, nor what they are like in form; for the factors preventing knowledge are many; the obscurity of the subject, and the shortness of human life."[9] Here, Protagoras questions the very existence of God. With these three claims Protagoras established individualism, rationalism, and atheism as being foundational to Western thought.

Contrary to Greek philosophical wisdom, in 1 Corinthians, Paul posits a wisdom that comes from God. God's wisdom is Christ.

> Where is the one who is wise? Where is the scribe? Where is the debater of this age? Has not God made foolish the wisdom of the world? For since, in the wisdom of God, the world did not know God through wisdom, God decided, through the foolishness of our proclamation, to save those who believe. For Jews demand signs and Greeks desire wisdom, but we proclaim Christ crucified, a stumbling block to Jews and foolishness to Gentiles, but to those who are the called, both Jews and Greeks, Christ the power of God and the wisdom of God. For God's foolishness is wiser than human wisdom, and God's weakness is stronger than human strength . . . . He is the source of your life in Christ Jesus, who became for us wisdom from God, and righteousness and sanctification and redemption (1 Cor. 1:20-25, 30).

The final moral consequence of Gentile rejection of God and their misguided wisdom, according to Paul, is that they have "exchanged the glory of the immortal God for images resembling a mortal human being or birds or four-footed animals or reptiles" (1:23). Paul, who would be knowledgeable of the history of Israel's idolatry and the prophetic tradition criticizing the idolatry of the nations, now turns to a description of contemporary Gentile idolatry (Is. 44:6-20).

Paul accuses the pagan world of false worship. Gentiles have substituted for their Creator, who should occupy the center of life and meaning for created things, mere idols. In essence, he argues that Gentile mental and moral darkness is evident by their perversion of God's glory through the worship of images of humans and animals. Indeed, based on Paul's worldview informed by the Old Testament, Gentiles have violated the first three of God's Ten Commands:

> Do not have other gods besides Me. Do not make an idol for yourself, whether in the shape of anything in the heavens above or on the earth below or in the waters under the earth. You must not bow down to them or worship them; for I, the Lord your God, am a jealous God, punishing the children for the fathers' sin, to the third and fourth generations of those who hate Me, but showing faithful love to a thousand generations of those who love Me and keep My commands (Ex. 20. 3-6 HCSB).

In Paul's first-century world, Greco-Roman religion was polytheistic. To an initial array of gods and spirits, Romans added both Greek gods and many foreign cultic deities. There were twelve major gods in the Greek pantheon: the Twelve Olympians. The Romans adopted and adapted many of these gods into a main pantheon of twelve deities called *Dii Consentes*. Under Greek influence, Roman gods became anthropomorphic, exhibiting such human characteristics as jealousy, love, deception, and lust.

The nature of religious practice in the first century was transactional. The gods were capricious and were placated in Roman worship by strict adherence to a rigid set of rituals, rather than by obedience to a moral code of behavior. Adherence to religious ritual was to be rewarded with the favor of the gods. The entire Roman religious system was based on superstition, but superstition then did not carry our modern negative connotation. By the time of Paul, many elite Gentiles no longer believed in the gods; their religious performance was more a political matter. During the reign of Caesar Augustus, the idea of deification of the emperor arose. Although Augustus resisted the Roman Senate's attempt to declare him a god, he was awarded this designation upon his death, an honor that was bestowed on many of his successors.[10]

With this depiction of Gentile idolatry, Paul argues that pagan culture in general, from Nimrod the Hamite to Cyrus, from Alexander the Great to the Caesars, and indeed all of Greco-Roman culture of the first century in particular, are in essence anti-God, hostile to its Creator. For Paul, Gentile "refusal to acknowledge and glorify God leads to a downward path: first, worthless thinking; next, moral insensitivity; and then, religious stupidity [idol-worship]."[11] Paul's critique of Gentile idolatry is anchored in the conviction that rival gods, whether ancient or modern, ultimately cannot satisfy (Is. 55:1-13). They cannot approximate the glory of God.

It is important in our discussion of ethnic issues between Gentiles and Jews in Rome to observe that unlike the Gentile laws that prohibited intermarriage on the grounds of ethnicity among the Greeks or status among the Romans, God's prohibition of Israelites marrying Gentiles was based *solely on the issue of idolatry.* Ethnicity was not a consideration; these laws were enacted because marriage to pagans would result in the rejection of Yahweh (Ex. 34:16; Dt. 7:3-11; Ezra 9:1 - 10:44).

Jewish corruption of this prohibition occurred during the Second Temple Period (538 B.C. – 70 A.D.). In response to the imposition of Hellenistic culture on Palestine by the Seleucids (ca. 198 B.C.), and especially the persecutions of Antiochus Epiphanes (ca. 215 – 164 B.C.),[12] Jewish nationalists, e.g., the Maccabees, and their scribal supporters, experts in the law, perverted the reason for the scriptural laws against intermarriage. These laws, which were designed to prevent idolatry and apostasy, were used instead to institute a practice to insure ethnic purity and ethnic exclusivity, i.e., ethnocentrism. In his criticism of Jewish sin, Paul exposes and condemns these attitudes (2:1-16).

In the same way, many Adventists have used Ellen White's statements on racial intermarriage to promote ethnocentrism, instead of her clearly stated motive: the prevention of controversy and the facilitation of the gospel mission of the church in nineteenth-century America. Adventist interpretations of her statements have been used to sustain ethnocentrism, in this case to maintain the myth of racial superiority. The reason for the prohibition, almost enshrined in doctrine, is that the white race is superior to the black race. Ellen White's numerous statements to the contrary are disregarded.[13]

Ellen White's writings have been and are being used in the twentieth and twenty-first centuries without regard to their nineteenth-century context. As mentioned earlier, the color line was a pervasive problem in nineteenth-century America. It was rooted in the notion that white people were of purer stock and were superior in every respect, including character, to people of color. This perspective was undergirded by pseudo-scientific justifications that rationalized racial separation and an unequal distribution of power and wealth.

A prime example of the salience of the color line in Adventist thinking since the nineteenth century that persists to the present day is our interpretation of Ellen White's position on interracial marriage. One of the most frequently quoted statements follows:

> But there is an objection to the marriage of the white race with the black. All should consider that they have no right to entail upon their offspring that which will place them at a disadvantage; they

> have no right to give them as a birthright a condition which would subject them to a life of humiliation. The children of these mixed marriages have a feeling of bitterness toward the parents who have given them this lifelong inheritance. For this reason, if there were no other, there should be no intermarriage between the white and the colored race.[14]

It is obvious that the counsel on interracial marriage had everything to do with the problems that would be generated for the children of such unions and the spread of the gospel in a hostile and sometimes dangerous cultural environment. These reasons are no longer valid. If the product of an interracial marriage can occupy the White House and the evangelistic efforts of interracial Adventist churches are successful, we can no longer maintain this improper use of Ellen White's counsel. Some Adventists, even prominent ministers, still hold that interracial marriage is tantamount to being "unequally yoked." This interpretation begs two questions. First, what is the nature of the inequality, i.e., who is the superior and who is the inferior in the relationship? And, if the full text is read, who is the "unbeliever"?

Accountable Now

Next, in a two-part argument, Paul describes God's response to Gentile rejection of God's glory and then provides a summary of the resulting moral corruption (1:24-32). Paul begins his description of God's reaction to Gentile sin with the words,

> Therefore, God gave them up in the lusts of their hearts to impurity, to the degrading of their bodies among themselves, because they exchanged the truth about God for a lie and worshiped and served the creature rather than the Creator, who is blessed forever! Amen. For this reason, God gave them up to degrading passions. Their women exchanged natural intercourse for unnatural, and in the same way also the men, giving up natural intercourse with women, were consumed with passion for one another. Men committed shameless acts with men and received in their own persons the due penalty for their error. And since they did not see fit to acknowledge God, God gave them up to a debased mind and to things that should not be done (1:24-28).

Using the conjunction, "therefore," Paul introduces the divine response to Gentile willful rejection of God's self-revelation. He repeats the phrase "God delivered them over" three times in this passage to describe God's present wrath against Gentile sexual sin (1:24, 26, 28; cf. 1:18). In other words, Paul describes God as allowing Gentiles to have their way in a direct response to Gentile rejection of God's person. God has figuratively stepped out of their way and given them over to their sinful desires.

Paul's statements are incomprehensible without first establishing that he assumes the Genesis creation narrative, especially humankind's creation in the image of God. According to the Genesis account, the image of God is *male and female*, two-in-one, corresponding to the divine three-in-one of the Godhead (Gen. 1:26-27; 2:4-25). In light of the creation story, Adam and Eve were created by God as image-bearers. As image-bearers, they were supposed to represent and perpetuate both dimensions of God's essential nature, *steadfast love and holiness* (cf. Ex. 34:5-7). In short, Adam and Eve were created with the Godlike ability for self-sacrifice and self-renunciation. They shared God's inner nature and thus God's glory.

In his summary of human sinfulness, Paul describes both Gentiles and Jews as falling short of the glory of God (3:23). Thus, sin causes human beings to fall short of God's creative intent, especially as it relates to sexuality. Unlike animals who mate based on instinct, Adam and Eve were given the ability to procreate as image-bearers (Gen. 1:28; cf. 1:22). The parenthetical statement of Moses, "Therefore a man leaves his father and his mother and clings to his wife, and they become one flesh. And the man and his wife were both naked, and were not ashamed," serves to emphasize that God created male and female (husband and wife) to experience holistic oneness, including sexual intimacy (Gen. 2:24-25).

D. R. Heimbach maintains that sexual intimacy as created by God has seven essential characteristics. Sex based on the image of God must be personal, exclusive, intimate, potentially fruitful, selfless, complex, and complementary.[15] In light of Paul's description of Gentile sexuality, we will address only two of these characteristics.

Sexual intimacy as created by God is complex or multidimensional. Human beings are created with spirits, souls, and bodies. God the Son created sex as a complex, multidimensional relationship that connects complex, multidimensional beings. The dimensions of sex are inseparable: each is essential to the whole at all times. Each affects the others, if one is denied or corrupted, sex as a whole is corrupted. The physical union of bodies is to be an expression of the deeper and more profound unity of human spirits and souls (mind, will, and emotion) made one in Christ. In other words, the outer connection of bodies is a *symbol* of the deeper connection of human spirits and souls.

Sexual intimacy is also complementary, i.e., it unites corresponding differences. Sex unites beings that are made for each other: differences that are both real and good. Males and females are different in ways that correspond; when united, these differences make something that is greater than what may be gained by simply adding sexual partners. "Sex is not for joining identical things, or just anything, or nothing at all."[16]

With this background, Paul's use of the refrain, "God delivered them over," becomes intelligible. For Paul, Gentile rejection and replacement of God at the center of life causes the corruption of humankind in its essence. Because Gentiles have rejected God's glory as revealed in creation, they inevitably reject God's image as male and female. Paul makes several interrelated claims about Gentile sexual sin. In so doing, he unfolds the consequences of God's stepping aside.

Paul says that God gave Gentiles over to the control of their sexual lusts: desire that flows from a darkened or corrupt heart (1:24; cf. 1:21; 1 Thess. 4:5-7). Paul argues that Gentiles are now motivated by a perverse sexual craving. Using the language of the Old Testament, he characterizes their sexual desire and behavior as "uncleanness" (6:19; cf. Lev. 18:22, 29; 20:13). And employing the cultural language of honor-shame, Paul describes their acts as "dishonorable."

It is telling that Paul later suggests that sin is a type of bondage. Believers are to be controlled by the Spirit, they are to "put on the Lord Jesus Christ," making no provision for the gratification of lust (6:16-23; 8:4-11; 13:14). In order that there will be no doubt about the reason for Gentile sexual perversion, Paul again uses the language of substitution. Gentiles have exchanged the "truth" embedded by God in the created order about human sexuality for a humanly constructed lie (1:25; cf. 1:23; Gen. 3:4-5). He affirms the truth of his own statement with an "Amen," literally, "let it be."

Paul sharpens his description of Gentile sexual perversion. He argues that God gave Gentiles up to degrading or dishonorable passions. Again, the idea is that of humans descending to a condition lower than that of God's original intent. Paul contends that same sex relations, both among men and women are contrary to nature. As previously stated, Paul's conviction turns on the belief that sexual intimacy between male and female is part of the created order (Gen. 1:26-27; 2:21–24; Mt. 19:4–6). While emphasizing homosexual sin, Paul continues his use of honor-shame categories in describing men having sex with men as a "shameless act" (1:26-27).

Here, it should be noted that although Paul views same sex relations as sin, he does not view it as being more egregious than any other sin; that he equates homosexuality with other vices is clear (1 Cor. 6:9-10; 1 Tim. 1:8-11). More important, Paul argues strenuously, against both many unbelieving Jews and Jewish believers of his day, that God loves all sinners and sent His Son to die in order that those who believe might be freed from the bondage of sin (5:6-8; 6:15-23).

As if for good measure, and as a way of summarizing his present argument, Paul uses his refrain for the final time, "God gave them over." For the third time he points out a cause and effect relationship. Gentiles "did not see fit to acknowledge God," therefore, God delivers them up to a debased mind, to doing things sexually "that should not be done." Here, there can be no doubt that Paul's language suggests a legal prohibition against Gentile sexual perversion (Lev. 18:22, 29; 20:13).

At this point, the question may be raised legitimately: Is Paul, a Jew and a former Pharisee, overstating the case against Gentile sexuality? Is there contemporaneous evidence for his charges? A brief depiction of Greco-Roman views and practices related to sexuality will serve to support Paul's description.

Greco-Roman "morality" in practice was informed by a radical separation between religion and ethics. While Greeks and Romans had no concept of sin as modern Christians know it, they did have their "moral" codes. It is ironic that Aristotle, who insists that there are no absolute moral standards, posits the idea of a moral life apart from the gods: a pagan righteousness by works.[17] Pagan priests in Paul's time did not function as moral guides; although moral philosophers, such as Martial and Juvenal, wrote about moral ideals, Greco-Roman society was characterized by licentiousness. The emphasis on sensuality was fueled by the Roman policy of "bread and circuses" to pacify the populace. The combination of violence and cruelty with sexual license that this policy dictated led to such popular amusements as crucifixions, gladiatorial contests, and combat with wild beasts. Sexual practices included orgies, prostitution, and pedophilia.[18]

Greco-Roman sexual mores differed significantly from ours. In the first-century world of permissive sexual ethics, Gentile men were expected to be attracted to both women and young males, including young boys and adolescents. The only restriction to satisfying the lust for young males, or females for that matter, was that they not be freeborn. Slaves or prostitutes of any age or gender were acceptable sexual partners for a Roman male as long as he took the dominant role.

The Greco-Roman male found a model in the Roman god Jupiter who was reported to have a strong erotic interest in attractive teenage boys. There was even same-sex marriage in the first century. The emperor Nero married a man, and this was not a cause of shame. Nero's second same-sex marriage, to his former slave Pythagoras, was considered shameful, however, because in this second ceremony Nero was the bride.

Same-sex relations were not considered immoral, nor did such acts constitute adultery in the context of a marriage. Among Romans, there was no concept of homosexuality in contrast to heterosexuality. In fact, no Latin words for these concepts exist. In a culture obsessed with virility, the important distinction was between penetrator and penetrated. The feminine, or shameful, role was that of being penetrated.

In this honor-shame culture, the ethos of aggressive masculinity implied by being the penetrator aligned with notions of honor and dominance, while being penetrated was frowned upon because it denoted the shameful status of submission and passivity. To Romans, masculinity was a highly sought-after virtue, and as long as the male was on the giving and not the receiving end, his masculinity was ensured. A Roman man could engage in sexual intercourse with both males and females as long as he assumed the dominant role.

Nero was shamed in his marriage to Pythagoras because Nero was taking the submissive role. By the same token, it was deplorable and illegal for young freeborn males to be the objects of adult male sexual attention, i.e., penetration, because this would damage the young male's pride and future reputation. Actors and other entertainers were viewed as shameful because they assumed the submissive sexual role with their patrons. Romans had a number of derogatory terms for a sexually penetrated male. A Roman man who desired the submissive role was thought to have a disease.[19]

In the Greco-Roman world, sex was regarded as an everyday necessity, such as food and drink. Therefore, sexual acts could be committed in plain daylight or within the view of servants; privacy was not a necessity. In Roman culture, sex was viewed as an animal instinct, something that emanated from natural bodily functions, and hence, did not entail any kind of obligation or bond between two people. Sharing a meal with another person had much more value and commitment than having sex. And yet, hyper-sexuality was condemned morally and medically for men and women. For Romans, the "disadvantage" or "inconvenience" of sex, especially for males, was that it might negatively affect or interfere with rational decision-making and action.[20] This description of Gentile sexuality justifies Paul's harsh criticism.

Paul employs a teaching device used by moral philosophers of his day: the vice list. Vice lists were to help adherents who conformed to a certain way of life, e.g., Stoicism, to distinguish between appropriate and inappropriate behavior. To close his description of Gentile sin, Paul uses a well-crafted vice list to catalogue Gentile depravity. He writes,

> They were filled with every kind of wickedness, evil, covetousness, malice. Full of envy, murder, strife, deceit, craftiness, they are gossips, slanderers, God-haters, insolent, haughty, boastful, inventors of evil, rebellious toward parents, foolish, faithless, heartless, ruthless. They know God's decree, that those who practice such things deserve to die—yet they not only do them but even applaud others who practice them" (1:29-32; cf. 1 Cor. 6:9-10; 1 Tim. 1:10).

Paul uses this catalogue of twenty-one vices to underscore the total moral corruption of the Gentile world of his time. This vice list emphasizes the Gentile focus on personal desire and self-gratification (cf. 2 Tim. 3:2-5; Jam. 1:14-15). It should not be missed that Paul concludes his list by again charging Gentiles with cultural arrogance. With the words, "yet they not only do them but even applaud others who practice them," he accuses Gentiles of not only practicing debauchery continuously, but reveling in the depravity of others (1:32b; cf. 1:18, 21-22).

A careful analysis of Paul's description of Gentile sin reveals an embedded progression. He moves from their rejection of the true God's self-revelation in nature, to the construction of an alternate idolatrous reality, and finally to moral corruption. Significantly, Gentile depravity includes same sex relations: the rejection and defacing of the image of God as male and female. Gentile suppression of truth results in comprehensive debauchery, a way of life in opposition to the Creator. Paul ends his description of Gentile sin with the ominous conclusion: "Those who practice such things are worthy of death" (1:32a NASB).

Again, the question may be raised: why does Paul begin his quest for reconciliation between Gentile and Jewish believers in Rome with a description of Gentile sin and its consequences? What is the significance of his portrait for achieving unity? There are at least three reasons for Paul's description.

With his depiction of Gentile sin, Paul is making a cultural charge against Gentiles as a whole, not just as individuals. Thus, he establishes the reality of corporate sin. Paul describes an attitude towards God and a resulting way of life embedded in Gentile culture. He suggests that all aspects of pagan life—its intellectual history, assumptions, values, beliefs, and practices—are tainted by sin. Throughout his portrait of Gentile sinfulness, Paul describes group traits expressed individually (1:18, 20-23, 29-32). Specifically, Paul hints of a *cultural arrogance, a prideful intentionality* against God's nature and creative purpose endemic among pagan Gentiles. Not only do they deliberately suppress the truth about God, they view their thought world as superior to that of others and their sinful behavior worth mimicking.

Next according to Paul, Gentiles take pride in their depravity. Gentile arrogance in the Greco-Roman period may have been based on the belief of Greeks that they were fated to bring wisdom and culture to the world and the conviction of Romans that they were fated by the gods to impose rule and order on the world.[21]

Nevertheless, in light of God's sovereignty, Paul views the Gentile way of life as marked by arrogance. The Gentile majority in Rome is reminded that Gentile culture stands under divine judgment, and this way of life deserves death, i.e., eternal separation from God (1:18, 32; 2:16; cf. 1 Cor. 7:31).

It is against this backdrop that Paul later admonishes believing Gentiles in Rome for their wrongheaded attitudes against all Jews, especially their Jewish brothers and sisters. He accuses Gentile believers of religious pride, of creating a misguided "ethnic theology" that informs their attitude and behavior towards the Jews in general and Jewish believers in Rome in particular, based on boastfulness, arrogance, and conceit. In addition, he warns these believers that if they persist in this sin, they too, like unbelieving Israel, will be "cut off," i.e., rejected by God (11:13, 18, 20, 22, 25).

Paul also, beginning with the first element of his thesis statement (the gospel of Christ is the power of God to salvation to the Jew first and also to the Greek), argues for the priority of Jews in the history of salvation (1:16; 9:4-5; cf. Jn. 4:22). Building on this premise, he again emphasizes the precedence of Israel in salvation, and adds that they will also be first in the final judgment of God (2:9-10). In light of Jewish priority, why then does Paul treat Gentile sin first? It is highly likely that Paul is attempting to undermine any idea among the Gentile majority of a political advantage in the body of Christ (12:3). There can be no doubt that Gentile believers enjoy a social advantage over Jews in Roman society. As mentioned earlier, Jews continued to experience the social shame associated with Claudius' expulsion.

However, Paul will forcefully remind Gentile believers that they are not the "olive tree"—a metaphor for the people of God—but simply "wild olive branches" grafted into faithful Israel (11:17-21). Paul says that Gentile believers should think of themselves as part of God's elect along with Jews who have experienced the mercy of God in Christ (8:28-30; 11:28-32). For Paul, any thought of dominance or political advantage is based on a misunderstanding of the nature of the body of Christ (12:3-21). As already mentioned, Paul begins his depiction of human sin and accountability by describing the Gentile majority in Rome. Is it possible that he is rhetorically placing the greater weight for reconciliation on those with the most political power and social advantage? Is he obliquely echoing the dictum of Jesus, "to whom much is given, much is required?" (Lk. 12:48).

There is a third and final way in which Paul's portrayal of Gentile sinfulness may aid his unifying purpose. As we have seen, Paul condemns Gentile sexuality, especially same sex relations. Given the different cultural backgrounds of believing Gentiles and Jews in Rome, how would they hear Paul's condemnation? Unlike the penchant among many Adventists to single out homosexuality as the worst possible sin, and the homophobia that unfortunately characterizes many personal interactions with homosexual people, Paul does not indicate that homosexuality is a sin that deserves especially harsh judgment. He lists this vice along with others that ultimately exclude a person from eternal life (1 Cor. 6:9-10; cf. 1 Tim. 1:8-11). Paul's teaching in this regard was likely to offend both segments of his audience, as it is likely to offend every contemporary segment of our modern congregations. While Paul soundly condemns homosexuality, he does not make this behavior the worst sin, nor does he enjoin disrespectful or hateful treatment of homosexual persons.

Why would Paul's counsel offend both Gentiles and Jews in his first-century audience? In 1 Corinthians, Paul warns his Gentile converts, many of whom would have previously engaged in same sex relations, that whether the man in question was the passive or the dominant partner, both were involved in shameful behavior (1 Cor. 6:9-10). Paul's aim was not to further shame the passive partner who may have had no choice in the matter. Paul unequivocally challenges the "moral" perception of the virile Roman male who has become a Christian to no longer feel free to express his sexuality however he pleases. E. Randolph Richards and Brandon O'Brien state,

> At the same time that Paul was setting a more restrictive sexual ethic than [Gentile] converts found comfortable (or fair), he also

> extended grace to people the Jewish converts were uncomfortable embracing in Christian fellowship. Jewish converts in the Roman churches would have been familiar with both the Levitical prohibitions against homosexual behavior and the Levitical punishment for that behavior. Their religious upbringing in Torah would have made it very difficult for them to believe that God could declare righteous anyone who had ever committed acts their Scriptures clearly labeled egregious sins. [22]

When his letter was originally read in the Christian assemblies in Rome, "Roman Christians were likely embarrassed by Paul's prudishness about sexuality, but the Jewish Christians were likely scandalized by Paul's willingness to extend forgiveness and fellowship to sinners."[23] Paul will later criticize both groups for constructing "theologies" and practices in keeping with their own cultural sensibilities or location (2:1-29; 11:13-36; 14:1-23). Presently, he turns to one of the major causes for discord among believers in Rome: a Jewish sense of advantage over Gentiles based on moral superiority and blindness to the Jews' own sinfulness.

Jewish Religious Pride and Judgmentalism

Now we encounter a rather complicated argument from Paul, describing and criticizing the judgmentalism of Jews towards Gentiles, which he characterizes as sin. Paul compares the partiality of the Jews with the impartiality of God. His purpose is to expose the bias of Jews towards Gentiles based on cultural pride and religious exclusivity and to make the point that God is without bias. Christ is God's impartial judge. All humanity, both Jews and Gentiles, are finally accountable to the Son. After describing Jewish hypocrisy and its misrepresentation of the character of God among the Gentiles, Paul begins to redefine what it means to be a Jew, and concludes with the corrective that no one is justified based on works of the law.

If pagan Gentiles are culpable before God in light of His self-revelation through creation, then for Paul, the unbelieving Jewish world stands under greater condemnation. In the passage 2:1 - 3:8, he argues that the covenant people, in spite of all their advantages, have also rejected the true God (3:1-2; cf. 9:4-5). Their rejection is far more egregious because of God's self-revelation that begins with the promise first made to Abram (Gen. 12:1-3; 4:13), codified in the Old Testament, and finally made incarnate in the person of Christ.

Paul substantiates his charges using three proofs: Jews have engaged in improper judgment that God will judge; they have failed to obey the law they profess; yet, God is faithful in spite of Jewish unfaithfulness. Paul's condemnation of Judaism is longer and more complex than his critique of Gentile sinfulness precisely because of the blindness caused by the Jewish misunderstanding of their call and privilege. We as Adventists also believe that we are the recipients of special blessings from God and that we have, as a result, special responsibilities in the last days. We must be careful unless we, like Israel, misunderstand the advantages of our unique call and privilege.

Paul begins his description of Jewish sin through the use of a rhetorical device called diatribe, a device he employs throughout his argument (2:1 - 3:8). Diatribe was a method of argumentation adapted by the Stoics that was in popular use in Paul's day, even within Jewish circles. This method places questions on the lips of a hypothetical opponent and then offers a rebuttal. It is believed that diatribe originated in the Greco-Roman classroom, where it was used to provoke learning and to exhort students to an alternative way of living. By anticipating a possible objection to his argument, the teacher puts the objection in the mouth of an imaginary opponent and then refutes it.[24]

Why does Paul choose this method of argumentation in his critique of Jewish sin? Because of the "legal" orientation of Pharisaic Judaism, among unbelievers and believers, Paul undoubtedly anticipates objections to any characterization of Jews as sinners. It is on this basis that he chooses a style of discourse designed to expose and meet Jewish objections. Using this teaching device, Paul begins,

> Therefore, you have no excuse, O man, every one of you who judges. For in passing judgment on another you condemn yourself, because you, the judge, practice the very same things. We know that the judgment of God rightly falls on those who practice such things. Do you suppose, O man—you who judge those who practice such things and yet do them yourself—that you will escape the judgment of God? Or do you presume on the riches of his kindness and forbearance and patience, not knowing that God's kindness is meant to lead you to repentance? But because of your hard and impenitent heart you are storing up wrath for yourself on the day of wrath when God's righteous judgment will be revealed (2:1-5 ESV).

Paul's critique in this passage is inexplicable without a brief description of Pharisaic Judaism's attitude towards Gentiles in the first century and its influence on Jewish Christianity.

First-century Judaism was a diverse society composed of three major "parties": Pharisees, Sadducees, and Essenes. Notwithstanding this diversity, all Jews agreed that their identity rested on three non-negotiable beliefs: (1) that the Jewish people were divinely elected as the chosen of God; (2) that Abraham, the exclusive father of the Jews, was God's partner in the covenant that involved God's gift of land; and (3) that circumcision was the sign of their covenant status (Gen. 12:1-3; 15:1-21; 17:1-14).[25] Pharisees and Essenes believed that people were righteous if they obeyed God's law—moral, ceremonial, and the oral traditions. Such people were not sinners based on their zealous keeping of the law.[26] In other words, Pharisees and Essenes taught and practiced *righteousness by works.* They believed that righteousness was attained through adherence to a legal standard.

Pharisaic Judaism in the first century was influenced by the teachings of two scholars: Hillel and Shammai. In the time of Jesus and Paul, Judaism was dominated by conservative Pharisees who followed the teachings and practices of the school of Shammai. After the destruction of the Temple in A.D. 70, the moderate school of Hillel became dominant. It is worth noting that Saul of Tarsus, later Paul the Apostle, studied under Gamaliel I, the grandson of Hillel, and became an ardent proponent of Pharisaic dogma (Acts 22:3; Phil. 3:4-6).

In Pharisaic thought, there were three classes of humanity: the unrighteous Gentiles, who were predestined for hell; the sinners, who were Jews not in full compliance with the law; and the observant Pharisees, who followed the law.[27] By the time of Jesus, there were several thousand Pharisees. Their name meant "pure" or "separated," and they followed an oral tradition that was not based in Scripture (Mk. 7:1-13; Mt. 15:1-9). They added to Torah a number of new ritual obligations that were designed to produce holiness. Pharisees attempted to expand to all spheres of life the ceremonial purity associated with the temple. The attitude of the Pharisaic Jew is epitomized in Jesus' parable of the Pharisee and the tax collector praying in the temple. The Pharisee prays, "God, I thank you that I am not like other people—greedy, unrighteous, adulterous, or even like this tax collector. I fast twice a week; I give a tenth of everything I get" (Lk. 18:11-12 HCSB).[28]

Paul's critique of Judaism rests primarily on a backdrop of the attitude towards Gentiles among the followers of the conservative school of Shammai. They believed that only the Hebrew descendants of Abraham were beloved by God. They did not attempt to convert Gentiles because salvation was thought to be restricted to Jews. These attitudes led the followers of Shammai to hate Gentiles, characterizing them as ritually unclean. Jews in Palestine particularly hated Samaritans, who were half–Jews (Jn. 4:9). Due to their popularity with the people, the followers of Shammai were able to pass 18 edicts that forced separation between Jews and Gentiles. Although the actual edicts have been lost, it is believed they forbade Jews from entering the houses of Gentiles and taught that Jews were ritually defiled by eating with, or even purchasing food from, Gentiles. The Apostle Peter, for example, cites the Pharisaic tradition prohibiting a Jew to associate with a Gentile (Acts 10:28).[29]

In the time of Paul, the followers of Shammai were extremely harsh and rigid in their religious prohibitions, even more so than their founder. Intensely patriotic, they hated the Romans and banned any association with anyone who contributed to Roman power or influence. While devotees of the school of Hillel generally encouraged the conversion of Gentiles to Judaism, Shammai's adherents were especially hard on proselytes, and discouraged conversions among the heathen Gentiles.[30]

Although attitudes towards Romans were diverse among the various groups, ranging from the pragmatic accommodation of the Sadducees to the revolutionary hostility of the Zealots, Jews resented all occupying forces—Assyrian, Babylonian, and Persian. Yet, the intense Jewish hatred of the Gentiles began with their reaction to the imposition of Hellenistic culture on Palestine by the Seleucids, particularly the actions of Antiochus Epiphanes IV (ca. 215-164 B.C.), a Syrian Seleucid tyrant who plundered the Temple in 169 B.C. Antiochus attempted to prohibit Jewish religious practices such as Sabbath-keeping, circumcision, and dietary restrictions. Under the leadership of the Maccabees, Jews revolted successfully against the Seleucids from 167 to 163 B.C.[31]

With this background, we can return to Paul's critique of what is most likely Pharisaic judgmentalism (2:1-5). Using the conjunction "therefore," Paul connects his present criticism to what was just said, especially his description of Gentile depravity (1:29-32). Employing diatribe, Paul creates an imaginary opponent: a Jewish moralist. Then, he makes a four-part case against Pharisaic judgmentalism. Paul first upbraids his imaginary opponent, "O man," for presuming to judge the Gentiles. Like the Gentiles who have no excuse for their sin in light of God's self-revelation in creation (1:20), Paul now suggests, possibly based on Torah, that this Jewish moralist, who possibly represents every Jew who judges Gentiles, should know better (Dt. 1:17; 16:19). Clearly, Paul implies that Jews as well as Gentiles are without excuse before God.

Paul next provides the evidence. He argues that his Jewish opponent's judgment of the Gentiles is invalid because "you the judge are doing the very same things" (2:1). In other words, Paul points out that the moralist himself is a sinner. In fact, for Paul, the sin of the moralist is worse because he does not practice what he preaches. Here, Paul indirectly charges his opponent with hypocrisy, a charge that Paul expands on later in this argument (2:17-24).

Then, with the words, "We know that the judgment of God rightly falls on those who practice such things" (2:2), Paul, assuming Jewish agreement with this point, reiterates the sinfulness of Gentile living and the certainty of God's judgment (1:18, 29-32). It is important to observe that when he says "we know," to the hypothetical moralist, Paul for the first time alludes to the fact that Jews are in possession of God's self-revelation through the written law (3:2; 9:4; cf. 1:2). Yet, Paul uses two rhetorical questions to drive home the disconnect between Jewish *knowledge* and their *actions.*

Paul's first question, "Do you imagine . . . that when you judge them that do such things and yet do them yourself, you will escape the judgment of God?" (2:3), is designed to emphasize Pharisaic hypocrisy and establish the principle that neither Jew nor Gentile will escape divine judgment. To say that Jews "do such things," does not imply that Jews engage in homosexuality or overt idolatry, rather that they are guilty of some of the attitudes decried in 1:29-31.[32] With his second question, "Or do you presume on the riches of his kindness and forbearance and patience, not knowing that God's kindness is meant to lead you to repentance?", Paul reminds the Jewish moralist of God's mercy, i.e., kindness and forbearance, towards the Jewish people (2:4; cf. 9:14-18; 11:32). Moreover, Paul chides his opponent for not appreciating the fact that God's mercy towards Jews should have produced repentance, literally, "a change of life," instead of judgmentalism towards Gentiles.

Finally, Paul identifies what he believes is the source of Pharisaic judgmentalism and its consequences. He accuses the Jewish moralist of having a "hard and impenitent heart" (2:5) The sense of the metaphor is to reject repentance, to refuse to turn to God.[33] It should not be missed that Paul's "heart" language is reminiscent of his earlier description of the source of pagan Gentile sin (1:21).

Paul ends his present discussion with his hypothetical opponent by warning that Pharisaic judgmentalism will result in God's wrath on the "day of judgment," clearly an allusion to the final judgment. Why will Jews, like Gentiles, experience the wrath of God? Gentiles have sinned by attempting to *dismiss* God; while, by judging the Gentiles, Jews have attempted to *diminish* God by usurping a prerogative reserved only to God. Thus, Paul ends with an implied contrast. Whereas God's *righteous* judgment is revealed in the final judgment (2:16), all Jewish judgment is unrighteous! Although Paul introduces the issue of Pharisaic judgmentalism using a hypothetical teaching device, he later makes it clear that the problem is real. Believing Jews in Rome are judging Christian Gentiles on issues ranging from the Sabbath to laws of ritual purity (14:10-23).

Accountable Then

Paul uses a cryptic argument to drive home his point against Jewish judgmentalism (2:6-10). He compares the "righteous" person with the "unrighteous" one, and asserts that in the final judgment, both will be judged based on their works. Is Paul here contradicting himself by suggesting that people are judged based on their works? No, not at all. Paul has already briefly established his understanding of "the obedience of faith," i.e., the faith that believers are to live by (1:5, 17), and will further demonstrate that genuine faith issues in submission to the Lordship of Christ (6:1-11). Spirit-enabled submission to Christ results in receiving the imparted righteousness of Christ. No doubt this is what Paul means by his dictum, "For we are his workmanship, created in Christ Jesus for good works, which God prepared beforehand that we would walk in them" (Eph. 2:10; cf. 8:5-30; 1 Cor. 12:1-2; Gal. 5:6, 16-26; Phil. 2:12-13).

Thus, works produced by the Spirit of Christ, the fruit of the Spirit, will be commended in the judgment, while *all unrighteousness,* including self-righteousness, produced through human effort, will be condemned. Both Jews and Gentiles will be condemned or commended using the same divine criterion (cf. Gal. 5:22-23).

It is important to observe that Paul appeals to God's judgment as the standard. He explains that although the Jewish moralist might be partial in his judgment, focusing on the conduct of immoral Gentiles, yet God is impartial, favoring neither Jew nor Gentile (2:11). In context, Paul is subtly warning the judgmental Christian Jews in Rome that their works will receive God's final condemnation (cf. 14:10-12). Finally, in his critique of Jewish attitudes towards Gentiles, Paul seems to bring his argument even closer to home (2:12-16). For the first time, he introduces the term *nomos*, "law," a subject to which he often returns throughout the letter. At this point, Paul heightens his claim related to divine impartiality. He explains that Gentiles and Jews will be judged based on the type of revelation received. Paul has already established that Gentiles would be judged based on God's self-disclosure through His creation (1:19-21). Now, he reiterates the claim that Gentiles have no excuse before God even though they have not had access to God's written law. Here, it seems that Paul is using the term law as a metaphor for the Old Testament (1:2), sometimes called "special revelation." Thus, he is able to conclude that Gentiles "who sinned without the law, will also perish without the law," while Jews "who sinned under the law, will be judged by the law" (2:12).

Paul reaffirms that all will be judged finally based on their works (2:6). Then using hypothetical language, he makes what would be viewed by any first-century Jew as an astonishing claim. He argues that Gentiles, who have not had access to God's written law, yet who act in keeping with the law's requirement, will not suffer disadvantage. Indeed, Paul asserts, "The law is written in their hearts" (2:15; cf. Jer. 31:33). Paul later develops his understanding of the need to experience the internalization of the law through the power of the Spirit at several critical points in his letter (2:25-29; 5:5; 6:17). What is astonishing in this passage is that Paul now applies this expectation of internalization of the law by Jews to Gentiles who have never received the written law of God.

He concludes his condemnation of Jewish judgmentalism by pointing out that God will be the final judge. It will be God who judges what *all people* have kept secret. According to Paul's gospel, this work of final or executive judgment will be accomplished through God's Son, Christ Jesus (2:16). It should be noted that according to Paul, the gospel includes both the announcement of salvation based on faith in Christ and the condemnation of sin. Believers, corporately and individually, are accountable to God in Christ. This raises the question, why does God the Father give final judgment to God the Son? In other words, why does Paul cast Christ as both Savior and Judge? (1:16-17; 3:21-26).

We must begin by establishing that Paul's assertion of Christ as judge is not limited to Romans. He makes the same claim more forcefully in 2 Corinthians. Paul writes, "For we must all appear before the judgment seat of Christ, so that each one may receive what is due for what he has done in the body, whether good or evil" (5:10; cf. Acts 10:42; 17:31; Rev. 19:11-21).

Paul's understanding of Christ as Judge is informed by the Old Testament and most likely by Jesus' own teaching. The Old Testament envisions the Messiah as a judge. The book of Judges chronicles a series of charismatic leaders who delivered the children of Israel from oppression due to their unfaithfulness to God. Christ is the antitype for these typical judges; He will bring eternal deliverance from sin to those who trust in Him. Isaiah 11:1-4 is a Messianic text that tells of One who will come from the stock of Jesse in Spirit of the Lord, a righteous Judge who will judge impartially and with equity. Jesus Christ is the fulfillment of this prophecy: the final perfect Judge.[34]

In this, Paul echoes Jesus when he states that the Father has given the authority to execute judgment to the Son. Jesus states that judgment has been given to the Son because He is the Son of Man, and as such shares human nature with His creation. Therefore, Christ is able to identify with human temptation, yet He took on human flesh without sin (Jn. 5:19-30; cf. 2 Cor. 5:21; Heb. 4:15).

Why does Paul emphasize that Christ will be the final judge? In context, Paul explains that Jewish judgment of Gentiles is improper, because it is based on hypocrisy; Jews are sinners before God. Their improper judgment of Gentiles is based on cultural bias—partiality. Given the situation in Rome, is Paul suggesting that partial judgment based on the ethnicity of the other will be condemned in the final judgment of Christ? On the other hand, Paul observes that God's proper judgment will be administered by a righteous God through God's righteous Son. Unlike Pharisaic judgment, God's final judgment, administered through Christ, is impartial, for Jews with the law, and for Gentiles without the law.

Paul has presented Christ as God's gospel, God's good news. Yet, God's salvation in Christ must include both God's righteousness and God's love, both justice and mercy. God's righteous nature must condemn sin. Before Paul can fully disclose Christ as Savior, he confirms that God's righteous judgment has been given to Christ.

Although it is often misunderstood in Adventism, Christ as Judge will be experienced in two ways. For those who reject God's gift of salvation through Christ, there is condemnation. This is the way that we typically think about final judgment. But for those in Christ who have trusted Him as Savior and Lord, Christ's judgment will be vindication (Jn. 5:22, 24). This truth is at the heart of Paul's assertion, "There is therefore now no condemnation for those who are in Christ Jesus. For the law of the Spirit of life has set you free in Christ Jesus from the law of sin and death" (8:1-2 ESV). Paul's affirmation just before his own death makes the point. "In the future, there is laid up for me the crown of righteousness, which the Lord, the righteous Judge, will award to me on that day; and not only to me, but also to all who have loved His appearing" (2 Tim. 4:8).

As Adventists we must ask: how does our explanation of the "Investigative Judgment" align with this critical insight? Have we focused on the condemnation for those who are not in Christ that is inherent in the judgment and failed to emphasize the vindication of those in Christ?

In summary, Paul is attempting to teach his audience that God's judgment in Christ is impartial, unlike that of the pious Jew, whose judgment of the Gentiles flows from an inherent cultural bias. Jews and Gentiles alike will be saved based on faith in Christ, but judged based on their works (1:17; cf. Eph. 2:10). Paul has made the point that pagan Gentiles experience the "present" judgment of God. Here, Paul makes it clear that both Gentiles and Jews will experience the future tribunal of Christ. In context, could it be that Paul is signaling that God will bring ethnocentric partiality into judgment? Is he subtly establishing the fact that all who practice bias or prejudice against the "other" will stand condemned before Christ in the final day? Does he want to drive home the point that the righteousness of God, i.e., God's wrath, will be revealed against ethnic sin?

Pharisaic Hypocrisy

Paul now moves from Pharisaic Judaism's misguided judgmentalism, and God's response to it, to a withering critique of their hypocrisy (2:17-29). Again using diatribe, Paul fashions the profile of an unbelieving devout Jew of his day, addressed as "You." His sketch exposes nine characteristics of first-century Pharisaic Judaism: the pious Jew (1) takes pride in Jewish identity, (2) finds comfort in the Mosaic law, (3) brags about "his" God, (4) knows the divine will, (5) has the ability to discern what is superior, (6) is trained in the law, (7) is confident of superiority to the "blind" Gentiles, (8) is able to instruct the immature Jew, and (9) has full possession of the knowledge and truth revealed in God's law (2:17-20).

Paul paints the picture of an observant Pharisaic Jew of the first century. This pious Jew is fully confident about his standing before God based on obedience to Torah, written and oral. *He is certain of his identity, message, and mission.* With this portrait, Paul places Jewish cultural pride and its sense of religious superiority on full display. Using colloquial language, we may describe Pharisaic Judaism as having "God in a box."

Paul now deconstructs his profile with four rhetorical questions that expose the hypocrisy of his imaginary opponent. These questions are designed to demonstrate the gap between Pharisaic profession and practice. Paul asks, "You then who teach others, do you not teach yourself? While you preach against stealing, do you steal? You who say that one must not commit adultery, do you commit adultery? You who abhor idols, do you rob temples?" (2:21-22 ESV). With these questions, Paul subtly charges the Pharisaic Judaism of his day with hypocrisy. Then he boldly concludes, "You who boast in the law dishonor God by breaking the law" (2:23; cf. Mt. 23:1-36). For the pious Jew, unbelieving or Christian, Paul's charge would be viewed as scandalous.

Therefore, Paul quotes the Jewish prophet Isaiah to support his negative assessment. "The name of God is blasphemed among the Gentiles because of you" (Is. 52:5). Paul's textual choice has contextual significance. He argues that Judaism has distorted the character of the true God and the nature of His law to such an extent that the pagan Gentile world now reviles the true God (2:24). Given the history of Western Christianity's exploitation based on ethnicity, religious intolerance, and racial prejudice, exemplified by the Crusades, the Spanish Inquisition, chattel slavery, and the Holocaust, one wonders if Paul's assertion can be modified to read, "The name of Jesus Christ is blasphemed among non-Christians because of you?"

It is notable that Paul, an ethnic Jew, criticizes the sin of his own people with honesty and stunning accuracy (cf. 11:1-10). His cultural critique would have been viewed by many Jews as a betrayal of group solidarity. Today, he would have been called a "sell-out." Nevertheless, Paul's willingness to expose the faults of Israel make his criticism of Gentile sin credible. Paul, like the God he serves, is impartial. He is no respecter of persons.

Paul concludes his condemnation of Jewish sinfulness with a complicated argument about circumcision that ends with a startling redefinition of what it means to be a true Jew (2:25-29; 9:6-9). His argument is incomprehensible to a 21st-century reader without an understanding of the meaning of the Jewish practice of circumcision.

As part of the covenant, God required that Abraham and his descendants be circumcised. Thus, circumcision was a *physical sign* of the covenant between God and Abraham (Gen. 17:1-27). In Judaism, circumcision was a symbol of Jewish election. It signified the Jews' special identity as the people of God. Circumcision served as a tangible demarcation between those who belonged to God (Jews) and those who did not (Gentiles).

With this background, Paul's reasoning, although complex, is understandable. Again, employing diatribe, Paul's argument goes something like this. Circumcision has value or significance only for a Jew who keeps the law. Yet, the Pharisaic Jew does not keep the law. He in fact is a lawbreaker (2:17-24). Therefore, because this devout Jew is a lawbreaker, he is no different from a pagan Gentile, who is uncircumcised.

Next, Paul reiterates the hypothetical point made earlier (2:14-15). If a Gentile without the written law keeps the law's requirements—the law written on the heart—then he will in fact be counted by God as a Jew, one of the circumcised. Moreover, the uncircumcised Gentile who keeps the law because it is written in his heart will judge the Jewish lawbreaker. How is this reversal possible? Paul explains: Gentile judgment is appropriate because this Pharisaic Jew has only an external religion based on "the letter of the law," its legal requirements (7:6), and physical circumcision, the external sign of the covenant (2:25-27).

Paul ends with an astonishing redefinition of what it means to be a Jew (2:28-29). He stresses his redefinition by echoing the teaching of Hebrew prophets on the subject of the "circumcision of the heart." In Deuteronomy 30:5-6, Moses wrote,

> The Lord your God will bring you into the land your fathers possessed, and you will take possession of it. He will cause you to prosper and multiply you more than He did your fathers. The Lord your God will circumcise your heart and the hearts of your descendants, and you will love Him with all your heart and all your soul so that you will live.

Here, as a part of Torah, Moses rehearses for the second generation of liberated Jews the covenant promise made with Abraham, Isaac, and Jacob. From the time of Abraham, Jews were required to perform the rite of circumcision themselves as a symbol of the covenant (cf. Ex. 12:44-49).

Now, Moses explains the deeper meaning of physical circumcision. Using "heart" as a metaphor for the place of human motivation, the seat of affection, emotion, desire, he envisions a time when God will circumcise or change the hearts of Jews throughout future generations. Further, Moses says that only this God-produced internal transformation would make it possible for the covenant people to respond to God with love issuing from their hearts and souls, i.e., their entire beings. This God-created change would be essential for the survival of the people so that they would live. It seems that Moses envisions by inspiration a time when physical circumcision, the external sign of being set apart in covenant relationship first given to Abraham, would be overshadowed by the circumcision of the heart. God would initiate internalization of the law as what it means to be set apart wholly to God (cf. 10:5-13; Jer. 31:33; Ezek. 36:26).

It is this Scriptural understanding of heart circumcision that Paul applies. He makes a radical claim by way of contrast. Paul asserts that a false Jew is one whose religion is outward or external. This type of Jew relies on physical circumcision, the external sign of covenant with God. His religion begins and ends with his own legal performance. By contrast, Paul's portrait shows what it means to be a true Jew (2:28-29; cf. Gal. 5:2-3).

Paul's description has three elements. Being a true Jew is primarily an inward or internal condition: transformation from the inside out. Next, Paul explains that to be a true Jew is chiefly a matter of heart. Paul argues for the necessity of heart circumcision performed by the Spirit of God. The spirit of the law is thus internalized. Paul will emphasize that this transformative work of the Spirit is diametrically opposed to transformation based on the letter, i.e., legal performance based on law keeping (7:6; 2 Cor. 3:6). Here, Paul lays the predicate for his explanation of how both corporate and individual sanctification are accomplished: both are wrought through the Spirit of Christ and are a work of the heart (10:6-13).

Finally, a true Jew does not seek praise or recognition from humans. His praise is from God. In context, Paul builds on this redefinition of true Jewish identity to establish that both believing Gentiles and Jews together are in reality God's covenant people. Although this redefinition is taken for granted by Christians in our time, for Jews of the first century, Paul's contention would have been viewed as outrageous, a betrayal of Jewish unique identity and privilege. Paul's redefinition of what it means to be a Jew leads us to wonder if we need to redefine what it means to be a true Adventist. Would our redefinition rest on the idea that a true Adventist is first and foremost one who lives a life of radical obedience to Christ in response to His love and then shares that love with others?

Now, in anticipation of Jewish objections to his depiction of sinfulness and divine judgment, Paul again trots out his imaginary opponent (3:1-8). Using what seems to be almost a "sleight of hand" argument, Paul poses a hypothetical Q and A with the imaginary opponent to establish an important principle for his audience in Rome. Paul's rhetorical goal is to assert the covenantal faithfulness of God to Israel in spite of the failure of Judaism to remain true to God (cf. 9:1 - 11:36).

Paul's argument is both developmental and dialogical. It moves from anticipated question to his response. In verse 1, the imaginary opponent raises two questions: "So what advantage does the Jew have? Or what is the benefit of circumcision?" Paul responds by arguing that the entire Jewish nation, through the covenant made first with Abraham and his descendants, had one decided advantage: the Jewish people "were entrusted with the spoken words of God" (3:2). With the expression, literally, "the sayings of God," Paul again refers to special revelation, and seems to suggest that the possession of Scripture gave Jews a decided advantage over Gentiles along with its concomitant responsibilities (1:2; 2:1-16; Ps. 147:19-20).

As a rejoinder, the opponent raises two additional questions. "What then? If some did not believe, will their unbelief cancel God's faithfulness?" (3:3). It seems clear that Paul places these questions in the mouth of his opponent to make a foundational claim on which he later builds (cf. 9:1 - 11:36). His response is unambiguous. Paul states emphatically that God is faithful in spite of Jewish unfaithfulness. Paul once and for all establishes what is for him an ontological fact: a statement of being. *God is true*, "even if everyone is a liar."

Paul quotes David to support his claim of divine faithfulness in response to the unfaithfulness of the Jews. "So that you may be justified in your words and triumph when you judge" (3:4; Ps. 51:4). In Psalm 51, David, as part of his confession after his sin with Bathsheba, acknowledges that in light of his own sin, any judgment by God is just.[35] By using this passage from the Old Testament, Paul not only bolsters his claim about God's faithfulness but also reasserts the rightness of the divine judgment against Pharisaic Judaism (2:1-5). As stated, Paul later develops the principle of the irrevocable faithfulness of God to Israel in order to challenge any actual or potential arrogance on the part of Christian Gentiles towards believing Jews in Rome (11:13-32).

Paul continues the imaginary interrogation by having his opponent raise two more questions in direct response to the claim of divine faithfulness. "But if our unrighteousness demonstrates the righteousness of God, what shall we say? That

God is unrighteous to inflict wrath?" (3:5). While acknowledging that to speak about God's unrighteousness makes no sense, and is merely for the sake of argument ("I am speaking in human terms") Paul seems to anticipate a possible convoluted question about his claim of divine faithfulness in response to Jewish sin. Some might contend that if Jewish unfaithfulness to the covenant serves to show divine faithfulness, then would not God be unjust in His judgment of the Jews?

In response, Paul uses an emphatic negation, "By no means!" and raises his own rhetorical question, "For otherwise, how will God judge the world?" This negation is designed to dispense with even the possibility of divine injustice (3:6). Nevertheless, Paul has his opponent posit a final question that continues the earlier absurd line of reasoning. The opponent asks, "But if by my lie God's truth is amplified to His glory, why am I also still judged as a sinner?"

Paul seems to sidestep his own hypothetical question to address an objection being made by actual opponents. "And why not say, just as some people slanderously claim we say, 'Let us do what is evil so that good may come?' Their condemnation is just" (3:8). Here, Paul moves from the imaginary to the real. He signals to believers in Rome, especially Jewish Christians, that the larger Jewish community, both unbelieving Pharisaic Jews and believing "Judaizers," finds his understanding of the gospel objectionable, especially his understanding of the role of the law in how righteousness is achieved (10:4; cf. 1 Thess. 2:14-16; Gal. 5:11-12; Acts 15:1-2).

There can be no doubt that Paul is now referring to what he views as slanderous accusations being made by Christian Jews who oppose his teachings. In the present discussion, Paul opines about being accused by some of antinomianism, i.e., opposed to the moral law. It seems that this is an actual charge leveled by his Jewish Christian opponents. Paul appears to make reference to the same accusation later in the letter when he asks, "What then are we to say? Should we continue in sin in order that grace may abound?" Again, he answers with an emphatic, "by no means!" (6:1-2; cf. 6:15).

Modern readers must understand that Paul is not paranoid. He is not imagining things. Before writing his letter to Roman Christians, Paul has been in a pitched battle with Jewish Christians, the so-called Judaizers. Paul's letter to the Galatians, written before Romans, reflects his ongoing conflict with the Judaizers (Gal. 5:12; 6:13).

Who were the Judaizers? They were Jewish Christians during the first century who sought to impose a traditional Jewish lifestyle and Jewish rituals on Gentile Christians. Not only did the Judaizers intend that Gentile Christians follow Jewish customs, Judaizers promoted the notion that salvation was attained in this way. Remember that all of the earliest Christians were Jews. Their males were circumcised, they practiced kosher dietary laws and regulations regarding ceremonial purity, they obeyed the oral tradition, and they worshiped in synagogues scattered throughout the Greco-Roman world and at the Temple in Jerusalem until its destruction in 70 A.D.

With the expansion of Christianity to the Gentile world, based on evangelism and persecution, Jewish Christians faced a serious question: was it necessary for a Gentile convert to first become a Jew in order to become a Christian? Those Jewish Christians, many of whom were Pharisees, who gave an affirmative answer to this question came to be known as the "circumcision party" (Acts 11:2; Gal. 2:12). They were generally followers of the conservative school of Shammai. Their position was vigorously opposed by others, such as Paul and Barnabas.

The merits of each position were debated at the "Jerusalem Council," and a compromise that required Gentile Christians to abstain from meat offered to idols, eating blood and blood saturated meat, and unchastity was reached (Acts 15:4-12, 23-29). Circumcision was not held to be necessary for Gentile Christians. In spite of the decision by the Jerusalem Council, the Judaizers or circumcision party continued to be active in the early Church, encountering and opposing Paul on his missionary journeys (Gal. 5:12; 6:13; 1 Cor. 5:12; 6:13; Phil. 3:2-3; Col. 2:16-17). In early Christianity, the Judaizers were sufficiently powerful to cause Peter and Barnabas to separate themselves from Gentile Christians in Antioch (Gal. 2:1-10). The apostle Paul was the most vocal opponent of the Judaizers.

As Jewish Christianity gradually decreased, the impetus of the Judaizers, the insistence that Gentile Christians must first become Jews in order to secure salvation, ceased. Jewish Christianity was significantly weakened by the destruction of Jerusalem and the ill-fated Bar Kochba revolt (132-135 A.D.) when Jewish Christians were persecuted by the insurgents.[36]

The theological problem that the Judaizers posed was their attempt to maintain both obedience to the law—Torah and the oral traditions—and faith in Christ as equally necessary for righteousness and therefore salvation. The doctrine of the Judaizers was erroneous in that it tried to mix grace and works.

Christian Jews in the first century were engaged in a sorting out process around issues of "continuity," what remains related to Torah—particularly ceremonial requirements—and "discontinuity," what is discarded in light of the new covenant made through the person and work of Jesus Christ (2 Cor. 5:16-17; Gal. 2:1-13). It just may be that Paul is attempting to head off possible objections to his gospel among Jewish believers in Rome.

Paul ends his imaginary dialogue with an imprecation directed to the actual opponents of his gospel. He says, "Their condemnation is deserved" (cf. Gal. 5:11-12). We should remember that Paul's overarching purpose is to bring about reconciliation and unity among the ethnically divided Gentile and Jewish Christians in Rome. How does his description of Jewish sin serve this purpose?

As with his criticism of the pagan Gentile world, Paul maintains that God's present wrath is also being visited on the unbelieving Jewish world. The Jewish minority in Rome is reminded that in spite of their covenantal advantages, Jews too have rejected the sovereignty of God and stand under divine judgment. By thus removing the basis for Jewish cultural pride, Paul undercuts any grounds for Jewish judgmentalism. He redefines what it means to be a Jew in a movement from ethnicity to the condition of the heart: a heart shaped by the Spirit.

The 21st-century application of Paul's admonition to the Roman Christians is both inescapable and disturbing. One of the most deceptive forms of idolatry is the idolatry of good things (cf. Mt. 7:21-23; Jn. 6:63). We are all aware of the possibility of the idolatry of bad things, such as fornication, or of neutral things, such as money. But are we aware of the potential idolatry of good things: making a good thing the ultimate thing? We know that anything that occupies the center of one's existence besides Jesus Christ has become an idol. Are some of us as Adventists, like the Pharisaic Jews of Paul's time, so devoted to law-keeping that it has become an idol? Later, Paul accuses Pharisaic Judaism in general, and the Judaizers in particular, of idolizing and thus perverting God's law (7:7-23).

While we were teaching a group of Adventist church members to give Bible studies, one woman became upset with the idea that salvation was based on faith in the merits of Christ rather than law-keeping. She said, "If I don't have the law, what do I have?" The response, "You have Christ," did not address her concerns. She left the meeting in tears and never returned to the group.

The Guilt of All Humanity

Now we come to Paul's final comments in this crucial section of his letter (3:9-20). Here, he depicts sin as that which is rooted in a cultural consensus—shared values, thought, and practices—all in opposition to God's self-revelation. For example, Paul portrays Gentile sin as that characterized by an idolatry that rejects the existence of the true God, resulting in both arrogance and moral depravity. On the other hand, he describes Jews as sharing a self-righteous judgmentalism resulting in a blind hypocrisy. Paul views sin as a power that exercises dominion, not just over the individual, but also over groups who embrace a common cultural identity. Paul is well aware of the danger of conformity to the "pattern of the world," to Greco-Roman culture (12:1-2). In fact, as we will see, Paul is aware of the fact that all sin, especially sin embedded in culture cannot be broken through human effort (8:1-30).

Mimicking God's impartiality, Paul characterizes sin as being common to all humans, not just the sin of Gentiles, or even of Jews, but sin as a component of the human condition. Sin is common to all. But what is Paul calling sin? Sin, for Paul, is falling short of God's creative intent. Sin is the congenital condition of all humanity, bequeathed by Adam. Grant Osborne puts it this way: All people have inherited corruption from Adam and then have participated in that sin. Therefore, they are guilty from two directions—the sinful nature inherited from Adam (passive sin) and their personal participation in that via their own sins (active sin).[37] Paul describes sin, both Gentile and Jewish, as group sin: sin embedded in their respective cultures.

More importantly, Paul views sin not just forensically, or legally, but personally. It is a breach of the essential relationship between human beings and God. It is a fundamental rejection of God's sovereignty, nature, and purpose. For Gentiles, sin is a rejection of God's self-revelation in creation. For Jews, sin is a rejection of God's self-revelation in Scripture. Moreover, falling short of God's creative intent is to fail to love both God and neighbors (Gen. 2:18; Dt. 6:5; Lev. 19:18). Could it be that this is why Jesus couples the two commands, "love God . . . love your neighbor as yourself," as what it really means to fulfill the law? (Mt. 22:37-40; cf. 13:10).

Ultimately, sin is the rejection of God's self-revelation in Christ, especially God's selfless love demonstrated in the cross. Paul later criticizes both Christian Gentiles and Jews for mutual improper judgment within the context of their religious squabbles. His conclusion: "Whatever does not proceed from faith [in Christ] is sin" (14:23 ESV).

Closing Arguments

Like a prosecutor giving a closing argument, Paul now concludes his deconstruction of Jewish superiority over Gentiles in matters of righteousness by raising two final questions and then giving his typical emphatic response. Both questions and responses are designed to enhance his leveling strategy in Rome. He writes, "What then? Are we better than they? Not at all; for we have already charged that both Jews and Greeks are all under sin" (3:9 NASB). It is important to observe that Paul here begins his final charge of human sinfulness by reversing the order of culpability (cf. 1:19:32). With the question, "Are we better than they?" Paul identifies himself as an ethnic Jew. Yet, following the impartial example of God (2:11), he indicts his own people first. Paul is no doubt aware of the responsibility that comes with spiritual advantage (3:1-2; cf. Lk. 12:48). Again the question, why does Paul find it necessary to name Gentile and Jewish sin in his quest for reconciliation and unity in Rome?

Later, Paul declares that the believing community is not immune to sin, i.e., life according to the flesh. It is an ever present danger for those in Christ (8:5-17). Yet, for Paul sin to be resisted, must be named, constantly exposed, whether it be individual or group sin (Eph. 4:15; cf. 1 Jn. 1:9). For example, we have already observed that Peter has embraced the oral tradition of the Pharisees related to ritual impurity caused by entering the house of a Gentile (Acts 10:28). Later, Peter, who had enjoyed table fellowship with Christian Gentiles, separated himself when members of the circumcision party (Judaizers) came to Antioch. Paul publicly names Peter's sin: his ethnocentric behavior. As an apostle of Christ, Peter is misrepresenting the gospel of Jesus Christ. It is not accidental that Paul's correction of Peter is preserved in Scripture. Paul calls sin by its right name, notwithstanding his cultural location (Gal. 2:11-14). More important, Paul names sin to establish the necessity of Christ's continuous grace in the lives of believers to free them from the continuous threat of sin.

Paul's purpose in exposing this common heritage is neither abstract nor theoretical. He believes that Gentile cultural arrogance and Jewish judgmentalism are by-products of their ethnocentric bias (cf. 11:13-24; 14:1-4). Without using the modern term ethnocentrism, Paul suggests that ethnic bias embedded in culture is a virulent form of sin that is at the core of Roman division. Paul's critique of sin raises several questions. Why is there no suggestion in the 28 fundamental beliefs of the Seventh-day Adventist Church[38] that ethnic, racial, tribal, or caste bias is sin? Why is there no clear Adventist "theology" that exposes ethnocentrism as violence against the person and work of Christ and antithetical to life in His body?

Nevertheless, so that neither Jews nor Gentiles in Rome would question the validity of his charge, Paul stacks seven passages from the Old Testament to support his indictment of universal human sinfulness. One should not miss the comprehensive scope or the inclusive nature of Paul's charges.

> There is no one righteous, not even one. There is no one who understands; there is no one who seeks God. All have turned away; all alike have become useless. There is no one who does what is good, not even one. Their throat is an open grave; they deceive with their tongues. Vipers' venom is under their lips. Their mouth is full of cursing and bitterness. Their feet are swift to shed blood; ruin and wretchedness are in their paths, and the path of peace they have not known. There is no fear of God before their eyes (3:10-18; cf. Ps. 14:1-3; 53:1-3; Ps. 5:9; Ps. 140:3; Ps. 10:7; Is. 59:7-8; Ps. 36:1).

There can be no doubt that Paul wants to drive home the point that Gentile and Jewish believers share a common heritage of sin, with or without the law, plain and simple.

Yet, in what might seem to be a digression from the thrust of his closing argument about universal sin, Paul returns to the subject of Judaism and the law (3:19-20). He makes two points: the first is to reiterate an important claim, the second is to lay a foundation for future clarification concerning the law (cf. 7:7-23). While restating that his Jewish kinsmen, "those under the law," have knowledge of the written law they possess, Paul maintains nevertheless that Gentiles and Jews, indeed the whole world, stand under God's judgment (3:19). Moreover, all will be speechless when arraigned in the divine court. His argument has come full circle (cf. 1:18).

Finally, building on his evidence from the Old Testament of *innate* universal sin and its resulting hopelessness (3:9-18), Paul asserts that "no one," neither Gentile nor Jew "will be justified before (God) by works of the law." Here and elsewhere in his letter, Paul uses the phrase "works of the law" as a pejorative for any attempt to secure righteousness based on obedience to the law (3:27-28; cf. 9:11, 32; 11:6). Paul views righteousness by works as a fatal flaw in Pharisaic Judaism and part of the reason why most of his Jewish kinsmen have rejected a gospel that announces Messianic salvation as a free gift (3:21-26; 10:1-4). He has already stated that "the just shall live by faith" (1:17). Here, he begins his clarification about the role of God's law in salvation with the words, "for through the law comes the knowledge of sin" (3:20).

If, as we believe, Paul is referring to both the moral as well as the ceremonial law, then we can begin to understand Jewish opposition to his teachings. Yet, the disruptive nature of his words, especially for a Jew (unbelieving or believing) living in the first century, can only be understood against the historical backdrop of Jewish thinking about the role of the law that developed in the era sometimes called the "Second Temple Period" (515 B.C. - 70 A.D.).

The subject of the law was fraught with confusion in Second Temple Judaism because of the different sects that were operative at this time; yet, in spite of this diversity, all Jews associated obedience to Torah as essential to righteousness and salvation. In addition, by the first century Jews had conflated the moral law, the ceremonial law, and the oral Torah, i.e., the traditions of the elders. Eventually, rabbinic Judaism would develop 613 commandments (365 negative and 248 positive) around the law designed to provide a hedge that would prevent any possibility of law-breaking. These traditions were in opposition to trusting in God for righteousness. For Paul, one of the primary functions of God's law is to provide a knowledge of sin. On this and many other points, Paul had issues with both believing and unbelieving Jews of his day.[39]

With his description of the sinful nature of the human condition, Paul destroys the idea of ethnic superiority (especially the Jewish sense of religio-ethnic superiority) by positing a common heritage of sin. Both Gentiles and Jews have fallen short of the glory of God. Thus, Paul proclaims that Gentiles and Jews alike are in need of a Savior.

Paul summarizes for the Roman believers the human condition they share. Although believers are justified or reckoned righteous through Christ, they are still vulnerable to conformity to the world, that is, fallen human culture, with its values, beliefs, and practices, whether Gentile or Jewish. Believers are to resist cultural norms through the power of the indwelling Spirit. The Spirit destroys the pernicious consequences of the fall and the reign of sin by producing the reign of Christ in the individual believer and the believing community. With this necessity clearly established, Paul now turns to justification through Christ alone—the essence of his gospel.

So What? Ethnic Warfare in the Northeastern Conference: An Eyewitness Account [40]

The following narrative is a verbatim account from a pastor who was present at the Northeastern Conference of Seventh-day Adventists Constituency Meeting.

There is an invisible line dividing the Northeastern Conference that becomes visible every four years when constituents come together to vote in officers. Sadly, this line has existed for quite some time. In this particular region, the demographics have shifted multiple times. At its inception in the 1940s the Northeastern Conference was predominantly African American. Later, a large wave of immigrants made their new home in the Northeastern Conference, and as a result, the balance of power started to shift. African Americans became the minority, which remains true to this day. Some Caribbean constituents had vowed to never allow an African American to be president again, claiming that they, African Americans, have plenty of other conferences where they can serve as president. Caribbean dominance lasted from 2000 to 2012.

Currently, another shift has taken place: language groups (Franco-Haitian, Hispanic, and Lusophone [Portuguese]) now make up one-third of the conference constituency. The largest of the language groups is Franco-Haitian, then Hispanic, followed by the Lusophone. Unfortunately, the different groups within Northeastern Conference have not become united in Christ. With each demographic shift, there has been a corresponding "culture war" for power, the most recent being that between the English-speaking (Caribbean) delegates and the Franco-Haitian delegates.

In June of 2012 the Northeastern Conference delegates elected the first Haitian president. On one side of the invisible line were delegates who opposed the idea of a Haitian president because of the perceived threat of a shift of power. Other opposing delegates questioned the qualifications of the nominee or believed that the nominating committee was biased.

On the other side of the line, language groups rallied behind their nominee. Throughout the day pronouns that highlighted the divide, "we" and "you," were used. The Franco-Haitian nominee eventually won, voicing the refrain, "It's our time." There was an eruption and delegates began cheering as if at a sporting event. A large number of delegates left after the brief celebration. However, controversy arose due to the manner in which the vote was taken, and so it appeared that there would be a need for another vote. Many of the delegates who had left found their way back. Ultimately, the original name was carried, much to the dismay of many delegates.

Pandemonium broke out at the reading of the final vote. Some delegates lifted chairs into the air as a cacophony of cheers filled the auditorium. Emotions were boiling over as delegates remained at appointed microphones requesting the attention of the chairman in a last-ditch effort to overturn the vote. Certain individuals even spoke over the prayer that was offered for the newly elected president and his family. Some senior pastors commented that they had never witnessed such an ugly meeting in all of the decades during which they had been members of the Northeastern Conference.

The emotions that boiled over on that day in 2012 would simmer during the next four years, increasing in temperature as the 2016 constituency meeting approached. Some members of the English-speaking delegation were determined to undo the result of the previous constituency meeting.

The 2016 meeting was a reaction to the 2012 meeting. A new name was nominated to serve as president—an individual of the English-speaking (Caribbean) delegation. The name was sent back, but then brought back by the nominating committee for a vote. The chairman called for a vote, which was taken by secret ballot, and the nominee was voted down.

The nominating committee went back into session and brought back another name. This individual was an African American. It should be noted that this individual was considered by many members of the conference as a candidate for president prior to the 2012 constituency meeting; but some believed him to be unfit to lead the Conference based solely on his ethnic background. When his name was read at the 2016 meeting, there was a unified negative response of "NO!" from one side of the invisible line.

The chairman called for a vote, which was again taken by secret ballot. While the vote was being tabulated, a senior pastor of the conference stood at a microphone and began berating the chairman in a most disgusting manner with a spirit that excited many while offending many others. He was almost removed. It should be noted that the spirit in which he spoke was not of Christ, to put it mildly. He recommended suspending the rules of order due to the opinion that the nominating committee was biased towards the incumbent Haitian president. The chairman agreed to entertain that motion once the vote was taken for the motion on the floor—the motion for the second recommendation of the nominating committee. The totals were read and the name was voted down with the number of those opposed being 666. The chairman communicated a sense of amazement as he read the number, and he chose to read it as "6-6-6." There was another mini-celebration.

From that point forward, it was voted to suspend the rules of order and eventually the incumbent Haitian executive officers were returned to office. After being elected, the president was allowed to recommend changes to the executive committee of the conference. Names of individuals who did not support the incumbent were removed and replaced with names of other individuals who had supported the incumbent.

Sadly, it seems as though there is no end in sight to the "cultural war" that rages within this conference. Man was in control of that constituency meeting, and God let them know by the vote that totaled 666 that our meeting was anti-Christ. At the end of the meeting, it was ignorantly stated that God's will had been done, a statement made from spiritual blindness. One day, God's will shall be done, but it was not done on that day.

According to other eyewitness accounts, at the height of the conflict, one of the delegates came to the microphone and suggested prayer; the delegate was shouted down by some of the others. Prayer was not offered.

How could this happen in Adventism? Because we have become so indifferent to group sin, some will say that this is simply "politics," "business as usual," or "boys being boys." Yet, these attitudes and behaviors must be named for what they are. They are sin, corporate sin, and as such, are demonic, an affront to the gospel of Jesus Christ. It should be acknowledged that these ethnic wars did not originate with Franco-Haitians. It has been an aspect of the politicization of God's work in this conference from its inception.

Moreover, many people of color, especially African Americans, sometimes act as if ethnocentrism, expressed as racism, is the exclusive province of whites. Although it cannot be understated that those of European descent have special culpability in this area, the fact is that ethnocentrism, and its corollary, prejudice, are basic to the human condition. They constitute sin, and as we will see, for Paul, the only solution is a Savior.

---

[1] Grant R. Osborne (ed.). *Romans.* The IVP New Testament Commentary Series. Downers Grove, IL: InterVarsity Press, 2004.

[2] Manfred T. Brauch. *Hard Sayings of Paul.* Downers Grove, IL: InterVarsity Press, 1989.

[3] C. N. Trueman. Romulus and Remus. August 16, 2016. *The History Learning Site.* www.historylearningsite.

[4] Bertrand Russell. *A History of Western Philosophy.* New York, New York: Simon and Schuster, 1945.

[5] Carol Poster. Protagoras. *Internet Encyclopedia of Philosophy.* iep.utm.edu.

[6] Jonathan J. Mark. Protagoras. *Ancient History Encyclopedia.* Published on September 2, 2009. *ancient.eu.*

[7] Poster.

[8] Protagoras. *Great Philosophers.* oregonstate.edu.

[9] Ibid.

[10] Ian Rutherford. Canonizing the Pantheon: The Dodekatheon in Greek Religion and its Origins. In Jan N. Bremmer and Andrew Erskine (eds.). *The Gods of Ancient Greece: Identities and Transformations* (online version). Edinburgh University Press, 2010; Roman Gods and Goddesses – Crystalinks www.crystalinks.com/romegods.html; Greek Mythology vs. Roman Mythology - Myths and Legends myths.e2bn.org/.../userstory20442-greek-mythology-vs-roman-mythology.html; Karl Christ. *The Romans: An Introduction to Their History and Civilization.* Translated by Christopher Holmes. Berkeley: CA: University of California Press, 1984; Everett Ferguson. *Backgrounds of Early Christianity* (2nd ed.). Grand Rapids, MI: Eerdmans, 1993; James S. Jeffers. *The Greco-Roman World of the New Testament Era: Exploring the Background of Early Christianity.* Downers Grove, IL: InterVarsity Press, 1999; Lesley Adkins and Roy A. Adkins. *Dictionary of Roman Religion.* New York, NY: Facts On File, 1996.

[11] J. A. Witmer. Romans. In J. F. Walvoord and R. B. Zuck (eds.). *The Bible Knowledge Commentary: An Exposition of the Scriptures* (vol. 2). Wheaton, IL: Victor Books, 1985, p. 443.

[12] George Foot Moore. *Judaism in the First Centuries of the Christian Era the Age of the Tannaim* (vol. 1). New York, NY: Schocken Books, 1974.

[13] Ellen G. White. *The Southern Work.* Washington, DC: Review and Herald, [1901] 2004, p. 9. "Note: these messages were written by Ellen G. White in 1896 and 1912. Repeated statements from her pen concerning racial relationships clearly indicate that her counsel on interracial marriage is not an issue of racial inequality; but essentially a question of advisability or inadvisability stemming from circumstances and conditions that could result in 'controversy, confusion and bitterness.' Ellen G. White has repeatedly reaffirmed her understanding of, and firm belief in, the equality of all races and the brotherhood of mankind." Ellen G. White Estate Trustees.

14 Ellen G. White. The Treatment of the Colored Race. Manuscript 7, 1896. Ellen G. White Estate.

15 D. R. Heimbach. *True Sexual Morality: Recovering Biblical Standards for a Culture in Crisis.* Wheaton, IL: Crossway Books, 2004.

16 Heimbach, p. 170.

17 Aristotle, *Nicomachean Ethics.*

18 E. Randolph Richards and Brandon J. O'Brien. *Paul Behaving Badly: Was the Apostle a Racist, Chauvinist Jerk?* Downers Grove, MI: IVP Books, 2016.

19 Ibid.

20 Everett Ferguson. *Backgrounds of Early Christianity* (2nd ed.). Grand Rapids: Eerdmans, 1993. See also Anthony Blond. *A Scandalous History of the Romans Emperors.* London: Constable Publishers, 1994.

21 James S. Jeffers. *The Greco-Roman World of the New Testament Era: Exploring the Background of Early Christianity.* Downers Grove, IL: InterVarsity Press, 1999.

22 Richards and O'Brien, pp. 134-135.

23 Ibid.

24 Stanley K. Stowers. *Letter Writing in the Greco-Roman Antiquity.* Philadelphia, PA: Westminster Press, 1996.

25 Craig A. Evans and Stanley E. Porter (eds.). *Dictionary of New Testament Background.* Downers Grove, IL: InterVarsity Press, 2000.

26 Vince Garcia. What You Never Knew About the Pharisees. *A New Christian's Handbook.* www.centralcal.com>christ.

27 Garcia.

28 Although there has been a modern attempt to rehabilitate the negative depiction of Pharisaic Judaism (the so-called new perspective), this profile we present is supported by Scripture (Mk. 7:13; Mt. 23:1-36; 15:1-20; Lk. 11:39-42). Contra E. P. Sanders. *Paul and Palestinian Judaism.* London: SCM Press, 1977. Also _____. *Paul, the Law, and the Jewish People.* Minneapolis, MN: Augsburg Fortress Press Publishers, 1985.

29 Garcia.

30Marcus Jastrow and S. Mendelsohn. Bet Hillel and Bet Shammai. *The Jewish Encyclopedia.* JewishEncyclopedia.com.; Heinrich Graetz. *History of the* Jews*: From the Earliest Times to the Present Day* (vol. 2). Charleston, SC: Nabu Press, 2010; Jonathan D. Brumberg-Kraus. Were the Pharisees a Conversionist Sect? Table Fellowship as a Strategy of Conversion. wheatoncollege.edu.

31Ferguson; See also George Foot Moore. *Judaism in the First Century of the Christian Era: The Age of the Tannaim* (vol. 1). New York, NY: Schocken Books, 1971.

32Thomas R. Schreiner. *Romans.* Baker Exegetical Commentary on the New Testament. Grand Rapids, MI: Baker Academic, 1998.

33 See Johannes P. Louw and Eugene A. Nida. *Greek-English Lexicon of the New Testament: Based on Semantic Domains.* Stonehill Green, UK: United Bible Societies, 1999.

[34] Gary Staats. *The Person and Work of Jesus Christ in Each Book of the Old Testament Seen in its New Testament Fulfillment.* Google Books: 2010.

[35] Osborne.

[36]David E. Aune. Judaizers. In W. A. Elwell and B. J. Beitzel (eds.). *Baker Encyclopedia of the Bible.* Grand Rapids, MI: Baker Book House, 1988; R. David Rightmire. Judaizers. *Baker's Evangelical Dictionary of Biblical Theology.* biblestudytools.com.

[37] Osborne, page 138.

[38] Ministerial Association, General Conference of Seventh-day Adventists. *Seventh-day Adventists Believe: A Biblical Exposition of Fundamental Doctrines* (2nd ed.). Boise, ID: Pacific Press, 2005.

[39] Ferguson and Moore.

[40] A verbatim perspective on the Northeastern Conference of Seventh-day Adventists Constituency Meeting, Camp Victory Lake, New York, June 5, 2016. From its inception in 1944 to 1988 the Northeastern Conference was led by African Americans, beginning with the presidency of Louis Bland and ending with that of Leonard Newton. In 1988, Stennett Brooks, from Nicaragua, was elected president. He served in this position until 2000, when the era of Caribbean dominance was initiated with the election of Don King. Caribbeans held sway until 2012, when Daniel Honoré, the first Haitian president, was chosen. He was re-elected in 2016.

CHAPTER THREE
The Savior

Romans 3:21 - 4:25

From the problem of universal sin, Paul now turns to God's solution in Christ. Paul demonstrates that just as Gentiles and Jews share not only a common heritage of sin, they now share a common salvation through Christ Jesus. Paul answers the question: how are sinful humans, whether Gentiles or Jews, made right with God? First, Paul describes God's declared righteousness through faith in Christ. Next, he explains and applies the principle of faith. And finally, he provides the iconic example of faith through the experience of Abraham.

God's Solution

In a concise statement, Paul articulates God's solution for human sinfulness and thus for the division among the believers in Rome, he writes,

> But now, apart from law, the righteousness of God has been disclosed, and is attested by the law and the prophets, *the righteousness of God through faith in Jesus Christ for all who believe.* For there is no distinction, since all have sinned and fall short of the glory of God; *they are now justified by his grace as a gift, through the redemption that is in Christ Jesus, whom God put forward as a sacrifice of atonement by his blood, effective through faith.* He did this to show his righteousness, because in his divine forbearance he had passed over the sins previously committed; it was to prove at the present time that he himself is righteous and that he justifies the one who has faith in Jesus (3:21-26).

In this passage, Paul uses the expression, "All have sinned and fall short of the glory of God," to summarize his depiction of the human condition (1:18 – 3:20). He has revealed that Gentiles and Jews alike have rejected the sovereignty of God and come under judgment. Therefore, to fall short of the glory of God is to come short of God's creative intent, i.e., God's intent in the creation of Adam and Eve in God's image (Gen. 1:26-27). The Divine image consists of three aspects: freedom that is self-limiting, unity in diversity—three yet one—and, most important, self-giving, self-sacrificing, self-renouncing love for the other. Paul, in 2 Corinthians, sums up the nature of God's glory revealed in Christ:

> And even if our gospel is veiled, it is veiled to those who are perishing. In their case the god of this world has blinded the minds of the unbelievers, to keep them from seeing the light of the gospel of the glory of Christ, who is the image of God. For what we proclaim is not ourselves, but Jesus Christ as Lord, with

> ourselves as your servants for Jesus' sake. For God, who said, "Let light shine out of darkness," has shone in our hearts to give the light of the knowledge of the glory of God in the face of Jesus Christ (2 Cor. 4:3-6; cf. 3:12-18).

Ellen White's comment on this passage is instructive.

> God's wonderful purpose of grace, the mystery of redeeming love, is the theme into which "angels desire to look," and it will be their study throughout endless ages. Both the redeemed and the unfallen beings will find in the cross of Christ their science and their song. It will be seen that the glory shining in the face of Jesus is the glory of self-sacrificing love. *In the light from Calvary it will be seen that the law of self-renouncing love is the law of life for earth and heaven*; that the love which "seeketh not her own" has its source in the heart of God; and that in the meek and lowly One is manifested the character of Him who dwelleth in the light which no man can approach unto.[1]

From Paul's perspective, God's intent after sin is to restore God's essential image in humanity—the Divine image revealed in the Son (cf. 8:29-30).

Paul sets out to demonstrate, once and for all, how God restores sinners, whether Gentiles or Jews, to right relationship with God's self and ultimately with others. Moreover, in context, Paul seeks to prove that, as it relates to *righteousness before God,* Jews have no advantage over Gentiles.

Yet, to fully appreciate the meaning and significance of this passage, two of Paul's previous assertions must be recalled. With these verses, Paul begins to develop his original thesis statement, "For I am not ashamed of the gospel; it is the power of God for salvation to everyone who has faith, to the Jew first and also to the Greek. For in it the righteousness of God is revealed through faith for faith; as it is written, 'The one who is righteous will live by faith'" (1:16-17).

In his thesis, Paul has already signaled that God's good news in Christ is the only means of salvation for both Jews and Gentiles. He has also established that his concern is not justification per se; believers are already justified. Rather, his concern is with sanctification, corporate and individual—how justified believers are to live by faith in Christ in community. More important, Paul uses the present passage as a corrective to his radical claim "for by works of the law no human being will be justified in His sight" (3:20).

Paul now stresses his point. He states, "But now apart from the Law *the* righteousness of God has been manifested" (3:21 NASB). Paul argues that God's righteousness, that is, God's ability to restore sinners to "rightness," or right relation with God has been revealed without Torah. Further, Paul asserts that his claim is neither novel nor heretical. He argues that "the law and the prophets," that is, the Old Testament, support his view.

How jarring this assertion would be for a first-century Jew of any stripe, even most Christian Jews, like those in Rome! As we have seen, Pharisaic Judaism and Christian Judaizers had distorted the role of God's law by making obedience to its requirements a prerequisite for salvation. They held that attaining righteousness and strict law observance were inextricably tied together. Furthermore, Pharisaic Jews had used God's law to retain the dividing wall between Jews and Gentiles, in short, as a pretext for ethnic prejudice (Eph. 2:14-15). Against this understanding, Paul maintains that the Old Testament, first given to the Jews, announces a solution for the problem of sin apart from the law (cf. 1:2; 9:1 - 11:36). He provides evidence shortly from the experiences of Abraham and David to support his claim (4:1-25; Gen. 15:6; 17:10-11; Ps. 32:1-2).

But now, with exquisite simplicity, Paul describes how God establishes right relationship between God's self and sinners. Paul asserts that new standing with God is achieved "through faith in Jesus Christ for all who believe" (3:22). With this statement, Paul clarifies for his Roman audience the common means by which God has secured their righteousness. Additionally, he subtly denounces the core belief of first-century Judaism: that righteousness before God is earned through human effort (cf. 9:30 - 10:4), and signals the way forward for believers in Rome.

How are Gentiles and Jews moved from standing under divine wrath to standing in right relationship with God? Paul's answer is concise and unequivocal: *"through faith in Jesus Christ."* Paul makes two claims that are central to his unifying purpose, i.e., his desire to establish common ground. Because God has provided a path to right relationship apart from the law, Jews have no advantage in righteousness before God (cf. 3:1-2). Also, faith—in short, trusting in God's saving initiative revealed in the life, death, and resurrection of Jesus Christ—is the only means by which God bestows righteousness on either Gentile or Jew. For Paul, righteousness, or right standing, is achieved through faith in the person and work of Jesus Christ from beginning to end.

However, Paul is making more than a soteriological point: a point related to salvation as a concept. His assertions, "to *all* who believe," "since there is *no distinction*," and "*they* are now justified by his grace as a gift," are all designed to convince believing Gentiles and Jews in Rome that they now enjoy a common salvation (5:12; 10:12). Just as they share a common sin story ("for all have sinned and come short of the glory of God") and were subject to God's wrath and impartial judgment, Gentiles and Jews now are made righteous before God in the self-same manner, through faith in Jesus Christ. Paul builds on this fundamental belief throughout the rest of the letter. At present, he moves to provide texture for his core belief.

Paul sketches a detailed picture of how God achieved right standing for Gentiles and Jews who have faith in Jesus Christ (3:24-26). Paul's description borrows both from the imagery of manumission, release from enslavement, and the Old Testament, specifically the Jewish tabernacle and the Day of Atonement. Paul's description supplies both the how and the why of God's actions in Christ.

Paul states, "Being justified as a gift by His grace through the redemption which is in Christ Jesus" (3:24 NASB). He uses the passive form of verb *dikaoō,* with the sense that believers "have been justified" by God. This phrase serves several purposes. It continues the idea of inclusion. Paul is making the case for a common justification of believing Gentiles and Jews. In addition, he uses the forensic or legal term justified, which means "declared righteous." This expression evokes the image of legal acquittal in a courtroom. Thus, for Paul, justification is a declaration of not guilty by God on behalf of believers.

Paul is here describing what is sometimes called "imputed" righteousness. It does not describe believers' actual condition, which still awaits sanctification or "imparted" righteousness through the Spirit (6:1 - 8:30). Moreover, Paul uses the passive voice to demonstrate that God's declaration of acquittal is God's unilateral act on behalf of both Jews and Gentiles. They are not active in this instance; both groups receive God's acquittal. This is important because Paul wants to stress the utter hopelessness of all human beings, including pious Jews, and the necessity of God's saving initiative, an act of love on behalf of sinners (cf. 5:6-10).

Therefore, Paul adds that believing Gentiles and Jews are justified "by his grace as a gift." The power of this statement demands context. We should remember that Pharisaic Judaism in the first century agreed that righteousness was attained through obedience to the Mosaic law. Thus, salvation for Jews was an entitlement, or a reward. Salvation was to be earned by good works.

Against this understanding, Paul posits the idea of justification as a gift. He employs his signature term "grace," which carries the meaning of "undeserved favor," to maintain that both right standing with God and the resulting salvation cannot be earned. Sinful Gentiles and Jews alike, who deserve death, must receive declared righteousness as a free gift. In fact, later in the letter, Paul makes the summary assertion that "the wages of sin is death, but the gift of God is eternal life in Christ Jesus our Lord" (6:23).

Now Paul turns to the *sine qua non* of his argument. Gentiles and Jews are justified "through the redemption that is in Jesus Christ." When Paul uses "redemption," he is using enslavement language, imagery that was very much a part of Roman culture. As mentioned earlier, it is estimated that by the end of the first century B.C., there were as many as two to three million slaves in Italy (35-40% of the population).[2]

Human bondage and the process of manumission—freedom from enslavement—which included a payment price, would have been very familiar to believers in Rome. Paul intentionally uses the language of bondage and freedom to describe how God achieves right standing for all who believe. He makes the compelling claim that God justified believing Gentiles and Jews "by or through" the redemption that is in Jesus Christ. The idea is instrumental: redemption is something that is done for sinners. Paul views Gentile and Jewish sinfulness as enslavement, a condition of bondage and helplessness without the possibility of unaided manumission or freedom.

For Paul, sin is an inexorable power for which humanity has no solution. Human sin encompasses both inherited and cultivated tendencies toward evil (5:12-21).[3] Paul's words are calculated to make Jesus Christ God's exclusive answer to the bondage of sin. He puts forth Jesus Christ as God's only means of securing human freedom. Through Christ alone, believing Gentiles and Jews now enjoy their right standing with God. They are reclaimed, rescued, and delivered from the dominion of sin through the price paid by Another (6:1-11; cf. 1 Cor. 1:30; Eph. 1:7; Col. 1:14).

Next, Paul broadens the scope of his discussion of redemption. He supplies both a past and present reason for why God acted in Christ to justify believing Gentiles and Jews (3:25-26). Using an image from the Jewish Day of Atonement, Paul argues that the substitutionary death of Christ demonstrates God's righteousness. He writes, "God presented Christ as a sacrifice of atonement, through the shedding of his blood—to be received by faith. He did this to demonstrate his righteousness, because in his forbearance he had left the sins committed beforehand unpunished" (3:25 NIV).

To fully understand Paul's meaning in this verse, one must first appreciate the dilemma that human sin created for God, a problem sometimes referred to as "the Fall" (1:18; Gen. 3:1-24). You will recall that God's essential nature has two dimensions: love and justice. In fact, Paul later reminds Gentile believers to consider both the "kindness and severity" of God (11:22). In other words, God, who is love, is also holy, God is merciful and yet just; thus the divine dilemma. How does God show divine love for fallen, sinful humanity, while at the same time maintaining divine justice? How does God satisfy the demands of God's own righteous nature? How does God demonstrate love for humankind and hatred for their sin? Drawing on language from the Jewish Day of Atonement, Paul depicts Christ as God's solution to the dilemma created by human sin (Lev. 16:1-34; 23:27-28).

Paul uses the term *hilastērion*, variously translated as "atonement," "propitiation," or "mercy seat" to portray God's solution in Christ. In the Septuagint, the Greek translation of the Old Testament, this term refers to the lid that covered the Ark of the Covenant on which God's presence resided (cf. Heb. 9:5). Once a year, on the Day of Atonement, the high priest would enter the most holy place to make atonement for his own sin and for the sins of Israel (Lev. 16:1-34). The high priest would take the blood of a sacrificed bullock and sprinkle it seven times on the mercy seat and seven times before it. It was through this symbolic ritual that, once a year, atonement or propitiation for sin was achieved. Israel confessed their sins, God pardoned their sins, and reconciliation between God and the people was accomplished.[4]

Douglas Moo explains,

> In the OT and Jewish tradition, this "mercy seat" came to be applied generally to the place of atonement. By referring to Christ as this "mercy seat," then, Paul would be inviting us to view Christ as the New Covenant equivalent, or antitype, to this Old Covenant "place of atonement," and, derivatively, to the ritual of atonement itself. What in the OT was hidden from public view behind the veil has now been "publicly displayed" as the OT ritual is fulfilled and brought to an end in Christ's "once-for-all" sacrifice.[5]

Although there are various interpretations as to how Paul applies the meaning of atonement language to Christ, context suggests that he is depicting Christ as the divine solution in two ways. Christ *voluntarily* appeases or satisfies the requirement of God's holiness and justice. God set Jesus forward as a sacrifice for atonement, but Christ is not a victim or an abused child. He participates collaboratively in the plan of salvation. He is not forced to assuage the wrath of a vengeful God. The Son of God, as God, voluntarily laid down His own life. God the Father and God the Son covenanted to save sinful humanity through the blood of Christ before the foundation of the world (Jn. 10:18; Rev. 3:8). God's nature is offended by sin. Indeed, Moses describes God as a consuming fire (Dt. 4:24; 9:3; cf. Heb. 12:29). Christ assuages the wrath of God deserved by sinners through His death, taking upon Himself God's righteous judgment. Christ becomes the payment for sin through substitution. He dies in the place of sinners (2 Cor. 5:21; cf. 1:18 - 3:20; 8:1).

In addition, based on Christ's death, those who believe, both Gentiles and Jews, are reconciled to God (5:1-11). With the justice demands of divine holiness satisfied, God is able to manifest God's love for sinners through the death of Jesus Christ (5:8). Thus, Paul argues that God demonstrates "His righteousness" through "restraint," or mercy, in the past by not destroying all sinners from the fall of Adam to death of Christ. By putting Christ on "public display," before the entire creation, including the cosmic powers (3:21, 26; cf. 8:31-39; Col. 2:13-15; Eph. 6:10-20), God's forbearance is vindicated.

Most important for his present audience in Rome, Paul asserts that God has an additional reason for the public display of Christ in death. "God presented Him to demonstrate His righteousness at the present time, so that He would be righteous and declare righteous the one who has faith in Jesus" (3:26 HCSB). Here, Paul reiterates the central claim of his argument. God justifies or declares righteous those who have faith in Jesus (3:21-22). Although Paul has made this claim earlier, there is now a difference.

It should be noticed that here for the first time in the letter, the name *Iēsous,* "Jesus," is used without reference to the titles "Christ" or "Lord" (cf. 8:11). Why this nuance? Could it be that Paul wants to emphasize the necessity of faith in the historical person and His sacrificial death? Does Paul seek to highlight that it is only through trusting in this name, literally "Jehovah is salvation," that righteousness is achieved? Is it possible that Paul uses the name *Iēsous,* which is equivalent to the Hebrew name "Jehoshua," or "Joshua," to equate present faith with final rest? We cannot be sure. But what is clear, for Paul, God's righteous nature is demonstrated in the counterintuitive act of declaring sinners righteous based exclusively on their faith in Jesus. Because of their common faith in Jesus, believers, Gentiles and Jews, now enjoy a new standing before God. In light of his focus on Christ's atonement as the answer for human sinfulness, why does Paul emphasize the death of Christ before appealing for reconciliation and unity in Rome?

The Atonement Applied

After explaining the significance of Christ's atoning sacrifice, and thus the significance of the cross—God's way of declaring righteous those who trust wholly in Christ Jesus—Paul applies his explanation to the current situation of divided believers in Rome. He does this through a series of rhetorical questions and their answers designed to continue his correction of faulty assumptions about faith and works, the identity of the people of God, and the role of the law.

Paul begins with three questions, followed by answers, and ending with a conclusion. "Then what becomes of boasting? It is excluded. By what law? By that of works? No, but by the law of faith. For we hold that a person is justified by faith apart from works prescribed by the law" (3:27-28 NASB). Paul's reference to boasting is no abstraction. He has already mentioned Jewish boasting over their knowledge about God, religious superiority over Gentiles, and possession of the law (2:17-29). Later, he reprimands believing Gentiles for what seems to be arrogant boasting about the plight of Judaism and the Gentiles' new standing with God (11:13-24).

Paul contrasts two principles to demonstrate that all human-centered boasting is disallowed in Christian community. Through these rhetorical questions, Paul sets works over against faith. His conclusion is simple and redundant: "a person is justified apart from works of the law" (3:20-26). You will recall that Paul uses the expressions "works" or "works of the law" pejoratively (2:15; 3:20, 27, 28; cf. Gal. 2:16; 2:16; 3:2, 5, 10). They are employed to denounce any attempt to secure righteousness, i.e., right standing before God, through law keeping. Paul again pounds home the point that faith in God's gift in Christ is the only basis for justification.

Next, Paul moves to the practical implications of his conclusion for the Roman believers. He uses two additional questions with one definitive answer. "Or is God for Jews only? Is He not also for Gentiles? Yes, for Gentiles too, since there is one God who will justify the circumcised by faith and the uncircumcised through faith" (3:29-30).

The questions, "Or is God for the Jew only?" and "Is He not also for Gentiles?" build logically on the previous conclusion, "for we conclude that a man is justified by faith apart from the works of the law," and all the other statements that level the playing field already established (1:6-7, 16-17). So, Paul's reasoning goes something like this. Jews had the law and Gentiles did not. If right standing with God is based on law-keeping, then God is only for the Jews. Therefore, only Jews can be saved. This, by the way, is what Pharisaic Judaism and Christian Judaizers believed and taught. A person had to be a Jew or become a Jew, i.e., a proselyte, through observance of the law in order to be saved (cf. Gal. 2:4, 12-16; 6:12-13; Phil. 3:2).

Because he has proven that God has justified those who have faith in Jesus apart from the law, Paul can emphatically answer that God is for "Gentiles too." Moreover, he affirms that God who is One—undivided—has provided only one way of accessing God's declared righteousness for both the circumcised and the uncircumcised. That way is faith alone: trusting what God has accomplished through the death and resurrection of Jesus Christ. Ever mindful of those Jewish opponents who have twisted his teaching about righteousness by faith apart from the law, Paul, again using diatribe, raises a final question and gives a decisive answer. "Do we then cancel the law through faith? Absolutely not! On the contrary, we uphold the law" (3:31).

As mentioned before, there can be no doubt that Paul has been accused by Jewish Christians of negating God's law by propagating the notion of right standing before God apart from the law. To this charge, he pleads not guilty. In fact, Paul later proves that his understanding actually upholds the law (4:3; 7:12, 14; 8:4; cf. 3:21). Given Paul's description of atonement through Christ and its application to the Roman believers, it seems appropriate at this point to raise a larger question. What does God accomplish through the death of Christ Jesus? For Paul, why the cross of Christ? In the present passage, Paul has just demonstrated that through Christ's substitutionary death, believers are declared righteous. Christ received the penalty for sin in the place of sinners (2 Cor. 5:21). Believers now experience right relationship with God. In addition, Paul argues that the righteous wrath of God has been satisfied. Divine wrath, through an act of grace, is replaced now by undeserved divine favor.

Yet, there is more. Later, Paul demonstrates that sin, death, and Satan have all been decisively defeated through Christ's death (5:12-21; 6:9-10; 8:31-39; 16:20; cf. 2 Tim. 1:10). For those in Christ, God has made all things new. Believers are part of the new creation (2 Cor. 5:17). Paul will show that believing Gentiles and Jews now have peace with God. They enjoy a new relationship with God the Father that results from Christ's sacrifice (5:1-11). But there is another accomplishment, a social dimension, made possible through Christ's death. Indeed, Paul's letter to the Romans moves inexorably to the exhortation, "welcome one another, therefore, as Christ has Welcomed you, for the glory of God" (15:7). The contours of this social necessity are described in Paul's letter to the Ephesians, a community of Gentile believers who seem to have either forgotten or rejected their common identity with believing Jews. Paul writes,

> So then, remember that at one time you Gentiles by birth, called "the uncircumcision" by those who are called "the circumcision"—a physical circumcision made in the flesh by human hands—remember that you were at that time without Christ, being aliens from the commonwealth of Israel, and strangers to the covenants of promise, having no hope and without God in the world. But now in Christ Jesus you who once were far off have been brought near by the blood of Christ. For he is our peace; in his flesh he has made both groups into one and has broken down the dividing wall, that is, the hostility between us. He has abolished the law with its commandments and ordinances, that he might create in himself one new humanity in place of the two, thus making peace, and might reconcile both groups to God in one body through the cross, thus putting to death that hostility through it. So he came and proclaimed peace to you who were far off and peace to those who were near; for through him both of us have access in one Spirit to the Father. So then you are no longer strangers and aliens, but you are citizens with the saints and also members of the household of God, built upon the foundation of the apostles and prophets, with Christ Jesus himself as the cornerstone. In him the whole structure is joined together and grows into a holy temple in the Lord; in whom you also are built together spiritually into a dwelling place for God (Eph. 2:11-22).

Although the full implications of Paul's description of the necessity of reconciliation between believing Gentiles and Jews based on Christ's death awaits later development, there is one social implication of the cross that stands out. Paul says that Christ made formerly divided Gentiles and Jews one "through His flesh." Together, they constitute "one new humanity." Paul's point is unmistakable. In Christ, Gentiles and Jews are one people. Together, they are the people of God. Therefore, division between believing Gentiles and Jews is a rejection of a central element of what God has accomplished in the death of Christ. Question: have we as Adventists forgotten the social necessity of the cross of Christ? Have we missed the social dimension of Christ's death through an unbalanced preoccupation with individual salvation?

A Common Ancestor

Paul, knowing that some in his audience will not be satisfied with his argument, turns to the Old Testament and to the Jewish patriarch Abraham to substantiate his case (4:1-25). Although Paul paints an idealized portrait in keeping with his purpose, the actual portrait of Abraham is anything but ideal. The choice of Abraham as a model raises the question: why does Paul enlist this particular "hero" from the Old Testament to support his claim that believing Gentiles and Jews are justified by faith in Christ apart from the law? Before this question can be answered, it is important to understand how Abraham was viewed in the Judaism of the first century.

Early Jewish authors (200 B.C. – 200 A.D.) posit two views of Abraham. In the first instance, Philo and Josephus, in their own attempt at cultural accommodation, present him as one who assimilated pagan, especially Hellenistic, culture. The second view presents Abraham as the discoverer and promoter of a radical monotheism in opposition to the polytheism of his pagan culture. In these texts, Abraham is one who resists and isolates himself from Gentile influences. In any event, Jews are admonished to follow Abraham as a model for living.[6]

The first view was a response to the challenge that the rise of scientific thinking and naturalistic philosophy presented to traditional Jewish belief in a personal God who created the world. This cultural challenge was countered by Philo and Josephus who found in Abraham the man who was able to see beyond the describable universe to a God who was above nature and not constrained by it. While there is no notion of idols or false gods in the Genesis account of Abraham, these writers credited him with seeing beyond the pagan cosmology of the time to posit a non-corporeal God, a wholly spiritual being, and setting himself against contemporary idolatry.[7]

The second view holds that at the age of three, Abraham considered the world of nature with its perfection, symmetry, coordination, and unity, and concluded that there must be an intelligent designer. Thus, Abraham discovered God. The Midrash on Genesis, from the second century A.D., says that Abraham's father was a manufacturer of idols. The child Abraham is said to have beheaded most of the idols with a hammer, which he placed in the hand of the one remaining idol. This led to a reprimand from his father, who was compelled to admit that Abraham's action was probably prompted by a realization that idols are only clay. Unlike his ancestors, Abraham saw a necessity to teach others about this monotheistic God. Abraham pitched his tent at a busy highway intersection where he could encounter and teach others, despite ridicule. He is said to have authored a 400-chapter book refuting idolatry.[8]

Four major themes about Abraham can be found in first-century texts.[9] First, is the emphasis on Abraham as the first monotheist, as described above. Second, is the idea that God established a covenant with Abraham through which his descendants are blessed. The covenant condition is obedience to the God who called Abraham out of his homeland and established a special relationship with him, changing his name from Abram, "exalted father," to Abraham, "father of many."[10] Third, Abraham's righteous character is presented, including his faithfulness, virtue, and piety. His progeny is blessed because of his loving relationship with God. Finally, Abraham is a keeper of the Mosaic law; in fact, the covenant was established when Abraham was circumcised. Abraham was held to have obeyed Torah so perfectly that his resulting surplus merits are available to his descendants.

With all of this, it is interesting to note that most Jews, past and present, view Abraham as the first Jew. But was Abraham a Jew? In spite of the fact that Jewish literature of the period viewed Abraham as their exclusive father—without reference to Ishmael and his descendants, or Keturah's sons, the Midianites—can his ethnic identity be established based on Scripture, or is it based on Jewish pride and their sense of exclusive identity?

A biblical examination of Abraham's ancestry reveals that he was a descendant of Eber (Gen. 10:24; 11:14), a descendant of Shem, whose descendants were called Hebrews. He was the father of Isaac, who was father of Jacob, or Israel (Gen. 35:10). Abraham was a native of Ur of the Chaldees. Thus, Abraham could rightly be designated as Shemite, Hebrew (Gen. 14:13), and Chaldean (11:28-31). However, there is no biblical indication that Abraham was a Jew. The Bible does not name him as a Jew or as the father of the Jewish people.

The plural term "Jews" is not used in the Old Testament until 2 Kings 16:6 to indicate people in the Southern Kingdom of Judah who were at war with Syria and its ally Israel. The singular term "Jew" is not used until about a century later where, in Esther 2:5, Mordecai is called a Jew, a Benjamite. In short, the term "Jew" in its accurate biblical sense was not in use until centuries after the death of Abraham.[11]

It is with this background that Paul now deconstructs Judaism's mythical portrait of Abraham for his Gentile and Jewish audience (4:1-25). In fact, building on his earlier redefinition of what it means to be a Jew (2:28-29), Paul now reimagines the identity of Abraham as the father of all those, Jew or Gentile, who are justified by faith in Christ apart from the law.

Paul introduces Abraham literally as "our ancestor according to the flesh." Then, with a rhetorical question and a hypothetical inference, he moves quickly past the issue of physical descent and signals how Abraham will function as a case study. Paul asks, "What then can we say that Abraham, our physical ancestor, has found? If Abraham was justified by works, he has something to brag about—but not before God" (4:1-2). How does Paul portray Abraham? Paul later uses Abraham to demonstrate that God has always justified a person solely based on faith in God.

Paul challenges his audience, especially the Jews in Rome, to consider the biblical portrait of Abraham our ancestor based on physical descent. From the outset of his recapping of this patriarch's story, Paul argues that Abraham has no grounds for boasting before God. You will recall that Paul has raised the issue of boasting already and has rejected it as lethal to Christian community (3:27). Paul's point is clear. If Abraham was justified by his works, he has a reason to boast. But if he is declared righteous based on his faith in God, he has nothing to crow about!

Paul strengthens his case by quoting Moses, "Abraham believed God, and it was credited to him for righteousness" (4:3; Gen. 15:6). Thus, Paul demonstrates that the Old Testament confirms that based solely on his belief in God, Abraham was credited by God with righteousness. It is important to note that Paul later uses this quotation about Abraham from Scripture as *prima facie* evidence to make his case. And from this passage, he uses an ancient mathematical or accounting term variously translated, "credit," "count," or "reckon" eleven times in his discussion of Abraham to drive home the point (4:1-25). Kenneth Wuest's simple explanation of how this term was used in the Greco-Roman world is helpful.

> [The term translated reckon] was used in early secular documents; "put down to one's account, let my revenues be placed on deposit at the storehouse; I now give orders generally with regard to all payments actually made or credited to the government." Thus, God put to Abraham's account, placed on deposit for him, credited to him, righteousness. The actual payment had not been made, the actual bestowal of righteousness had not been consummated, and for the reason that our Lord had not yet paid the penalty of man's sin and had not yet been raised from the dead. Abraham possessed righteousness in the same manner as a person would possess a sum of money placed in his account in a bank.[12]

It is critical to understand that Paul uses the accounting term credited almost interchangeably with the legal term justified; the only difference is that as an Old Testament figure, Abraham's credited righteousness anticipated full payment through the death of his "seed," Jesus Christ (Gen. 22:18). Additionally, as with the term justified, Paul uses the passive voice to indicate that the righteousness credited to Abraham was God's unilateral act on behalf of a sinner (cf. 3:24).

Paul illustrates the principle of credited righteousness (4:4-5). He uses a hypothetical example contrasting works and faith. Paul reasons that when a person works, he or she has the right to expect payment. Indeed, the person is owed payment; it is not a gift. Conversely, when a person does not work, but believes God "*who declares the ungodly to be righteous*" righteousness is not owed. It is credited; it is a gift. With this hypothetical example, Paul makes two points. The first is obvious. Abraham's righteousness was a gift from God; it was not earned. The second point is subtle and is made through inference. Abraham was ungodly when he was counted righteous by God (Gen. 15:6). Could it be that Paul uses insinuation because he knows how Abraham is idolized among first-century Jews?

In any event, Paul moves from illustration to quotation to support his argument. He quotes King David, another Jewish icon, to bolster his claim that righteousness is credited by God to the account of sinners who believe. Paul quotes Psalms 32:1-2: "Blessed are those whose iniquities are forgiven, and whose sins are covered; blessed is the one against whom the Lord will not reckon sin" (4:7).

Many commentators speculate that Psalm 32 is a song of repentance written by David after he sinned with Bathsheba. Whether or not this is the context of the psalm, the reason Paul appropriates David's words of repentance is clear. Both Abraham and David, while sinners, had righteousness credited to their accounts by God. Moreover, Paul chooses this psalm because it reinforces his thesis that a person is declared righteous based on faith in Christ (3:21-26). In a sense, Paul seems to view his presentation of Christ as propitiation and David's psalm as describing the same reality. Psalm 32 uses the language of forgiveness, sins covered, and sins not reckoned. These are the very elements used by Paul to claim that believers are declared righteous through the sacrificial death of Jesus Christ (3:23-26). Is it possible that Paul includes David as a witness because he, unlike Abraham, is a true Jew?

Returning to Abraham's justification story, yet, ever mindful of his purpose, Paul now moves to application. He demonstrates that Abraham was justified before he was circumcised (4:9-12). Extending the idea of blessedness from the psalm, he raises the rhetorical questions, "Is this *blessing* only for the circumcised? Or is it also for the uncircumcised?" If one recognizes that here circumcised and uncircumcised are used as metaphors for Jews and Gentiles, then Paul's questions again focus attention on the commonality of Jews and Gentiles before God.

Building on Genesis 15:6, Paul reminds Roman believers that he has already established that faith was credited to Abraham for righteousness. Now, he raises the issue of timing. Using two additional questions, Paul makes the definitive and astounding claim that when Abraham was justified, that is, credited as righteous by God, *he was not a Jew but a Gentile!* He writes, "In what way then was it credited—while he was circumcised, or uncircumcised? Not while he was circumcised, but uncircumcised" (4:10). One wonders how beleaguered Christian Jews in Rome received this clarification.

But Paul does not stop with this disturbing revelation; he further explains that Abraham, a Gentile, was reckoned righteous before he received physical circumcision. In fact, Paul maintains that Abraham later received the sign of physical circumcision as a seal of the righteousness that he had already been given through faith (Gen. 17:1-14). Why this sequence of events? Paul provides two interrelated reasons (4:11-12). He begins by arguing that God justified Abraham while a Gentile so that he would be the father of all future Gentiles who would be declared righteous by faith. Paul then continues his deconstruction of the significance of being a physical descendant of Abraham. Earlier in the letter, redefining Jewish identity, he wrote, "For a person is not a Jew who is one outwardly, and true circumcision is not something visible in the flesh. On the contrary, a person is a Jew who is one inwardly, and circumcision is of the heart—by the Spirit, not the letter" (2:28-29; cf. 9:6-8).

Now, Paul argues that the Gentile Abraham, before physical circumcision, also became the father of Jews who have his same faith. Paul's point is clear. Physical circumcision that became the sign of Jewish ancestry was never sufficient. Abraham, to whom God credits righteousness, is the father of all who are justified by faith. Paul is not engaged in abstract musing about Abraham and circumcision. His treatment is purposeful. Paul's aim is to demonstrate that divided Gentiles and Jews in Rome share Abraham as their common progenitor, their common "spiritual" father. Paul later builds on this claim at critical points in the letter (4:17; cf. 9:1 – 11:36; 15:1-13).

Paul evokes the promise made by God to Abraham that his descendants would inherit the land of Canaan (4:13; Gen. 17:1-8). Paul examines the promise to bolster his claims related to justification by faith. He argues that Abraham and his descendants did not receive the promise through the law: shorthand for "works of the law" (3:20). Rather, they received it in the same manner that one receives credited righteousness; they received the promise through faith. It should be noted that Paul extends Abraham's experience of credited righteousness to his descendants. This extension makes it necessary to identify Abraham's "true" progeny (cf. 9:8).

In verses 14-17, Paul again challenges the idea of Jewish privilege based on physical descent from Abraham. He reasons, "If it is the adherents of the law who are to be the heirs, faith is null and the promise is void" (4:14). He uses the expression, literally, "those of the law" to identify unbelieving Jews who are physical descendants of Abraham, those who seek to attain righteousness through legal obedience to Torah (cf. 10:1-4). Paul's argument is explicit: if Jewish legalists are Abraham's heirs, "then faith is made empty and the promise is canceled."

It seems that Paul does not want to be misunderstood. He realizes that both his understanding of the role of the law and his redefinition of Jewish identity will cause consternation among those of Jewish descent, even possibly those in Rome. Therefore, he again attempts to clarify the law's function. He has already demonstrated that "through the law comes a knowledge of sin" (3:20). Now, he adds that "the law produces wrath" and reiterates that there is no recognition of sin without the presence of law (4:15). Paul later explains that all the negative effects induced by the law of God are not based on any defect in the law, but on the innate deficiency of sinful human nature (7:7, 10-25; cf. 5:12-21).

For now, Paul returns to his present argument and his purpose for writing the letter. He concludes that God's promise of an inheritance came through grace and faith, not through the law. Now, Paul exposes his central claim. God guarantees the promise of inheritance apart from the law in order that the promise would be for *all* of Abraham's descendants, both believing Jews and Gentiles—not just for Abraham's natural descendants, but for those with his faith in God. Therefore, Paul contends, "He is the father of us all in God's sight" (4:16b-17a).

To support his claim, Paul quotes Genesis 17:5: "I have made [Abraham] the father of many nations." With these words from the Old Testament, Paul reinforces the new reality of common paternity. For Paul, believing Gentiles and Jews in Rome are one people with one father (4:17a; cf. 4:11-12). Although found in the Old Testament, Paul's claim would have been scandalous to a first-century Jew who viewed Abraham as the exclusive father of the Jewish people.

Paul now summarizes Abraham's story in light of his faith in God. He articulates the significance of Abraham's experience as the archetypal figure of faith for the Roman believers. Through his recapitulation of Abraham's relationship with God, Paul provides an exquisite definition of experiential faith. He makes three interrelated claims about Abraham's faith and ends with God's response (17b-22).

Paul states that Abraham believed in the unlimited ability of God. "He believed in God, who gives life to the dead and calls things into existence that do not exist." One wonders if Paul is referring to Abraham's decision to sacrifice Isaac at God's word, reasoning that "God was able to raise him from the dead" (Heb. 11:19; Gen. 22:1-19).

Next, Paul describes the tenacity of the patriarch's faith. He says, Abraham believed, "hoping against hope, so that he became the father of many nations according to what had been spoken So will your descendants be" (4:18-19). There can be no doubt that Paul is here referring to God's promise to give Abraham a son in his old age (Gen. 17:19; 18:10). That Abraham hoped against all hope speaks to the impossibility of the promise being fulfilled based on natural circumstances. Paul states that Abraham "considered his own body to be already dead (since he was about 100 years old) and also considered the deadness of Sarah's womb, without weakening in the faith" (4:19 HCSB). In other words, when there was no physical evidence on which to base his hope, Abraham continued to believe. He did not allow physical circumstances, his age, or Sarah's barren condition, to undercut his faith. He discounted temporal reality in light of the promise of God. It is based on the steadfastness of his faith in what God spoke that Abraham became "the father of many nations" (Gen. 17:5).

Paul finishes his portrait of Abraham's faith by identifying its source. Paul states, "No distrust made him waver concerning the promise of God, but he grew strong in his faith as he gave glory to God" (4:20). It is just now that Paul reveals a central concern of his letter. He does this by way of contrast. Paul affirms that Abraham rejected unbelief in God's promise. Rather, he grew strong. Literally, he was given strength in his faith. Paul uses a verb that can mean to "strengthen, become strong" in order to signal that God not only justified Abraham through faith, but Abraham was also sanctified through faith In context, Paul wants to demonstrate that

Abraham experienced the process of sanctification as he gave glory to God. Abraham grew strong in faith as he focused on God's glory: God's splendor and majesty. Abraham did not indulge in unbelief, instead, he became absorbed in the inner excellency of Yahweh. It is through his communion with God that Abraham "was fully convinced that what [God] had promised He was also able to perform" (4:21 HCSB).

For Paul, spiritual growth is no small matter. He uses the language of sanctification as he ends his description of Abraham's faith. Paul depicts this faith as active rather than passive. Abraham's faith, i.e., his receptivity to God, grew stronger as he continually responded to God's self-revelation. By beholding, Abraham was changed (cf. 2 Cor. 3:18). Although Abraham struggled like all saved sinners—going to Egypt without a word from God and lying to Pharaoh and Abimelech about Sarah to save his own skin—from the time he left his father's house in response to the divine command to his victory of dependence on Mt. Moriah, Abraham *lived by faith in Yahweh* (cf. 1:17). Later, Paul exhorts the divided community in Rome to follow in Abraham's footsteps. They too must grow simply through faith in Christ (6:1 - 8:30; 12:1 - 15:13; cf. 1:11-12).

Paul concludes his portrait of Abraham's faith with a statement describing the divine response. He ends where he began by again merely quoting Genesis 15:6, confident that he has made his case: "Therefore his faith 'was reckoned to him as righteousness'" (4:22). Paul closes with commentary on Genesis 15:6, drawing a direct analogy between Abraham's justification and that of all believers (4:23-25). And his reason for choosing Abraham becomes crystal clear. "Now it was credited to him was not written for Abraham alone, but also for us. It will be credited to us who believe in Him who raised Jesus our Lord from the dead" (4:23-24).

Here, Paul posits his summary claim. Abraham, the individual, serves as model for "us," i.e., for all believers, whether Jews or Gentiles, especially those in Rome. The experience of being credited or declared righteous is not unique to Abraham. God, who raised the believers' Lord, Jesus Christ, from the dead, has justified Abraham and his true progeny, both Gentiles and Jews. Finally, Paul reiterates two facts about Jesus Christ on which he later builds (1:4; 3:24; cf. 5:1). "He was delivered over to death for our sins and was raised to life for our justification" (4:25 NIV). Paul begins and ends his argument with emphasis on Christ's substitutionary death (3:21 - 4:25). In the coming discussion, Paul will further expose the implications of Christ's death and His present status as the Risen Lord for those in Rome. In the next chapter of this book, we will turn to the real thrust of Paul's letter. He presents the communal and individual implications of believers being declared righteous through faith in Jesus Christ to show how Gentiles and Jews must share a common sanctification.

So What? The Experiment

We entered a university church filled with young people and a good number of more mature worshippers. The students in attendance as well as those leading the worship service represented many ethnicities. The music was a mixture of genres including the Oakwood University *Aeolians*. This was a Deep Sabbath, a campus exchange between Oakwood and Southern Adventist universities. The sermon by the pastor was based on Jesus' end-time prediction in Matthew 24; the emphasis was on the idea that the love of many *believers* would grow cold and the need for more than propositional truth. Pastor John Nixon stressed the necessity in the Adventist church for Christ's love among believers. The congregation was attentive and enthusiastic; many had notebooks ready to take sermon notes. We were impressed by the preaching of Christ's righteousness accepted by faith, by the diversity of the students who led in worship, by the inclusiveness of the liturgy, and by the spiritual nature of the service. We inquired about the background of *Renewal*, and Nixon, former senior pastor of the Southern Adventist University Church in Collegedale, Tennessee, provided the following reflections.

The Birth of Renewal at Collegedale Church

When it became obvious that many students were not attending either of the Sabbath morning worship services of our church, the eight-member pastoral staff of Collegedale Church decided to do something. As it happened, one of our pastors was doing research for his dissertation on the dilemma of young adults between the ages of 18 and 25 leaving the church. Some of his research helped to inform our intent. We decided to start a collegiate worship service. The main reason the pastoral staff thought of the need for a collegiate service, something the church at Southern Adventist University never had before, was the perception that biblical preaching was missing. It wasn't an entertainment initiative.

Interested in being up-to-date and relevant but with insufficient time to conduct a study, the university chaplain conducted an informal survey. He contacted clerks from fourteen Adventist churches in the university vicinity and asked for a headcount of the number of students who attended their Sabbath services. After making his calculations, he informed us that there were at least 1000 students who were not attending church services anywhere. This information fueled our motivation.

Over the next few weeks in our staff meetings and on our annual pastoral retreat, we developed a plan and a process for initiating a college worship service. Seeking God's will in the matter, we prayerfully tried to take everything into consideration—logistics, timing, advertisement, and most of all, the reaction we expected to get from church leaders. We knew there'd be pushback and we agreed that when it came, we would "stick to our guns." This was too important to let go because of political considerations. Our plan was to meet with key leaders before bringing a proposal to the church board.

As we met with the board of elders, the Sabbath School divisions, the music committee and others, we met strong opposition. They expressed concerns about giving the students control, about allowing their music into the sanctuary, about how the service would affect the Sabbath school times. But the biggest objection came when we informed the leaders that we intended to give the collegiate service prime time. It had to take place at 11:30. It was unreasonable to expect students to come to an 8:30 service. The reaction against this part of the proposal was so strong that some of the pastors started suggesting that the church wasn't ready for this change, that we should withdraw the plan and try to bring it back another time. I reminded them that we had anticipated this very opposition and decided beforehand that when it came, we would not back down. This strengthened the resolve of some.

Through perseverance, we were able to get the church board to approve the proposal. The collegiate worship service began. The students named it Renewal. *We did a headcount every Sabbath and after nine months we were able to report to the church in business session that the average student attendance was between 900 and 1000. Why was* Renewal *so successful?*

Looking back on how the collegiate worship service began and how it progressed, I can identify at least four key factors that accounted for the enthusiastic student response.

(1) Priority
When the students saw that we were making them and their needs first, they were moved to respond. At the time, there were a few small student groups that met on Sabbath independently. They closed on their own, and the 11:30 service in the church became the focus. The service itself, and especially the time at which it was held, showed that the community considered them important.

(2) Trust
Worship at the Collegedale Church had always been a "sacred cow." We took pride in the tradition and sophistication of our worship services—the organ, the orchestra, the singers, the players, the professionals, the mildly academic sermons. This was the service that was broadcast live on the university radio station. Everyone knew this would change with the collegiate service. But we trusted the students and they were inspired to show themselves worthy of our trust.

We formed a student worship committee that would meet once a week to plan the service of the following week. It was chaired by a college student and populated by college students as well. They chose the members and they were inclusive. One pastor was assigned to meet with the committee to answer questions and give direction. The students were in charge. Over time, membership on the team became a coveted position. They were not required to follow any worship formula. They were free to be creative. There were only two stipulations. First, out of respect for the church's historic worship tradition, drums would not be included among the instruments. There would be no trap set in the sanctuary. Second, the pastor would stay in control of the pulpit. He would preach for both services and when a guest speaker was desired, he would give the final approval. The students accepted these qualifications without complaint.

(3) Affirmation
As time went on, the students saw that their worship service was an important part of the spiritual life of the community. Not only did we give them frequent praise, but the adult attendance at their service increased. Every innovation they tried wasn't successful. But they learned from their mistakes as we continued to support them and praise their efforts.

(4) Proclamation
The students reported that they were willing to shut down all their alternative worship services on campus because the Renewal worship had Christ-centered preaching. These millennial Adventists responded to Paul's gospel emphasis: Christ and Him crucified. They wanted to know more about Jesus and how to have an actual relationship with Him.

There was fruit for their labors. As they attended a worship service that was spiritually grounded in Christ and relevant to their life experiences, students responded to calls for repentance. Light was received. Lives were transformed. Some were baptized.

We do not know what became of this experiment. But given the fact that the Seventh-day Adventist Church in the so-called "first world" is losing young adults in unprecedented numbers, several questions may be raised. Why did young adults from various ethnic backgrounds respond to preaching focused on Christ and His atoning sacrifice? Is the death and resurrection of Christ central to Adventist thought and practice? What can we as a church learn from the Christ-centered experiment in worship at Collegedale Church?

---

[1] Ellen G. White. *The Desire of Ages.* Mountain View, CA: Pacific Press, 2011, p. 19.

[2] David J. Williams. *Paul's Metaphors: Their Context and Character.* Peabody, MA: Hendrickson Publishers, 1999, pp. 111-140.

[3] See Ellen G. White. *Christ's Object Lessons.* Hagerstown, MD: Review and Herald, 1941.

[4] See Leon Morris. *The Atonement: its Meaning & Significance.* Downers Grove, MI: IVP Academic, 1983; Grant R. Osborne *Romans.* The IVP New Testament Commentary Series. Downers Grove, IL: InterVarsity Press, 1997.

[5] Douglas J. Moo. *The Epistle to the Romans.* The New International Commentary on the New Testament. Grand Rapids, MI: William B. Eerdmans, 1996, p. 232.

[6] Gerald F. Hawthorne, Ralph P. Martin, and Daniel G. Reid (eds.). *Dictionary of Paul and His Letters.* Downers Grove, IL: InterVarsity Press, 1993.

[7] Ibid. See also Jon D. Levenson. *Inheriting Abraham: The Legacy of the Patriarch in Judaism, Christianity, and Islam.* Library of Jewish Ideas. Kindle Edition. Princeton University Press.

[8] Abraham—the First Jew: Why is Abraham considered the first Jew? Ask the Rabbi. aish.com. Accessed Jan. 11, 2016; Peta Jones Pellach. *Abraham and the Covenant.* ILS Israel and Judaism Studies, 2006.

[9] Hawthorne and Martin.

[10] Pellach.

[11] John C. Green. *A Light Upon Abraham: A Matter of Definition.* Hope of Israel Ministries. www.hope-of-israel.org.

[12] Kenneth Wuest. *Wuest's Word Studies in the Greek New Testament.* (2nd ed.). Grand Rapids, MI: William B. Eerdmans, 1980.

CHAPTER FOUR
The Peace

Romans 5:1 - 8:39

Paul turns from a description of believers' shared justification through faith in Christ and His substitutionary death to the implications for Christian community. He now begins to shape a mosaic of believers' shared life in Christ. Paul describes the scope of Christian life from "peace to *parousia*."[1] In short, he sets before the divided Roman communities a comprehensive vision of life in Christ beginning with peace or reconciliation to God and ending in reunion with God, i.e., glorification. Through the use of reconciliation language, Paul provides the predicate for his summary exhortation to unity among believers in Rome. After describing Christ's victory as the second Adam and the "reign of grace," Paul discloses the very heart of his letter. He introduces the means and necessity of holistic sanctification: participation in the death and life of Christ. Finally, Paul establishes the Holy Spirit as the means by which believers receive the resurrection life of Jesus Christ. Jews and Gentiles together are members of God's family and co-heirs with Christ. They are more than conquerors through His love.

Peace With God Through Christ[2]

Paul makes a comprehensive case for the need of corporate sanctification in Rome (6:1 – 8:39; cf. 1:11-12). He builds his argument on the belief that Gentiles and Jews now enjoy peace with God. They have moved from being under God's wrath to being reconciled to God. Paul puts it this way,

> Therefore, having been justified by faith, we have peace with God through our Lord Jesus Christ, through whom also we have obtained our introduction by faith into this grace in which we stand; and we exult in hope of the glory of God. And not only this, but we also exult in our tribulations, knowing that tribulation brings about perseverance; and perseverance, proven character; and proven character, hope; and hope does not disappoint, because the love of God has been poured out within our hearts through the Holy Spirit who was given to us. For while we were still helpless, at the right time Christ died for the ungodly. For one will hardly die for a righteous man, though perhaps for the good man someone would dare even to die. But God demonstrates His own love toward us, in that while we were yet sinners, Christ died for us. Much more then, having now been justified by His blood, we shall be saved from the wrath *of God* through Him. For if while we were enemies we were reconciled to God through the death of His Son, much more, having been reconciled, we shall be saved by His

> life. And not only this, but we also exult in God through our Lord Jesus Christ, through whom we have now received the reconciliation (5:1-11 NASB).

These verses function as a hinge passage, summarizing Paul's argument thus far, especially his description of how God declares believers righteous based on faith in Christ's substitutionary death, and then leading to a description of the benefits of justification. Before we unpack the meaning of these verses and their implications for the divided community, we must clarify how Paul structures this passage. He uses a literary device called chiasm to repeat and emphasize claims made in verses 1-2 with verse 11. Using this device, Paul begins his discussion by emphasizing that all believers now have peace with God and therefore present and future confidence (5:1-2), and ends in verse 11 repeating the same idea by stating that all believers may be confident of future glory because they have reconciliation with God through Jesus Christ.[3] Paul thus employs a common structural device to establish his central claim: believing Gentiles and Jews now enjoy peace, or reconciliation, with God through Christ.

Paul introduces his argument describing the shared benefits of justification with the words, "therefore, having been justified by faith, we have peace with God through our Lord Jesus Christ" (5:1 NASB). Using the conjunction "therefore," Paul ties his previous discussion of God's declaration of righteousness for those who have faith in Jesus with the present argument (3:21 - 4:25). He explains this with the words, "having been justified by faith." With this simple phrase, Paul speaks volumes. Justification is now assumed for all believers, both Gentiles and Jews; this new standing with God was not achieved by human effort, but rather by God's saving initiative through the death of Christ for those who trust (1:17).

Critical to the present discussion, Paul equates believers' present status of justification with the phrase that controls the entire passage "we have peace." This clarification is important for what follows. Justification, peace, and reconciliation describe the same reality in Paul's language of salvation (5:1-2, 10-11). Yet, there is a significant distinction. We have already seen Paul using justification language to depict believers' legal acquittal. The idea is that of a courtroom where a verdict has been rendered and a new standing declared. By bringing forward the reality of justification, Paul is still describing believers' new forensic standing before God (3:21-26; 1:17). But now, with the metaphors peace and reconciliation, he moves from a legal depiction to that of intimate interpersonal relationship. Paul evokes a picture of divine-human friendship. It is possible that he has Abraham's intimate relationship with God in mind (4:1-25; cf. 2 Chron. 20:7; Is. 41:8; Jam. 2:23).

Paul maintains that far from being under the threat of God's wrath (1:18; cf. 8:1), *all believers* now "have peace with God," or put another way, "have now received the reconciliation through our Lord Jesus Christ." Thus, for Paul, peace and reconciliation are interchangeable ideas. Along with the verbs, "we have," and "we received," Paul uses plural verb and pronoun forms throughout the passage to assert the central corporate claim that justified Gentiles and Jews together now share a new relational standing with God.

Indeed, Paul establishes relational peace with God through the death of Christ as one of the unearned benefits or common possessions—access, hope, and love through the Spirit—already received from God by justified believers (5:1-5). For Paul, *eirēnē,* meaning "peace," "is the first and most characteristic of the benefits received by believers."[4] Rather than the first century Roman idea of peace achieved through war and domination, the *Pax Romana* of Caesar Augustus, Paul seems to have in mind the Old Testament concept of *shalom* (Is. 54:10, 13). As such, "peace is not just the absence of war or cessation of hostilities; it involves, like the Hebrew word *shalom*, an all-inclusive experience of well-being. This well-being is not to be seen as an internal, subjective state but as an objective reality that comes into being when people [and] their God . . . are in right relationship."[5]

Whereas Roman peace was achieved by Augustus through the use of violence against the other, Paul maintains that believers have been given peace through a different type of Lordship. Jesus Christ, the believers' Lord, voluntarily accepts violence and death to accomplish their peace (cf. 1:4, 7; 4:24). It is this understanding of peace that accounts for the fact that in a subsequent letter, Paul personifies the concept of peace, and asserts, "For He Himself [Jesus Christ] is our peace who made both groups one [believing Gentiles and Jews]" (Eph. 2:14 NASB; cf. Phil. 4:7; Is. 9:6).

For our purpose of demonstrating Paul's desire to foster reconciliation and unity in Rome, it is important to observe that Paul "is also able to conceive of peace in an ethical, relational sense, resulting in believers acting in peace, i.e., living out in their interactions with others the peace they have received"[6] through Christ (14:19; cf. 1 Cor. 14:33). Paul later develops this ethical understanding more fully.

Building on the reality that justified believers have peace with God, Paul identifies a second benefit already received by believers. He writes, "We have also obtained access through Him by faith into this grace in which we stand" (5:2). Here, he connects the second possession, "access" with grace. Earlier, Paul has argued that believers are justified freely by God's grace. In other words, they are declared in right standing without merit; justification is undeserved (3:24). He asserts that believers who stand in grace, undeserved favor, also have access to God. It has been observed "that the metaphors of access and standing invoke images of the approach to God in the sanctuary or the ruler in a royal court."[7]

The rhetorical force of Paul's claim is simple yet profound. Through Christ, believers have direct access to God the Father; there is no longer any need for a human high priest or mediator (cf. Lev. 4:3-21; 16:14-15; Heb. 9:1-28). Believers share entrance into the presence of God (Eph. 3:12). Yet, this communal aspect to access to God is often ignored. While writing to predominantly Gentile house-churches in Asia Minor, Paul makes an astonishing claim. "He [Christ] came and preached peace to you who were far away and peace to those who were near. *For through him we both have access to the Father by one Spirit"* (Eph. 2:17-18 NIV).

Paul makes several points. He suggests that Jesus in His incarnation proclaimed peace to both Gentiles, "you who were far away," and Jews, "those who were near." Then he argues that through Christ, presumably through His death, believing Gentiles and Jews together have "access to the Father by one Spirit." Is Paul revisiting a subtle point made by Jesus, when He taught His disciples to begin prayer with the invocation, "*Our* Father in heaven," (Mt. 6:9)? For Paul, is it possible for either Gentiles or Jews in Christ to go before the Father without love or concern for the other? Does Paul's assertion to Ephesus, "For through him we both [Gentiles and Jews] have access to the Father by one Spirit," challenge our modern and postmodern individualistic understanding of relationship with God?

Paul identifies "hope or confidence" as the third benefit received by justified believers. In addition, he argues that believers can properly "boast" in their "hope of sharing the glory of God" (5:2b-4). "Paul's use of hope has two aspects . . . . believers are confident that they will participate, or share in, a future that will be animated by 'the glory of God,' i.e., God's eschatological salvation (cf. 8:18). To hope is to be assured of a future with God."[8] Additionally, with the phrase "not only so, but also," Paul introduces the second paradoxical aspect of hope: "affliction" that produces mature hope. Paul makes this point using another literary device called chain syllogism, which places the emphasis on the last element in the chain.

Therefore, according to Paul, believers can boast because they "know that *affliction* produces endurance, endurance produces proven character, and proven character produces hope" (5:3a-4 NIV). "Paul's intent is to assert that believers not only have confidence that anticipates a glorious future with God, but that afflictions for the believers have the paradoxical effect of strengthening their hope. Hope is tested and approved in the present situation. Confidence in the future, which is developed in present affliction, is for Paul the believer's legitimate ground for boasting"[9] (cf. 2:17, 23; 3:27; 4:2).

For Paul, the association of present and future hope with affliction does not represent idle theological musing. One has only to review a list of Paul's personal hardships for Christ to see this point. For example, in comparison to those whom he views as false apostles in Corinth, Paul writes,

> Five times I have received from the Jews the forty lashes minus one. Three times I was beaten with rods. Once I received a stoning. Three times I was shipwrecked; for a night and a day I was adrift at sea; on frequent journeys, in danger from rivers, danger from bandits, danger from my own people, danger from Gentiles, danger in the city, danger in the wilderness, danger at sea, danger from false brothers and sisters; in toil and hardship, through

> many a sleepless night, hungry and thirsty, often without food, cold and naked (2 Cor. 11:24-27; cf. 8:35-39).

In this light, Paul will end his discussion of the certainty of future glory with the conviction, "Now if we are children, then we are heirs—heirs of God and co-heirs with Christ, if indeed we share in his sufferings in order that we may also share in his glory" (8:17 NIV).

Concluding his list, Paul exposes the final benefit of justification shared by believers. He links this benefit to hope and describes its two dimensions: God's love through the gift of the Spirit. Paul writes, "and hope does not disappoint us, because God's love has been poured into our hearts through the Holy Spirit that has been given to us." (5:5).

Now for the first time, using explicit language, Paul introduces the gift of the Holy Spirit (cf. 1:4). Later in the letter he argues that the Spirit is God's essential gift, given to believers for both corporate and individual sanctification (7:6; 8:1-30). Here, Paul presents the Holy Spirit as the indispensable gift through which believers have received the love of God.

Before explaining this important claim in the letter, it is critical to observe how Paul relates mature hope, just described, to God's love received through the Spirit. Paul asserts first that believers' "hope does not disappoint." The NRSV translation, although accurate, does not carry the full import of the original language. The NIV offers the more literal translation "hope does not put to shame."

As we have seen, Paul's world was characterized by the Roman honor-shame value system, in which shame was to be avoided at all costs. Paul has just argued that the believers' present hope is matured through affliction. He recognizes that in Greco-Roman society, affliction is associated with shame. With the words "hope does not put to shame," Paul continues to undercut this dominant Greco-Roman value. Affliction may be the ground of shame for pagans or for the unbelieving Jews, but for believers, suffering for Christ's sake paradoxically constitutes their ground for boasting (5:3-4). How is this true? What is the basis for this claim? For Paul, the reason that believers' hope does not cause shame is profoundly theological. Paul says it is "because God's love has been poured into our hearts through the Holy Spirit that has been given to us" (5:5b). Paul bases his conviction solely on the love of God received through the Spirit.

Yet, how is Paul using the expression "the love of God" and what does it mean? The phrase, the love of God, can be interpreted in two ways: (1) believers' love for God, or (2) God's love for believers. Based on the thrust of his argument thus far with his emphasis on God's beneficence towards justified believers (1:1-4), Paul here has God's love for believers in mind.[10] But, the question remains, how are we to understand what Paul means by the expression, the love of God? Paul's use of this expression can best be explained by contrast with pagan ideas about the relationship of the gods to humans.

We should remember that Greeks and Romans understood their gods anthropomorphically: gods shared human characteristics, emotions, and behavior. In addition, they were often capricious. Fearful of the unpredictability of their gods, pagans concentrated on the idea of *tychē*—fate or luck. Hence, their common greeting, *chairein*, or "best wishes." We saw that Paul adapted this typical greeting by modifying it in the introduction of his letters to "grace and peace," emphasizing believers' personal and compassionate relationship with God. Pagan Greeks and Romans, on the other hand, could not conceive of a personal relationship with their gods; they could only hope to appease them through scrupulous adherence to ritual.

For Paul, God's love for believers, given through the Holy Spirit, is the opposite of the capriciousness of pagan gods. From the outset, in the greeting of the letter, Paul asserts that believers are literally, "loved ones of God." Moreover, believers do not have to speculate about God's intent towards them. Paul greets his Roman audience with the assurance that they have received both grace and peace from God their Father and from the Lord Jesus Christ (1:7).

It is important to recall that the dimensions of love and justice are held in tension in the nature of God. In context, the meaning of God's *agapē,* God's unconditional, sacrificial "love" for the sinners revealed in the death of Christ, is best described in the conclusion of Paul's doxology in praise of God that is fully developed later (8:31-39). Paul writes,

> Who can separate us from the love of Christ? Can affliction or anguish or persecution or famine or nakedness or danger or sword? As it is written: "Because of You we are being put to death all day long; we are counted as sheep to be slaughtered." No, in all these things we are more than victorious through Him who loved us. For I am persuaded that not even death or life, angels or rulers, things present or things to come, hostile powers, height or depth, or any other created thing will have the power to separate us from the love of God that is in Christ Jesus our Lord! (8:35-39).

Paul uses the same word, affliction, to introduce the process of mature hope and to begin a list of potential threats (5:3; 8:35). How is this possible? Paul's understanding of the love of God received through the Spirit by justified believers can best be summed up with the words *eternal security in Christ the Lord.* Because believers' holistic interests are now secure in Christ, absolute freedom from fear—past, present and future—is experienced (cf. 2 Tim. 1:7; 1 Jn. 4:16-19). In Christ all threats, temporal and cosmic, have been defeated (8:31-39; Col. 2:15). Believers' lives are now "hidden with Christ in God" (Col. 3:3). God's love is the essential benefit, which Paul says is continuously poured out in *the hearts of all believers* through the Spirit.

This is the reason Paul can assure believers that their confidence will not be put to shame: the Holy Spirit, the conduit of God's love, provides comprehensive safety. Believers, confident in the fact that they cannot be separated from this love, are free to love others unconditionally. Divine generative love creates love for God in believers (cf. 2 Cor. 5:14) and also love for others. Thus, for Paul, there is an ethical dimension of God's love. One cannot receive God's love without extending it.

As with the benefit of peace with God, the love of God received through the Spirit must become the love of God extended, especially in the believing community. Paul expands the ethical requirement of love later in the letter. For now, one of his maxims, "let love be genuine," will suffice (12:9). Paul urges believers in the Roman community to *let the love of God* extended to one another be sincere, without pretense. With this pithy saying, Paul begins to describe for all believers in Rome the essence of true Christianity (12:10; 13:8-10; cf. 1 Cor. 14:1a; Jn. 13:34-35).

For Paul, God's love extended is not an isolated ethical teaching directed exclusively to the believers in Rome. In other letters, he depicts the operational necessity of communal love. For example, in his letter from a Roman prison to the Philippians where rival leaders are modeling arrogance rather than the humility of Christ, Paul admonishes the entire community with the words,

> If then there is any encouragement in Christ, any consolation *from love*, any sharing in the Spirit, any compassion and sympathy, make my joy complete: be of the same mind, having the *same love*, being in full accord and of one mind. *Do nothing from selfish ambition or conceit, but in humility regard others as better than yourselves.* Let each of you look not to your own interests, but to the interests of others. *Let the same mind be in you that was in Christ Jesus* (Phil. 2:1-5).

We should note the accent on communal compassion, selflessness, and humility, all after the pattern of Jesus Christ. The same themes are echoed in Paul's "love hymn" written to the fractious Corinthians. The commentary provided by the Amplified Bible is helpful.

> Love endures with patience *and* serenity, love is kind *and* thoughtful, and is not jealous *or* envious; love does not brag and is not proud *or* arrogant. It is not rude; it is not self-seeking, it is not provoked [nor overly sensitive and easily angered]; it does not take into account a wrong *endured.* It does not rejoice at injustice, but rejoices with the truth [when right and truth prevail]. Love bears all things [regardless of what comes], believes all things [looking for the best in each one], hopes all things [remaining steadfast during difficult times], endures all things [without weakening]. Love never fails [it never fades nor ends] (1 Cor. 13:4-8a).

In context, Paul argues that the spiritual gifts of prophecy and knowledge will be terminated at Christ's second coming. Only God's love, the seminal fruit of the Spirit, is eternal (1 Cor. 13:1-3, 8b; Gal. 5:22).

Nevertheless, the love of God received by believers and enjoined on them awaits a definitive description (5:6-8). In these verses, Paul contrasts the new standing of believers, just described, with their past condition apart from faith in Jesus. He has already reminded them of their shared heritage of sin (1:18-3:20). Now he constructs a concise profile of the fallen human condition in order to help believers in Rome fathom the love of God revealed in the death of Jesus Christ.

Paul begins with the assertion, "For while we were still weak, at the right time Christ died for the ungodly" (5:6). He presents a negative descriptive progression that culminates with the word "enemies" to capture human separation from God (5:10). In this verse, he uses two adjectives, "weak" or "powerless," and "godless" or "impious," to describe the human condition. It seems that Paul uses the initial phases of his profile to reinforce the critical point that believers had no part in effecting their change in status from old to new (cf. 2 Cor. 5:16-17).

Believers' new life with God is accomplished by the death of Christ. Paul sets in bold relief the profound nature of Christ's death, contrasting the absurdity of Christ's death with the undeserving condition of those for whom the act was performed. This is the rhetorical function of the words, "Very rarely will anyone die for a righteous person, though for a good person someone might possibly dare to die" (5:7). Paul's point is clear. He emphasizes Christ's readiness to die by comparing what a reasonable person might possibly do in a more favorable situation.[11]

Paul exposes the heart of his present argument. He states, "But God demonstrates His own love for us in this: while we were still sinners, Christ died for us" (5:8). Paul has made the claim before about the efficacy of the death of Christ for believers' justification, hinting divine benevolence (3:25-26). Yet, what is only implied earlier is now made perfectly clear. *Paul establishes that the demonstrable locus of God's love is the death of Jesus Christ.* Building on his claim that God's love for believers through the Spirit is a present possession (5:5), Paul now inextricably links the demonstration of the love of God with the cross of Christ. With this assertion, Paul explains what seems to be absurd: the death of Christ for weak and godless people. Paul reasons that the death of Christ, and by inference His resurrection (cf. 4:24-25; 5:9-10), *demonstrates* or *proves* God's *own* love for believers. The sense is continuous and emphatic.

Here, Paul discloses fundamental convictions (5:8). By asserting, "God proves His own love," Paul reaffirms that it is God's initiative that has given believers new life (3:21-26). He presents the same conviction in 2 Corinthians 5:17-18a, "So if anyone is in Christ, there is a new creation: everything old has passed away; see, everything has become new! All this is from God" (cf. 8:3).

Paul continues his negative profile of believers before faith in Jesus. Believers were not only weak and godless but "sinners." Paul may have volitional lawlessness in mind (cf. 1:18). Sinners, not the righteous, were the passive recipients of new life with God. God revealed in Christ is the only God in antiquity whose love is demonstrated in the pursuit of fallen humanity, those in opposition to God. Roman religion depicted humans in pursuit of their gods through ritual appeasement and the acquisition of favor through offerings.

Most important, Paul locates the demonstration of God's love for believers definitively in the death of Christ. Paul's linkage between God's love and Christ's death raises several questions. Is there something more about the death of Christ revealed in His life? Does Christ's love displayed through His incarnation reveal something about the love of God? Again, we turn to Paul's letter to Philippi. It is in this letter that Paul describes the divine motive. He writes,

> Make your own attitude that of Christ Jesus, who, existing in the form of God, did not consider equality with God as something to be used for His own advantage. Instead He emptied Himself by assuming the form of a slave, taking on the likeness of men. And when He had come as a man in His external form, He humbled Himself by becoming obedient to the point of death—even to death on a cross (2:5-8).

Paul describes the voluntary condescension of Jesus Christ, his downward mobility for the sake of sinful humans. Central to Paul's description is his observation that Christ, the God-Man, emptied Himself of status and power to save sinners. In fact, Paul says "God made him who had no sin to be sin for us, so that in him we might become the righteousness of God" (2 Cor. 5:21). Are we to conclude that Christ's condescension for the sake of the undeserving other is a revelation of God's essential nature? Is the cross an exclamation point on the way Christ lived? Are we not simply reflecting on a mystery, God's self-giving love through the Son for creatures in open rebellion? It sometimes seems that with our Adventist emphasis on propositional truth we miss the real significance of God's profound love for us and its necessity for our well-being. A brief story illustrates this point.

We met a young woman at an Adventist institution a few years ago. We will call her Maria. She had been reared in a strict, conservative Adventist home. Her mother, who had been brought up in a brothel, was converted to Adventism; and possibly as a reaction to her upbringing, became very focused on correct behavior. The dictums of Ellen G. White were often repeated in Maria's home, e.g., guarding the edges of the Sabbath. In rebellion against her mother's legalism, Maria left the church for a few years to "sow her wild oats." When she came back to the church, Maria fell into a pattern of legalism that rivaled that of her mother. She found no joy or assurance in her practice of religion, and this was manifested in numerous physical complaints.

In conversation with Maria one evening, we shared the three-fold affirmation that the Father gave Jesus at His baptism: "You are my son, *my beloved*, in whom I delight." We emphasized that all who have faith in Christ share in these affirmations. Maria almost lost her mind. She said that she had never heard before how much God loved her. She quickly shared this good news with others in the facility, both Adventists and non-Adventists, and organized a series of Bible studies for us to teach them more about this amazing truth.

Is it possible, based on legalism and our emphasis on propositional truth, that many Adventists suffer from a "divine love deficiency?" Could it be that a lack of experience with the affirming love of God that banishes insecurity, lack of identity, and fear may lead to the chronic practice of ethnocentrism in the church with its false assurance of cultural identity and superiority?

In the third part of his argument, Paul asserts the certainty of future salvation based on the reality of believers' new standing with God (5:9-11). He repeats and amplifies the claims made by employing a literary device used in Jewish legal argumentation called *qal wahomer*, meaning "light and heavy," in which one proceeds from a statement of lesser weightiness to one of greater weight.

Paul continues his exposition with the words, "Much more surely then, now that we have been justified by his blood, we will be saved through Him from wrath" (5:9). For Paul, the lesser part of the argument already established has two parts. Believers have been justified and therefore enjoy a new standing of peace with God (5:1-2). In addition, the means by which believers have been justified is by His blood, in short, through the death of Christ (5:6-8).

It is important to understand that Paul can describe believers' new relational standing with God as lesser only from the perspective of the greater reality of future salvation, thus the greater claim, "We will be saved through Him from wrath." Believers can have full confidence in the present as they anticipate future salvation based on their new standing with God through Christ. The emphasis of Paul's lesser-to-greater argument is that believers in Rome, both Gentiles and Jews, who now possess a new standing with God, can be fully confident of a future free from condemnation (cf. 8:1).

Paul continues his lesser-to-greater explanation, but this time intensifies his assertion by using an "if . . . how much more surely" construction. Paul writes, "For if while we were enemies, we were reconciled to God through the death of his Son, much more surely, having been reconciled, will we be saved by his life" (5:10). For Paul, the lesser clause of the argument is, "For if while we were enemies we were reconciled to God through the death of His Son." In this clause, Paul makes several important moves.

He completes the negative profile of believers apart from faith in Jesus (5:6): "weak and godless," and "willful" sinners (5:8). Now Paul uses the more powerful term "enemies" to conclude his description (5:10). This depiction of believers' shared condition apart from faith in Jesus is designed to create a negative crescendo. The terms Paul uses move from the fairly gentle characterization of "weak" to the more severe depiction of "sinners," and culminates in the even more emotionally-charged designation of "enemies."[12] Paul heightens the force of his argument by describing the past condition of believers as enemies of God.

Paul then establishes that while being enemies, "we [believers] were reconciled to God" (5:10). He has made the same argument earlier using the term justified (5:1; cf. 3:21-25). In keeping with the relational benefit "peace with God" (5:1), Paul uses the verb "to reconcile." The sense of the verse is that God has taken the sole initiative to reconcile believers and bring them into a new relationship with God. Believers, former enemies, are the passive recipients of God's past beneficence. "Note the two directions—hostility from the unbeliever due to sin and hostility from God due to his judgment on sin. But as a result of Christ's death, that hostility has been removed from both sides, a new relationship has ensued."[13]

Paul ends the lesser clause by reasserting the means through which believers are reconciled. He repeats his belief that the death of Christ was God's means, or instrument, thus maintaining the central conviction of the entire passage (5: 1-8).

Next, with the phrase "how much more surely," Paul develops the comparatively greater claim that "having been reconciled, we [believers] will be saved by His life." Again the believers' salvation is depicted as a future, but certain, reality accomplished through the death of Christ. Yet, now Paul places the accent on the certainty of believers being "saved by His life." If it is stipulated that Christ's death refers to His crucifixion, then "His life" must refer to Christ's resurrection life (cf. 4:25). It seems likely that Paul has in mind the present intercessory work of Christ in tandem with the Holy Spirit (8:26-27; Heb. 7:25).[14]

As in the previous lesser-to-greater argument (5:9), Paul's burden is comparative. Believers' present situation, here reconciled, is viewed as inferior when compared with their eschatological salvation. Believers can be confident of future salvation based on the death and resurrection of Jesus Christ.

Paul concludes his case for the certainty of believers' salvation by again using the formula "not only so, but also" (cf. 5:3). With these words, Paul signals that in addition to all that has been said, he has something more to say, "we even boast in God through our Lord Jesus Christ, through whom we have now received reconciliation" (5:11). In actuality, this verse functions as a summary of the entire passage (5:1-10).

Paul emphasizes believers' ground for boasting: earlier, in mature hope and future confidence, here, in God (cf. 5:3-4). We should remember that Paul has earlier corrected improper boasting on the part of Jews who placed confidence in their ability to obey the law (2:17, 23). The implication is that boasting in ethnicity or social status is unacceptable for Paul; believers can only boast legitimately about what God has done in Christ (1 Cor. 1:29, 31)[15]

Paul ends by reiterating, through the use of reconciliation language, the central claim of his argument. Through the Lord, Jesus Christ, believers now *together* enjoy a new relationship with God (5:1-2, 6-8, 9-10; cf. 4:25). Paul began the passage by describing the new situation of believers with the word peace. He ends by asserting that believers are no longer hostile towards God. Indeed, through Christ, believers have been reconciled, they have moved from being God's enemies to being God's friends.

Before moving to Paul's final formal treatment of justification by comparing Adam and Christ (5:12-21), we raise several questions central to the thesis of this book. If, as we have demonstrated, "justification and reconciliation are metaphors describing the same fact,"[16] why then does Paul shift metaphors? With this passage, characterized by relational language of peace and reconciliation with God (5:1-11), how does Paul attempt to address the ethnic division of believers in Rome?

To begin addressing these questions, we must return to Paul's Greco-Roman context. It is important to understand that the topic of reconciliation was not unique to Romans or Paul's other letters (cf. 2 Cor. 5:11-21; Col. 1:15-20; Eph. 2:11-22). In fact, the subject of concord or reconciliation was a dominant theme in Greco-Roman rhetoric and diplomacy. As early as the fourth century B.C., Aristotle's treatise, *Rhetoric*, identified the issue of war and peace, i.e., reconciliation, as one of the five most important subjects of deliberative rhetoric, a type of speech designed to persuade hearers to decide on a future course of action.[17]

By the first century A.D., concord, or unity, within a political body was considered a part of the general topic of war and peace, and was addressed as the opposite of factionalism in the rhetorical handbooks used to educate males of the upper strata. Reconciliation discourse was used to persuade factionalized groups to embrace unity. Examples of discourse urging unity among divided groups during the time of Paul include the speeches of Dio Chrysostom and Aelius Aristides to various cities in Asia Minor. These cities were culturally similar and close geographically to cities Paul addressed in his letters.

For the purpose of our study, the point is that concord or reconciliation discourse reflected a universally recognized political value in Greco-Roman culture that was applied to city-states as well as smaller social units.[18] It is highly likely that Paul's Gentile and Jewish audience would have understood his initial use of reconciliation discourse as a subtle appeal to unity after a period of factionalism within the community.

With this historical backdrop, we can now address how Paul used peace and reconciliation language to urge unity among believers in Rome (5:1-11). Careful analysis reveals how his reconciliation language functioned. As already mentioned,

Paul uses the discourse of "peace with God through Jesus Christ" and "we were reconciled to God through the death of His Son" in an attempt to create common ground between Gentile and Jewish believers. He does this by contrasting their status apart from faith in Jesus with their new life with God by faith. Justification, peace, and reconciliation, which are descriptive of the new situation of believers, stand in stark contrast to their former status, characterized as being under the power of sin, divine wrath, and judgment.

Paul continues by using reconciliation language as part of his discourse of inclusion through which he develops the notion of a shared primary identity among believers in Rome, thus fostering unity. As we have seen, Paul in his introduction has already identified believers as those "called to belong to Jesus Christ," "beloved of God," and "called saints" (1:6-7). Now, Paul argues that believers have in common a new relationship with God through the death and resurrection of Jesus Christ (cf. 1:16-17; 3:21-26). This new status is described as justified, peace, access into the grace in which we stand, and reconciled. Further, believers share both a present and future hope and the love of God in their hearts through the gift of the Holy Spirit (5:1-11).

Most important, Paul uses reconciliation discourse in this passage in an effort to *prepare* Gentile and Jewish believers for his communal exhortations in general (12:1 - 15:13), but especially his direct exhortation for unity between Gentiles and Jews at the close of his formal argument. Later Paul makes the summary appeal:

> Welcome one another, therefore, just as Christ has welcomed you, for the glory of God. For I tell you that Christ has become a servant of the circumcised [Jews] on behalf of the truth of God in order that he might confirm the promises given to the patriarchs, and in order that the Gentiles might glorify God for his mercy. As it is written, "Therefore I will confess you among the Gentiles, and sing praises to your name"; and again he says, "Rejoice, O Gentiles, with his people"; and again, "Praise the Lord, all you Gentiles, and let all the peoples praise him"; and again Isaiah says, "The root of Jesse shall come, the one who rises to rule the Gentiles; in him the Gentiles shall hope." May the God of hope fill you with all joy and peace in believing, so that you may abound in hope by the power of the Holy Spirit (15:7-13).

At this point, the question raised earlier can now be addressed: why did Paul change from the metaphor of justification (legal) to that of reconciliation (relational)? Although several explanations are possible, based on the overall argument of the letter, there can be no doubt that Paul uses vertical reconciliation language. In other words, language that describes reconciliation with God is used to establish a *grammar* for later exhortations, i.e., horizontal reconciliation within the Roman community (14:1 - 15:13).

What is meant by a grammar? Here, we define a grammar as a necessary premise or fact on which later argumentation depends.[19] Wayne Meeks provides an example of how a passage functions as the premise for subsequent argumentation. He suggests that Paul presents what we may call a grammar in Romans 2:1: "Therefore, any one of you who judges is without excuse. For when you judge another, you condemn yourself, since you, the judge, do the same things." In this verse, Paul maintains that human judgment is inappropriate because all stand under the impartial judgment of God. This premise or grammar is used as a basis for Paul's later exhortation against believers judging one another in Rome (14:1-23). For example, "Who are you to pass judgment on servants of another? It is before their own lord that they stand or fall" (14:4).

Thus, Paul ties the prior premise to the later exhortation: judgment of other believers should be ruled out because they belong to God, and all stand under God's impartial judgment to be executed by the Son.[20] This idea can be expressed from the perspective of so-called Pauline ethics. According to this framework, Paul bases his exhortation, what believers should do, on what God has already done in Christ. This ethical paradigm is sometimes called in Pauline studies the indicative and the imperative.[21] Based on this construct, because God is the impartial judge (indicative or fact), believers are not to judge one another (imperative or exhortation).

It is our contention that Paul's peace and reconciliation language (5:1-2, 11) functions as a grammar most specifically for the summary exhortation of 15:7: "Welcome one another, therefore, just as Christ has welcomed you, for the glory of God." As we will demonstrate later, Paul's entire letter can be summed in his final Christological premise and exhortation: because believers in Rome have been welcomed, accepted, or received, by Jesus Christ, they are to welcome one another. *There can be no doubt that Paul believes that the ethnocentrism being practiced among believers in Rome is a denial of reconciliation with God through the Lord Jesus Christ, one of the benefits of justification* (cf. 1 Jn. 4:20).

Given the divided situation in Rome, is Paul raising an implicit question, how can Gentile and Jewish believers, who possess divine love through the Spirit, love made visible in the Cross, be at war with each other? In light of the death of Christ, will justified believers in Rome follow the example of God? Will they take the initiative through the power of the Spirit to be reconciled to perceived enemies? At what point will we as Adventists come to understand that without reconciliation across ethnic and racial lines there can be no genuine reconciliation with God?

The Reign of Sin Broken

Paul now compares Adam and Christ (cf. 1 Cor. 15:20-22, 45). This comparison serves as the conclusion of his formal treatment of justification in the letter (5:12-21; cf. 1:16-17; 3:21 - 5:11). In these verses, Paul portrays Adam as the father of all sinful humanity. Earlier, he depicts Abraham as the father of all those justified by faith (4:1-25). Paul shows that Gentiles and Jews alike share another common progenitor, Adam, and that they in common inherit his sinful nature. Conversely, Paul demonstrates that through the obedience of Christ, specifically, His sacrificial death, the power of sin, that is, "the reign of death," has been broken for justified believers. This claim will be foundational to Paul's explanation of sanctification in general, and corporate sanctification in particular, through the power of the Spirit (6:1 - 8:30; 12:1 - 15:13).

Although sometimes viewed as complex, Paul's argument is simplified if the tools he uses are understood. He employs three literary devices to make his case. (1) Paul again uses the Hebrew argumentation technique called *qal wahomer*, "light to heavy," often translated "much more" (5:15-19; cf. 5:9-11); (2) He employs typology to argue that Adam, from the Old Testament (Gen. 1 - 3; 1 Chron. 1:1), serves as a symbolic representation of Christ (5:14); and (3) Paul adopts a popular first-century rhetorical device called *synkrisis*, "the comparison of opposites,"[22] to demonstrate the superiority of Christ and His work to Adam and his sin.

Paul's argument has three parts. Paul provides a statement of the problem related to Adam's sin (5:12). Then he delineates the historical prevalence of sin (5:13-14). Finally, through comparison, Paul identifies the resolution for the problem of sin through Jesus Christ, the believers' Lord (5:15-21).

Paul begins using the phrase, literally, "because of this," to tie the present argument to the previous discussion of the benefits of justification, that is, reconciliation to God through Christ and thus the assurance of a glorious future (5:12a). Next, with the words, "through one man sin entered into the world, and death through sin, and so death spread to all men, because all sinned" (5:12b NASB), Paul identifies the contours of the issue to be addressed. His statement of the problem has several critical dimensions.

Paul immediately assigns culpability for sin's entrance into the world to one man: Adam. Notably, the transgression of Eve from the Genesis fall narrative is not mentioned (Gen. 3:6-7). It is possible that Adam's disobedience to God's direct command given before the creation of Eve is in view? (Gen. 2:16-17). Yet, in assigning exclusive responsibility to Adam, Paul sets up his comparative intent in the passage. He later demonstrates that the resolution of the problem is through one man (5:15-21). In addition, Paul's language seems to be designed to establish Adam as the progenitor of all sinful humanity. Earlier in the letter, Paul describes the reality of Gentile and Jewish sin (1:18 - 3:20), now he identifies sin's source.

Paul establishes a causal sequence of events that issues from Adam's sin, the first of which is death, that is, human mortality. Paul maintains this cause-effect linkage throughout the passage. It is noteworthy that Paul makes no distinction between physical and spiritual death. He seems to suggest that holistic death is innate to the human condition.

Using the words, literally, "pass through," Paul argues that Adam's sin was transmitted to all humans. Although debated, it seems likely that Paul intends the transmission of Adam's sinful nature to all humanity. This is probably what Paul means with the words, "and were by nature, children of wrath, like the rest of humankind" (Eph. 2:3b; Ps. 51:5). In other words, according to Paul, Adam's sinful nature became both congenital and universal.

Paul addresses individual culpability. Not only has sin been bequeathed from Adam to all humans, but all humans "have sinned and fallen short of the glory of God" (3:23). Paul's point? As human beings, both Gentiles and Jews chose to participate in sin and are therefore responsible.

Now with the parameters of the problem clearly identified, Paul adds two clarifications related to sin and the law. He writes, "Sin was indeed in the world before the law, but sin is not reckoned when there is no law" (5:13). Paul states that sin predates God's giving of the law on Mount Sinai (Ex. 20:1-17). Paul may be stressing the time sequence between the entrance of sin and the coming of the law in order to highlight the consequences of unfettered sin, "death reigned" (5:14), and to be able to argue later that the coming of the law had the effect of "multiplying sin" (5:20).

Paul next explains that sin cannot be "reckoned" or "registered" against humans when there is no law. Here, Paul seems to reiterate the claim that through the law comes a knowledge of sin, and therefore specific accountability (3:20; cf. 4:15). This too he builds on at the close of his argument (5:20-21). With the words, "Nevertheless death reigned from Adam until Moses," Paul introduces the rubric "death reigned," to describe death as the tangible expression of sin's power (5:14). He uses the verb meaning to "rule, be king" to heighten the idea of the dominance of sin through death over all humanity, from Adam, when sin is introduced, to Moses, through whom the law was given. Paul's point is simple: even before sin is counted, death asserts absolute control. The concept of the reign of death is critical throughout the present argument because Paul sets it over and against a superior power that he calls "the reign of grace" (5:21). Furthermore, Paul demonstrates that believers' submission to God's reign is the essence of sanctification (6:1-23).

Next, Paul emphasizes the scope of death's reign. He makes the point that death reigned, "even over those who did not sin in the likeness of Adam's transgression" (5:14). Paul recognizes that Adam's sin was a violation of a direct command from God, and Adam experienced death as the consequence of willful, premeditated sin (Gen. 2:16-17; 3:6-7). It seems that Paul's goal is to stress the indiscriminate nature of death's reign, encompassing the disobedient like Cain and the obedient like Abel (Gen. 4:1-9). Certainly, Paul is mindful of the fact that according to the Old Testament, between the time of Adam and Moses, only Enoch has escaped the dominion of death (Gen. 5:21-24).

Paul discloses the perspective on which his succeeding comparative argument will be founded (5:14b). He establishes that his analysis is based on the view that Adam serves as a "type or pattern" of "the One to come," i.e., Christ. Thus, Paul signals that his remaining argument will be "typological." In salvation history, Old Testament persons, events, and institutions are presented as "types" that point to their "antitypical" fulfillment in Christ. For example, the Exodus, as a symbol of liberation, prefigures the final deliverance of the people of God in Christ.[23]

Paul employs a literary device, in verses 15-21, that was used widely in his day called *synkrisis*. As we have seen, this method of argumentation was used to compare opposites through contrast. In addition, Paul argues again from "light to heavy" (5:9-11). Adam serves as a negative type or representation. This contrast is designed to establish the superiority of Christ. Paul's comparative argument has three parts: 15-17, 18-19, 20-21.

He compares Adam's sin and its consequences with the superior work of the sacrifice of Christ (5:15-17). He begins his argument with the words, "But the free gift is not like the trespass. For if the many died through the one man's trespass, much more surely have the grace of God and the free gift in the grace of the one man, Jesus Christ, abounded for the many" (5:15). Paul establishes the basic elements for his comparison, contrasting what he calls the gift with the trespass. His argument is straightforward, moving from light to heavy. He reasons as follows: if it is true, and it is, that through Adam's sin many died (5:12), then how much more, through Jesus Christ's gift, that is, His sacrificial death, has God's grace overflowed to many. Paul's first point of comparison is simple. Christ's self-sacrifice, i.e., His act of grace, is superior in quality to Adam's sin.

Paul adds an additional element by contrasting the benefits of the gift with the consequences of sin. He writes, "Nor can the gift of God be compared with the result of one man's sin: The judgment followed one sin and brought condemnation, but the gift followed many trespasses and brought justification" (5:16 NIV). In short, Adam's sin resulted in divine judgment and condemnation, while the gift—Christ's sacrificial death, despite many trespasses—resulted in justification (cf. 5:6-8). Verse 17 functions as a comparative summary with the critical reiteration, "For if by the transgression of the one, death reigned through the one, much more those who receive the abundance of grace and of the gift of righteousness will reign in life through the One, Jesus Christ" (NASB). Here again, Paul underscores his point using light to heavy argumentation. His logic is clear. If through Adam's sin death reigned, and it did; then, how much more through Christ will those, believers, who received abundant grace and the gift of righteousness that is justification, reign in life?

Paul reintroduces the reign motif of verse 14. There, he argued that because of Adam's sin, "death reigned from Adam to Moses." Now, Paul establishes the reality of two opposing reigns: the reign of death through Adam versus the superior reign in life made possible through Christ. Paul will shortly embellish the meaning of Christ's reign (5:20-21; 6:1-23).

He ends the direct comparison between Adam and Christ by contrasting the universal implications of their actions (5:18-19). Using the expression "so then," Paul ties his present assertions to the previous verses. He argues, "Just as one trespass resulted in condemnation for all people, so also one righteous act resulted in justification and life for all" (5:18). Paul reaffirms his previous claim about the reach of Adam's trespass. Through his one act, all humanity fell under divine condemnation (5:12). Then, picking up the threads of his Christological portrait thus far, Paul asserts, conversely, that "one righteous act," that is, Christ's death, leads to justification and life for all.

With the words translated, "life for all," Paul seems to have in mind the universal offer of justification through faith in Christ and new life in Christ as a consequence of being declared righteous (5:21; cf. 3:21-26). To close his comparison of the two Adams, Paul restates for emphasis the comparison of verse 18 using different language. "For just as through one man's disobedience the many were made sinners, so also through the one man's obedience the many will be made righteous." Paul maintains the substance of his contrast while exchanging terms. Adam's one act is now characterized as disobedience, literally, to "refuse to listen" and those under condemnation are again called sinners (5:12).

Conversely, Christ's one act is now described as obedience. And through Christ's sacrificial act, Paul says the justified will be made righteous (5:16). In this verse, Paul uses the significant term "made," literally, "stand as constituted," twice.[24] First, with the claim that through Adam's disobedience many were *made* sinners, Paul echoes the claim that Adam's sin was transmitted through his sinful nature (5:12). In his second use of the term, through Christ's "obedience the many *will be made righteous*," Paul adds a critical clarification. Justified believers are to receive additional imparted righteousness, i.e., sanctification. As with justification, believers will be the passive recipients of sanctification from God through the obedience of faith (1:5; 6:1 - 8:30).

Paul ends his comparison with an eye towards both the sanctification and the final glorification of believers, both made possible through Christ (5:20-21). Building on the foregoing argument, Paul again raises the issue of the law in relation to sin (5:13-14). He says that "the law came in, with the result that the trespass multiplied." Paul builds on his basic understanding of the primary function of God's law, which is to provide a knowledge of sin (3:20); through the law sin is registered or charged (5:13). In this verse, Paul adds that with the introduction of law, sin increases. He later explains this phenomenon as a problem, not of the law, but of fallen human nature (7:7-25). For now, Paul uses this fact to continue his light to heavy comparison. His point is that "where sin multiplied, grace multiplied even more." Paul emphasizes not only the supremacy of grace over sin, but also its excess.

Finally, Paul sums up his comparison by contrasting the two opposing reigns. He writes, "So that, just as sin reigned in death, so grace might also reign through righteousness leading to eternal life through Jesus Christ our Lord" (5:21). He concludes his argument by personifying both sin and grace. Again sin, introduced by Adam, is depicted as a ruler or king exercising its dominion over all humanity through death, not just physical but spiritual (cf. 5:14, 17). Now, with his audience in mind, Paul briefly discloses the resolution for the problem of sin and death. He posits the reign of grace through righteousness. Paul's closing point is simple yet profound. Sin reigned in death through Adam. Now, because of God's righteousness (1:17; 3:21), grace is able to rule through Jesus Christ, the believers' Lord (1:4; 4:25; 5:1, 11). Moreover, the reign of grace through Christ will result in sanctification and in glorification, i.e., eternal life (8:3-30).

Before turning to Paul's discussion of sanctification, a question may be raised in light of his use of the concept of grace in this passage. Is Paul using the term grace in a new way? Previously, Paul used grace to connote God's undeserved favor given for believers, especially through the death of Christ (3:24). In addition, Paul describes justified believers as now having access to God because they stand in grace, or divine favor (5:2). Yet, in this passage, beginning in verse 17, Paul seems to associate grace with the *God-given ability or power now available to justified believers.* He appears to suggest that it is through an excess of grace, i.e., divine power, that believers are able to reign in life. Paul personifies grace as having the ability to multiply and to reign. In both instances, grace is described over and against the power of sin and the reign of death. Also, in both instances, Paul argues that grace is a superior power (5:20-21). This view of grace as a power seems to stand behind Paul's description of his encounter with Christ after his prayer for personal deliverance.

> Because of the surpassing greatness of the revelations, for this reason, to keep me from exalting myself, there was given me a thorn in the flesh, a messenger of Satan to torment me—to keep me from exalting myself! Concerning this I implored the Lord three times that it might leave me. And He has said to me, "My grace is sufficient for you, for power is perfected in weakness." Most gladly, therefore, I will rather boast about my weaknesses, so that the power of Christ may dwell in me (2 Cor. 12:7-9; cf. 1 Cor. 15:10; 2 Tim. 2:1; 1 Pet. 4:10).

Paul speaks of grace as divine power. We believe that this understanding of grace as the power of Christ now available to justified believers is essential to Paul's explanation of sanctification.

In light of the situation in Rome, why does Paul compare Adam and Christ? The goal of Paul's comparison is to contrast two heads, representative figures, and therefore two families. Adam is the head of sinful humanity, "those who live with the effects of [his] sin," while Christ is the head of all those justified by faith, "who live with the effects of Christ's atoning sacrifice."[25] More than this, Paul demonstrates that Christ overturns the perpetual damage done by Adam for those who trust in Christ. Justified Gentiles and Jews now have a new Head, Jesus Christ. Through Christ, *the power of sin has been broken*, believers may walk in newness of life (6:4). Believing Gentiles and Jews are members of a new family whose Head is Christ (cf. 8:12-17; Eph. 2:15-16; cf. Col. 1:13)

Participation with Christ

Paul now turns to the pressing question that gave birth to his epistle to the Romans; we saw this query in the thanksgiving of the letter (cf. 1:11-13). Indeed, much of his discussion thus far has been preparatory to the question (3:21 - 5:21), how are justified believers to live between the times, that is, from the point of justification by faith to the *parousia,* or second coming? In much of the discussion that follows, Paul addresses the subject of spiritual growth, i.e., sanctification, not just of the individual but also of believers in community (6-8:30; 12:1 - 15:16; 16:1-20). Soon he will zero in on the ethnic and religious division in Rome in an attempt to foster unity. Through his initial explanation of the gospel (1:16-17), Paul has demonstrated that believing Gentiles and Jews share a common heritage of sin and divine condemnation (1:18 - 3:20).

More important, he has shown that both groups now share a common justification. Based on faith in the substitutionary death of Jesus Christ, they have been declared righteous by God apart from the law (3:21 - 4:25). Believers now together share a new standing with God; they have been reconciled and share the hope of future glory (5:1-11). In addition, Paul has demonstrated that believers, Gentiles and Jews, are now no longer under the reign of sin. Through the death of Christ, sin's dominion, introduced by Adam, has been broken. Believers now experience the reign of grace through the Lord Jesus Christ (5:12-21).

Now, in a two-part argument, awash with metaphors, Paul begins to outline the contours of the new life in Christ (6:1-23). Using two dominant images, death and slavery, he takes up the question of sanctification, particularly corporate holiness. How are justified believers to live? His answer is as follows: believers, through faith in Christ, are to live as people who have died to sin and now live though participation with Christ (6:1-14); believers are to live as people who are slaves of God (6:15-23).

Paul sets up his discussion of sanctification by echoing his earlier dialogue with an imaginary opponent (6:1-3, 15; cf. 2:1-5, 17-24). He uses two rhetorical questions and an emphatic answer to address possible Jewish objections. Paul writes, "What should we say then? Should we continue in sin so that grace may multiply?" Most likely, Paul is concerned that some of his Jewish audience and their supporters might misconstrue his prior statement, "The law came along to multiply the trespass. But where sin multiplied, grace multiplied even more" (5:20). Paul closes the door on this possibility with the emphatic answer, "Absolutely not!"

He then raises questions that serve as the introduction to his description of the new life in Christ. "How can we who died to sin go on living in it? Do you not know that all of us who have been baptized into Christ Jesus were baptized into his death?" (6:2b-3). These questions, loaded with content, are central to Paul's understanding of sanctification. So, in the discussion that follows (6:4-14), Paul answers his own rhetorical questions. He uses the symbols of baptism and crucifixion to argue that justified believers cannot continue in sin because, simply put, they have died to sin.

Paul evokes the death and resurrection of Jesus Christ as the model for how justified believers are to live (1:17). Yet, he does not view the passion of Christ as simply exemplary. Paul argues for the realty of an actual, twofold participation for believers. He states,

> Therefore we have been buried with him by baptism into death, so that, just as Christ was raised from the dead by the glory of the Father, so we too might walk in newness of life. For if we have been united with him in a death like his, we will certainly be united with him in a resurrection like his (6:4-5).

Paul's assertions are rich with meaning. Using the death and resurrection of Jesus as his paradigm, Paul states, what is for him, a past fact about the experience of all believers, then provides its purpose (6:4). In other words, Paul first argues that justified believers have been buried with Christ through baptism into death. Here, baptism serves as a potent metaphor for participation in the death of Christ. Consequently, Paul begins his description of sanctification with the image of death. Believers have died. For Paul in this passage, baptism, or immersion in water, is a symbol of burial, of death, not just forgiveness of sin (cf. Acts 2:38).

Believers share in the death of Jesus Christ. For Paul, justification means first that believers are dead to their former sinful ways. As we will see, for Paul this symbolic death language has practical implications for believers living in the Roman communities. Next, Paul provides the purpose for identification with Christ in death. Believers have been put to death, *so that, just as Christ was raised from the dead by the glory of the Father, so we too might walk in newness of life.* Here, Paul exposes the second vital dimension of sanctification. Believers participate in Christ's death in order to partake of His resurrection life. The reception of the actual life of Christ is what Paul has in mind when he uses the phrase, "walk in newness of life." Yet, Paul's description of the process of moving from death to life is significant. With the words "just as," Paul again uses the experience of Jesus as the model for believers' sanctification. It should be noted that he says, "Christ was raised from the dead by the glory of the Father." What does Paul mean? How does it relate to the sanctification of believers?

We must observe that Paul says that Jesus was the passive recipient of resurrection life. He was raised from the dead. Moreover, using cryptic language, Paul supplies the means by which Jesus received resurrection life: "by the glory of the Father." Literally, Jesus is raised from the dead by the "glorious power" of God the Father.[26] If, as we believe, Paul is referring to God's Spirit as the person and power responsible for Christ's resurrection, then this analogy is vital for Paul's understanding of how the ongoing process of sanctification is achieved (1:4; 8:11).

Paul's point is basic to his understanding of the process of growth in Christ. Just as Jesus Christ was resurrected by the power of God, that is, the Holy Spirit, by the same means, believers are enabled to walk in newness of life. Paul later develops the indispensable role of the Holy Spirit in sanctification (8:1-30). For now, his point seems to be that believers experience regeneration; they receive the imparted righteousness of Christ, not through human effort, but by the power of God (cf. Eph. 2:8-10).

Paul restates the reality of believers' participation in both the death and resurrection life of Christ with an additional clarification (6:5). In his analogy, Paul does not equate Christ's resurrection with the resurrection of believers. Christ's resurrection is paralleled with believers' experience of new life. Thus, when Paul says, "If we have been joined with Him in the likeness of His death, we will certainly also be in the likeness of His resurrection," he is saying that participation in Christ's death in the present guarantees participation in the future resurrection of the body (1 Cor. 15:12-49).

Seemingly, Paul's argument that believers' new life in Christ must be characterized by death and then life is so important that he shifts metaphors to make essentially the same point. Paul continues to describe how believers have died to sin (6:6-11). Now, adding specificity, he employs the images of crucifixion and slavery to reinforce the necessity of both death and life in the process of sanctification. Paul states, "We know that our old self was crucified with him so that the body of sin might be destroyed, and we might no longer be enslaved to sin. For whoever has died is freed from sin" (6:6-7). Paul argues from what he believes is a fact of believers' past experience, and then identifies the purpose.

For Paul, literally, as a part of justification, "our old man together was crucified" with Christ; this is a known fact. What does Paul mean? Specifically, what does he have in mind with the metaphor, "our old self" and the fact of its death? For Paul, "our old self" refers to the common sinful self before faith in Jesus (1:18 - 3:20; cf. 3:23-26), a self that lived under the unfettered control of sin introduced through Adam's transgression (5:17-19, 21).

To be crucified with Christ is to experience the death of ego. In Galatians 2:20, Paul provides his paradigmatic testimony, "I have been crucified with Christ; *and it is no longer I who live,* but Christ lives in me; and the *life* which I now live in the flesh *I live by faith in the Son of God,* who loved me and gave Himself up for me" (NASB). In addition, Paul can conceive of our old self as the "collective sinful self," the self that expresses itself through a common sinful worldview that includes values, attitudes, and practices opposed to God, and ultimately to God's self-revelation in Jesus Christ (1:18 – 3:20). It is this cultural, societal manifestation of the collective old self that Paul has in mind with the exhortation to the Romans,

> Therefore, I urge you, brethren, by the mercies of God, to present your bodies a living and holy sacrifice, acceptable to God, which is your spiritual service of worship. *And do not be conformed to this world,* but be transformed by the renewing of your mind, so that you may prove what the will of God is, that which is good and acceptable and perfect (12:1-2; cf. 1 Jn. 2:15-17).

Paul admonishes the believers in Rome to reject conformity to the Greco-Roman world in very specific ways in view of God's mercies received in Christ (12:1-15:13). In fact, Paul says that all human systems are under divine judgment and are passing away (1 Cor. 7:31). According to Paul, being crucified with Christ expresses itself both individually and collectively.

Yet, in context, Paul reminds believers of the death of the old self in solidarity with the cross of Christ in order to emphasize two related purposes and their effect: "in order that sin's dominion over the body may be abolished, so that we may no longer be enslaved to sin. For whoever has died is freed from sin" (6:6b-7). Paul restates claims made in his comparison between Christ and Adam. Because of Christ's victory over Adam's trespass, the power of sin, its rule, has been broken. Through identification with Christ's death, believers are no longer to live as enslaved to sin (5:17-19, 21). Indeed, Paul asserts that the effect of death is freedom. He returns to the metaphors of slavery and freedom shortly to emphasize the necessity of divine Lordship (6:15-23).

Paul continues to restate and accentuate all that has been said about solidarity with Christ in death and the resulting life (6:8-11). However, he summarizes his argument with a Christological claim. "The death he died, he died to sin, once for all; but the life he lives, he lives to God" (6:10). Paul's point is clear. Through His sacrificial death in solidarity with sinners, Christ broke the power of sin and death, once and for all, for those who believe (5:12-21; cf. 2 Cor. 5:14-15, 21; Heb. 7:27; 9:12, 26–28; 10:10). In addition, Paul asserts that now through His resurrection, Christ lives eternally in the presence of the Father. On the basis of this overarching claim on which sanctification rests, Paul issues to the believers in Rome his first apostolic command. "So you also must consider yourselves dead to sin and alive to God in Christ Jesus" (6:11). Paul's command is predicated on the example of Christ (6:4).

Believers who are sanctified through the power of God's Spirit must engage in two related activities. Believers, based on Christ's victory over sin, must reckon themselves dead to sin. They must appropriate Christ's triumph. But solidarity with the death of Christ is not sufficient. Believers must count themselves "alive to God in Christ Jesus" (6:11b). For the first time Paul uses the expression that captures the fullness of believers' identity: believers are in Christ. They share an inextricable union with Him (cf. 8:1; Jn. 15:1-16). It is on the basis of this union and the reality of Christ's resurrection that believers are exhorted to consider themselves "living to God." Although a bit esoteric, Paul is about to explicate the meaning of being alive to God in Christ.

With the exhortation for believers to reckon themselves dead to sin and alive to God firmly in place, Paul issues related commands (6:12-14). These commands have implications for his ongoing clarification of the relationship between law and grace. He states,

> Therefore do not let sin reign in your mortal body, so that you obey its desires. And do not offer any parts of it to sin as weapons for unrighteousness. But as those who are alive from the dead, offer yourselves to God, and all the parts of yourselves to God as weapons for righteousness (6:12-13).

Paul personifies sin as a ruling power and admonishes believers to reject its holistic dominion, even its evil insinuation. Through Christ, believers are to resist sin's reign over their finite beings.

Paul continues his exhortation with both a negative and a positive admonition. Negatively, believers are not to offer any member of their bodies as tools of unrighteousness (cf. 1:18). Positively, believers, as those who are now alive, are to offer their bodies to God and each member to God as instruments of righteousness. With his dual exhortation, it seems as if Paul creates a "freedom from" and "freedom to" tension that should actuate the lives of believers.

Paul builds on his earlier contrast between the reign of sin and the reign of grace (5:21). "For sin will not rule over you, because you are not under law but under grace" (6:14). Paul explains why sin has lost its mastery over believers. He can assert that believers are no longer under the rule of sin based on Christ's victory over Adam's sin (5:17, 21). In addition, Paul argues that believers, unlike unbelieving Jews, are no longer under the rule of the law (Gal. 6:16-25). Paul has already explained that the law provides knowledge of sin and paradoxically increases sin based on sinful human nature (3:20; 5:20; cf. 1 Cor. 15:56). Later, he demonstrates why Pharisaic Judaism's distortion of the role of the law is lethal (7:7-23). For now, Paul demands that believers, who are being sanctified, are under the rule of grace.

Having made a comment about the limitation of the law for sanctification, Paul anticipates vehement opposition from most Jews—believers and unbelievers (6:1; cf. 3:8). In order to forestall misunderstanding, he relies on two rhetorical questions and his emphatic disclaimer. "What then? Should we sin because we are not under law but under grace? Absolutely not!" (6:15).

With this negation, Paul is now in the position to explain his understanding of the rule of grace. He does this indirectly by analogy, using the metaphor of slavery (6:16-23). Paul has used this image before. As a part of his self-identification, at the beginning of the letter, he introduced himself as a slave of Christ. What is more, in describing the common identity of Gentiles and Jews in Rome, Paul maintained that Roman believers are called to belong to Christ (1:1, 6).

In the present discussion, Paul has already broached the subject of slavery, arguing that believers who participate in Christ's death are no longer enslaved to sin (6:6). Now Paul expands his use of the image of slavery to explain an aspect of new life in Christ, beginning his clarification with the question, "Don't you know that if you offer yourselves to someone as obedient slaves, you are slaves of that one you obey—either of sin leading to death or of obedience leading to righteousness?" (6:16). It seems that Paul starts with this question to alert his audience in Rome to the reality that there are competing forces at work seeking mastery over believers. Believers, who have died with Christ, must now live with this awareness. Believers must always recognize to whom or what they offer obedience. This is critical, because implicit in Paul's question is the assumption of human slavery and the present reality of rival masters. For Paul, it seems that the only question is to whom should believers offer their submission.

Accordingly, he spells out the consequences of obedience to sin versus obedience to God (cf. 6:13, 22). Although a bit ambiguous, Paul seeks to explain that obedience to sin as a master results in death, while obedience to God issues in righteousness, i.e., Godlikeness or sanctification (6:19; cf. 1:17; 3:21). In verses 17-18, using the Roman believers' past slavery to sin as his reference point (1:18 - 3:20), Paul thanks God for their acceptance of the gospel (1:8). He reminds believing Gentiles and Jews that they received the truth in the heart (cf. 2:29). In addition, he reaffirms the fact that Roman believers have been liberated from slavery to sin and are now enslaved to righteousness.

As we have already seen, Paul is not the founder of the communities in Rome so he takes every appropriate opportunity to build the ethos of his mixed audience (1:2, 5-7, 8-15). Paul also recognizes that later in the letter, he will identify some implications of the gospel that will be difficult for both Gentiles and Jews to hear (15:15; cf. 10:1-4; 11:11-24; 14:1-23).

Paul seems to pause to acknowledge the imperfection of explaining sanctification using slavery for his analogy. He states, "I am using an example from everyday life because of your human limitations" (6:19a NIV). Before Paul continues his analogy, he concedes that slavery, although a common occurrence in Greco-Roman life, is not a perfect metaphor for new life in Christ because while believers are slaves to God, paradoxically, they experience the utmost freedom (6:22; 1 Cor. 9:1-23; cf. Mt. 11:28-30; Jn. 8:36). In addition, slavery to God does not do justice to the rich complexity of Paul's understanding of believers' relationship to God. While it is true that believers are slaves, it is also true that they are beloved of God, adopted sons and daughters, heirs and joint heirs with Christ, God's children, and the elect of God (1:7; 8:14-17, 28-30).

So, although limited, the slavery image serves his present purpose, and Paul continues, "For just as you once presented your members as slaves to impurity and to greater and greater iniquity, so now present your members as slaves to righteousness for sanctification" (6:19b). Paul uses believers' former enslavement to sin and its pattern—uncleanness to lawlessness to greater lawlessness—to exhort them now to offer themselves to enslavement to righteousness, that is to God, and its result: sanctification (6:3, 17-18, 22). For the first time, Paul actually uses the term "sanctification," i.e., holiness, although he has made oblique references to it before (1:11-12, 17; 5:1, 11, 15, 17). How does Paul use this term?

We must remember Paul's context. First-century Pharisaic Jews understood holiness as separation from Gentiles, sin, and licentiousness.[27] They believed that holiness was achieved by rigid adherence to the law—written and oral—rather than through a personal relationship with God. It is notable that at the height of the righteousness by faith debate in 1888, Ellen White warned Adventists about allowing the law to overshadow Christ.

> This message was to bring more prominently before the world the uplifted Saviour . . . *Many had lost sight of Jesus* . . . . The message of the *gospel of His grace* was to be given to the church in clear and distinct lines, that the world should no longer say that *Seventh-day Adventists talk the law, the law, but do not teach or believe Christ* . . . . Unless he makes it his life business to behold the uplifted Saviour, and by faith to accept the merits which it is his privilege to claim, the sinner can no more be saved than Peter could walk upon the water unless he kept his eyes fixed steadily upon Jesus. *Now, it has been Satan's determined purpose to eclipse the view of Jesus and lead men to look to man, and trust man, and be educated to expect help from man.* For years the church has been looking to man and expecting much from man, but not looking to Jesus, in whom our hopes of eternal life are centered. Therefore God gave to His servants [Jones and Waggoner] a testimony that presented the truth as it is in Jesus, which is the third angel's message, in clear, distinct lines.[28]

For Paul, salvation, deliverance by God through Christ from the holistic reign of sin and death, has three phases: justification, sanctification, and glorification. We will treat glorification later in the discussion (8:18-30).

Phase one of salvation is justification through faith in Christ. In this stage, God declares a sinner righteous because the sinner trusts God's word for rescue, especially God's word in the death and resurrection of Jesus Christ. This is the stage where God imputes righteousness based on the blood of Christ. Believers are acquitted and covered with Christ's righteousness. Believers now enjoy the benefits of justification: peace and reconciliation, access to God, present and future hope, and the experience of the love of God through the Spirit. In addition, through Christ, the second Adam, the reign of sin has been broken for justified believers (3:21 - 5:21).

Phase two of salvation is sanctification. It assumes justification by faith in Christ and is a continual participation in both the death and resurrection life of Christ made possible by the Spirit of God. In this stage, God imparts righteousness through the obedience of faith, i.e., relational obedience (1:5). Through the power of the Spirit, believers gradually reckon themselves as dead, they submit to the reign of God—Father, Son and, Spirit—both corporately and individually. Yet, while justification is God's grace bestowed on the individual, sanctification is more. It is also God's creation of a communal mosaic, a holy people (Lev. 11:44; 1 Pet. 1:16).

Unlike Pharisaic Judaism, Paul's use of holiness language refers to all believers, both Jews and Gentiles. Paul can use holiness to refer to the group "in general (8:27; 16:2), at Rome as a whole group (1:7) and as individual house churches (16:5), at Jerusalem (15:25-26, 31)."[29] Paul, as mentioned earlier, does not conceive of righteousness, and therefore salvation, independent of community. An exclusively individualistic concept of salvation, at the expense of a parallel corporate view, is an unfortunate by-product of the European Enlightenment and cultural accommodation during the Protestant Reformation. Individualistic salvation may be described as an emphasis on the independence of the individual from the body in terms of spiritual life. Sanctification made available through the Spirit covers the individual, the family, and the church. Justified believers are called to exhibit the holiness of God, not just as individuals, but also as a community (cf. Ex. 19:6; 1 Pet. 2:9).[30]

In addition, through the Spirit of God, dead believers progressively receive the resurrection life of Christ. They are raised by the Spirit to walk in newness of life. Believers receive the very life of Christ, the fruit of the Spirit (6:4; cf. Gal. 2:20; 5:22-23). What is resurrection life? *It is the actual impartation of the death and life of Jesus Christ through the work of the Spirit.* This is why Paul in his summation of the salvation process argues, "Those whom [God] foreknew He also predestined to be conformed to the image of His Son" (8:29). This is the meaning of Paul's all-encompassing claim, "Christ in you, the hope of glory" (Col. 1:27; cf. 3:9-10; 2 Cor. 3:17-18; Eph. 2:10; Phil. 2:5-11). For Paul, the impartation of the life of Christ through the Spirit is both the means and the goal of sanctification.

Paul uses a final "when, but now" argument to cement his emphasis on the necessity of slavery to God. He states,

> When you were slaves of sin, you were free in regard to righteousness. So what advantage did you then get from the things of which you now are ashamed? The end of those things is death. But now that you have been freed from sin and enslaved to God,

> the advantage you get is sanctification. The end is eternal life (6:20-22).

This time, Paul reminds his audience in Rome of their former loyalty to sin and their present freedom with regard to righteousness. He reminds believers of *the fruit* of their former enslavement and its residual shame. Yet, his reminders only serve to enhance the reality of their present standing. Believers have been liberated from sin through the death of Christ and are now slaves of God.

This new slavery also has its own fruit. It leads to sanctification, and even more, to eternal life. Paul ends his initial description of sanctification, the reign of grace, with a summary assertion that serves to contrast the results of opposing enslavements, "For the wages of sin is death, but the gift of God is eternal life in Christ Jesus our Lord" (6:23). Paul's point is clear: the reign of sin ends in death, but through Christ's reign, through His Lordship, God gives eternal life.

Paul's description of sanctification as enslavement to God raises questions, both ancient and modern. Why does Paul drive home the necessity of enslavement for his audience in Rome? Is it possible that Paul understands the tenacity of cultural sin expressed as ethnic enmity and its ongoing threat to the new life in Christ? We have acknowledged the difficulty of slavery as a metaphor for contemporary Christians living in the West, yet what are the consequences of rejecting its application for the life of believers? What are the consequences of neglecting the substance of Paul's teaching, especially as it relates to the acceptance of the ethnic other?

These questions bring to mind a dinner we enjoyed at the home of an Adventist leader some years ago. The dinner guests were ethnically and racially mixed. The question we discussed was the feasibility of racial unity in Adventism. A famous Adventist evangelist offered the following "wisdom": there can be no racial unity in the Adventist church until the time of trouble. When we must run to the foxholes together, then there will be unity. This evangelist is not the only Adventist leader who has expressed this notion to us. It is interesting that as Adventists, especially in evangelism, we never bring up the foxhole explanation for any other sin, e.g., alcoholism, adultery, or smoking. We teach that these sins must be abandoned now, but not ethnocentrism. We left unexamined at that table the possibility that Adventism has not submitted to its Master. His teaching with regard to ethnocentrism is plain. Is it possible that we are a people without a Lord?

Unfinished Business

Before addressing the means by which sanctification is achieved, Paul returns to his discussion of God's law and its distortion in Pharisaic Judaism and among the Judaizers (7:1-25). In this argument, he stresses the powerlessness of the law for sanctification. Paul picks up a thread introduced earlier but left undeveloped. He has stated, "For sin will not rule over you, because you are not under law but under grace" (6:14). In order to treat his upcoming argument, it is important to clarify what Paul means with the phrase "you are not under law but under grace." Paul's use of the preposition "under" is critical. He is saying that believers are no longer, like unbelieving Jews, ruled by the law. They are no longer under its reign or lordship. He has asserted that believers are now under the rule of grace; they are slaves of God (6:22). When writing to believers in Galatia, Paul puts it this way:

> But before faith came, we were kept in custody under the law, being shut up to the faith which was later to be revealed. Therefore the Law has become our tutor *to lead us* to Christ, so that we may be justified by faith. But now that faith has come, we are no longer under a tutor. For you are all sons of God through faith in Christ Jesus (Gal. 3:23-26 NASB).

It is extremely important that Paul does not say that the law has no role in the lives of his audience. He has already shown that God's law provides a knowledge of sin, and increases sin based on sinful human nature (3:20; 5:20). Paul's simple point is that God did not give His law to justify or to sanctify. The law was not given by God to save, period. As we will see, Paul envisions those under the Lordship of Christ as having the law internalized, it is "written on their hearts." Ultimately, believers are to be constrained by the love of Christ (8:1-2; 2 Cor. 5:14).

Paul's legal clarification is most likely directed to the Jewish minority in Rome (7:1-25). Like many unbelieving Jews, Jewish believers in Rome have depended on the law—Torah and the oral traditions—as a means of securing righteousness. It seems that this distortion of the role of the law has served as a ground for Jewish boasting and feelings of superiority over Gentile believers (2:1-11). In addition, it seems that a focus on the oral law has reinforced Jewish exclusivity (14:1-23). Thus, for Paul, Jewish misunderstanding of God's law and the use of oral tradition serve as major impediments to reconciliation between believing Gentiles and Jews. Paul's argument concerning the limitation of the law for new life in Christ is made in two movements: (1) believers are dead to the law, married to Christ (7:1-6); and (2) the law is inadequate as a means of sanctification (7:7-25).

Paul introduces the thorny subject of the law's limitations with the rhetorical question, "Or do you not know, brethren—for I am speaking to those who know the law—that the law has authority over someone as long as he lives?" (7:1). With the address, literally "brothers," i.e., "brothers and sisters," and the reference to knowledge of Torah, Paul signals that he is speaking directly to those of Jewish ancestry in Rome, his kinsmen according to the flesh (9:3; cf. 10:1; 11:1). As he becomes increasingly more direct in his admonitions, Paul later finds occasion to speak directly to the Gentile majority (11:13-24).

Paul begins his clarification of the limitations of God's law by using an illustration. He employs the marriage union to convince the Jewish minority to fully embrace their new life in Christ. Paul writes,

> For a married woman is bound by law to her husband while he lives, but if her husband dies she is released from the law of marriage. Accordingly, she will be called an adulteress if she lives with another man while her husband is alive. But if her husband dies, she is free from that law, and if she marries another man she is not an adulteress (7:2-3).

Paul's illustration is based on Jewish civil law. A married woman is legally bound to her husband as long as he is alive. But she is no longer bound to him when he dies. Therefore, if she gives herself to another man when married, she is considered an adulteress. But if her husband dies, she is free from that law by which she was bound. Now if she gives herself to another, she is not an adulteress.

Paul applies his illustration directly to his Jewish audience. He states, "Likewise, my brothers, you also have died to the law through the body of Christ" (7:4). Paul has argued that believers have died to sin (6:2). Now he tells Jewish believers that they have also died to the law through participation in the death of Christ (7:5a; cf. 6:15). For a first-century Jew of almost any stripe, these words would have been viewed as blasphemy, but Pharisaic Jews, in particular, viewed themselves as "disciples of Moses" (Jn. 9:28). They, like their sympathizers, the Judaizers, were wedded to the law.

It is no doubt against this backdrop that Paul shares with Christian Jews the twofold purpose of death to the law. He states, "So that you may belong to another, to him who has been raised from the dead in order that we may bear fruit for God" (6:5b). Jewish believers are no longer bound to the law so that now they may belong exclusively to Christ, their resurrected Lord. Christ is their new husband. Paul again uses the language of enslavement. His point seems to be that believers "cannot serve two masters" (Mt. 6:24). Also, believers may now bear fruit to God. Here, he echoes his earlier language of sanctification (6:22; Gal. 5:22-23).

Paul reminds his Jewish kin of the negative consequences of being under the rule of law. He again argues that before justification, "while we were living in the flesh," that is, while we Jews lived based on sinful nature received from Adam, "our sinful passions, aroused by the law, were at work in our members to bear fruit for death" (7:5; cf. Phil. 3:3-4; Gal 6:13). Paul's analysis is critical. Jews who expected righteousness through adherence to the law were disappointed. Why? Because the law could not change sinful passions, i.e., the sinful human nature. In fact, the law arouses it (cf. 5:20).

Finally, with the words "but now," Paul exposes the central claim of his illustration. He writes, "But now we have been released from the Law, having died to that by which we were bound, so that we serve in newness of the Spirit and not in oldness of the letter" (7:6 NASB). Maintaining the marriage imagery, Paul argues that Jewish believers, like a widow of a deceased spouse, have been released from the rule of the law, because they have died to what held them (cf. 7:2). In fact, Paul identifies the critical purpose for believers' death to the law. It is so that Jewish believers may serve in the new way of the Spirit and not in the old letter of the law. Paul again uses slavery language. He employs a verb, which means literally, "to slave," in order to contrast the sanctifying power of the Spirit with the old rule of the law (cf. 6:4, 22; 2 Cor. 3:6). Eventually, Paul develops this critical theme: the essential role of the Holy Spirit in sanctification (8:1-30).

Aware of the sensitivity of his Jewish audience to the subject of the law, Paul moves quickly to justify his illustration and its application (7:7-13). He does not want to leave the false impression that the law is in any way flawed. Paul wants to make it crystal clear that the problem is not God's law but indwelling sin, i.e., sinful human nature.

Paul uses the rhetorical question, "What should we say then?" to alert his audience to a critical development in the argument (7:7; cf. 3:5; 6:1). Then he poses a second question that serves as the focus of his discourse with his typical unequivocal negation. "Is the Law sin? May it never be!" (7:7a NASB). It seems clear that Paul understands the possibility of misunderstanding raised by his assertion, "The law came in to multiply the trespass" (5:20) and his claim that believers have been released from the law (7:6), thus his question: is law sin? The question is a serious one because it seems that Paul's Jewish Christian opponents have made just this accusation against his gospel (Gal. 2:4, 12; 6:12; cf. Phil. 3:2; Act. 15:1, 5).

So that there is no confusion among Roman believers, Paul addresses the issue head-on. Paul establishes his premise and suggests an example. He writes, "On the contrary, I would not have come to know sin except through the Law; for I would not have known about coveting if the Law had not said, 'You shall not covet'" (7:7b NASB). Building on his earlier claim that through the law comes a knowledge of sin, Paul seems to suggest that the law provides not only cognitive, but experiential knowledge of sin (3:20). No doubt mindful of Judaism's understanding of the tenth commandment of the Decalogue, i.e., sinful desire as of root of all sin, Paul now uses part of this commandment, "You shall not covet," to make his case (Ex. 20:17; Dt. 5:21).[31] In using this example, there can be no doubt that Paul has the moral law in mind when he discusses the limits of the law for sanctification.

Paul uses his example both to defend the law and to begin to expose indwelling sin as the real culprit (7:8-11). He makes several related points. Personifying sin, Paul argues that it uses the command not to covet to produce in him various types of coveting. Thus, he concludes that sin is dead, that is, there is no awareness of sin, without the law. Paul then observes that without consciousness of sin produced by the law, he was alive while in sin. But when the commandment came, sin revived; therefore, he died. Why? Because the commandment reveals and condemns sin. Next, Paul opines that the commandment did not deliver what he had expected. He anticipated life but the commandment, in fact, brought death. As we have seen, Paul believes that Pharisaic Judaism has promulgated this erroneous expectation of the law. And last, Paul restates the power of sin. It causes a person to think he or she can obey the commandment, but this is a deception of sin, because the law kills.

His example concluded, Paul exposes the goal of his present argument. He exonerates God's law, arguing, "So the law is holy, and the commandment is holy and just and good" (7:12). Paul attempts to establish that the problem is not the law, but sin. His claim is emphatic. The entire law of God is holy. And each commandment is holy and just and good. With the conjunction "therefore," Paul summarizes his argument, tying up the final loose end. Once again, he uses a rhetorical question and emphatic denial, "Did that which is good become death to me? May it never be!" Paul reiterates the claim just made that the law is good. He has already shown that it is sin that produces death (5:12). Yet, he emphasizes that sin takes opportunity through the law to produce death, revealing the malevolence of sin (cf. 5:20).

With the case for the law and against sin firmly established, Paul now provides a graphic illustration that would resonate with his Jewish audience in Rome (7:14-23). He describes the dilemma of the observant Jew who seeks holiness through obedience to the law. In sum, Paul depicts the conundrum for a devout Jew: embracing the rule of law and yet discovering that sin continues to reign (cf. 7:25b).

The Pharisaic Dilemma

Because of his use of the first person singular, "I" throughout this passage, some scholars conjecture that Paul is describing his own experience as a Pharisaic Jew before justification (7:7-25).[32] This is not likely because Paul's self-description in other letters offers no hint of a personal dilemma created by attempting to obey God's law. In fact, Paul maintains "Although I myself might have confidence even in the flesh. If anyone else has a mind to put confidence in the flesh, I far more . . . regarding the righteousness that is in the law, blameless" (Phil. 3:4, 8). This description argues for Paul's complete self-deception as a Pharisee under the law (cf. Jn. 9:40-41).

What is clear is that Paul is not describing the experience of a believer because from the outset, he depicts this person as one who is under the reign of sin and under the rule of the law (7:14, 17, 23, 25a). Paul has just demonstrated that for believers, the power of sin has been broken and the rule of the law has been abolished (5:12-21; 6:1-23). In fact, believers no longer struggle with the law, they have died to it (7:1-6). Believers still experience the struggle between the flesh and the Spirit. Yet, they are confident of victory through God's Spirit (Gal. 5:16-21; cf. 8:1-30). Therefore, this discussion assumes that Paul is describing the dilemma of a hypothetical Pharisaic Jew bent on pursuing righteousness through works of the law (3:20; 10:1-3). For ease of description, we will maintain Paul's use of the first person singular in our discussion of this passage. Paul sketches the dilemma (7:14-23), and then provides resolution (7:24-25).

Paul introduces the dilemma, "For we know that the law is spiritual, but I am made out of flesh, sold into sin's power" (7:14). He maintains the contrast already established between the law and sin. Evoking Jewish knowledge about the true nature of the law, he restates the conclusion of his previous argument: "The law is spiritual, holy, just and good" (cf. 7:12). Next, by way of contrast, Paul affirms his inherent condition as "fleshly," or carnal (cf. 7:5). Further, he describes himself as having been sold into sin's power. Paul's use of a metaphor depicting enslavement to sin and his description of complete impotence, should not be missed.

Now, Paul begins to outline the inner contours of his predicament. He views the contradiction in his own behavior as a mystery. He admits, "For I do not understand what I am doing, because I do not practice what I want to do, but I do what I hate." Paul describes himself as a person obsessed with his own behavior. Then, almost as a parenthesis, he argues that this contradiction between desire and action affirms the goodness of the law (7:16).

Paul exposes what he believes is the core of his dilemma. He writes, "So now I am no longer the one doing it, but it is sin living in me. For I know that nothing good lives in me, that is, in my flesh. For the desire to do what is good is with me, but there is no ability to do it" (7:17-18). Here, Paul subtly suggests that Pharisaic Judaism has not accounted for the fundamental problem created by Adam's sin and its spread to all humanity (5:12-21). He makes it abundantly clear that he is under the power of indwelling sin. With the words, "I am no longer doing it," Paul implies the loss of volition to the power of sin and again acknowledges his flesh as the problem. Then he exposes the deeper enigma, the disconnect between his knowledge and his behavior. Paul gives cognitive assent to what is good, but he lacks the power to perform it.

Paul repeats for emphasis the dilemma just described (7:19-20). Then, he identifies what he believes is the crux of Jewish dilemma. Still, in the hypothetical first person, Paul states, "So I find it to be a law that when I want to do what is good, evil lies close at hand. For I delight in the law of God in my inmost self, but I see in my members another law at war with the law of my mind, making me captive to the law of sin that dwells in my members" (7:21-23). Paul's argument seems complicated. However, it is simplified if one understands that he is describing his discovery of a principle that stands behind the Jewish conundrum related to the law. He describes it first as an internal conflict between his desire to do what is good with the existence of indwelling sin. Paul restates the conflict with more specificity. The fact that internally, his delight in God's law exposes two opposing laws. On the one hand, there is the law of his mind that wants do good, while on the other, the law of sin is controlling his members, his entire being. Paul has painted a picture of the Pharisaic dilemma that demands resolution. As we will see, for Paul, this is no abstract matter. He believes that Jewish misunderstanding of the law is an issue in their inability to accept fully believing Gentiles (14:1-12; cf. 2:1-5).

Paul provides the resolution to the Jewish conundrum: "Wretched man that I am! Who will rescue me from this body of death? Thanks be to God through Jesus Christ our Lord!" (7:24-25a). On behalf of all unbelieving Jews, Paul acknowledges his wretched condition. Then he thanks God for deliverance through Jesus Christ, the believers' Lord.

Paul later repeats the same dilemma of unbelieving Jews and suggests the same resolution with these words:

> Brethren, my heart's desire and my prayer to God for them is for *their* salvation. For I testify about them that they have a zeal for God, but not in accordance with knowledge. For not knowing about God's righteousness and seeking to establish their own, they did not subject themselves to the righteousness of God. For Christ is the end of the law for righteousness to everyone who believes (10:1-4 NASB).

Possibly to emphasize the problem and introduce his detailed solution, Paul now provides a summary statement of the Jewish dilemma related to the misuse of God's law. "So then, with my mind I am a slave to the law of God, but with my flesh I am a slave to the law of sin" (7:25b).

Paul has put a nail in the coffin of the heretical notion of righteousness by works of the law. He identifies the Holy Spirit as the power necessary for sanctification. For Paul, the law is powerless to sanctify, because of sinful human nature. He has demonstrated to his Roman audience, especially the Jews, that the power for reconciliation does not come through the observance of the law.

Are we as Adventists still dealing with the Pharisaic dilemma? Consider the story of the rich young ruler (Mk. 10:17-22). He earnestly desired eternal life. Even Jesus acknowledged that he had kept the law from his youth. Yet, when confronted with the radical choice to accept Jesus as Lord, the young man went away sorrowful. It is far easier to keep the dictums of the law than to submit to a Lord. Many can adhere to the letter of the law based on willpower. But the surrender, the death to self and the agenda of the self that is necessary for accepting the Lordship of Christ is another matter. When will we as a church take seriously the commands of Jesus: "Love one another as I have loved you" and "love your enemies?"

Christ's Life Through the Spirit

Paul moves from his description of the dilemma created by Jewish misapplication of the law to God's solution. Thus far, Paul has shown the futility of Pharisaic Judaism and the Judaizers' quest for holiness based on life under the law. He has demonstrated that there is no flaw in God's law; rather the problem is with indwelling sin. Jewish law keepers who anticipated life through obedience to the law have, in fact, experienced death. They are powerless against sin. Paul says that this outcome should have been expected because the letter kills; it does not provide life. The law condemns sin. It reveals the need of a Savior.

Paul now exposes his entire Roman audience to the reality of God's means of sanctification for those in Christ Jesus (8:1-39). It is at this point that he develops the vital role of the Holy Spirit in spiritual growth. He has already suggested that it was the Spirit who raised Jesus Christ from the dead (1:4; cf. 6:4). In addition, he has disclosed that justified believers now serve in the newness of the Spirit and not based on the letter of the law (7:6). Yet, for Paul, what exactly is the work of the Holy Spirit in salvation? More specifically, what is the Spirit's role in a community divided based on ethnicity?

Probably, the most comprehensive biblical description of the work of the Holy Spirit is found not in the letters of Paul, but in John's gospel. In the so-called "Farewell Discourse," before His crucifixion, Jesus describes for His eleven disciples the role of the third person of the Godhead (Jn. 13:31 - 16:33).

Jesus calls the Spirit another Comforter or Helper. The Spirt dwells with believers so closely that it is as if Jesus takes up residence within them. Thus, Jesus can say of the Spirit's coming to believers, "I will come to you" (Jn. 14:16-18). The Spirit's role is to teach Jesus' followers all things and to remind them of what He has taught them. "The Spirit will not provide qualitatively new or independent revelation, but will bring to light the meaning and significance of the revelation imparted by Jesus"[33] (Jn. 14:26).

John calls the Holy Spirit "the Spirt of Truth" who, along with the disciples, will testify of Jesus. The Spirit will participate with believers in missionary outreach, bearing witness about Jesus (Jn. 15:26). In addition, the Spirit will judge the world. As prosecutor, the Spirit will convict the world by providing evidence of the world's guilt in three ways: of sin, in that the world does not believe in Jesus; of righteousness, in that the Spirit, in His legal function, convicts the world of the righteousness of Jesus; and of judgment, in that the ruler of this world, the archenemy of Jesus, and those who follow him, both demon and human, now stand condemned. This is the only work, according to Scripture, that the Spirt will perform in the world (Jn. 16:8-11).

Finally, the Spirit will continue the revelatory ministry of Jesus to believers, guiding them into all truth regarding God's character and ways. The Spirit will act only on the pattern set by Jesus, and will tell His followers what is yet to come. The Spirit will help believers to understand their present in light of what Jesus has revealed about the Father in the past. The Spirit collaborates with the Father and the Son in presenting the full revelation of God. The Son gives glory to the Father and the Spirit gives glory to the Son. Because Jesus is the full revelation of God, the Spirit takes from what is Jesus' and declares it to His believers (Jn. 16:12-15).[34]

Although written some forty years after Romans, Paul would not have quibbled with John's record. In fact, he would have affirmed the words of Jesus. Yet, Paul's description of the Spirit's work in this letter addresses the situation within the Roman church. Paul uses several names to identify the third person of the Godhead: Spirit of holiness, the Spirit, Holy Spirit, the Spirit of God, and the Spirit of Christ. However, in his letter to the Romans, Paul's central concern is to emphasize that it is the Spirit who gives new life, i.e., the life of Christ, to believers. Paul argues that new life in Christ, the reception of His imparted righteousness, is achieved only through the power of God's Spirit.

To understand Paul's description of the Spirit's work in the present discussion, we must recognize that he is building on a critical assertion made earlier in the letter, "And hope does not disappoint, because the love of God has been poured out within our hearts through the Holy Spirit who was given to us" (5:5 NASB). Rightly understood, Paul has laid the predicate for sanctification. Justified believers may be confident from peace to *parousia* because they now possess the gift of God's love through the indwelling Spirit, the essential benefit necessary for spiritual growth. Paul shows later that it is the Spirit that mediates to believers God's love revealed in the person and work of Jesus Christ. This mediation of Christ through the Spirit is God's means of sanctifying believers, both as individuals and as a community. As the Spirit's mediation of Christ is received among God's people, reconciliation and unity are the result.

After reiterating the certainty of believers' new standing in Christ, Paul describes the work of the Spirit in sanctification and indirectly suggests the process by which reconciliation and unity can be achieved in the assemblies in Rome (8:1-30). Seemingly, enraptured by the plan of salvation, Paul ends his description of the Spirit's work with praise to God the Father through Christ (8:31-39).

He opens with a definitive statement about the new reality of believers. Paul writes, "Therefore, there is now no condemnation for those who are in Christ Jesus" (8:1). With the use of the conjunction "therefore," Paul states a claim already established. The wrath of God has been assuaged through the substitutionary death of Christ (3:25; cf. 1:18; 2:5, 8). Justified believers no longer stand under divine condemnation counted through the law (5:12-16; 7:6). They enjoy reconciliation with God (5:1-11). To be in Christ is Paul's shorthand for describing a transfer from one dominion to another, from life under the reign of sin to life under the reign of grace (5:12-21; cf. Col. 1:13). The phrase "in Christ" sums up the primary identity of believers (6:11; cf. 1:6-7; 5:1-2, 9-11). It serves to gather all believers into one body where *"there is neither Jew nor Gentile,* neither slave nor free, nor is there male and female, for you are all one in Christ Jesus" (Gal. 3:28; cf. 12:3-8). All believers, whether Gentiles or Jews, are now free to love, because they are secure in Christ. It is this common identity that Paul now reinforces.

Yet, in order that none will be deceived as to the means by which new life in Christ is maintained, Paul identifies the Holy Spirit. Here, Paul is unambiguous. He asserts, "For the law of the Spirit of life in Christ Jesus has set you free from the law of sin and of death" (8:2). Paul exposes his audience in Rome to the power of sanctified living. His claim has two dimensions. He maintains that there are two opposing principles at work the law of the Spirit of life in Christ and the law of sin and of death. Then he asserts the ability of the Spirit to break the power of sin and death. In fact, Paul is arguing that for those in Christ, the Spirit has broken the dual reign. The Spirit has set each believer free from the power of sin and death. Believers share this common freedom in Christ.

Paul establishes the law of the Spirit of life as the *sine qua non* for sanctification. God's exclusive means of producing the imparted righteousness of Christ both in the individual and in the believing community is through the Spirit. Just as the Second Person of the Godhead was the active agent in creation (Col. 1:15-16; Jn. 1:3), the Holy Spirit is the active agent in sanctification (cf. Gen. 1:2). God the Father, through the Spirit, must continually impart the life of Christ to justified believers. Paul wants the Roman believers to appreciate that only the Spirit is able to create newness of life (6:4; 7:6). This principle is critical to Paul's understanding of how reconciliation and unity are ultimately achieved.

Now, in order to provide absolute clarity, Paul exposes a radical juxtaposition between the law's inability and God's ability. Paul says, "For what the Law could not do, weak as it was through the flesh, God did" (8:3a NASB). He again addresses the inability of the law to produce holiness, because it is limited by the flesh. With awe-inspiring clarity, he asserts the divine solution to the problem of the law's inability based on indwelling sin. His remedy: "God *did*." His point is emphatic. What the law could not do and was not intended to do, God did. How did God address the dilemma created by the righteous demands of the law and human sinfulness? Paul answers, "He condemned sin in the flesh by sending His own Son in flesh like ours under sin's domain, and as a sin offering" (8:3b HCSB). Paul now affirms once and for all that God's response to the problem of sin is Christ. God has provided holistic salvation through the Son. Earlier, Paul demonstrated that God justifies those who believe through the death of Christ (3:21-26). Now he extends God's solution to sanctification. Believers are also made righteous through faith in Christ.

Next, Paul describes the purpose for Christ's sacrificial death. Christ died "so that the righteous requirement of the Law might be fulfilled in us, who do not walk according to the flesh but according to the Spirit" (8:4 NASB). Paul makes two critical moves. First, in context, he explains that God, through the death of Christ, satisfies God's own just requirement of the law, for the law condemns, it requires death for sin (6:23; cf. 1 Tim. 1:9; Lev. 20:1-27). Moreover, the law's requirement is holiness—a requirement that the law demands but cannot produce (8:3; cf. 7:7-13). Paul's point is that through Christ's death, God has made fulfillment possible *in us,* that is, in believers. In other words, through the death of Christ, God made internalized holiness available to all believers (cf. 2:28-29).

Paul moves now to delineate the crucial requirement for sanctification. He does this by establishing a contrast between two ways of being, not just behaving: the flesh versus the Spirit (Gal. 5:16-17). Paul uses the expression, literally, "walking around" in the Spirit to stress that sanctification is not achieved through the life lived according to the flesh, but life according to the Spirit.

Although Paul clarifies the two ways of living throughout the rest of the passage, it is important to note his use of the term "the flesh." In some cases, he uses the flesh in a neutral way to describe human beings or the human race (11:14; Gal. 2:16; 1 Cor. 1:29). In other cases, Paul uses the flesh in morally negative ways: human nature in open rebellion against God, or as human nature independent of God that relies on culturally-based value systems.[35]

In the present context, his emphasis is on life lived according to human cultural value systems (cf. 12:1-2). Life according to the flesh is any attempt to live independently of God's saving work in Christ. It encompasses the embracing of any worldview that is not centered in Christ. In fact, Paul later sums up life according to the flesh with the assertion, "For whatever does not proceed from faith is sin" (14:23). Ethnocentrism is thus by definition life according to the flesh, because it is the negative human evaluation of others in comparison to one's own ethnic group. For Paul, "ethnocentrism" in Rome was expressed as Jewish judgmentalism toward Gentiles or Gentile arrogance towards Jews (2:1-16; 11:13-24; 14:1-23).

Paul now builds on the contrast between Adam and Christ, between the "reign of sin and death" and "the reign of grace" (5:12-21). He describes two classes of people who embrace opposing ways of living (8:5-11). Paul uses the categories "according to the flesh" and "according to the Spirit" to depict dramatically the conflict between those who live their lives in Christ and those who live their lives opposed to God. As we will see, Paul uses his description of life according to the Spirit to create a grammar for applied sanctification for believers in Rome. He is mindful that life according to the flesh remains a potential threat to those in Christ. Thus, his exhortations to justified believers on how to live in the believing community and in Greco-Roman society assume life lived according to the power of the Spirit (12:1 - 15:13).

In this passage, Paul contrasts human thought and its ontological consequences with life according to the Spirit. He establishes the two opposing ways of living, "For those who live according to the flesh think about the things of the flesh, but those who live according to the Spirit, about the things of the Spirit" (8:5). He describes not merely two different ways of thinking, but two different life orientations. On the one hand, those who exist according to the flesh are obsessed with what is carnal or earthly: life lived in accordance with the desires of fallen, sinful human nature that is opposed to God (cf. 7:5, 18, 25). In his letter to the Galatians, Paul describes this orientation with these words:

> Now the works of the flesh are obvious: fornication, impurity, licentiousness, idolatry, sorcery, *enmities, strife, jealousy, anger, quarrels, dissensions, factions,* envy, drunkenness, carousing, and things like these. I am warning you, as I warned you before: those who do such things will not inherit the kingdom of God (Gal. 5:19-21).

In general, life according to the flesh in Paul's day took the form of adherence to cultural values and practices such as the honor-shame system, social stratification, and an emphasis on ethnic identity and privilege. As depicted in the above vice-list, life according to the flesh can find expression personally as well as socially.

On the other hand, those who live according to the Spirit focus on the things of the Spirit. Indeed, believers must reject the Greco-Roman value of self-mastery through reason (paganism) and law (Judaism).[36] They must experience the paradox of voluntary submission to the Spirit of Christ. Paul describes this paradox in Philippians 2:13: "Work out your own salvation with fear and trembling; for it is God who is at work in you, enabling you both to will and to work for his good pleasure." This is precisely what Paul has in mind with the use of language that implies the leading of the Spirit (cf. Gal. 5:16-18, 24).

Yet, it is important to point out that Paul's view of life according to the Spirit is not behaviorally focused. For Paul, life according to the Spirit is another way of describing who believers become through the impartation of the life of Christ. As opposed to the flesh, Paul in Galatians describes Christ's life imparted by the Spirit.

> By contrast, the fruit of the Spirit is love, joy, peace, patience, kindness, generosity, faithfulness, gentleness, and self-control. There is no law against such things. And those who belong to Christ Jesus have crucified the flesh with its passions and desires. If we live by the Spirit, let us also be guided by the Spirit (Gal. 5:22-25).

"The fruit of the Spirit" is simply another way that Paul describes the character of Christ mediated to justified believers through the Spirit. Richard Blackaby's comments are significant. He states,

> The moment you became a Christian, the Holy Spirit began a divine work to produce Christ's character in you. Regardless of who you are, the Spirit works from the same model, Jesus Christ. The Spirit looks to Christ in order to find the blueprint for your character. The Spirit will immediately begin helping you experience and practice the same love that Jesus had when He laid down His life for His friends. The same joy He experienced will now fill you. The identical peace that guarded the heart of Jesus, even as He was being beaten and mocked, will be the peace that the Spirit works to instill in you. The patience Jesus had for His

> most unteachable disciple will be the patience that the Spirit now develops in you. The kindness Jesus showed toward children and sinners will soften your heart toward others. There will be a goodness about you that is only explainable by the presence of the Spirit of God. The Spirit will build the same faithfulness into you that led Jesus to be entirely obedient to His Father. The Spirit will teach you self-control so that you will have strength to do what is right and to resist temptation. All of this is as natural as the growth of fruit on a tree. You do not have to orchestrate it on your own. It automatically begins the moment you become a believer. How quickly it happens depends upon how completely you yield yourself to the Holy Spirit's activity.[37]

Although Blackaby limits his observations to the Christian individual, Paul has in mind not only individuals, but a people characterized by Christ's love, joy, peace, and so on—a community infused with the life of Christ (cf. 12:9-21). Soon after, Paul reminds the Roman believers that Christ's character is produced with a condition; believers must share His suffering (8:17-18; cf. 5:3-5).

Paul reiterates the diametrically opposed ways of existence with their results. "For the mind-set of the flesh is death, but the mind-set of the Spirit is life and peace" (8:6). Here, it seems that Paul's goal is to emphasize the radical difference in outcomes. For Paul, those who exist in order to gratify fallen human nature will experience non-existence, the second death, while those who live in and through the Spirit can anticipate glorification, eternal existence with God.

Paul now launches a scathing critique against existence according to the flesh. He writes, "For the mind-set of the flesh is hostile to God because it does not submit itself to God's law, for it is unable to do so. Those who are in the flesh cannot please God" (8:7-8). Paul makes two claims about those still under the reign of sin. First, all fleshly living is in opposition to God. He uses the language of enmity or hatred of God. To exist in the flesh is to live as God's enemy. Life according to the flesh demonstrates its hostility to God in the rejection of God's law. Those in the flesh are unable to yield to God's law. This claim raises questions. Does Paul's description include both paganism and Judaism? Do both unbelieving pagans and unbelieving Jews reject submission to God's law? Are both "bad flesh" and "good flesh" hostile to God and His law? Clearly, from Paul's perspective, the answer to all these questions is an emphatic "Yes" (1:18 - 3:20; cf. Tit. 3:2-8).

Paul has already demonstrated that both Gentiles and Jews fall under God's judgment. Yet, he has taken great pains to show that even the devout Jew, while attempting to obey the law, unwittingly rejects God's law and is unable to submit. This too is life according to the flesh (7:7-23; 10:1-3; cf. Jn. 3:5-8; 6:63). As Paul clarifies later in the letter, God's law is summed up in one ethical claim, "Love does no wrong to a neighbor; therefore, love is the fulfilling of the law" (13:10). Paul makes clear that all fleshly living is unpleasing to God. He will later directly address ethnocentrism and its consequences in Rome. For now, it is important for him to establish that God is not pleased with any manifestation of life according to the flesh.

What does life according to the flesh look like in Adventism today? Perhaps this example will help. We had just finished a presentation on spiritual leadership with workers in a black conference. Evidently, we had crossed an imaginary line, because the next speaker, a retired leader, stressed the need to hold onto our historic grievances as black Adventists. Then he preceded to recap the Lucy Byard story mentioned in our introduction.

The Lucy Byard incident is universally known and frequently cited among African American Adventists, many of whom do not even know her name. Her tragic story was one of the catalysts for the formation of black ("Regional") conferences in the Seventh-day Adventist Church. Mrs. Lucille (Lucy) Byard (1877-1943) was a member of the Jamaica Long Island Seventh-day Adventist Church. A musician, she played the piano and organ and directed the church choir. When she became ill in 1943, her husband enlisted the help of Pastor Jeter Cox to arrange for her to be treated at the Seventh-day Adventist Washington Sanitarium. After traveling by train from New York with her husband, Mrs. Byard was seen in the emergency room at the Sanitarium. Apparently, the admissions personnel assumed the light-skinned Byards to be white. But when the personnel noticed that Mr. Byard had designated their race as black on the admissions documents, Mrs. Byard was refused admission to the Sanitarium. Although she was gravely ill, her husband rushed her by taxi to Freedman's Hospital at Howard University, but it was too late. Mrs. Byard died of pneumonia.[38]

This is a terrible chapter in our history as Adventists; a life was lost because of racism. And every time racial reconciliation is brought up with black Adventists this story is rehearsed. It is as if this particular wrong can never be forgiven. The need for white Adventists to repent and to confess and ask forgiveness for the death of Lucy Byard is glaring and long overdue. But Christian forgiveness, ultimately, needs no confession from wrong doers; believers forgive because they have been forgiven by God through the death of Christ (Eph. 4:31-32; cf. Mt. 6:9-15; 18:21-35).

The account of the murders in Charleston, South Carolina, is instructive. As you recall, the Charleston church shooting (also known as the Charleston church massacre) occurred at the historic Emanuel African Methodist Episcopal Church in downtown Charleston, South Carolina, on the evening of June 17, 2015. Nine people were killed by a white supremacist terrorist during a prayer service, including the senior pastor (and state senator) Clementa C. Pinckney. Three other victims survived the shooting. The gunman, Dylann Roof, when later arrested was found to have espoused racial hatred on a website; and in a manifesto published before the violence, he confessed to a hope that his action would ignite a race war.[39]

What was remarkable about this incident was the reaction of church members, especially the families of the victims. At a bond hearing bereaved family members were allowed to address the killer. One by one they lined up to offer forgiveness to the impassive Roof; they said that they were praying for his soul and hoped that he would find salvation. Newspaper columnist John Dickerson made the following prescient statement: "It was neither expected nor explicable, that forgiveness. Such forgiveness is unseen in the animal world, is illogical in the rational world, is nonsensical to common human nature. Such forgiveness is humanity at its most human, or perhaps its most divine."[40]

We know that the church and families' forgiveness *was* divine. Only the Spirit of Christ could inspire such an action. But we, as Adventists, must ask ourselves some hard questions. When will white Adventism corporately, especially in North America, repent and confess for the death of Lucy Byard and the systemic injustice it represents?[41] When will black Adventists, especially African Americans, forgive this past example of corporate sin? When will we finally forgive white Adventism for her death? And when will we all recognize that the lack of repentance, confession, and forgiveness is life according to the flesh and as such a rejection of Christ?

Paul describes the practical reality of life in the Spirit, and by so doing he exposes the Spirit's essential work. He states,

> However, you are not in the flesh but in the Spirit, if indeed the Spirit of God dwells in you. But if anyone does not have the Spirit of Christ, he does not belong to Him. If Christ is in you, though the body is dead because of sin, yet the spirit is alive because of righteousness. But if the Spirit of Him who raised Jesus from the dead dwells in you, He who raised Christ Jesus from the dead will also give life to your mortal bodies through His Spirit who dwells in you (8:9-11 NASB).

Paul articulates the significance of his comparison between the flesh and the Spirit with specific regard to the situation of believers in Rome. He builds on his earlier claim that believers, through Christ's death, have been transferred from the reign of sin to the reign of grace (5:12-21). He emphasizes that believers have moved from life dominated by the flesh to life in the Spirit. For the first time, Paul uses the language of indwelling related to the Spirit. He has discussed indwelling sin as the defining characteristic of life in Adam. Now he asserts that the possession of the indwelling Spirit is the definitive mark of those who belong to Christ.

Paul makes an important claim that can only be understood if one recognizes that with the word "if," he is describing the present condition of believers and its consequences. Paul is saying that because Christ is in believers, even though their physical bodies are subject to death because of sin, their spirits are alive because of their shared justification (5:12, 17, 20; cf. Eph. 2:1-5). Because believers possess the same Spirit who had the power to raise Christ from the dead, they can be certain that this self-same Spirit will give them the resurrection life of Christ (cf. 6:1-5).

In context, what is Paul saying about the work of the Spirit? As the Spirit alone could raise Jesus from the dead, so only has the Spirit the power to give life in the present to believers. In other words, sanctification is the work of divinity. For Paul, the life that the Holy Spirit gives is Christ Himself, i.e., Christlikeness. The life of Christ mediated by the Spirit is the spiritual power to resist and overcome sin. Paul's depiction of life and its source is radically different from "the Jewish belief that life is found in the words of the law"[42] (cf. Jn. 5:38-39).

With his description of the work of the Spirit, Paul is not engaged in empty rhetoric. There are important implications here in his exhortations to reconciliation and unity that are addressed later in the letter. Paul does not urge believers to act in their own strength or simply based on a legal standard. Rather, because of Christ's indwelling through the Spirit and the security of God's love that this implies, believers possess Spirit-enabled power in the present to resist fleshly living, including ethnocentrism. Sin's power is broken through the indwelling Spirit of Jesus Christ (8:31-39; Phil. 4:13). This is why the power of the Spirit is necessary for reconciliation and unity.

Paul's portrayal of the Holy Spirit as the power for reconciliation and unity in the body of Christ echoes an important truth implicit in the Farewell Discourse of Jesus, and especially His High Priestly Prayer (Jn. 13:31 - 17:26). After assuring His disciples that He would be present through the Spirit to comfort, enable, and guide, Jesus prays for Himself, the eleven apostles, and all believers until the second coming. As a part of His prayer for end-time believers, Jesus makes two critical points (Jn. 17:20-26). First, He prays for a unity among believers that is analogous to the oneness between the Father and the Son. *This is the only means by which unbelievers will come to believe that the historical Jesus is indeed Christ, the Savior of the world.* For Jesus, this is the essence of evangelism (Jn. 13:34-35), not baptismal statistics or propositional truth.

Then Jesus suggests that this type of divine oneness among believers cannot be achieved through human effort. Even with the best of intentions, the oneness that God intends cannot be manufactured through programs, structural charges, politics, legislation, or public relations. Jesus maintains that divine oneness, like salvation itself, comes from above. It comes from Christ's Spirit (Jn. 3:3; 6:63). Genuine reconciliation and unity is a gift from God, thus the indispensable role of the Holy Spirit.

Again, with the transitional conjunction "therefore," and with the use of familial language, "brothers and sisters," Paul seeks to bolster the common identity of the believers in Rome and emphasize the community's obligation to God in response to salvation (8:12-17). He is fully aware that although believers have been set free from the reign of sin, the possibility of existence according to the flesh remains a genuine threat. While believers should not experience the struggle of unbelieving Jews or

Judaizers, between the flesh and the law, because believers have died to the law, nevertheless, the struggle between the flesh and the Spirit is real, even for those in Christ.

Paul reminds believers that those who have been justified through Christ and who walk according to the Spirit are not debtors to the flesh, to live according to its dictates. As Paul brings his description of the work of the Spirit in producing shared holiness to an end, he again stacks language of common identity (cf. 1:6-7; 5:1-11). Both Gentiles and Jews are debtors, not to the flesh, i.e., self-gratification and human cultural systems, but to God through the Spirit. Paul's words are not abstract but contextually relevant. Later in the letter, Paul admonishes Gentile and Jewish believers to reject conformity to the pattern of the Greco-Roman world: its values, attitudes, beliefs, and practices. He is not concerned with whether the conformity emanates from Gentile culture or Jewish culture. His concern is that those in Christ reject life according to the flesh and with renewed minds live according to the Spirit in response to God's mercy in Christ (12:1-2).

Paul reiterates the fact that death is the consequence of fleshly living. Then he moves to a critical theme of his present argument. Paul now introduces the necessity of Spirit-produced death of the body. He states, "But if by the Spirit you put to death the deeds of the body, you will live" (8:13). Paul has already made clear that new life in Christ is characterized by participation in Christ's death and has hinted that this is the work of the Spirit (6:4). What was hinted is now made explicit. Paul demands that believers are to participate with the Spirit in destroying the practices of the body.

Indeed, he argues that it is by this Spirit-aided death that believers paradoxically live. In writing to the Galatians, he describes this paradox: "I have been crucified with Christ; and it is no longer I who live, but Christ lives in me; and the *life* which I now live in the flesh I live by faith in the Son of God, who loved me and gave Himself up for me" (Gal. 2:20 NASB). What Paul has experienced as an individual, he now enjoins on the Roman communities. Paul's use of body includes the human spirit, soul, and body, that is, the whole person (1 Thess. 5:23). Paul views Spirit-produced death as vital to sanctification. As we have seen and will see, Paul's call to participate in the death of Christ through the Spirit is not just to the individual but to the entire community. Moreover, when Paul speaks of putting to death the deeds of the body there can be no doubt that he has in mind the virulent ethnocentrism that now divides Roman believers.

Paul now turns to the goal of his present discussion. He wants to emphasize that through the Spirit, Roman believers share a common identity, with its present privileges and challenges, and a glorious future inheritance. Paul exposes Gentile and Jewish believers to the criterion for divine sonship. He writes, "For *all* who are being led by the Spirit of God, these are sons of God" (8:14 NASB). Paul's words take on added relevance in light of the cultural contexts of both Roman and Jewish audiences.

For Roman believers, the term "son of God" was in common parlance. It was used as a reference to the Caesars. Octavian (Caesar Augustus) used the term "Caesar, son of the divine one" on coins bearing his image in order to establish his authority by making a connection between himself and his deified predecessors. Thus, Octavian presented himself as one who had inherited the name of Caesar and was the son of the god, Julius Caesar.[43]

In Judaism, the term "sons" or the concept of "sonship" was often used to identify the descendants of Abraham, the children of Israel (Ex. 4:22; Ps. 29:1). Sonship was determined by ancestry. Thus, in the time of Paul, the criteria for sonship among Jews was physical descent and religious practice.[44] By contrast, Paul argues that to be sons of God is determined solely by submission to the Spirit, simply put, all those who have been justified, who are now led by the Spirit, whether Gentiles or Jews. In other words, all believers are children of God to the extent that they relinquish complete control to the Spirit of God.

With the words, "For you did not receive a spirit of slavery to fall back into fear, but you received the Spirit of adoption, by whom we cry out, "*Abba*, Father!" (8:15 HCSB), Paul expands his understanding of what it means to be sons of God. He subtly contrasts proper enslavement to God with believers' former slavery to the reign of sin, which issued in fear. In another letter, Paul claims that "God has not given us [believers] a spirit of fear, but of power, love and sound judgment" (2 Tim. 1:7). Indirectly, Paul seems to have in view the threat and ultimate powerlessness of Satan against those in Christ, who live by the Spirit (cf. 8:31-39; 16:20). Yet, Paul's deeper, familial point is to affirm that all believers have received the Spirit of adoption.

Paul connects two claims. He says that the Spirit of God adopts all believers, both Gentiles and Jews into God's family. There is no other means of access. Adoption was common in the time of Paul, so his audience would have been very familiar with this practice. The Greek word used by Paul means literally, "to make [someone] a son." Almost entirely exclusive to males, adoptees could come from families of equal status to the adopter or could have been former slaves. Most of the Caesars were adopted by their predecessors. Adoptions were initiated for reasons of childlessness, estrangement from the biological heir, reinforcement of political connections, enhancement of family social status, and interfamilial alliances. Adoption in the Greco-Roman world was viewed very positively. There were four effects of adoption: change of family, change of name, change of home, and new responsibilities and privileges. "The adopted son became a member of the family, just as if he had been born of the blood of the adopter; and he was invested with all [of its] privileges."[45] The adopted son received full rights to succession and the capacity to inherit.[46]

Some would argue that the adoption metaphor supersedes and transforms Paul's use of the metaphor of slavery. Yet, there is no evidence in the letter to support this idea. In fact, as you will recall, Paul introduces himself to the believers in Rome as a slave of Christ (1:1). It would be understood that Paul views the standing of believers paradoxically, including both enslavement and adoption. Believers are willing slaves but more than slaves, they are members of God's family. Enslavement to God is necessary to navigate in a world characterized by sin. However, believers understand that slavery to God while in the mortal body produces genuine freedom (1 Cor. 9:1-23).

Then Paul relates this new familial standing of believers accomplished through the Spirit with deep emotional intimacy. Believers "cry out, Abba, Father." Paul uses the terms, one Aramaic, the other Greek, to express believers' dependence on God as Father. Thus, he appeals to both Gentile and Jewish members of the community. Some have observed that the word "Abba" was used by Jewish children as a term of endearment and should be translated with the English "Daddy." Others reject this claim on the grounds that this translation reads modern sensibilities into the text. Nevertheless, there can be no doubt that Paul envisions a deep intimacy between the Father and believers through the Spirit (cf. Gal. 4:6; Mk. 14:16).

Paul develops the further implications of this intimacy. He argues that the Spirit has the additional responsibility of personal confirmation of the believers' familial status. Paul says, "The Spirit Himself testifies together with our spirit that we are God's children" (8:16 NASB). Here, it seems that Paul argues for agreement between the Holy Spirit and the believer's spirit.

Yet, the goal of the Spirit's witness is to assure believers, both Gentiles and Jews, that they are children of God. Thus, they are all siblings in Christ. Further, Paul begins to expose the profound future implications of membership in God's family. He writes, "And if children, also heirs—heirs of God and coheirs with Christ—seeing that we suffer with Him so that we may also be glorified with Him" (8:17 HCSB). In this verse, Paul establishes a future fact with a condition. He identifies the joint benefit of being adopted through the Spirit into God's family as His children. Believers, Gentiles and Jews together, are heirs.

Although Paul appropriates the inheritance language familiar to both Roman and Jewish cultures, his thoughts are not temporal. Believers are heirs of God and coheirs with Christ. They will share in an eternal inheritance bestowed by God their Father. In addition, believers will participate in the inheritance allotted to God's only true heir, Jesus Christ. Yet, the anticipated inheritance associated with sanctification has a temporal, Christological condition. Believers *together* must share the suffering of Christ (cf. 5:3). Paul seems to suggest that just as Christ entered into His glory through suffering, believers are to follow His path to glorification *together*.

Paul's familial language in this passage is purposeful. It must be understood against the backdrop of Roman division. All common identity language, "debtors," "children of God," "heirs of God," and "joint heirs with Christ," is used to heighten the rhetorical pressure for submission to Spirit-produced reconciliation and unity.

Paul wants Roman Christians to understand that in light of the cross, believers constitute one family different from those who live according to the flesh. Thus, the primary responsibility of the Holy Spirit is to produce one people conformed to the image of God's Son (8:29).

A Shared Future

Finally, Paul moves his audience in Rome from a focus on sanctification, individual and corporate, to glorification, their shared future with God (8:18-25; 15:13). He continues to build on the theme of the certainty of future hope in spite of the reality of present affliction, first introduced as a benefit of justification (5:3-4). Paul seems to reflect on his own suffering for Christ (8:18; cf. 2 Cor. 11:23-29). He then compares his own present suffering and by extension the suffering of all believers to their glorious future (cf. 8:17). Based on this comparison, Paul determines that the present distress of believers is insignificant when compared with the glory to be revealed (cf. 1:17; 2 Cor. 4:17). Paul uses a form of the verb "to groan" and the noun "sigh" to depict metaphorically the tension between present suffering and future glory. He first describes the groans of both the creation and believers, and then explains the necessity of the Spirit's groaning on behalf of those in Christ (8:19-28).

Paul makes the cryptic statement, "For the creation eagerly waits with anticipation for God's sons to be revealed" (8:19). He personifies God's creation and suggests that the creation is waiting for the children of God to be "unveiled." In other words, the creation awaits the glorification of believers. Paul recalls the fall of Adam and Eve in Eden and God's curse on the creation as a consequence (8:20-22; cf. Gen. 3:17-19). He then argues that God subjected the creation to decay in the expectation that both the creation and the children would experience freedom from corruption.

Still using personification, Paul states, "We know that the whole creation has been groaning as in the pains of childbirth right up to the present time" (8:22 NIV). Here, Paul uses imagery of a mother in childbirth to describe the condition of the creation as it awaits freedom from corruption. He depicts the creation as groaning with labor pains from the time God subjected it to futility until the present when it waits for liberation.

Paul now turns his focus from the groaning of creation in anticipation of freedom to the present situation of believers. He argues that like the creation that groans, believers who have received the "first fruits of the Spirit" groan internally as they await a final adoption (8:23; cf. 5:5; 2 Cor. 1:22). Paul has used the metaphor of Spirit adoption to affirm that believers are God's children. Now he uses adoption as a metaphor for the redemption of the believers' resurrected bodies (1 Cor. 15:12-58).

Paul builds on his earlier comments that as a result of justification, believers "rejoice in the hope of the glory of God" (5:1-2; 8:24-25). He explains that the hope of bodily resurrection is part of salvation. It seems that Paul's purpose is to clarify the nature of future hope. He argues that hope is not based on what is seen. Hope received by believers as a consequence of justification does not rely on sensory experience (cf. 5:1-11). Like the hope possessed by Abraham, believers' hope focuses on the unseen, that is, God and the promises in Christ, and is therefore patient. It is characterized by endurance (cf. 4:18).

Paul discloses the role of the Spirit as believers groan awaiting final redemption (8:26-28). He pictures the Spirit as the constant helper of believers in their pervasive frailty (cf. Jn. 14:25). He states, "In the same way the Spirit also helps our weakness" (8:26 NASB). Paul views weakness as part of the ongoing condition of those who have been justified and who await glorification (cf. 1 Cor. 2:1; 2 Cor. 12:7-10). He identifies prayer as a primary example of weakness for believers as they wait for redemption. In fact, Paul stresses that believers' petitions are misguided, making the intercession of the Holy Spirit necessary. It is in this context that he says that the Spirit acts as a go-between or representative before God, interpreting the prayers of believers with the Spirit's wordless groaning.

In an attempt to clarify the working of the Spirit as an intercessor on behalf of believers, Paul describes the cooperation of God the Father and God the Spirit while believers pray as individuals and in community. He has established that believers do not know for what to pray. Yet God, who knows the hearts of believers, their motivations and affections, also knows the mind of the Spirit. In turn, the Spirit intercedes on behalf of the saints, literally, "in accordance with God," that is, with God's will. Through this divine collaboration, the ignorance of believers in prayer is counterbalanced.

Paul seems to recognize the mysterious nature of his description of the workings of God on behalf of believers. Therefore, he moves to a definitive statement of assurance. He writes, "And we know that in all things God works for the good of those who love him, who have been called according to his purpose" (8:28). His point is that in the end, in spite of present suffering, which is not good, believers can be confident that God is continuously at work producing eternal good (cf. 5:1-10). Paul refers to the formative language of calling from his introduction to describe believers. There, they are identified as "called to belong to Christ" and those "called to be saints" (cf. 1:6-7). Here, Paul adds that believers have been called according to God's purpose. As we will see in what follows, Paul employs the language of divine election. All of this is the semantics of corporate holiness.

Paul concludes his description of the threefold groaning—of the creation, of believers, and of the Spirit—in anticipation of bodily redemption with the reason believers can be confident that the final outcome will be for their good. He again uses a literary device called chain syllogism to make the point that believers will experience glorification, their shared destiny (cf. 5:3-5a). Paul states, "For those whom he foreknew he also predestined to be conformed to the image of his Son, in order that he might be the firstborn within a large family. And those whom he predestined he also called; and those whom he called he also justified; and those whom he justified he also glorified" (8:29-30).

In this passage, two facts are assumed about God. With the use of the phrase "have foreknowledge of" or "to choose beforehand," Paul assumes both God's sovereign foreknowledge, that is, God's omniscience and God's right to choose beforehand based on knowledge. And in a related assertion, Paul assumes that God had intimate knowledge of all those who would respond by faith to the gift of salvation through Jesus Christ (3:21-26; 11:2; cf. Eph. 1:4). It is on the basis of God's knowledge of those who would trust God's salvation through Christ that Paul now adds that God "predestined" or "determined beforehand" that these believers, both Jews and Gentiles, would "be conformed to the image of His Son." In addition, Paul envisions a progressive conformity to the image of God's Son. Thus, he argues that Christ as "the firstborn" will bring many conformed "brothers and sisters" into glory (cf. 8:15-18). "The use of the word 'many' signals the fulfillment of the Abrahamic covenant, in which 'all nations' were blessed in Abraham (Gen. 12:3). In the Old Testament, Israel was God's firstborn (Ex. 4:22), but now we see that Jesus Christ is God's firstborn, and one becomes part of God's family through union with him."[47]

It is important to note that for Paul, "conformity to the image of Christ" is both the language and goal of sanctification made possible by the Spirit (8:29; cf. 2 Cor. 3:18; Col. 3:10; Gen. 1:26-27). Additionally, the fostering of Christlikeness is Paul's goal in writing to Roman believers. His desire for their growth is the reason for his detailed explication of the gospel of God. From the outset, Paul has sought to undermine ethnic and religious factionalism by explaining God in Christ. He knows that genuine reconciliation and unity in Rome can only be achieved through the impartation of the life of Jesus Christ (1:8-13; 6:1-23; cf. Eph. 4:11-16).

Finally, Paul completes his chain. He adds that those predestined before time began are the called, or elect, of God. Believing Gentiles and Jews are God's elect, an idea that would be scandalous to the first-century Jew (1:6; cf. 9:11, 24-25). Jews viewed Israel as the elect of God. According to Paul, believers can have confidence in the fact that those who God called, God justified and will also glorify (3:21-26). Paul's vocabulary of God's foreknowledge and predestination is a part of his understanding of divine election. God's sovereign right to elect becomes critical to his later discussion concerning true Israel. Paul later argues that God knew the full number of both Jews and Gentiles who will be saved by faith in Jesus (9:1 - 11:36; cf. esp. 9:11, 24-25; 11:2).

Paul's point is that from beginning to end, from before time to eternity, it is God—Father, Son, and Spirit—Who works for the good of God's children. Paul's argument has come full circle. God, through the death and resurrection of Jesus Christ, has justified believers. God, through the Spirit, is sanctifying believers by imparting to them the resurrection life of Christ. God will certainly glorify all those who continue to trust God's love revealed in Jesus (3:21 - 8:30). This is the shared reality for all those in Christ.

Paul's instruction on sanctification through the Spirit is far more than theological abstraction. It is part of his announced desire to strengthen believers in Rome (1:11-12). Paul's teaching on the impartation of the life of Christ to believers through the Spirit is vital to his purpose of reconciling Gentiles and Jews. He has demonstrated that power for holiness is not provided through the law, through knowledge of what is right. For Paul, the power for holiness manifested in reconciliation and unity must come from the Spirit of God, the same power that raised Jesus Christ from the dead (1:4; 6:4; 8:11). It is the Spirit that gives believers newness of life, the very life of Christ. And it is only through the Holy Spirit that oneness will be achieved among believers in Rome.

More than Conquerors

Paul ends his description of the Spirit's work of mediation of the life Christ to the Romans with a doxology, a hymn in praise of God (8:31-39). Yet, Paul's praise to God for what God has accomplished in Christ seems to be tempered by the reality of a potential threat to the wellbeing of believers (cf. Eph. 6:10-20). Paul is acutely aware that Satan, the adversary, will continue to harass believers until *parousia.* Thus, Paul designs his doxology to assure believers in Rome that Satan is in fact defeated (16:20; Col. 2:15). He praises God because believers are more than conquerors through Jesus Christ. They enjoy absolute security based on divine love. Paul's praise has two stanzas: the potential threat (8:31-34) and God's love in Christ (8:35-39).

Paul again uses a series of rhetorical questions both to introduce his doxological argument and to announce its theme (8:31-34). He uses the question "if God is for us, who is against us" to affirm God's faithfulness on behalf of believers and to suggest a real threat. With the assertion and question "He who did not spare His own Son, but delivered Him over for us all, how will He not also with Him freely give us all things?" (8:32 NASB), Paul offers irrefutable evidence of God's faithfulness and love for believers. The fact that God sacrificed God's own Son for believers is positive proof that God will continue to provide everything necessary for their salvation (3:21-26; 5:6-8, 10).

Paul again employs questions interspersed with answers to hint at the identity of the adversary and to expose God's solution (8:33-34). He uses judicial imagery to heighten the force of his argument. Paul poses the question, "Who can bring a charge against God's elect?" (8:33a). This question has its precedent in the Old Testament. In Zechariah 3:1-5, Joshua the High Priest stands before the Angel of the Lord in filthy clothing. Satan stands next to Joshua to accuse him. The Lord rebukes Satan and removes Joshua's guilt (cf. Job 2:1-6; 2 Cor. 2:11; Rev. 12:10). Paul has already identified justified Gentiles and Jews as God's elect (8:30). His question, therefore, seems calculated to alert believers to the seriousness of the threat.

Paul now undercuts the force of the Satanic peril, exposes God's solution for human guilt, and draws attention to the impotence of the Accuser. He writes, "It is God who justifies. Who is to condemn? It is Christ Jesus, who died, yes, who was raised, who is at the right hand of God, who indeed intercedes for us" (8:33b-34). God's answer for the guilt of the elect is declared righteousness, "God justifies." Paul's point is that based on the substitutionary death of the Son, God remains just in justifying all those who trust in Jesus (3:21-26). In light of God's sovereign grace, Paul's query, "Who is the one who condemns?" may also be rendered "Who is the one condemning?" In other words, Paul questions Satan's right to bring continuous accusations against the elect based on the judicial provision made by God for believers' sins. Satan's accusations against those in Christ are all the more absurd given the fact that the threat of God's condemnation has been removed (8:1-2). Paul drives home this point. He exposes God's comprehensive solution against any Satanic charge leveled at the elect. *God's eternal answer is Christ* (cf. Rev. 14:6-12).

Paul has already established that God has given final judgment to the Son (2:16). Now, he makes several claims about Christ as God's all-inclusive solution. "Christ Jesus is the One who died." Paul seems to have in mind penal substitution. Christ died in the place of believers, thus fulfilling the requirements of the law (3:24-25; 5:8; cf. 2 Cor. 5:21). "Christ has been raised." God has demonstrated His power over death. Christ is the firstborn of many who will participate in the eschatological resurrection (1:4; 6:4, 8, 11). Christ, the risen and ascended Lord, "is at the right hand of God." He occupies the position of absolute power (cf. Eph. 4:8). Along with the Spirit, Christ intercedes on behalf of believers (cf. 8:26-27; cf. Heb. 12:25).

Paul moves from the threat of Satanic accusation to God's pervasive security for believers based on the love of Christ (8:35-39). Paul begins his enthusiastic praise with the rhetorical question, "Who can separate us from the love of Christ?" (8:35). The implied answer to the question is "No one!" Paul intensifies the rhetorical force of his first question with a second, listing possible threats to believers' temporal existence. He queries, "Can affliction or anguish or persecution or famine or nakedness or danger or sword?" (8:35b; cf. 5:5). Here again, the implied answer to the question is "Nothing."

In what seems to be a digression from his argument, Paul quotes from Psalm 44:22, "For your sake we are being killed all day long; we are accounted as sheep to be slaughtered." (8:36, cf. Is. 53:7; Zech. 11:4-7). He seems to reflect on his own sacrifices as an apostle of Christ and potentially what faithfulness might cost believers (8:17-18; cf. 1 Cor. 3:9-13; 2 Cor. 11:23-29). Yet, notwithstanding real and potential suffering, Paul provides a definitive answer to his own question. Can any threat on earth separate believers from Christ's love? His answer is an unequivocal "No!" Moreover, Paul contends that temporal adversity actually provides the predicate for victory (cf. 5:3-4). Using military imagery most often associated with

Caesar, Paul demands that believers are "more than conquerors" through Christ and His love, a love demonstrated for all time through His death (8:37; cf. 5:6-8).

Finally, Paul shares his own unshakable conviction with the believers in Rome. His prose becomes poetic as it takes on the air of boundless celebration. He writes,

> For I am convinced that neither death, nor life, nor angels, nor rulers, nor things present, nor things to come, nor powers, nor height, nor depth, nor anything else in all creation, will be able to separate us from the love of God in Christ Jesus our Lord (8:38-39).

Paul lists every conceivable threat to believers, both natural and supernatural. Nevertheless, he concludes that separation of believers from the love of God in Christ Jesus is impossible. All believers, Gentiles and Jews, are eternally safe through their Risen Lord.

So What? The Apology

One of the best-kept secrets in Adventism took place on June 20, 2015, in Cassopolis, Michigan. Have you heard about it? It occurred during the celebration of the 70th anniversary of the Lake Region Conference of Seventh-day Adventists at the annual camp meeting at Camp Wagner. The Lake Region Conference is one of the five conferences in the Lake Union Conference. The other conferences are the state conferences for Michigan, Wisconsin, Illinois, and Indiana; they are predominantly white conferences. The Lake Region Conference is a black conference that serves primarily the black constituents who live in the states covered by the white conferences.

So what happened? Elder Don Livesay, president of the Lake Union Conference, addressed the Sabbath morning congregation at Camp Wagner, flanked by his fellow officers: Gary Thurber, executive secretary; Glynn Scott, treasurer; and Carmelo Mercado, general vice-president. The purpose of Livesay's remarks was to issue an apology to the black members of the Lake Region Conference for the racism, both past and current, that has been a part of their experience in the Seventh-day Adventist Church.

Here are a few highlights of Livesay's 12-minute message.

Reading from a prepared statement, Livesay cited racial discrimination as one of the three reasons for the formation of black, i.e., regional, conferences 70 years ago.

> *A review of the conversations in the early-to-mid-1940s reveals key reasons why that major change and approach to the ministry to the Black community took place. It was seen that the mission to the Black individuals in this country would be more effective with Black conferences. It was seen that*

leadership development could progress better with Black conferences. But we all know there was an additional factor.

A simple, honest look at the segregated church of the past—the segregated General Conference cafeteria, the Negro Department of the General Conference that was first directed by White men, the segregated hospitals that led to the death of Lucy Byard, [48] *the dismissive attitudes and actions—these, and more, issues were also major contributors to the establishment of the Regional work.*

He then acknowledged the wrongs that had been done, without equivocation.

Let us recognize that the Church at that time failed the Black community . . . who stayed true to the message and mission of this Church in spite of its deep and many failures. Some might attempt to excuse the behavior of the Church, through those years, because of the culture of society of that specific time. One could say that the White church, the White members, the White leadership merely reflected what was going on around us; but God has not called His Church to reflect the evil of the world. God has called the Church to reflect His character, to treat each other in love, with the Golden Rule, in respectful ways, and to honor each other as all of God's children.

But Livesay moved beyond acknowledging the failures of the past; he addressed present wrongs.

But if only, if only, our failures were just in the past. The election of President Barak Obama would seem, by many, as a monumental step in progress of crossing over the barrier of race relations. It was a point in history that many, both Black and White, thought would never happen. But it is clear that even that significant event did not mean that we have arrived. Awareness of our lack of racial equality and social justice has been heightened, and Black lives have been needlessly and carelessly taken in Ferguson, New York, Baltimore and other locations, both recently and through the years past, and now even in Charleston.

In a poignant moment, Livesay read the names of each of the nine members of the historic Emanuel African Methodist Episcopal Church, in Charleston, South Carolina, who had been shot and killed by a young white supremacist as they came together for a mid-week prayer and Bible study service. This tragedy had occurred in the week just before the Lake Region camp meeting convened.

Then Livesay came to the climax of his remarks, the apology. It was received with applause and an "Amen" chorus.

So as we celebrate 70 years of the Lake Region . . . I come to you with my fellow officers of the Lake Union with a heart that compels us to not only bring our joy in the success of Lake Region but also to bring a personal and an

> *official apology to our brothers and our sisters of the Lake Region Conference on behalf of the Seventh-day Adventist Church of the Lake Union.*
>
> *We apologize with sorrow for the failures of the Church in regard to race for individuals disrespected, for the lack of time taken to understand, for the mistreated, the leadership marginalized, and for students of our college who were only able to sit with Black students in the cafeteria, for Lucy Byard, and for the slowness, reluctance and the stubbornness to do the right thing. We are sorry that we as a Church did not rise above the sins of society that day, and we are sorry for the lack of progress our Church has made in the last 70 years in the establishment of the Regional work.*

Then Livesay committed himself and the Lake Union to an ongoing effort to engage and foster the kind of racial interaction that would lead to change.

> *Our apology is from our hearts, but we recognize an apology is not enough. We are also committed to seek deeper, more meaningful understanding of each other, more sensitive approaches, more inclusive and stronger partnerships that will make us more united as God's people and for His cause, that we may come closer together, march together arm in arm, then and now, and then someday together into the Holy City to spend eternity with our God and with each other.*

On behalf of the Lake Region Conference, president Clifford Jones thanked Elder Livesay and accepted the apology. Jones offered to work together aggressively, vigorously, and intentionally to eliminate racism in the Church.

What has been the response to Livesay's apology? Unfortunately, it has been disappointing. In the first place, it never went viral. This is the first time in the history of the Seventh-day Adventist Church that a comprehensive apology has been issued on behalf of a major church entity for the racism that black members have suffered in North America. It is true that Alfred C. McClure, late president of the North American Division, apologized on his own behalf at the Race Summit that the General Conference convened October 27-30, 1999.[49] But his apology was not an officially authorized statement, and it has been said that he was criticized for issuing it.

Some white leaders have said that Livesay's initiative was a distraction from Adventist mission. Some blacks have said that Livesay's apology was a political move that he hoped would propel him into the presidency of the North American Division. The logic of this reasoning escapes us, but this is what was said. Most people that we have talked with since that day, have never heard that there was an apology. When we share the video with them, most blacks are amazed and frequently tearful, as were some in the congregation that heard it first-hand.

Livesay's response has been superb. Led by the Lord, he engaged in meaningful conversations with black members that were prompted by his apology. He felt compelled to provide a platform for black Adventists to tell their painful stories and for white Adventists to listen. He called a meeting on October 1, 2016, at the Berrien Springs Village Seventh-day Adventist Church, for this sharing and listening to take place.

Livesay's apology leaves us with a number of questions. Why did this example of Spirit-led leadership not go viral? Amid the rhetoric of Adventist identity, message, and mission, and given our ethnic, racial, tribal, and caste divisions, why are reconciliation and unity not on the General Conference agenda? Is it time for those in authority to lead the church in repentance and confession all over the Adventist world, e.g., Russian and Ukrainian, Hutu and Tutsi, Jamaican and Haitian, Afrikaner and Zulu, African American and Caribbean, French and German, Japanese and Chinese, Mexicans of European descent and Mestizos, Argentinian and Brazilian, Brahmin and Dalit?[50]

We contend that the scope of Livesay's apology must be extended beyond the confines of the Lake Union Conference. It goes to the heart of the corporate repentance, confession, forgiveness, and love that are needed in the church worldwide. Virulent ethnocentrism, which is vitiating the heart of Adventism, must be named for the sin that it is and abandoned through the power of the Spirit, whether it be racism in North America and South America, nationalism in Europe, caste in India, or tribalism in Africa.

---

[1] J. Paul Sampley. Romans in a Different Light: A Response to Robert Jewett. In David M. Hays and E. Elizabeth Johnson (eds.). *Pauline Theology, Volume III: Romans.* Minneapolis, MN: Fortress Press, 1995, p. 122

[2] The content of this section (5:1-11) adapted from Gregory J. Allen. *Reconciliation in the Pauline Tradition: Its Occasions, Meanings, and Functions.* Doctoral Dissertation. Boston University, School of Theology, 1995.

[3] Paul J. Achtemeier. *Romans.* Interpretation: A Biblical Commentary for Teaching and Preaching. Louisville: John Knox Press, 1985.

[4] Theodore Pulcini. On Right Relationship with God: Present Experience and Future Fulfillment, An Exegesis of Romans 5:1-11. *St. Vladimir's Theological Quarterly* 1992; 36(1 & 2): 67.

[5] Werner Foerster. "*eirēnē.*" In Gerhard Kittel, Geoffrey William Bromiley, and Gerhard Friedrich. *Theological Dictionary of the New Testament* (vol. 2). Grand Rapids, MI: Eerdmans, 1976, pp. 406-420.
[6] Allen, p. 36.

[7] James D. G. Dunn. *Word Commentary, vol. 38a, Romans 1-8.* Dallas, TX: Word Books, 1988, pp. 249-250.

[8] Allen, p. 42. See also Werner Kümmel. New Testament Exegesis. In O. Kaiser and W. G. Kümmel (eds.). *Exegetical Method: A Students' Handbook*. New York: The Seabury Press, 1963, pp. 35-69.
[9] Ibid. p. 43.

[10] C. K. Barrett. *Epistle to the Romans.* Harper's New Testament Commentaries. New York: Harper & Row, 1957.

[11] Ibid.; Allen, p. 46.

[12] Pulcini.

[13] Grant R. Osborne (ed.). *Romans.* The IVP New Testament Commentary Series. Downers Grove, IL: InterVarsity Press, 2004, p. 135.

[14] John F. Walvoord and Roger B. Zuck (eds.). *The Bible Knowledge Commentary: An Exposition of the Scriptures by Dallas Seminary Faculty.* (New Testament Edition). Wheaton, IL: Victor Books, 1983.

[15] John E. Toews. *Believers Church Bible Commentary: Romans.* Harrisburg, VA: Herald Press, 1991.

[16] Barrett, p. 108.

[17] Aristotle, Rhetoric 1.4.7; also see George A. Kennedy. *New Testament Interpretation Through Rhetorical Criticism.* Chapel Hill: University of North Carolina Press, 1984.

[18] Margaret M. Mitchell. *Paul and the Rhetoric of Reconciliation: An Exegetical Investigation of the Language and Composition of I Corinthians.* Louisville, KY: Westminster/John Knox Press, 1991.

[19] Allen, p. 59.

[20] Wayne A. Meeks. Judgment and the Brother. In Gerald F. Hawthorne and Otto Betz (eds.). *Tradition and Interpretation in the New Testament: Essays in Honor of E. Earle Ellis.* Grand Rapids, MI: Eerdmans, 1987.

[21] Victor P. Furnish. *Theology and Ethics in Paul.* Nashville, TN: Abingdon Press, 1968.

[22] Christopher Forbes. Paul and Rhetorical Comparison. In J. Paul Sampley (ed.). *Paul in the Greco-Roman World: A Handbook.* Harrisburg, PA: Trinity Press, pp. 134-171.

[23] Paul Achtemeier. *Interpreter's Dictionary of the Bible: An Illustrated Encyclopedia.* (supplementary volume). Nashville, TN: Abingdon Press, 1976.

[24] Walvoord and Zuck.

[25] Osborne, p. 141.

[26] Johannes P. Louw and Eugene A. Nida. *Greek-English Lexicon of the New Testament: Based on Semantic Domains.* Stonehill Green, UK: United Bible Societies, 1999.

[27] Geoffrey W. Bromley. *Theological Dictionary of the New Testament (Abridged – Little Kittel).* Grand Rapids, MI: Eerdmans, 1985.

[28] Ellen G. White. *Testimonies to Ministers and Gospel Workers.* Washington, DC: Review and Herald, 1923, pp. 90-91.

[29] Peter Oakes. Made Holy by the Spirit: Holiness and Ecclesiology in Romans. In Kent E. Brower and Andy Johnson (eds). *Holiness and Ecclesiology in the New Testament.* Grand Rapids, MI: William B. Eerdmans, 2007, pp. 175.

[30] Ibid. See also Robert J. Banks. *Paul's Idea of Community: The Early House Churches in Their Cultural Settings* (rev. ed.). Peabody, MA: Hendrickson Publishers, 1994.

[31] Thomas R. Schreiner. *Romans.* Baker Exegetical Commentary on the New Testament. Grand Rapids, MI: Baker Academic, 1998.

[32] For full discussion see Douglas J. Moo. *The Epistle to the Romans.* Grand Rapids, MI: Eerdmans, 1996, pp. 424-427.

[33] Andreas J. Kostenberger. *John.* Baker Exegetical Commentary on the New Testament. Grand Rapids, MI: Baker Academics, 2004, p. 442.

[34] Ibid.

[35] Gerald F. Hawthorne, Ralph P. Martin, and Daniel G. Reid (eds.). *Dictionary of Paul and His Letters.* Downers Grove, IL: InterVarsity Press, 1993.

[36] Stanley K. Stowers. Paul and Self-Mastery. In Sampley.

[37] Richard Blackaby. *Experiencing God Day by Day.* B&H Publishing Group. Kindle Edition, Locations 2851-2852, 2006.

[38] See Naomi R. Allen. Memories of My Grandmother, Lucille Byard. *North American Regional Voice* (August 1987), 4-5. blacksdahistory.org. August 2013; Benjamin Baker. Death in D.C.: Lucy Byard, 1943 (an excerpt from the book *Crucial Moments*). *Adventist Review,* n.d.; Bert Haloviak. Impact of SDA Eschatological Assumption on Certain Issues of Social Policy. Race Summit Workshop Presentation. October 27, 1999. "The Next Best Plan"—Formation of Black Conferences, pages 12-14. *Adventist History Library. http://www.adventistarchives.org/docs/AST/Race_Relations.pdf.*

[39] *Church Massacre Suspect Held as Charleston Grieves. The New York Times. June 18, 2015*; *Connor, Tracy. Dylann Roof Indicted for Murder in Charleston Church Massacre. NBC News, July 7, 2015*; Nine Dead in Charleston Church Massacre. *MSNBC, June 17, 2015.*

[40] John S. Dickerson. Charleston victims wield power of forgiveness: Column. *USA Today,* June 21, 2015; Mark Berman. "I forgive you": Relatives of Charleston church shooting victims address Dylann Roof. *Washington Post,* June 19, 2015.

[41] Lake Union Conference of Seventh-day Adventists president Don Livesay apologized for the death of Mrs. Lucy Byard to the members of the Lake Region Conference on June 20, 2015, on behalf of the Lake Union Conference. But the Seventh-day Adventist Church as a whole as never apologized for her death.

[42] Kostenberger, p. 220.

[43] Oakes, pp. 167-183.

[44] Kostenberger.

[45] Septimus Buss. *Roman Law and History in the New Testament.* London: Rivingtons, 1901.
[46] Charles H. Welch. Adoption: An Alphabetical Analysis. LW Publications. bibleunderstanding.com; Sarah Julien. Coming Home: Adoption in Galatians and Ephesians. *Quodlibet Journal*; 5(2-3, July 2003).

[47] Schreiner, pp. 453-454.

[48] See Naomi R. Allen. Memories of My Grandmother, Lucille Byard. *North American Regional Voice* (August 1987), 4-5. blacksdahistory.org. August 2013; Benjamin Baker. Death in D.C.: Lucy Byard, 1943 (an excerpt from the book *Crucial Moments*). *Adventist Review,* n.d.; Bert Haloviak. Impact of SDA Eschatological Assumption on Certain Issues of Social Policy. Race Summit Workshop Presentation. October 27, 1999. "The Next Best Plan"—Formation of Black Conferences, pages 12-14. *Adventist History Library. http://www.adventistarchives.org/docs/AST/Race_Relations.pdf.*

[49] Jonathan Gallagher. Adventist Church Holds Race Summit. November 1. 1999. Silver Spring, MD: *Adventist News Network*. The Race Summit, held October 27-30, at the General Conference headquarters in Silver Spring, Maryland, convened a broad representation of lay members, church pastors, educators, and other leaders to discuss issues of race relations that confronted the church in all areas. The meeting, initiated through the impetus of Dr. Rosa Banks, was sponsored by the North American Division of Seventh-day Adventists under the leadership of its president, Alfred C. McClure. The activities of the summit included presentations, work groups, seminars, and interpersonal interaction among the participants. We made a presentation on racial reconciliation in Romans during the meeting. Kermit Netteburg, church spokesperson, said at the time: "The Church in North America has recognized the need for such a frank and open discussion on race relations. This summit is part of an intentional strategy to provide forums to better aid racial harmony, and the recommendations adopted will assist the Church in its inclusive attitude of racial harmony." A critical presentation during the meeting was made by Tony Campolo, noted Baptist pastor, author, sociologist, and public speaker. It happened that an exhibit of the paintings of Harry Anderson was on display during the summit. Most Adventists from ethnic minorities are well aware that in Anderson's work Jesus is a blond, blue-eyed European, that all angels are white, and that only whites are going to heaven. Campolo began his remarks with a severe criticism that such inaccurate and insensitive paintings were being highlighted at a meeting focused on reconciliation and inclusivity. His loving rebuke left this Adventist audience in silent embarrassment. Summit participants worked in groups at the end of the meeting to develop action plans in a number of areas of church activity that were reported to the group as a whole. Recommendations included the development of a strategic plan that would consider ecclesiastical structure, church congregations, and a program of education that would present "practical pathways to inclusivity." The mood at the end of what was sometimes a painful meeting was optimistic, and we all looked forward to the implementation of the voted recommendations. What was the result? Nothing. No official mention of the summit and its recommendations was ever heard again. Even though in the words of spokesperson Netteburg, the church recognized a need for frank discussion and a strategy to address racial issues, the church has been silent to this day.

[50] Dalit, officially Scheduled Caste, is the term formerly known as "Untouchable," that describes people born into the caste system of India that deems them as impure and less than human. They face many types of social discrimination, especially in rural areas. Dalits are subjected to numerous human rights violations, often without recourse to a legal system that turns a blind eye to beatings, torture, rape, humiliations, and even lynching. Police are often implicated in illegal raids, beatings while in custody, and failure to investigate complaints. Dalits compose most of the poor and illiterate members of Indian society; because they are considered impure, men and women are consigned to perform the "unclean" and menial jobs in society, e.g., cleaning latrines and sewers by hand, clearing away dead animals, and heavy agricultural work. Some are bonded to work as slave laborers to pay off debts that were incurred generations ago. Hindus believe that a person is born into one of four castes of descending status: Brahmins are priests and teachers, Kshatriyas are rulers and soldiers, Vaisyas are merchants and traders, and Sudras are laborers. Dalits are literally outcastes. They are not even a part of the caste system. The discrimination that they face on a daily basis is intensified for Dalit women who are subjected to rape and gang-rape, forced into ritual and commercial prostitution, and sometimes murdered for offenses committed by male family members. See Hillary Mayell. India's "Untouchables" Face Violence, Discrimination. *National Geographic News*, June 2, 2003; Julie McCarthy. The Caste Formerly Known as "Untouchables" Demands a New Role in India. Goats and Soda:

Stories of Life in a Changing World. npr.org; Editors of the *Encyclopaedia Britannica*, Untouchable: Hindu Social Class. *Encyclopaedia Britannica.*

CHAPTER FIVE
The Mercy

Romans 9:1 - 11:36

Before he can develop some of the practical implications of sanctification through the Spirit for believers in Christ (12:1 - 15:13), Paul first addresses God's faithfulness to the promises made to Israel: promises made to the patriarchs, Abraham, Isaac and Jacob. In this part of his letter, Paul turns to the Old Testament to validate his inclusive interpretation of God's gospel. He demonstrates that because God is faithful to God's promises, there is hope for unbelieving Israel. Their hope is through faith in their Messiah, Abraham's Seed. It is within this context that Paul addresses the arrogance of the believing Gentile majority towards Jews in general and towards Christian Jews in Rome in particular, i.e., blatant ethnocentrism. He exposes his believing audience to the mystery of divine election in which believing Jews and Gentiles are included in the people of God solely based on divine mercy in anticipation of the fulfillment of the divine promise. Paul shows that Scripture witnesses to God's saving plan for both Jews and Gentiles through Christ. In a comprehensive explanation of Scripture, Paul shows his audience in Rome that God's plan from the beginning was calculated to produce one people, the elect, both Jews and Gentiles, based on faith in Christ.

Israel's Tragic Heritage

Paul begins his argument with an expression of his deep concern over the present plight of unbelieving Israel because they have rejected their promised Messiah. Yet, his concern is framed by an affirmation of his identity in Christ and submission to the Spirit. He writes,

> I am telling the truth in Christ, I am not lying, my conscience testifies with me in the Holy Spirit, that I have great sorrow and unceasing grief in my heart. For I could wish that I myself were accursed, *separated* from Christ for the sake of my brethren, my kinsmen according to the flesh (9:1-3 NASB).

It is noteworthy that Paul's words exhibit pathos for Israel that recalls the intercession of Moses on Sinai for the idolatrous Israelites (Ex. 32:30-32). Indeed, Paul even entertains the horror of being "cut off from Christ" for the benefit of his flesh and blood, the people of Israel.

Based on these verses, two major points can be made. It should be carefully observed that Paul does not reject the reality of his Jewish ethnic identity (cf. 11:1). He is emphatic about his concern for *his* "kindred." He is an ethnic Jew (cf. Phil. 3:4-9). Nevertheless, with the qualification "according to the flesh," Paul maintains that he does not view his ethnic identity as having any priority in his life. It is not of primary importance (2 Cor. 5:16-17; 1 Cor. 9:20). As you will recall, Paul has plainly asserted that his primary identity is in Christ (1:1). Moreover, he has argued that "in Christ" is in fact the defining identity of all believers (1:6; 6:11; 8:1-2). And, unlike the first apostles, Paul is not concerned about the political fortunes of Israel (Acts 1:6-8). His lament is far more significant and farsighted. Paul's concern is riveted on Israel's salvation.

It seems that Paul's anguish is exacerbated by the fact that the unbelieving Israelites have wasted their privileges. Thus, Paul reaffirms Israel's covenantal birthright as the people of God (9:4-5; cf. 3:1-8). With the Old Testament as a possible template, Paul lists seven God-given possessions of Israel including adoption, the glory, the covenants, the giving of the law, the worship or temple service, the promises, and the patriarchs (9:5a; cf. 8:15; 11:28; Gen. 12:1-3; 15:18; Ex. 4:22; 20:1-17; 24:17; 26:30; Jer. 31:31-34).

Paul ends his rehearsal of Israel's heritage by establishing that Christ was of Israel, "according to the flesh" (cf. Jn. 4:22). Then, he asserts that Christ is "God over all" (9:5b). Here, Paul picks up the human-divine tension he created between Jesus as the Messiah, as a descendant of David according to the flesh, and the fact that Jesus Christ is also the Son of God (1:3-4). It should be remembered that Jesus' claim of divinity was an abomination to most first-century Palestinian Jews and ultimately a primary reason for His execution (cf. Jn. 10:30-33; 19:7).

God's Sovereign Choice

Paul maintains that despite Israel's unfaithfulness, notwithstanding its squandered privileges, God remains faithful to God's promise made to Israel (9:6-13). His discussion is complex. Paul begins by establishing God's enduring faithfulness. He states, "It is not as though the word of God had failed" (9:6a). It is important to observe that Paul's belief in the irrevocable nature of the "word" of God serves as the bedrock for his entire argument (cf. 11:29). In context, Paul wants to demonstrate that God keeps the promise made to Israel (cf. Num. 23:19-21).

Yet, possibly sensing that his assertion demands clarification considering Israel's present condition of apostasy, Paul reiterates his redefinition of what it means to be a "true" Israelite. He writes, "For not all Israelites truly belong to Israel, and not all of Abraham's children are his true descendants (9:6b-7a). Earlier, Paul made the radical claim that physical circumcision alone did not make one a Jew. He insisted that a true Jew is determined inwardly, through circumcision of the heart, made possible by the Spirit (cf. 2:28-29). Building on this assertion, Paul now makes the jarring claim that being a descendant of Abraham does not make a person an Israelite. He makes a distinction between Abraham's physical descendants and his "actual" descendants based on the promise. One can only imagine the reaction of Jewish Christians in Rome as Phoebe read this part of the letter (16:1-2).
As usual, Paul quotes from Scripture to support and expound on his claims (cf. 1:2, 17). Nowhere else in his letters does Paul concentrate so many Old Testament

quotations and allusions as in this argument (9:1 – 11:36). "To [Paul] Scriptures are holy and prophetic; they constitute the very oracles of God, and they were 'written . . . for our learning'"[1] (1:2; 3:1-2; 4:3; 15:4). Why this concentration? It seems that Paul wants to show that his understanding of the gospel is rooted in God's word. He now demonstrates throughout the passage that the Old Testament reveals God's plan to reconcile believing Jews and Gentiles into one people, the elect of God.

In this vein he begins, writing, "It is through Isaac that descendants shall be named for you" (9:7b; Gen. 21:12). Paul adds a critical nuance to his argument. He subtly asserts that the true "seed" or descendant would be traced through Isaac rather than Abraham's physical descendants. With this claim, Paul is now able to draw his conclusion. "[I]t is not the children of the flesh who are children of God, but the children of the promise are regarded as descendants" (9:8 NASB). We should remember that Paul has just argued that those led by the Spirit are children of God (cf. 8:14, 16-17). Now, he maintains that to be a true Israelite is determined based on God's promise and not on physical descent from Abraham. One might ask at this point, what is Paul doing to Jewish identity? Why is he so determined to make Jewish cultural heritage of no effect?

Building on this conclusion, Paul uses several illustrations to support his argument and expose his seminal assertion: to be an Israelite is not determined according to the flesh, but is solely based on *God's promise and sovereign selection* (cf. 8:14; 28-30). We will examine one of these illustrations in detail: Isaac and Rebekah.

Paul depicts the experience of the Abraham and Sarah to assert that the birth of Isaac, a physical impossibility for them, became a reality solely based on the promise of God. Paul's larger point may be inferred. To be a true Israelite one must come through the line of God's promise.[2] God's promise supersedes physical descent.

Paul moves on to the experience of Isaac and Rebekah to round out his claim about what it means to be an Israelite.

> Nor is that all; something similar happened to Rebecca when she had conceived children by one husband, our ancestor Isaac. Even before they had been born or had done anything good or bad (so that God's purpose of election might continue, not by works but by his call) she was told, "The elder shall serve the younger." As it is written, "I have loved Jacob, but I have hated Esau" (9:10-13; cf. Gen. 25:23; Mal. 1:2-3).

Paul's goal in using the illustration of Isaac and Rebekah and the birth of their twin sons is critical to the argument that follows. But this example can only be understood by recalling Paul's brief but significant comments about divine election.

He stated,

> For those whom he foreknew he also predestined to be conformed to the image of his Son, in order that he might be the firstborn within a large family. And those whom he predestined he also called; and those whom he called he also justified; and those whom he justified he also glorified (8:29-30).

Paul used this passage to establish God's sovereign foreknowledge and pre-ordaining of those who would trust God's salvation provided through the sacrificial death of Christ. He argued that believers are the called, or elect, of God.

Now, in the present discussion, Paul uses the promise to Rebekah to reiterate God's sovereign right of election. This is why he emphasizes God's election of Jacob rather than Esau before their birth, prior to the time either child engaged in good or bad behavior. Paul wants to underscore that God's selection of Jacob was "so that God's purpose of election might continue." He concludes that divine election is not based on works but solely on God Who calls (9:11b). Thus, Paul's reason for using this illustration becomes clear. He seeks to establish that God's sovereign right of election extends to Israel solely based on God's purpose and the promise made to the patriarchs.

Again, sensing possible objections to his argument concerning the election of Israel, Paul contends that God is just in His selection of Israel (9:14-24a). In his typical style, Paul again joins the argument with two rhetorical questions and an emphatic negation. "What then are we to say? Is there injustice on God's part? By no means!" (9:14).

Paul then uses two quotations from the Old Testament to explain both the sovereignty and justice of God (9:15-18). First, he quotes Moses: "I will show mercy to whom I will show mercy, and I will have compassion on whom I will have compassion" (9:15; Ex. 33:19). With this quotation, Paul appropriates the coupled verbal ideas, "to have mercy on" and "compassion on," to describe an intrinsic aspect of God's nature (cf. Ex. 34:6-7; Phil. 2:27; Tim. 1:13, 16).

Indeed, Paul later in the letter uses the cognate noun, "mercies" to sum up all God has accomplished for believers in Christ. It is because of God's mercies through Christ that Paul exhorts Gentile and Jewish believers to present their bodies as living sacrifices and reject conformity to the ethos of the Greco-Roman world. Moreover, it is based on God's mercies through Christ that believers are renewed by the Spirit and are enabled to discern the will of God (12:1-2).

From this quotation of Moses, Paul extrapolates the conclusion. "So then it does not depend on human will or effort but on God who shows mercy" (9:16). With these passages, Paul seeks to confirm God's absolute sovereignty. He argues that

God is free to show mercy and compassion to whomever God pleases. Why this conclusion? What purpose does it serve?

Paul has already demonstrated that all humanity, both Gentiles and Jews, have sinned by rejecting God and deserve extinction, the second death. He has proven that Judaism is misguided in its belief that strict observance of the law is decisive in salvation. Now, he rejects physical descent from Abraham as the basis for election and establishes *God's mercy* as the sole criterion. Paul's teaching on the mercy of God proves pivotal throughout the remaining discussion (9:18, 23; 11:30-32; cf. 12:8; 15:8-9).

For the New Testament writers in general, and for Paul in particular, Christ crucified is God's supreme act of mercy (3:21-26; 5:6-8; Eph. 2:4-5; cf. 1 Pet. 1:1-4; 2:10). Paul explains this mystery that unites the Old and New Testaments with the words,

> [God] saved us, not on the basis of deeds which we have done in righteousness, but according to His mercy, by the washing of regeneration and renewing by the Holy Spirit, whom He poured out upon us richly through Jesus Christ our Savior, so that being justified by His grace we would be made heirs according to *the* hope of eternal life (Tit. 3:5-7 NASB).

Thus, according to Paul, God's mercy through Christ has made possible God's grace through Christ. What does this mean? If mercy lies in not giving all sinners the death they deserved from Adam to the cross, then how was God able to do this? Mercy emphasizes the idea of divine restraint. A righteous God is able to pass over sin only because God's mercy rests on the promise (3:25). The Old Testament begins with the promise of Christ's substitutionary death. He would satisfy the penalty for sin (Gen. 3:15). The sentence of death announced in Eden would have been executed were it not for divine mercy made possible through the divine promise (Gen. 2:17).

Yet, God's mercy through Christ anticipated fulfillment. God can give sinners who believe in Christ grace they do not deserve based on the reality of His death. Again, Paul's emphasis on mercy is strategic. He wants Roman believers to understand that from the beginning, for Jews and Gentiles alike, the plan of salvation was established on divine mercy (11:30-36).

Next, Paul cites another passage from Moses. This time, he uses the experience of the Egyptian Pharaoh of the Exodus to illustrate his claim of divine sovereignty. He writes, "For the scripture says to Pharaoh, 'I have raised you up for the very purpose of showing my power in you, so that my name may be proclaimed in all the earth'" (9:17; Ex. 9:16). As with his previous quotation, Paul draws a conclusion. "So then, He shows mercy to those He wants to, and He hardens those He wants to harden" (9:18). Through this example, Paul again makes the point that God is free

to show mercy to whom God chooses. Yet, he makes the additional point that God has the sovereign right to harden, literally, "make stubborn," those who reject God's persistent entreating as Pharaoh did (cf. Ex. 4:21; 7:14 - 11:10; 14:4, 8).
No doubt Paul realizes the potential confusion related to his claim of God's sovereignty in showing mercy to some and hardening others. Therefore, Paul takes up the issue of divine sovereignty and human culpability (9:19-21). Again, Paul seems to anticipate questions that may arise in his audience. He states, "You will say to me then, 'Why then does he still find fault? For who can resist his will?'" (9:19). Paul places two questions in the mouth of the imaginary speaker. These questions are designed to highlight the tension between God's sovereignty and human responsibility. In other words, if a sovereign God makes the critical choices, then how can God hold humans responsible? Who can resist God's will?[3]

Instead of addressing these esoteric questions, Paul responds with several questions designed to point out the absurdity of this line of inquiry. "But who indeed are you, a human being, to argue with God? Will what is molded say to the one who molds it, 'Why have you made me like this?' Has the potter no right over the clay, to make out of the same lump one object for special use and another for ordinary use?" (9:20-21; cf. Is. 29:16; 45:9). Paul's questions are calculated to stress the absolute sovereignty of God as Creator over the creature and therefore God's right to show mercy and to judge creation. Paul employs the analogy of a potter and a lump of clay to emphasize the point, arguing that God has the sovereign right to create some humans for honor and others for dishonor. Paul's point is straightforward: the creature has not the right to question the Creator.

Paul continues his rather complicated argument using two hypotheticals, one a statement, and the other an application question. *The question is devised to make the central point of his present argument.* He states,

> What if God, desiring to show his wrath and to make known his power, has endured with much patience the objects of wrath that are made for destruction; and what if he has done so in order to make known the riches of his glory for the objects of mercy, which he has prepared beforehand for glory—including us whom he has called, not from the Jews only but also from the Gentiles? (9:22-24).

Paul uses his hypothetical statement to again reveal God's reasons for enduring with much patience the objects of wrath. God's reasons are "to show his wrath" and "to make known his power." (cf. 1:18). Paul, using the phrase "much patience," exposes an additional quality of God's nature, even towards the objects of wrath. Here, he uses the term "patience" to demonstrate that God is not partial or arbitrary in judgment (cf. 2:4, 11). Paul's subtle point is that God has demonstrated patience towards the objects of wrath, i.e., Gentiles and Jews who would ultimately reject God's sovereignty, kindness, and salvation (2:5).

Now, with his hypothetical question, Paul suggests that there is an additional and more important reason for the forbearance of God. God's wrath is restrained "in order to make known the riches of his glory for the objects of mercy, which he has prepared beforehand for glory" (9:23). Paul clearly equates the objects of mercy with those God has prepared beforehand for glory. The objects of mercy are God's elect, "even us, whom he also called" (24a NIV; cf. 8:29-30). Paul ends his hypothetical question with a definitive statement that exposes the goal of his argument. God's elect, the called, are not from the Jews only but also from the Gentiles. In a clear, unambiguous statement, Paul declares that Christian Jews and Gentiles together are God's elect. They are one called people. Paul soon after develops this inclusive understanding of divine election and its implications (11:1-36).

But for now, Paul uses the Old Testament to bolster his claim. He stacks three quotations drawn from Israel's prophetic tradition to support the assertion that both Jews and Gentiles constitute the elect of God (9:25-29). Paul first quotes Hosea, "Those who were not my people I will call 'my people,' and her who was not beloved I will call 'beloved.' And in the very place where it was said to them, 'You are not my people,' there they shall be called children of the living God" (Hos. 1:10). Paul uses this citation to demonstrate that Scripture predicted the inclusion of Gentiles among the people of God. Gentiles will be called the one having been loved, the children of God (9:25-26; cf. 8:16-17).

To this citation, Paul adds two quotations from the prophet Isaiah,

> And Isaiah cries out concerning Israel, "Though the number of the children of Israel were like the sand of the sea, *only a remnant of them will be saved;* for the Lord will execute his sentence on the earth quickly and decisively." And as Isaiah predicted, "If the Lord of hosts had not left survivors to us, we would have fared like Sodom and been made like Gomorrah" (9:27-29; cf. Is. 10:22-23; 28:22).

Paul uses Isaiah to make two important points. He proclaims that although Israel cannot be numbered based on God's promise made to Abraham, only a remnant of Israel will be saved (cf. 11:5; Gen. 22:17). Thus, Paul argues based on prophetic utterance, that there is an unfaithful and a faithful Israel. It is only the faithful, or remaining, Israel that constitutes the other part of God's elect. In other words, only a remnant of the Jewish people will be saved (cf. Is. 49:18; 50:40; Amos 4:11). Paul amplifies Isaiah's first quotation with the second. His point is that it was based on an act of God that a remnant from Israel survived. If not for divine mercy, Israel's fate would have mirrored that of Sodom and Gomorrah.

With the use of the Old Testament, Paul demonstrates that a number of Gentiles would become part of God's chosen people and that a remnant of Israel would be saved. Through prophetic Scripture Paul proves that believing Gentiles and Jews are God's people. It is noteworthy that Paul anchors his argument for unity among believers in Rome squarely in Scripture. He does not appeal to cultural tradition, philosophical speculation, or political necessity. For Paul, believing Gentiles and Jews are one community as part of God's saving plan.

The Unbelief of Israel

Paul shifts the discussion for the moment from God's sovereignty to Israel's failure (9:30 - 10:13). He now identifies the central reason for national Israel's present state of alienation from God. Paul makes his case by arguing that unbelieving Israel has rejected God's way of righteousness. He signals a change in his argument with the rhetorical question, "What should we say then?" (9:30; cf. 4:1; 6:1; 8:31; 9:14). From an historical perspective, Paul contrasts two different approaches to securing righteousness, and thus salvation. Paul describes the approach of Gentile believers. He states, "Gentiles, who did not strive for righteousness, have attained it, that is, righteousness through faith" (9:30a). Paul argues that believing Gentiles are part of a people who did not pursue right relationship with God (1:19-32), nevertheless, they obtained righteousness by faith. Although left unstated, Paul has already established that the righteousness of God, both imputed and imparted, is attained through faith in Jesus alone (9:30b; cf. 1:17; 3:21-26). Paul's point is that Gentile believers, like those in Rome, trust in what God has achieved through His Son and have attained righteousness.

Conversely, Paul depicts the approach to attaining righteousness practiced in Judaism. He writes, "But Israel, who did strive for the righteousness that is based on the law, did not succeed in fulfilling that law. Why not? Because they did not strive for it on the basis of faith, but as if it were based on works. They have stumbled over the stumbling stone" (9:31-32). With vivid brevity, Paul identifies the reason why unbelieving Israel did not achieve the righteousness they pursued. He says, "Because their pursuit of righteousness was based on the law." Paul makes it crystal clear that Israel is in its present condition of alienation from God because they did not pursue righteousness through faith! Rather, Israel attempted to secure righteousness by works (cf. 2:1 - 3:8; 7:14-24; 10:3).

Paul uses a cryptic image to identify the ultimate cause for Israel's failure. He maintains, "They stumbled over the stumbling stone" (9:32b). Paul uses the metaphor "the stumbling stone" to represent Jesus Christ. Although enigmatic here, Paul makes the direct connection in a letter to the Corinthians. He states, "For Jews demand signs and Greeks desire wisdom, but we proclaim *Christ crucified, a stumbling block to Jews* and foolishness to Gentiles, but to those who are the called, both Jews and Greeks, Christ the power of God and the wisdom of God" (1 Cor. 1:22-24; cf. Mt. 21:44). His claim is simple yet devastating. Unbelieving Israel has rejected its long-anticipated Messiah (cf. 9:5).

Once again, Paul turns to the Old Testament to support his claim. "See, I am laying in Zion a stone that will make people stumble, a rock that will make them fall, and whoever believes in him will not be put to shame" (9:33; 28:16; Is. 8:14). Paul quotes from Isaiah's prophecy to identify the tragic condition of present Israel. They stumble and fall over Christ. Next, he provides the solution, "Whoever believes in Him will not be put to shame." Paul now makes this very case.

Again, with pathos, Paul addresses the plight of unbelieving Israel (10:1-3). Possibly, speaking directly to his Jewish audience in Rome, Paul states his deep concern for Israel, but this time he insists that his distress is over Israel's salvation. He states, "Brothers and sisters, my heart's desire and prayer to God for them is that they may be saved" (10:1). Next, he describes the paradoxical dilemma of unbelieving Israel (10:2). Paul can bear witness that Israelites possess a zeal or jealousy for God (cf. Phil. 3:6). Yet, he concludes that their zeal was misguided; it was not according to knowledge. Paul uses a term that means precise or correct knowledge based on divine revelation (Eph. 1:17; Col. 2:2).

Paul describes what he believes is the *operational* cause for Israel's failure along with its consequences. Israel has rejected its Messiah. Now, Paul exposes the specific mechanism by which this rejection occurred and its effect. He states, "For, being ignorant of the righteousness that comes from God, and seeking to establish their own, they have not submitted to God's righteousness" (10:3). In this verse, Paul makes three important claims. He says Judaism is ignorant of the righteousness that comes from God. The sense is continuous. Their ignorance persists (cf. 3:21 - 4:25).

Paul suggests that Judaism has misinterpreted its own Scripture, especially Torah, a claim that he develops soon after (10:5; cf. 3:2). Then Paul argues that Judaism has attempted to replace God's means of righteousness with a counterfeit system; "they attempted to establish their own righteousness." And last, Paul describes the consequences of Israel's misguided theology and praxis. He concludes that to the present time, Israel has not submitted to God's way of reestablishing right relationship between God and sinners.

Paul now makes one of the most startling categorical statements in his letter (10:4). By doing so, he summarizes an essential aspect of the Christology that permeates his entire gospel. Paul states, "For Christ is the end of the law for righteousness to everyone who believes." The meaning of Paul's assertion is disputed because the term *telos*, "end," has two basic meanings. It can mean "end" with the sense of termination or cessation at some point in time. *Telos*, can also carry the sense of the "fulfillment" or "goal" towards which something moves.[4] Although the second meaning is possible, with the sense that the law pointed to Christ and finds its goal in Him, the context requires that Paul's assertion be understood with the sense of termination.

It is important to remember that Paul has just compared the means by which believing Gentiles have attained righteousness with that of unbelieving Israel. Gentiles have attained righteousness through faith in Jesus, while most Israelites have rejected Christ and His atoning work. Paul says explicitly that Israel, being ignorant of the righteousness that comes from God, sought to establish their own counterfeit system of righteousness based on law (10:3; cf. 7:7-23; 9:30-32). It is against this backdrop that Paul argues that "Christ is the end of the law *for righteousness* to everyone who believes." Grant Osborne makes the point succinctly: "Paul is saying then, that Christ has put an end to any attempt to achieve righteousness by means of the law. Salvation is by faith in him alone, and the works of the law in that sense are at an end."[5]

This clarification is critical because Paul is not arguing for the termination of God's law as it relates to its proper function. He has made it clear that the law is not nullified by faith, on the contrary, the law is upheld. In addition, he has characterized the law as "holy, righteous, good" and "spiritual" (3:31; 7:12, 14). More important, at several points in his letter, Paul has identified the law's God-given function. Paul said that "through the law comes a knowledge of sin" (3:20). He contends that because of sinful human nature, the law came in to multiply trespasses (5:20).

In his letter to the Galatians, Paul identifies the law's supreme function. "The law, then, was our guardian until Christ, so that we could be justified by faith" (Gal. 3:24). Based on this partial evidence, it is impossible for the conclusion to be drawn that Paul is arguing for the termination of the proper role of God's law. As stated above, Paul is arguing, especially for his Jewish audience, that God's law was never designed to provide righteousness, either imputed or imparted, culminating in salvation.

It is for this very purpose that God sacrificed God's Son (1:17; 3:21-26). Therefore, according to Paul it is because of Israel's ignorance, that is, their intentional rejection of God's righteousness through Christ, that they are in their present condition of alienation. Israel misinterpreted Scripture because they did not interpret it through Christ (1 Cor. 2:1-5; cf. Jn. 5:39-40; Lk. 24:27, 44-45). Rather, they attempted to remake the Messiah in their own cultural image. Are we as Adventists unwittingly guilty of the same ignorance?

Several years ago, Pastor Lee Venden preached a series of sermons on the seven churches of Revelation 3 for the 3ABN Anchors of Truth program. In the first sermon, entitled "Hot, Cold, or Warm," on the message to the church at Laodicea, Venden focused his remarks on the all-sufficiency of Christ for our salvation. During the sermon, he related an experience he had at a camp meeting in Alberta, Canada. After preaching on how we are saved by the merits of Christ alone and not by our good works, Venden was approached by an older man who poked him in the chest. The man stated emphatically that staying out of trouble gained him brownie points in heaven. He said, "I don't have time for daily time with Jesus that you are talking about, and I don't need it."

Later in the sermon, Venden related a story from his days as a local church pastor. About six church leaders, including elders and board members, sent a letter to the conference president. The writers complained that they were tired of every sermon being about Jesus. They said, "What we would like is some good, old-fashioned Seventh-day Adventist preaching for a change." They called for Venden to preach the "truth." Venden interpreted the message of these disgruntled members to mean that they wanted him to hit his congregation with the "truth" again and again. The conference president shared the letter, and his response, with Venden. The president said to the unhappy members, "I'm looking forward to the day when I get complaints like yours from every church in my conference. I want Jesus to be first and foremost in every church. I want Jesus to be the theme of every congregation." Venden concluded, "It's wonderful to work for a boss like that."[6]

As we return to Paul's argument, he supports with Scripture his claim that Christ is the end of the law for righteousness to everyone who believes. He quotes numerous passages from the prophets, including Moses, Isaiah, and Joel (10:5-13). With these quotations, Paul contrasts righteousness based on works of the law with righteousness based on faith in Jesus. He first appeals to Moses to establish righteousness by works as the negative element in his contrast. He reminds his audience that in Leviticus, Moses writes, "The person who does these things will live by them" (Lev. 18:5).

Paul employs this cryptic quotation to highlight the exacting nature of God's law. A person must keep the law perfectly to claim righteousness based on the law; such a person "will live by them" (cf. 1:17). In other words, if the person who pursues righteousness through obedience to the law violates one command, the person has broken all the commands (cf. James 2:10). Paul may have had in mind the misguided rigor and absurdity of Pharisaic Judaism of the first century. As mentioned, Rabbinic Judaism would eventually identify 613 commands from Torah that the pious Jew had to obey to attain righteousness before God (cf. Mt. 11:28; 23:4).

Paul's inference is simple. The law must be kept perfectly to claim righteousness, if that righteousness is based on the law. Yet, Paul has demonstrated that no one with Adam's fallen nature has perfectly obeyed God's law (3:23; 5:12-21). What is Paul's implied conclusion? Righteousness by works of the law is an impossible pursuit and a corruption of the divine intent (3:20, 21-26, 28; 9:31-32). Moreover, the person who pursues righteousness based on the law, a standard that cannot be achieved, remains under the law's curse, i.e., its penalty against sin (cf. Gal. 3:12-13). As stated above, Paul laments the fact that this has been the zealous but ignorant quest of most of his kinsmen in Israel (9:1-3; 10:1-3).

Next, Paul reinterprets a quotation from Deuteronomy to contrast righteousness that is based on faith with righteousness that is based on the law (10:6-8). His use of the Mosaic law is unintelligible to a modern audience without the full quotation and its original context. Moses wrote,

> Surely, this commandment that I am commanding you today is not too hard for you, nor is it too far away. It is not in heaven, that

> you should say, "Who will go up to heaven for us, and get it for us so that we may hear it and observe it?" Neither is it beyond the sea, that you should say, "Who will cross to the other side of the sea for us, and get it for us so that we may hear it and observe it?" No, the word is very near to you; it is in your mouth and in your heart for you to observe (Dt. 30:11-14).

Paul quotes freely from Moses' charge to the Israelites poised to enter Canaan. Moses prophesied blessings for faithfulness and curses for disobedience. Although Israel would face affliction if they forsook God, they could be restored to prosperity if they returned. Since they had the word of God in their present situation, they had no need to ask that hit be brought down from heaven or that someone should have to cross the sea to bring it to them.

In the same way that the word of God was near to Israel, so Paul contends, the same was true in his generation. Christ had come in the flesh, had died, and had been resurrected. There was no need for anyone to ask that He be brought down (His incarnation) or that he be brought up from the dead (His resurrection). The message of righteousness by faith was near, available and accessible, to Paul's audience. He was, in fact, proclaiming this word to them.[7] As Paul has demonstrated, there is no need for arduous human effort to attain God's righteousness. Paul's argument is that God through the incarnation, life, death, and resurrection of Christ has made righteousness accessible, in fact, it is God's free gift (3:21-24; cf. Tit. 3:7).

Now, with a rhetorical question and a quotation, Paul states, "But what does it say? 'The word is near you, on your lips and in your heart'" (10:8a; Dt. 30:14). Paul continues his appropriation of the final instruction of Moses to Israel as they prepared to enter Canaan. Building on the accessibility of God's command to choose life, Moses reminds the Israelites of the need for God's command to be internalized in the "mouth" and the "heart." It is important to note that Moses began his final instruction to the second generation with the clarification that covenant fidelity, that is, *relational obedience,* would only be made possible through God's internal work, through the "circumcision of the heart." It is based solely on God's internal initiative, that Israel would come to love Yahweh with all their hearts and souls and therefore experience life (30:6; cf. Jer. 31:33; Ezek. 36:26; 2:28-29).

Paul makes a subtle transition from Moses and Israel to his Roman audience. His move is complex. While righteousness by works cannot make Christ accessible, righteousness by faith teaches, "The word is near you, in your mouth and in your heart" (10:8a). With the use of the term "word" or "message," Paul moves from Moses' emphasis on the "law" in Deuteronomy to the "gospel" he proclaims.[8] He writes, "This is the word of faith that we proclaim: If you confess with your mouth, 'Jesus is Lord,' and believe in your heart that God raised Him from the dead, you will be saved" (10:8b-9 HCSB).

Paul provides a summary of the gospel he preaches. He identifies the word of faith, that is, righteousness by faith in Christ alone as the content of his proclamation so none in Rome will be confused. Next, he elaborates by pinpointing the two related conditions by which salvation is achieved. First, Paul says, "If you confess with your mouth, 'Jesus is Lord.'" Paul again sets forth the necessity of the Lordship of Jesus Christ for salvation. He has established that salvation is a gift from God. Now it seems that he seeks to expose the essence of the obedience of faith (1:5; 16:26).

Earlier in the letter, as part of his description of the new life in Christ, Paul used the metaphor of slavery to God. He showed that slavery to God is paradoxically freedom from sin and the means by which sanctification, and ultimately eternal life, are secured (6:15-23). Thus, the genuine confession "Jesus is Lord," which is only possible through the Spirit, is to acknowledge both the divinity of Jesus Christ and submit absolutely to His Lordship in every aspect of life (9:5; 1 Cor. 12:3; cf. 2 Cor. 4:5; Phil. 2:11; Eph. 5:20-21).

Now Paul moves to the concomitant condition for salvation. You must believe in your heart that God raised Him from the dead. Paul has made this point before. The same Spirit that raised Jesus is able to give believers newness of life (1:4; 6:4; 8:11). In addition, he echoes the need for internalization of the word of faith in the heart that is only possible through the work of the Spirit (cf. 2:28-29; Dt. 30:14).

As he prepares for application, Paul reverses the order of the content of his proclamation, setting forth the actual sequence in salvation. "For one believes with the heart and so is justified, and one confesses with the mouth and so is saved" (10:10). In other words, after believing in the heart the word of faith, righteousness through Christ alone, righteousness is declared or imputed. Then, the Spirit produces the transformative confession, "Jesus is Lord," which results in salvation: imparted righteousness—sanctification—and ultimately glorification.

Finally, Paul makes his application to Roman believers. He quotes Isaiah to demonstrate the inclusive scope of his claim about righteousness and salvation through Christ. "The scripture says, 'No one who believes in him will be put to shame.' For there is no distinction between Jew and Greek; the same Lord is Lord of all and is generous to all who call on him" (10:11-12). Paul reiterates his assertion that hope in Christ will not put believers to shame (1:16; 5:5). Yet, Paul's core point is that there is no distinction in the way that Jews and Gentiles are to acquire righteousness and thus salvation. He declares Christ's Lordship over all, both Gentiles and Jews, and that His graciousness is extended to all believers (3:22, 29).

Paul adds one more quotation to strengthen his claim about the inclusive scope of salvation through faith in Jesus Christ. He states, "For everyone who calls on the name of the Lord will be saved" (10:13; Joel 2:32). For Paul, "everyone" or "all" identifies believing Gentiles and Jews. Believers can be confident that if they call on the name of the Lord, they will be saved. We should again note Paul's emphasis on the Lordship of Christ. This is no mere abstract emphasis. Paul later makes a pointed exhortation to believing Gentiles and Jews in light of the Lordship of Christ (11:13-32; 14:1-23).

Israel Rejects the Gospel

Paul abruptly returns to his concern for Israel's salvation (10:14-21). He continues to lament the fact that most of the people of Israel have not called on the name of the Lord because of unbelief (10:13; cf. 9:30-33). Indeed, they have rejected the message of righteousness by faith in Christ. Paul later employs a plethora of Scripture to substantiate his case.

He raises a series of rhetorical questions designed to describe Israel's opportunity to hear the word of faith and their culpability in rejecting it. He queries, "How then will they call on Him in whom they have not believed? How will they believe in Him whom they have not heard? And how will they hear without a preacher? How will they preach unless they are sent?" (10:14-15a). With these questions, Paul uses reverse order to describe the process by which a person comes to faith in Christ. He creates a visual image of the of the evangelistic process, beginning with the need for a preacher to be sent and culminating with the need for people to believe in Christ as Lord.

Paul believes that Israel has been exposed to this process. Yet, as is now his pattern, Paul uses a citation from Scripture to elucidate the necessity of the evangelistic process. He states, "As it is written, 'How beautiful are the feet of those proclaiming good news'" (10:15b; Is. 52:7). But here is the heart of the matter: although Israel has heard, "not all have obeyed the good news" (10:16a). Paul seems to argue that unbelieving Israel has heard the message of righteousness by faith in Christ, leading to eternal life, and has rejected it (cf. 10:8b-10).

No doubt Paul understands the gravity of this assertion, especially for his Jewish audience in Rome. Therefore, he uses several quotations from Scripture designed to substantiate his claim. First, Paul quotes Isaiah's question, "Lord, who has believed our message?" (10:16b; Is. 53:1). Using this question, it seems that Paul is simply reinforcing what he has already said about Israel's rejection of the prophetic message regarding salvation through Christ (10:16a). Yet, the significance of this citation is that Paul suggests that the gospel was first announced in the Old Testament by the prophets to Israel (1:2, 16; 3:21). This connection is supported by the fact that Paul summarizes the essence of his gospel proclamation with the words, "So faith comes from what is heard, and what is heard comes through the word of Christ" (10:17). Ostensibly, Paul's purpose is to anchor his gospel proclamation in the gospel message of the Hebrew prophets (10:8-9).

Still seeking to demonstrate Israel's culpability, Paul raises a rhetorical question, gives an answer, and provides a proof text. "But I ask, 'Did they not hear?' Yes, they did: Their voice has gone out to all the earth, and their words to the ends of the inhabited world" (10:18; Ps. 19:4). He argues that unbelieving Israel alone is responsible for its present state of separation from God. They have no excuse because they have heard the universal gospel announcement.

Paul moves from proving Israel's responsibility based on hearing the gospel to their accountability since they understood it (10:19-21). He raises the additional question, "Did Israel understand?" Although the implied answer is yes, Paul turns to quotations from Moses and Isaiah to make his case. He writes, "First, Moses said: I will make you jealous of those who are not a nation; I will make you angry by a nation that lacks understanding. And Isaiah says boldly: I was found by those who were not looking for Me; I revealed Myself to those who were not asking for Me" (10:19-20; Dt. 32:21; Is. 65:1). With these quotations, Paul reiterates claims already made. Using Moses' prediction, he makes the point that God would use Gentiles who lacked understanding, which Israel possessed and rejected, to make Israel jealous.

And with the prophecy from Isaiah, Paul makes the point that the Gentiles without understanding would find God. In fact, God's self-revelation would be manifested to the Gentiles without their request. It would be an act of grace (cf. 9:30-31; 3:21-26). Lastly, Paul closes and emphasizes his present argument. He again quotes Isaiah to accentuate Israel's responsibility in rejecting their covenant God. "But to Israel he says: All day long I have spread out My hands to a disobedient and defiant people" (10:21; Is. 65:2). Paul's condemnation of unbelieving Israel is sharpened by contrast with believing Gentiles. Gentiles, who did not pursue God, heard the gospel and found God while Israel heard and understood God's good news in Christ, yet rejected it!

A Remnant from Israel

Paul shifts his discussion once again. He demonstrates that not all of Israel rejected the gospel (11:1-10). In fact, Paul argues that God preserved a remnant from Israel through a sovereign act of grace. Using what is now his typical device, Paul signals a transition in his argument by raising a question and providing an emphatic response. "I ask, then, has God rejected his people? By no means!" (11:1a). Paul's question and categorical answer, literally, "let it not be," are designed to qualify his previous discussion. He seeks to impress upon this audience, both Gentiles and Jews, that in the plan of God, the total rejection of Israel is simply impossible.

Paul uses himself as exhibit A to support his claim. He states, "I myself am an Israelite, a descendant of Abraham, a member of the tribe of Benjamin" (11:1b). Paul reminds his Roman audience that he is in fact an Israelite and lists his partial pedigree (cf. Phil. 3:5-6). It is important to observe that for the first time, Paul directly identifies himself as an ethnic Jew. As we have seen, Paul's introductory identification focused on his primary identity, his identity in Christ (1:1; cf. 7:1; 9:3).

Now, Paul answers his original question, "Has God rejected his people?" with a qualification. He argues, "God has not rejected His people He foreknew" (11:2). Here, it is critical to recall that Paul has already established that God, based on divine omniscience, knows all who would respond to the saving initiative through God's Son (8:29). In the present discussion, Paul declares that despite Israel's general rejection of the gospel, *God knew beforehand those Israelites who would respond to the message of salvation through Christ.* In other words, God foreknew the elect of Israel (cf. 8:29-30). Paul later returns to this claim in the argument (11:25-27).

For now, Paul bolsters his declaration regarding God's foreknowledge of a Jewish elect with an illustration from Scripture. He states,

> Do you not know what the scripture says of Elijah, how he pleads with God against Israel? "Lord, they have killed your prophets, they have demolished your altars; I alone am left, and they are seeking my life." But what is the divine reply to him? "I have kept for myself seven thousand who have not bowed the knee to Baal" (11:2-4; 1 Kg. 19:10-14, 18).

Paul uses what would have been a familiar story to both Jews and former proselytes in the audience to make a critical point about God's elect in Israel.

In his retelling of the story, Paul repeats Elijah's plea against apostate Israel. Yet, for Paul's argument, the response of God to His despondent prophet, "I have kept for myself seven thousand who have not bowed the knee to Baal," is definitive. His point is obvious. Elijah was correct in his characterization of idolatrous Israel. Nevertheless, he was incorrect in his belief that he alone remained faithful to Yahweh. Paul exposes the point of his scriptural illustration. He states, "In the same way, then, there is also at the present time a remnant chosen by grace" (11:5 HCSB).

With this critical assertion, Paul makes three claims that will serve as a foundation to the rest of his argument (11:11-36). Paul maintains that just as God knew the faithful in Israel in the time of Elijah, God at the present time has foreknowledge of all believing Israelites (11:26). Then Paul uses the term translated "remnant" only here in his letter (cf. 9:27).[9] The Greek word he uses is found nowhere else in the New Testament. The term "remnant" as used by Paul literally means, "a residue," "the small part that is left after most is removed."[10] Elijah and the faithful seven thousand Israelites in the time of Ahab and Jezebel illustrate Paul's usage. In context, Paul argues that there is a present remnant from Israel: believing Israelites who have heard the gospel and responded to their Messiah (cf. 9:5).

In Pharisaic Judaism, remnant theology stressed the idea of foreordination based on righteousness by works. Likewise, Rabbinic Judaism stressed study and observance of the law.[11] In Greek usage, "remnant" referred to human remains, the leftovers from a meal, or an interval in music. But more specifically, in the Septuagint, "remnant" was used to mean survivors, the remnant of the people. In the Old Testament, the remnant has a double reference to sifting and deliverance, with the implications of a great judgment but also the comfort of salvation. In the messages of the prophets, the elements of destruction, salvation, and responsibility dominate. The "concept stands in the context of three acts of divine revelation: the election of the people, the calling of the prophets, and the promise of the Messiah."[12]

With his final claim, Paul merges the reality of a remnant out of Israel with the sovereign activity of God (9:14-24). He ties the Jewish remnant with God's overall act of election that includes Gentiles, all made possible through Christ (10:11-13, 20; cf. 8:29-30; 3:21-26). In this regard, Gerhard Kittle's comments are helpful.

> Believing Israel within the new community is the remnant. The cutting away of merely natural Israel displays God's judgment, but the preservation of a remnant of Jews among believing Gentiles displays his mercy and faithfulness. The focus is on God's free action, but in view of the general unbelief of Israel a place is also found for the responsibility of Israel.[13]

Paul moves immediately to shore up the connection between election and grace. He states, "And if by grace, then it cannot be based on works; if it were, grace would no longer be grace" (11:6 NIV) Paul has made this distinction between grace and works before (3:20, 27-28; 9 11, 32), but this time his goal is to emphasize God's gracious election of a remnant of Israel. Although Jews are the physical descendants of Abraham and possess covenant privileges, their salvation is undeserved.

Paul exposes a distinction between two classes of Israelites: the unbelieving and the elect (11:7-10). He introduces the distinction with a question and a statement. "What then? Israel failed to obtain what it was seeking" (11:7a). Paul builds on the earlier assertion, "But Israel, pursuing the law for righteousness, has not achieved the righteousness of the law" (9:31). Thus, for Paul it is *unbelieving Israel* who failed to obtain what it was seeking. In other words, most of Israel pursued righteousness through the law and were disappointed (cf. 9: 30; 7:7-12). By contrast, Paul argues "but the elect did find it" (11:7b). His point is that a Jewish remnant of which he is a part has found genuine righteousness that comes from God through faith in Jesus, while unbelieving Jews, "the rest," were hardened. God is said to have hardened both Pharaoh, a Gentile pagan, and unbelieving Israel because of persistent rejection of the divine will (cf. 9:16-18). Paul's point? Unbelieving Gentiles and Jews are culpable. They have rejected divine patience.

Paul uses several quotations from the Old Testament to demonstrate unbelieving Israel's continuous rejection of the gospel and its consequences (11:8-10). He combines two passages to illustrate the consequences of Israel's dismissal of God's entreaty. Paul blends the words of Moses and Isaiah to say that God gave apostate Israel a spirit of insensitivity, eyes that cannot see and ears that cannot hear, not just in the past, but to this day (11:8; Dt. 29:4; Is. 29:10; cf. 1:24-27). Finally, Paul quotes

David to embellish his point. "Let their table become a snare and a trap, a stumbling block and a retribution for them; let their eyes be darkened so that they cannot see, and keep their backs forever bent" (11:9-10; Ps. 69:22-23). Here, Paul suggests two additional consequences of Israel's rejection of God's Christ. Israel's rituals, which should have been a blessing, pointing them to their Messiah, became a curse. And finally, Israel would become unable to comprehend God's word and would live in subjection to Gentiles. In Paul's words, "their backs [would] be bent forever" (11:10b NIV).

Naming Gentile Sin

Paul now moves from Israel's present culpability for rejecting righteousness through Christ to their future hope. He takes up the fate of unbelieving Israel. In doing so, he challenges the embryonic "ethnocentrism" of Gentile believers in Rome. Thus, Paul begins to disclose, especially for his Gentile audience, God's inclusive plan for believing Jews and Gentiles in Christ (11:11-24). Paul will now speak boldly to the Gentile majority. Yet, he will speak the truth in love (cf. 15:15-16; Eph. 4:15).

Again, employing his typical question and answer formula, Paul exposes the thrust of his new line of argument. "So I ask: Did they stumble that they might fall? By no means!" (11:11a). Paul uses the metaphorical language of stumbling to characterize Israel's rejection of Jesus Christ (9:32-33; cf. 1 Cor. 1:23). He couples this understanding with a verb meaning "to fall down" to suggest the idea of permanence. Paul's question may be paraphrased thus: is unbelieving Israel's rejection of Jesus Christ irrevocable? And to this question, he answers with an emphatic "No!"

Paul now redefines the meaning and purpose of Israel's failure. He argues, "Rather, because of their transgression, salvation has come to the Gentiles to make Israel envious. But if their transgression means riches for the world, and their loss means riches for the Gentiles, how much greater riches will their full inclusion bring!" (11:11b-12, NIV). This redefinition makes two important points, one straightforward the other complex. Paul argues first that Israel's rejection of Christ has provided an opportunity for salvation to be announced to the Gentiles (1:5-6, 13-15; 15:15-16). This in turn will have the effect of creating jealousy for salvation in unbelieving Israel (cf. 10:19). Paul's second assertion, "Now if their stumbling brings riches for the world, and their failure riches for the Gentiles, how much more will their full number bring," requires contextual explanation.

It is important to appreciate that Paul's redefinition of Israel's failure assumes a previous argument. Paul has argued that God works creatively for the good of the elect, those that love God, those whom God foreknew (8:28-30). Moreover, Paul has demonstrated that a remnant of Israel is part of the elect known by God (11:5). So, Paul's present argument must be understood against the backdrop of his belief that there is an elect that is made up of both Jews and Gentiles. And only God knows the full number from each group (11:12; 11:25b). It is *only* with this understanding that his argument becomes intelligible.

In the present passage, Paul insists that there is a "fullness" or a full number from Israel. His point is that God can accomplish God's saving purpose for the elect of Israel notwithstanding the failure of unbelieving Jews (11:7). This clarification provides the interpretive key to Paul's disputed assertion, "A hardening has come upon part of Israel, until the full number of the Gentiles has come in. *And so all Israel will be saved"* (11:25b-26a).

Paul now turns to a critical moment in the discussion (11:13-24). For the first time in his letter, he speaks directly to the Gentile majority in Rome. Paul has spoken directly to his Jewish kinsmen about judgmentalism and their distortion of God's law (2:1, 17; 7:1). Now, he speaks directly to Gentile believers about their attitudes and actions towards Jews. Again, Paul employs diatribe as a teaching device. He uses metaphorical argumentation to unfold God's plan for the elect, both Jews and Gentiles.

Paul begins his appeal to Gentile believers in Rome with a direct address. He states, "Now I am speaking to you Gentiles. In view of the fact that I am an apostle to the Gentiles" (11:13a HCSB). Paul speaks to Gentiles as a group, not just as individuals. It is most likely that the Gentiles that Paul refers to are of Italian or Roman descent. In addition, Paul begins by appealing to his authority as an apostle of Christ sent specifically to the Gentile world (cf. 1:1, 6, 13-15; 15:15-16). He speaks boldly, not as an ethnic Jew, representing the interests of his people, but as one sent by Christ for the salvation of Gentiles (1:6; 15:15-16). He speaks for their good in Christ.

Paul continues to show the vital connection between Jews and Gentiles in the plan of God and therefore the reason for his evangelistic strategy. He writes, "I magnify my ministry, if somehow I might move to jealousy my fellow countrymen and save some of them. For if their rejection is the reconciliation of the world, what will *their* acceptance be but life from the dead?" (11:13b-15 NASB). It seems that Paul implies that in cooperation with the purposes of God towards Israel, his ministry to Gentiles is calculated to provoke Israel to envy. He contends that the goal of this intentional provocation of his own people, according to the flesh, is salvific. His desire is to save some of them (10:1; cf. 1 Cor. 9:19-22).

Paul's use of the subjunctive mood, literally, "might save," and an indefinite pronoun, "some," is significant. With the use of this construction, Paul signals that the salvation of Israel remains a future possibility; it is not yet a fact. Furthermore, Paul expects only some to respond. This clarification should inform further any interpretation of Paul's cryptic words, "And all Israel will be saved" (11:26). In addition, Paul's statement and rhetorical question, "For if their rejection is the reconciliation of the world, what will *their* acceptance be but life from the dead?" merely echoes what has been said previously with a slight nuance. Earlier, Paul argued that Israel's rejection of Christ provided an opportunity for salvation to be announced to the Gentiles (11:11b-12). Here, he emphasizes God's rejection of unbelieving Israel as a consequence of their refusal to accept salvation through Christ. Yet, Paul's point is that since God's rejection meant the reconciliation of believing Gentiles, Israelites who accept Christ will experience spiritual resurrection, that is, life from the dead (11:15b; cf. 6:1-4; 5:1-11; Lk. 15:24, 32).

With two allegorical illustrations, Paul seeks to unfold for the Gentile majority critical aspects of what is called salvation history (11:16-24). Most modern commentators use this passage to undergird the view that the Jewish nation as God's chosen people will be restored.[14] The statement, "And so all Israel will be saved," is used to support this interpretation (11:26). As we will demonstrate, Paul's overall argument does not support this meaning.

Paul's purpose is not theoretical, abstract, or esoteric. Instead, he confronts a practical problem that feeds the division among believers in Rome. Furthermore, he now tackles an issue that threatens the Gentiles' new life in Christ. Their salvation is at stake (cf. 8:9-11).

Paul begins his corrective with an illustration based on Mosaic law. "If the part of the dough offered as firstfruits is holy, then the whole batch is holy" (11:16a). Many views have been suggested as to Paul's meaning in this passage. However, the entire argument and immediate context seem to require an allegorical interpretation. Paul most likely uses the "first fruits" of dough to represent Israel's patriarchs, especially Abraham, and the "whole batch" or "lump," to refer to the elect of Israel, that is, Abraham's spiritual descendants (4:1; 9:5; 11:1-6; cf. Num. 15:17-21). With this understanding, Paul's foundational assertion becomes clear. Gentile believers must understand that Abraham and the Jewish patriarchs, as the firstfruits were holy, i.e., set apart to God. Moreover, their faithful Jewish progeny, like the 7000 Israelites who did not bow to Baal, are also holy, God's elect, a remnant saved by grace (cf. 11:4-5).

Paul uses another complementary illustration from nature to expand on his first image (11:16b). With the words, "And if the root is holy, so are the branches," Paul simply replaces "firstfruits" and "whole batch" with "the root" and "the branches." Thus, with the root and branches imagery, Paul again has both Abraham and his faithful descendants, the elect of Israel, in mind.

In what follows, Paul shifts metaphors. Building on his root and branches image, he states, "But if some of the branches were broken off, and you, a wild olive shoot, were grafted in their place to share the rich root of the olive tree, do not boast over the branches. If you do boast, remember that it is not you that support the root, but the root that supports you" (11:17-18).

Before we can appreciate how Paul uses this metaphorical language to instruct his Gentile audience, historical context is in order. The olive tree was valued in Paul's

world for its fruit, oil, and timber. It also had symbolic significance through associations with fruitfulness and athletic success. But for Paul, like the fig and the vine, the olive tree represented Israel (see Jer. 11:16; Hos. 14:6). The Jews in Paul's time would have viewed the olive tree as a symbol of exclusiveness; Israel was the planting of God. Gentiles were separate; they had no part in the commonwealth of Israel.[15]

Using the figurative language, "But if some of the branches were broken off, and you, a wild olive shoot, were grafted in their place to share the rich root of the olive tree," Paul makes three points (11:17). First, he employs the image of broken-off branches to acknowledge and reiterate the fact that God has rejected unbelieving Israel because of their rejection of Christ (cf. Jer. 11:16; Jn. 15:2). Second, Paul uses the metaphor of a wild olive branch to depict believing Gentiles (cf. 1:19-32). Finally, he reminds Gentile believers in Rome that they "were grafted in among them and have come to share in the rich root of the cultivated olive tree." It is vital to unpack Paul's symbolic language.

Based on the context, Paul explains to believing Gentiles that they were grafted in, or joined with, faithful Israel. The language suggests that the grafting in of believing Gentiles occurred as a sovereign act of God, part of the divine mystery (16:25; Eph. 3:1-6). It seems that Paul wants to remind Gentile believers that they were not first in salvation history. Many Jews, like Paul himself, came to believe in their Messiah. They were not broken off (1:16; 11:1-5). More important, for what will follow, Paul asserts that Gentile believers now share in the nourishing root. Believing Gentiles enjoy the benefits, which have accrued from faithfulness of the Jewish patriarchs, especially Abraham and his faithful Jewish progeny. Here, it is quite possible that Paul is echoing the words of Jesus to the Samaritan woman, "Salvation is from the Jews" (Jn. 4:24). In summary, it seems evident that Paul uses the image of the olive tree to remind Gentiles in Rome that through God's grace, they were joined with God's Jewish elect, the faithful of Israel.

Yet, Paul changes his tone and language. For the first time in the letter, he issues an apostolic command to his Gentile audience and identifies a substantial part of the reason for division in Rome. He exhorts, "Do not be arrogant towards the branches" (11:18a). Earlier, in his list of Gentile vices, Paul used the word "arrogant" to describe a basic attitude of pagans that results from their separation from God (1:30; cf. 2 Tim. 3:2). Here, there can be no doubt that Paul admonishes Gentile believers in Rome about their group attitude towards the branches, that is, Jews, both believers and unbelievers. Twice in this passage and nowhere else in his letters, he uses a Greek verb, which can mean, "to boast, brag against, exult over" (11:18).

He appropriates the word "boast" from Greco-Roman culture with a range of meanings to include, to degrade another, to despise, and to have more power.[16] James, the apostle and brother of Jesus, uses the same term in his letter to describe the attitude of triumphing over others or bragging against another within the believing community (Jam. 2:13; 3:14). Paul demands, as an apostle of Christ, that Gentiles in Christ reject their corporate animus towards Jews. He chastises Gentiles for their desire to create a new exclusivity based on ethnicity. Yet, Paul's exhortation raises the question, why are Gentile believers in Rome hostile towards Jews?

Although anti-Judaism was widespread during the time of Paul, specific views and criticisms varied widely. As we have seen, a number of authors commented on Jews and Judaism during the late republic and early empire, e.g., Cicero, Horace, Ovid, Seneca, and Juvenal. Jewish practices and characteristics that came under criticism included such things as Sabbath-keeping and the worship of an unseen God. Jews were seen as a threat to Roman society. Tacitus, a conservative Roman historian who wrote somewhat after the time of Paul, summed up the complaints against Jews this way: "They sit apart at meals, and they sleep apart, and although as a race, they are prone to lust, they abstain from intercourse with foreign women; yet among themselves nothing is unlawful. They adopted circumcision to distinguish themselves from other peoples by this difference."[17]

James Walters adds other complaints from Tacitus: "They export their money to Jerusalem; they separate themselves from all other peoples and practice circumcision in order to distinguish themselves; they proselytize non-Jews; they are misanthropic, god-haters, un-Roman, and anti-family."[18] Jewish rites and customs were characterized as contrary to the glory and dignity of Rome. Jews were criticized as politically influential and vicious in lobbying for their cause. Peter Schafer argues that the Roman attitude towards Jews was more complex than a simply negative perspective. He sees both attraction and repulsion, which were embodied in fear of Jews as well as the growing appeal for Judaism among Romans. Some Roman authors, like Varro, were very sympathetic to Jewish beliefs, while even severe critics, like Tacitus, were respectful.[19]

Jews, as well as other foreign immigrants in Rome, clustered together in regions of ethnic concentration for mutual support and security. Archeologists have identified such areas of Jewish settlement in ancient Rome, centered around temples. The significance of ethnic pockets lies in the failure of immigrants to dissolve into the Roman melting pot. [20]

We have already seen that Paul's letter to Rome was partly occasioned by the expulsion of Jews from Rome by the emperor Claudius in 49 A.D., and their repatriation in 54 A.D. under Nero (Acts 18:1-3; cf. 16:3). What would have been the effect of these circumstances on Roman Jews? The consequences of Claudius' expulsion on Jewish identity in Rome must have been considerable. As has been established, Roman culture was characterized by a quest for honor and the avoidance of shame. For Gentiles and Jews alike, Jewish banishment from Rome, the imperial city, would have been considered highly shameful. There can be little doubt that upon their return, Jews would have been viewed by Gentiles as pariahs, *personae non gratae,* "unwelcome persons." It is highly doubtful that Gentile believers in Rome would have been immune from the prevailing prejudice.

However, there is another possible reason, closer to home, for Gentile antagonism towards Jews. Before the expulsion, it is believed that the Christian assemblies in Rome had a decidedly Jewish character. Leadership, theology, and liturgy would have had a distinctly Jewish flavor. This situation would have changed radically by the repatriation of Jews in 54 A.D. Gentile believers, now the majority, would have been firmly in charge. The evidence in the letter supports this conclusion. Paul subtly criticizes Jewish believers for judgmentalism, religious boasting, and a law-oriented understanding of worship and salvation (2:1-11, 17-29; 3:27-28; cf. 14:1-10). At this point in the letter, he admonishes believing Gentiles, the new majority, about their haughtiness and possibly about their law-free and impersonal understanding of Christian faith (cf. 12:3-8; 14:1-9, 20-23; 15:7-13; 16:1-16). With this clarification, we can continue Paul's admonition to the Gentiles in Rome.

Paul again uses figurative language to highlight his apostolic command. He writes, "If you do boast, remember that it is not you that support the root, but the root that supports you" (11:18b). Paul continues his salvation history argument to show Gentiles the irony of their bragging. He suggests that Gentile arrogance towards Jews is wrongheaded and should be rejected on the grounds that the Gentiles' very existence and continued well-being is based on Jewish faithfulness, like Abraham—the root—and not vice versa (4:1-25).

Paul continues his critique of Gentile pride by anticipating and deconstructing what might be the response of Gentile believers to his warning. "You will say then, 'Branches were broken off so that I might be grafted in'" (11:19). It seems that Paul anticipates that some Gentiles will use the fact of God's rejection of Israel as a justification for their attitude of superiority towards Jews. Ironically, Paul agrees with this soteriological conclusion. Gentile believers would be correct in observing that unbelieving Israelites were broken off because of unbelief (11:20a). Gentiles are also correct in their understanding of faith as the ground of their salvation.

However, Paul argues that the Gentile believers in Rome should not misread the implications of their correct understanding of salvation (11:20b). He begins his corrective with a double imperative. Speaking directly to Gentiles, he says, "Do not be arrogant," literally, "do not highly think." Paul demands that Gentile believers reject conceit in their thinking about their Jewish siblings. It must no longer be a part of Gentiles' way of living (cf. 12:3, 16). For Paul, the arrogant thinking of believing Gentiles towards Jewish believers and unbelievers is incompatible with life in the Spirit. It represents life according to the flesh (8:3-9; cf. 1 Tim. 6:17). Rather, Paul admonishes believing Gentiles to fear, or be in awe. As we will see shortly, Paul uses the term fear in the sense of respect or reverence for God's person.

Paul explains why Gentiles are to fear. Referring to his allegorical illustration, he warns, "For if God did not spare the natural branches, He will not spare you either"

(11:21). Paul builds on what he has said about God's impartiality earlier in the letter. Using diatribe, he has warned Jews against being judgmental towards Gentiles. Now he upbraids believing Gentiles on the same basis. Paul again sets before his audience the impartiality of God (cf. 2:1-5, 11).

Paul's reasoning is succinct and cogent. If God did not spare unbelieving Israel, the natural branches, Gentile believers should understand that God will not spare them either. *The threat of divine rejection is unmistakable.* Paul sharpens his point, warning Gentiles of the dire consequences of maintaining their attitude towards Jews. Paul calls on Gentiles in Rome to reflect on the tension in God's nature and its implications. He writes, "[Consider] then the kindness and the severity of God: severity toward those who have fallen, but God's kindness toward you, provided you continue in his kindness; *otherwise* you also will be cut off" (11:22).

With this second imperative, Paul commands Gentile believers to reflect deeply on the two essential attributes from which God acts: kindness and severity. Paul reiterates that God has demonstrated severity towards unbelieving Israel and kindness towards believing Gentiles. There can be no doubt that Paul has in mind God's saving act of benevolence through Christ (3:21-26; 5:6-8).

Paul's point is not esoteric but specific and contextual. He argues that God's continued kindness towards believing Gentiles is conditional. It is predicated on Gentile kindness. Paul makes the condition abundantly clear: "provided you [the Gentiles] continue in *His* kindness." It is important to recall that Paul is not partial in his insistence that believers extend the kindness of God received to others, especially believing brothers and sisters. Using indirect language, he has already reminded believing Jews that God's kindness precludes judgmentalism, presumably directed towards Gentiles (2:1-4, 11; cf. 14:1-23).

In addition, Paul issues a terrifying warning to Gentile believers: "Otherwise you too will be cut off" (11:22b). Paul's words to the believing Gentile majority are direct and unequivocal. He is saying in effect: If Gentiles persist in their arrogant attitude towards Jews in Rome, if they fail to extend God's kindness to both believing and unbelieving Jews, then they will experience the same fate as unbelieving Israel; "you too will be cut off," or rejected from God's family (cf. 2:5-10; 8:15-17). You will forfeit salvation. *To remain ethnocentric in attitude and practice is a clear indication that one is not part of God's elect.*

Paul equates the ethnic arrogance of believing Gentiles towards Jewish believers and unbelievers with *the unbelief* of Israel. He views their attitude and the resulting behavior as virulent corporate sin. Why? Paul realizes that group or individual pride is a rejection of the divine nature (1:18 - 3:20; cf. Prov. 6:16-19). He knows haughtiness will eventually lead to the rejection of God's saving love in Christ Jesus. Furthermore, Paul's warning to Gentiles must be understood in light of what he has said about the sanctifying work of the Spirit, corporately and individually.

If Gentile believers persist in their arrogance towards Jews, they are rejecting the Spirit's impartation of the righteousness of Christ, the fruit of the Spirit (Gal. 5:22). For Paul, this is to live according to the flesh. In context, Paul's goal is to warn believing Gentiles that if they do not receive and extend the kindness of God demonstrated in the death of Christ, even for enemies, they like unbelieving Israel, will be rejected by God (5:6-8, 10; cf. 2 Cor. 3:18).

Many African American Adventists can recall an incident that goes like this. A white Adventist pastor has been invited as the guest speaker for the Sabbath sermon at a black Adventist church. After the song of meditation by the choir, the guest pastor introduces his sermon with the following remark, "I really loved that music. When we get to heaven, I'm going to come over to your side to hear you sing." The speaker has no inkling that what he intended as a compliment is profoundly insulting to his audience. In fact, it demonstrates ignorance of the implications of the gospel. This incident is not an apocryphal description; we have both experienced this first-hand, as have many other North American black Adventists. It reflects a pervasive attitude among us as a church. Do we as Adventists appreciate the seriousness of persisting in ethnocentrism, racism, tribalism, and caste? *Do we really understand that salvation is at stake?*

Finally, Paul exposes Gentile believers to the deeper implications of his allegorical illustration (11:23-24). He wants Gentiles to begin to appreciate the fact that there is still hope for unbelieving Israel. Thus, his discussion moves from present reality to potentiality. Paul argues, "And even those of Israel, if they do not persist in unbelief, will be grafted in, for God has the power to graft them in again" (11:23). Paul maintains that if Jews do not persist in unbelief, literally, "untrust" in God's saving act in Christ, then God has the power to graft them back into their olive tree. Using again a lesser-to-greater argument, Paul bolsters his claim through comparison. "For if you have been cut from what is by nature a wild olive tree and grafted, contrary to nature, into a cultivated olive tree, how much more will these natural branches be grafted back into their own olive tree" (11:24).

Paul's allegorical argument is simple. If some Gentiles were taken from their wild olive tree and contrary to nature were grafted into a cultivated olive tree, i.e., the elect of Israel, then how much more will Israelites, natural branches, when they trust in their Messiah be grafted into their own olive tree. Paul seems to emphasize that because Israelites are not foreign to their own heritage, their integration into elected Israel will be comparatively easy (9:4-5; 11:1-2). For Paul, all that is needed is the lifting of the veil from the mind and the heart. That veil is removed in Christ (2 Cor. 3:14-18).

God's Mystery Disclosed

Paul continues his direct address to Gentile believers in Rome. He moves from warning against ethnocentrism to the disclosure of a mystery (11:25-32). Paul shares with his audience, especially Gentiles, God's covenantal purpose for all His elect, both *Jews and Gentiles.*

Paul couples a disclosure formula with his ongoing corrective. He writes, "For I do not want you to be ignorant, brothers, of this mystery—so that you will not be conceited" (11:25a). Paul uses this disclosure devise, "I do not want you to be ignorant," to signal to Gentile believers that he is about to share a significant insight (cf. 1 Thess. 4:13). He calls what he is about to reveal to Gentiles "this mystery," something previously hidden, but now made known by God (cf. 16:25; Eph. 3:3-5, 9).

Paul's disclosure is designed to undercut the conceit of believing Gentiles (cf. 11:18-20). Gentile believers must comprehend God's revealed purpose so that they will no longer be literally, "wise in yourselves" (11:25; cf. 12:3). Paul, an ethnic Jew, while admonishing Gentiles for their arrogance towards Jews, still refers to them as brothers and sisters (cf. 8:12-17). This is the very same familial language used by Paul to address Jewish believers in Rome (7:1).

It is on this basis that Paul speaks prophetically, revealing God's future purpose for His elect, both Gentiles and Jews. He states, "A hardening has come upon part of Israel, until the full number of the Gentiles has come in. And so all Israel will be saved" (11:25b-26a). Although debated, Paul's disclosure must be interpreted in light of his previous argument, especially his statement, "And all Israel will be saved."

Paul makes three claims in his disclosure of God's mystery, and each claim rests on facts already established. Israel's rejection of God's saving purpose in Christ has resulted in a partial hardening. Also, Israel's partial hardening came to allow "the fullness," that is, the full number of Gentiles to be saved. And Paul's third claim: just as there is a full number of Gentiles, there is a full number of Israel. Thus, "all" Israel will be saved.

All three claims are consistent with Paul's earlier argument. He has already established that God in omniscience foreknew the elect, that is, all those, both Jew and Gentile, who would respond by faith to God's salvation in Christ. Therefore, Paul has argued that it is God who justifies, sanctifies, and glorifies the elect (8:28-30). In addition, Paul has already established that Israel's rejection of the message and their Messiah was not either total or final. He has demonstrated that God has a Jewish remnant and that Israel's rejection of the gospel has allowed God's salvation to be announced to the Gentiles. Moreover, he has argued that the inclusion of Gentiles would have the effect of making Israel jealous for their Messiah and salvation (11:1-12). The result of their envy would be the inclusion of the full number from Israel (11:12, 28). Based on this previous argument, Paul's cryptic statement, "and all Israel will be saved," can only mean: and "all" of the elect from Israel will be saved, that is, their full number.

As if he is mindful of the possibility of being charged with self-serving exaggeration, Paul uses citations from Isaiah and Jeremiah to support his claim. He quotes, "'Out of Zion will come the Deliverer; he will banish ungodliness from Jacob.' 'And this is my covenant with them, when I take away their sins.'" (11:26b-27; Is. 59:20-12; Jer. 31:31-34). Paul employs two Messianic prophecies, which depict Israel's future. First, he uses Isaiah, who foretells the coming of the Messiah, "the Deliverer" who Himself removes Israel's godlessness (cf. 1:18).

Next, Paul appropriates Jeremiah's prediction of an additional covenant. In context, Jeremiah predicts that God would make a new covenant with Israel and Judah that would be different from the covenant made on Sinai. The new covenant would be predicated on God's changing the hearts of Israel (2:28-29; 12:1-2; cf. 1 Thess. 5:23). God's new saving work would be internally focused rather than on Israel's misunderstanding of the old covenant, which was externally focused. Jeremiah envisions a time when each Israelite would move beyond just correct teaching or knowledge to an intimate relationship with Yahweh. For Paul, these predictions of God's saving initiative in Christ on behalf of Israel's elect have begun.

Finally, Paul again reiterates for Gentile believers the counterintuitive relationship between Gentiles and Israel in God's plan of salvation. He ends his present argument as he began, demonstrating that salvation for both Jews and Gentiles is based solely on the sovereign mercy of God (11:28-32).

Paul describes Israel's paradoxical relation to the gospel and divine election. He states, "Regarding the gospel, they are enemies for your sake, but regarding election, they are beloved because of the patriarchs" (11:28). In this passage, Paul argues that the gospel had the initial effect of causing most of Israel to become enemies of God and God's saving purpose in Jesus Christ. Yet, there was an additional effect: through their rejection, the gospel of Christ came to the Gentiles. With this, Paul simply is summarizing what he has already argued. Israel's rejection has meant Gentile inclusion (11:11-12).

Paul also declares that God has not totally rejected Israel based on election. As he has before, he now argues that the elect of Israel is loved because of the patriarchs, Abraham, Isaac, and Jacob (cf. 9:5). Paul explains to believing Gentiles how Israel's rejection of God and God's election of Israel are possible. He writes, "For the gifts and the calling of God are irrevocable" (11:29). With these cryptic words, Paul articulates a principle about God. Because God is sovereign, God's call or election of Israel, despite their rejection, is irreversible. Yet, God is able to fulfill the promise to the patriarchs through the elect of Israel (11:1-10).

Paul ends the present discussion by reiterating, especially for the Gentiles in Rome, the mystery of God's saving plan. He states,

> Just as you were once disobedient to God but have now received mercy because of their disobedience, so they have now been

> disobedient in order that, by the mercy shown to you, they too may now receive mercy. For God has imprisoned all in disobedience so that he may be merciful to all (11:30-32).

Paul's closing argument, in these verses, to his Gentile audience is inexplicable without recalling his foundational assertion in the letter. Paul builds on a previous argument to demonstrate that election of either Gentiles or Jews is based ultimately on an act of divine mercy. Earlier he wrote,

> But now, apart from law, the righteousness of God has been disclosed, and is attested by the law and the prophets, the righteousness of God through faith in Jesus Christ for all who believe. For there is no distinction, since all have sinned and fall short of the glory of God; they are now justified by his grace as a gift, through the redemption that is in Christ Jesus, whom God put forward as a sacrifice of atonement by his blood, effective through faith. *He did this to show his righteousness, because in his divine forbearance he had passed over the sins previously committed; it was to prove at the present time that he himself is righteous and that he justifies the one who has faith in Jesus* (3:21-26).

As you recall, Paul makes several claims that are vital for an understanding of God's election and mercy. Most significantly, Paul establishes that God's righteousness is disclosed through faith in Jesus Christ for all who believe, whether Jews or Gentiles. In addition, God makes no distinction between Gentiles and Jews as it relates to salvation, because all have sinned. Also, God's love and righteousness find their seminal expression in the death of Jesus, an act of penal substitution that assuaged the righteous wrath of God against all humanity. And Paul lastly claims: God demonstrated God's righteousness by passing over the sins previously committed by both Gentiles and Jews. God could forebear by not executing judgment in anticipation of the substitutionary death of Christ. Because of Christ, God showed mercy to all humanity, both Gentiles and Jews.

It is on this basis that Paul explains to his Gentile audience in Rome the mystery of salvation (11:30-32). He wants believing Gentiles to appreciate the fact that both Gentile and Jewish believers, indeed all humanity, have been disobedient and deserve the sentence of death (1:18 - 3:20). Yet, God has acted mercifully on behalf of all who trust God's salvation through Christ. God's mercy has been extended to both Gentiles and Jews. In context, Paul's subtle point is that because of God's mercy, Gentile arrogance and conceit toward the Jewish minority is to be rejected. It is anathema for those in Christ.

In summary, Paul's point is unmistakable. Both Gentile and Jewish believers have been disobedient. They have fallen short of the glory of God. Yet, both Gentile and Jewish believers are included in God's elect based on divine mercy. Christ died on behalf of both. Indeed, God could extend mercy to believing Gentiles and Jews through the death of Jesus Christ.

Given Paul's explanation of salvation history to those in Rome, can we as Adventists continue to treat ethnocentrism as an insignificant matter? From Paul's biblical perspective, ethnocentrism is a rejection of God's eternal plan to create one new humanity, the elect in Christ (Eph. 2:16). Those who promote division based on ethnicity, race, tribe, or caste are on the side of Satan in the cosmic struggle that has already been won by Christ; they are on the losing side (16:20; Eph. 6:10-20).

Finally, Paul again raises his voice in doxology (11:33-36; cf. 8:31-39). He again praises God, this time for the inscrutable plan in Christ for saving the elect, both Jews and Gentiles. Paul concludes, "O the depth of the riches and wisdom and knowledge of God! How unsearchable are his judgments and how inscrutable his ways!" (11:33). Paul appropriates a collage of Scriptural citations to echo his praise of God's sovereign ways in Christ Jesus, ending in benediction. "'For who has known the mind of the Lord? Or who has been his counselor?' 'Or who has given a gift to him, to receive a gift in return?' For from him and through him and to him are all things. To him be the glory forever. Amen" (11:36; cf. Job 41:11; Is. 40:13; Jer. 23:18).

So What? The Sermon[21]

We, along with friends, watched and listened in amazement as Alex Bryan, senior pastor of the Walla Walla University Seventh-day Adventist Church, preached the gospel of Jesus Christ in response to students' concern with the movement Black Lives Matter. The context for their questions about the quality of black life in America grew out of a rash of shootings of innocent, unarmed blacks by police officers across the nation.

In a sermon, historic in Adventism, entitled, "Ask Anything: Racism," Bryan attempted to articulate the social implications of the cross for post-modern America in general and the Adventist church in North America in particular. He opened his remarks by saying that no other sermon in the "Ask Anything" series had generated so much reaction as his intention to address this topic. Comments such as, "Why are you even addressing this subject?" were not uncommon.

Bryan took as his text for the morning Matthew 9:36, "When he saw the crowds, he had compassion on them, because they were harassed and helpless, like sheep without a shepherd." He stressed the notion that Jesus *saw* the crowds and that led to His compassion. Throughout the sermon, as Bryan moved from one disturbing assertion and fact to another, he echoed the refrain, "Open your eyes," challenging his congregation to see the "crowds," the racial other, those who are disadvantaged and vulnerable.

Bryan deconstructed a myth, as Paul does with the myth of Abraham for the Jews of his time, naming and exposing the proverbial elephant in the room for North American Adventism: racism. He cited only a few of the hundreds of biblical texts that address God's concern for the marginalized, concluding that there can be no true Christian peace if any group is marginalized—that this, in fact, is at the heart of what it means to be a Christian.

Using a timeline that ranged from 1619, when the first black slaves were brought to these shores, to the present, Bryan described 400 years of abuse heaped on black people. In an effort to understand personally the plight of blacks during slavery, he viewed the film, *12 Years a Slave*, the true story of Solomon Northrup, and stated that it made him physically sick for hours. Bryan quoted Abraham Lincoln, in 1864, "If slavery is not wrong, then nothing is wrong." In the same vein, he also quoted James White, in 1862: "It is the darkest and most damning sin upon this nation."

Then, Bryan took his congregation on a tour of the hallowed sites of American democracy, the revered edifices along the Mall and other locations in the capital city. He began with the White House, but then noted that it was built partly by slave labor. He went on to consider the Washington Monument, also built partly by slave labor, in honor of George Washington who owned 317 slaves. Moving to the Jefferson Memorial, Bryan noted that the most eloquent voice of the equal rights of all men owned 200 slaves. In fact, stated Bryan, for the first 250 years of this nation, blacks were viewed as animals to be used by the white majority; and that for 100 years, following their emancipation by the Civil War, blacks suffered the functional slavery of Jim Crow. He cited the 2000 blacks that were lynched and the denial of voting rights at the end of the Reconstruction. He mentioned the 1887 disparities in black vs. white life expectancy (33 vs. 47 years) and the appalling black infant mortality rate of one in nine. He reminded his audience that interracial marriage was illegal in a time when blacks were essentially non-citizens.

From 1964, the beginning of the Civil Rights era, until 2016, Bryan described a checkered record: black/white disparities in household income, high school dropout rates, college graduation rates, infant mortality, life expectancy, deaths by homicide, the perception of how blacks are treated in the society and whether this is a problem, incarceration rates, and the length of prison sentences. He summarized the social inequities saying that it is as if blacks and whites are living in two different countries [largely influenced by structural, or institutional, racism].

Bryan exposed white male privilege with an illustration about how anyone, including himself, can win any foot race given a sufficient head start. Being a white male threw him so far down the track that there were many hurdles he did not have to endure. He illustrated this notion with several telling examples: white males comprise 43 of 44 of American presidents, 98% of United States senators, 94% of Supreme Court justices, 94% of Fortune 500 CEOs, and 92% of major sports team owners. But of most significance, although whites are only approximately 5% of the Adventist church worldwide, 100% of General Conference presidents have been white males [most from North America], this despite the fact that since 1920, North American whites have been in the minority in the Adventist church.

Decrying the tendency among whites to ignore the problem in the vain hope that it will go away, Bryan challenged whites in the congregation to exhibit the first act of compassion: to cross the street and have a conversation with one who is marginalized. He stated, "If we are broken in one place, we will be broken in all places."

Bryan described Ellen White's last trip to a General Conference Session in 1909. Broken in health, the 81-year-old prophet went out of her way on the journey from California to Michigan to address black congregations and visit black institutions, such as the school in Huntsville, Alabama, that would become Oakwood University. Arriving at the world meeting, she delivered 11 sermons, one of which was titled "Our Duty to the Colored People."[22] She thanked God that she had not neglected them as she travelled to the meeting, and stated, "You may feel that you make sacrifices, but if you go where I have been, in the highways and hedges, your compassion would be stirred by what you see." Bryan stated, "The true spirit of Adventism is not exclusion but inclusion," again challenging his primarily white audience to "find someone not like us and ask them to tell their story."

Ending on a humorous note that became deadly serious, Bryan talked about his young son who has chosen to root for a football team other than the one Bryan had supported all his life. He showed a picture of them together: his son wearing a jersey different from his father's. Bryan then suggested to the next generation of Adventists, the young people in his congregation, that they did not have to wear the same jersey of those who came before them. The metaphor was clear and compelling.

Bryan's sermon was received with a standing ovation, starting with the choir of young people sitting behind him, followed by the young people in the audience, and then with some reluctance the older generation.

Adventist identity, message, and mission cannot be realized in the way that Christ intended without a profound unity in Christ's body based on reconciliation achieved through the Spirit of Christ. To proclaim authentically the messages of the three angels, Adventism worldwide must experience what Paul calls "truth working through love." We must reject our political discussions, ethnic group power, and self-determination. We must acknowledge that white male privilege in Adventism continues to usurp the authority given by God the Father to His Son. Nevertheless, as in the early church, the Holy Spirit is able to direct the body of Christ in *all things*, including structure and governance, if the church is willing to submit.

What has been the Adventist response, black and white, to Bryan's sermon? In large part, a deafening silence. When we shared the sermon with some in the black community we got a cynical response: "This is only empty rhetoric." But troubling questions remain.

Was this just a sermon, or is this message, this confession, critical to reconciliation and unity in the Adventist church? Is white male privilege in Adventism a major impediment to reconciliation and unity? Can Jesus be Lord in Adventism unless and until white male privilege is confessed and abandoned through the Spirit? Can the church truly participate with Christ in His mission to the world without those who have carnal power and privilege acknowledging and rejecting such privilege? Will the young adults—mostly white in Bryan's audience, and in the Adventist church worldwide—take up his challenge and live by faith in Christ? We have no way of knowing. Only Christ's Spirit knows. Yet, what we do know is that on October 8, 2016, for approximately 40 minutes, we listened to a white Seventh-day Adventist minister stand in an Adventist pulpit and announce the good news of the Cross.

---

[1] E. Earle Ellis. *Paul's Use of the Old Testament.* Eugene, OR: Wipf and Stock, 1981. According to Ellis' tabulation, Paul quotes or alludes to the Old Testament 31 times in 9:1 - 11:36.

[2] John F. Walvoord and Roger B. Zuck (eds.). *The Bible Knowledge Commentary: An Exposition of the Scriptures by Dallas Seminary Faculty.* (New Testament Edition). Wheaton, IL: Victor Books, 1983.

[3] Ibid.

[4] Frederick William Danker and Walter Bauer. *Greek-English Lexicon of the New Testament and Other Early Christian Writers* (3rd ed.). Chicago, IL: University of Chicago Press, 2001.

[5] Grant R. Osborne (ed.). *Romans.* The IVP New Testament Commentary Series. Downers Grove, IL: InterVarsity Press, 2004, p. 266.

[6] Sermon by Lee Venden, "Hot, Cold, or Warm" 3ABN Anchors of Truth. Published on April 12, 2014. In his sermon Venden charges that Adventists often attempt to substitute a personal relationship with Jesus Christ in three ways: (1) external goodness, (2) intellectual understanding of truth, and (3) theological purity and doctrine. He quotes Ellen White, on counsel of the true witness leading to shaking. The counsel of True Witness is an increased focus on Jesus (see Ellen G. White. *Early Writings,* Washington, DC: Review and Herald, p. 70).

[7] J. A. Witmer. Romans. In Walvoord and Zuck, pp. 480–481.

[8] Ibid, p. 269.

[9] In Romans 9:27, Paul quotes Isaiah 10:22-23; 28:22, where he uses a related Greek term also translated "remnant." Logos Bible Software. *The Lexham Theological Wordbook.* Bellingham, WA: Lexham Press, 2011.

[10] The Lexham Theological Wordbook.

[11] Geoffrey W. Bromley. *Theological Dictionary of the New Testament (Abridged – Little Kittel).* Grand Rapids, MI: Eerdmans, 1985.

[12] Ibid, p. 524.

[13] Ibid, pp. 525-526.

[14] Walvoord and Zuck.

[15] David J. Williams. *Paul's Metaphors: Their Context and Character.* Peabody, MA: Hendrickson Publishers, 1999; Gerald F. Hawthorne, Ralph P. Martin, and Daniel G. Reid (eds.). *Dictionary of Paul and His Letters.* Downers Grove, IL: InterVarsity Press, 1993.

[16] Johannes P. Louw and Eugene A. Nida. *Greek-English Lexicon of the New Testament: Based on Semantic Domains.* Stonehill Green, UK: United Bible Societies, 1999.

[17] Tacitus. *Histories* 5.5.

[18] James C. Walters. *Ethnic Issues in Paul s Letter to the Romans: Changing Self-Definitions in Earliest Roman Christianity.* Valley Forge, PA: Trinity Press International, 1993, referencing Tacitus, Tacitus. *Histories* 5.4-5.

[19] Peter Schafer. *Judeophobia: Attitudes Toward the Jews in the Ancient World.* Cambridge, MA: Harvard University Press, 1997.

[20] Walters.

[21] Retrieved from Walla Walla University Church website. Sermon by Alex Bryan, Senior Pastor, October 8, 2016.

[22] This message was originally given at the General Conference session of 1891.

CHAPTER SIX
The Welcome

Romans 12:1 - 15:13

Paul now moves to the practical implications of the gospel of God for estranged Gentile and Jewish believers living in Rome. Building on his explanation of the gospel, Paul exhorts Gentiles and Jews to live in response to what God has accomplished in Christ. He moves from general exhortation for community living, to its application in the larger pagan society, and then to specific issues dividing Gentile and Jewish believers, such as disputed matters. He encourages Roman believers to embrace applied sanctification made possible through the Spirit of Christ. Yet, Paul does not introduce a new form of works righteousness. As he has already established and now makes specific, believers in Rome are to live in response to God's gracious activity in the person and work of Christ. Finally, with the words, "Therefore, welcome one another as Christ has you, for the glory of God," Paul summarizes the rhetorical purpose of his entire letter. While urging the strong—Gentiles—to bear the burdens of the weak—Jews—Paul uses Christ as the supreme example of one who sacrificed Himself for the other for the glory of God. He urges the believing communities in Rome to follow the example of Christ.

Life in the Body of Christ

Paul turns from his direct admonition to Gentiles in Rome to an appeal that embraces the entire community (12:1-21). "I urge you therefore, brothers and sisters, by the mercies of God, to present your bodies as a living sacrifice, holy and acceptable to God, which is your spiritual worship" (12:1-2). With these words, Paul establishes the premise that will govern his discourse through the remainder of his formal argument (12:1 - 15:13). He makes several rhetorical moves to call the believers in Rome to proper mutual life in Christ.

Paul uses the conjunction "therefore" to signal that what he is about to say must be understood in light of all that has been said before (12:1a; cf. 1:18 - 11:36). He uses familial language, literally "brothers and sisters," to address the whole Roman community, both Gentiles and Jews. As you recall, Paul, like other moral teachers of his day, employs a didactic device that later would be called the indicative and the imperative. Simply described, the indicative represents God's facts in Christ, while the imperative asserts God's claims in Christ based on His saving work.[1]

In antiquity, moralists used this device to couple a command, the imperative, with the basis for the command, the indicative. Two examples illustrate how this teaching device functioned. In the book of Exodus, Moses, on behalf of God, gives the Ten Commandments to Israel (Ex. 20:3-17). These ten imperatives were to serve as the legal criteria for the covenant made at Sinai. However, prior to the giving of the Commandments, God had established the basis on which the commands were to rest. God says to Moses,

> Thus you shall say to the house of Jacob, and tell the Israelites: You have seen what I did to the Egyptians, and *how I bore you on eagles' wings and brought you to myself.* Now therefore, if you obey my voice and keep my covenant, you shall be my treasured possession out of all the peoples. Indeed, the whole earth is mine, but you shall be for me a priestly kingdom and a holy nation. These are the words that you shall speak to the Israelites (Ex. 19:3-6).

Moses was to explain to the Israelites that obedience to the covenant commands, *the imperative,* was to be understood in light of *God's indicative,* "I bore you on eagles' wings and brought you to myself." The Israelites were *to do* in response to what *God had done.* As if to stress the importance of the indicative, Moses repeats an element of God's earlier statement as the preamble to the giving of the ten commands. "Then God spoke all these words: I am the Lord your God, who brought you out of the land of Egypt, out of the place of slavery" (Ex. 20:1-2). The imperatives that follow are to be understood and obeyed based both on God's identity as Israel's covenant Lord, and on what God had done on behalf of God's people as an act of sovereign love.

In Philippians, Paul exhorts believers to maintain this same tension. "Therefore, my beloved, just as you have always obeyed me, not only in my presence, but much more now in my absence, work out your own salvation with fear and trembling; for it is God who is at work in you, enabling you both to will and to work for his good pleasure" (Phil. 2:12-13). Paul reminds believers of their obedience to his apostolic message as a representative of Christ. He then urges them, the imperative, to rigorously pursue salvation. Yet, he provides a corrective, possibly to thwart the legalism of the Judaizers who are attempting to infiltrate the community (Phil. 3:1-4; cf. Gal. 5:12). With the indicative, "for it is God who is at work in you," Paul insists that believers are to pursue salvation because God is actually at work, enabling believers through the Spirit both to will and do! The indicative makes possible the imperative.

In Romans, Paul describes the practical dimensions of communal sanctification for believers in Rome (12:1a). He establishes the contours of life in the body of Christ by using the same formula. He begins with the imperative: "I exhort you, brothers and sisters . . . to present your bodies as a living sacrifice." Paul uses a verb that may be translated, "urge, exhort, appeal" to signal a shift in his discourse. He has exhorted Gentile believers earlier (11:18, 20). Now, he begins his appeal to all believers in Rome with a foundational exhortation. He urges believers "to offer your bodies as a living sacrifice."

Paul uses symbolic language drawn from the Jewish sacrificial service where the priest offered animal sacrifices as a substitute for the sins of the covenant people (cf. Lev. 4:1 - 5:19; cf. Heb. 7:23-28). He appropriates this image to urge Gentile and Jewish believers to offer their whole bodies to God: to live lives in community based on sacrifice, service, and mutual love (cf. 12:3-21; 1 Thess. 5:23). Paul's exhortation to sacrificial living is not new. He has used the symbolic language of burial, crucifixion, and enslavement to enjoin believers to participate in the death and resurrection life of Christ as the very essence of both communal and individual sanctification (6:1-23).

Yet, Paul does not seek to establish a new legalism, a new righteousness by works. He qualifies his exhortation with his foundational indicative, "by the mercies of God." With this phrase, Paul clarifies the impetus and capacity for sacrificial living. He repeats the meta-narrative that runs through the first eleven chapters of his letter (1:1 - 11:36); put succinctly, God has acted in the death and resurrection of Jesus Christ to save both Gentiles and Jews who believe (3:21-26).

Earlier in the letter, Paul has established the necessity for God's mercy through Christ (1:18-3:20). Believers, like all humanity, were under the wrath of God. They deserved divine judgment for sin culminating in the second death, i.e., eternal separation from God (1:18; 6:23). Yet, believers have been rescued from the condemnation of God's law because Christ satisfied the righteous requirements of the law through His death (3:21-31; 8:3-4). Believers now stand in right relationship with God because of God's mercy in Christ (5:1-11).

Without directly mentioning the name of Jesus Christ, Paul establishes God's mercies, God's undeserved act of love in Christ, as the basis for proper sacrificial living. Indeed, Paul continues his liturgical image by defining spiritual worship, which is life holy and acceptable to God, as simply a response to God's mercies in Jesus Christ. *The result is a life of praise that flows from continual submission to God.* Rightly understood, "through the mercies of God" serves as the formative indicative for all exhortations to follow. For Paul, all sacrificial living on the part of believers is a continuous response to God's undeserved love given in Christ (5:6-8; cf. 2 Cor. 5:14).

In sum, Paul's appeal "to present your bodies as a living sacrifice," and his basis, "by the mercies of God," are foundational to his final argument for reconciliation and unity among believers in Rome (cf. 15:30; 16:17). Later Paul brings his letter to a close with a series of exhortations built on this implied indicative. In fact, he culminates his formal argument with the summary imperative and indicative, "Welcome one another, therefore, just as Christ has welcomed you to the glory of God" (15:7; cf. 14:1). Believers are to extend to others what they have received from God in Jesus Christ.

Building directly on his foundational indicative, "in view of God's mercies," Paul uses two contrasting imperatives to exhort believers in Rome. He states, "Do not be conformed to this age, but be transformed by the renewing of your mind" (12:2a). Paul has established this contrast earlier in the letter by juxtaposing life according to the flesh with life in the Spirit (8:3-11). In this passage, Paul specifically admonishes Roman believers to reject, on the one hand, life based on Greco-Roman culture, whether Gentile or Jewish, while on the other hand, he encourages believers to embrace transformed life through the Spirit. Paul has already suggested the shape of conformity to his age, the Greco-Roman world. He has depicted two expressions of life lived opposed to God (1:18 - 3:9).

Paul offers first a scathing critique of Gentile culture. Although ancient and modern historians emphasize the achievements of Hellenization and Romanization, for Paul, Gentile culture in the first century was characterized by idolatry, the wanton rejection of the true God, and the veneration of man—the attempt to replace God with the individual and things produced by individuals (1:18-32). Closely related to idolatry was the Roman quest for personal honor and the avoidance of shame. This central cultural value created a stratified system in Roman society. Social stratification perpetually designated some as superior and others as inferior.

Paul views Gentile living as a consequence of their rejection of God (1:24, 28). He has already painted a Gentile lifestyle marked by the value of bread and circuses and its resulting debauchery (1:24-32). Roman culture emphasized the material life and the priority of entertainment that featured acts of sex and violence, both a corruption of the image of God.

Second, while many Hellenized Jews participated in the excesses of Greco-Roman culture, you will recall that Pharisaic Jews in the first century attempted to preserve a culture based on their belief in their exclusive covenant identity and status based on the Mosaic law and the oral traditions. Pharisaic Judaism devalued Gentiles as outsiders to God's covenantal regard.

Paul's criticism of Jewish culture is no less derisive than is his critique of Gentile society. He has accused Jews of attempting to replace God by sitting in judgment of others, especially Gentiles (2:1-5). Paul has derided Judaism for its hypocrisy and misrepresentation of God, its materialism, and its attempt to secure salvation through the works of the law (2:17-18; 3:20; cf. Lk. 16:14; 17:26). Most important, Paul has exposed Judaism's portrayal of God's attitude towards Gentiles. He has demonstrated that believing Gentiles, along with believing Jews, are within the scope of God's covenantal care in Jesus Christ and members of one family.

Paul's exhortation against conformity to Roman culture is specific to his age. He believes that all human structures, with their values, attitudes, and practices are under divine judgment and are passing away (1 Cor. 7:31-32; cf. 1 Jn. 2:15-17). He implies that aspects of Greco-Roman culture have contributed to the ethnic schism among believers in Rome. But the question must be raised: how does Paul view culture?

Kathryn Tanner's definition of culture helps us to begin an answer to this question:

> Insofar as it is specific to a particular group of people, a culture tends to be conceived as their entire way of life, everything about the group that distinguishes it from others, including social habits and institutions, rituals, artifacts, categorical schemes, beliefs and values. Thus, "culture is essentially a construct that describes the total body of belief, behaviors, knowledge, sanctions, values and goals that mark the way of life of a people . . . . In the final analysis it comprises the things that people have, the things they do, and what they think."[2]

Tanner further maintains, "Cultures are conventions in the sense that they are human constructions. 'Everything . . . created by man, in the process of living, comes within the concept of culture.'"[3]

"Paul saw very clearly that being in Christ by faith decisively altered a person's spiritual relationship to everything in this earthly existence: to law, to death, to the created world and all its orders—including all elements of culture."[4] The new human being in Christ has been set free from all matters that pertain to earthly existence alone. Paul himself had experienced both death and resurrection—he had died to his old way of life, thought patterns, and value system. Faith relocates the Christian into a reality that is not centered in any empirical reality found in this world.

We have established that Paul views Greco-Roman culture as life according to the flesh, a product of Adam's fallen human nature. Yet, Paul's writings expose a paradox in his understanding of culture. The following statements display Paul's enigmatic thinking about the relationship between Christ and culture: "1) In Christ, culture doesn't matter. 2) In communicating Christ, culture matters a great deal."[5] We will examine each statement.

Paul writes to the church in Galatia,

> For in Christ Jesus you are all children of God through faith. As many of you as were baptized into Christ have clothed yourselves with Christ. There is no longer Jew or Greek, there is no longer slave or free, there is no longer male and female; for all of you are one in Christ Jesus. And if you belong to Christ, then you are Abraham's offspring, heirs according to the promise (Gal. 3:26-29).

For those in Christ, there are only two groups: those who belong to Him and those who do not. However, God chose Abraham and his descendants to play a special role in salvation history. But, being a part of Israel does not confer any spiritual superiority. As we have seen, faith in Christ makes one just as much a child of Abraham as those who can claim physical descent. Race, tribe, language, and specific culture all become matters of indifference in the relationship with God for those who are in Christ. In short, they transcend culture.

Sinful nature motivates us to elevate our particular cultural understandings, practices, and preferences as better than those of others, as the only right way. The temptation to regard other cultures as inferior is the very essence of ethnocentrism. Biblically, it is described as a lack of neighborly love. We must ask ourselves how ethnocentric thinking affects how church leaders and missionaries are trained. Do curricula, specifically courses on preaching and worship, reflect hidden bias that emphasizes one culture or another, rather than the poetry, music, and communication styles of a variety of potential host cultures?

In Christ we have come to a place that transcends all human culture. From this perspective we have an opportunity to view the sinful bias that we have toward our own particular culture: a bias that is so deeply ingrained that we may not always be aware of it ourselves.[6]

> We are free to probe the issue of whether we have been more bound to the culture we came from than [we have] been concerned about the culture we're preaching to. God's truth is the be-all and the end-all, not our culture, not our history, not our own way of doing things, however sublime it may seem to us. In Christ, culture doesn't matter.[7]

The paradox is that culture matters a great deal in communicating Christ. Paul writes to the church in Corinth,

> For though I am free with respect to all, I have made myself a slave to all, so that I might win more of them. To the Jews I became as a Jew, in order to win Jews. To those under the law I became as one under the law (though I myself am not under the law) so that I might win those under the law. To those outside the law I became as one outside the law (though I am not free from God's law but am under Christ's law) so that I might win those outside the law. To the weak I became weak, so that I might win the weak. I have become all things to all people, that I might by all means save some. I do it all for the sake of the gospel, so that I may share in its blessings (1 Cor. 9:19-23).

Although we are free, we willingly make ourselves slaves in order to win our neighbors to Christ. Our personal and group cultural preferences no longer matter; what matters is faith working in love (Gal. 5:6). Paul exemplified this in his ministry. He consistently acted to remove stumbling blocks to the acceptance of the gospel, adapting his style and content so that only sin and grace, Christ and Him crucified, the resurrection of the dead, and the final judgment—non-negotiable matters—were in view. He remapped people's thought worlds so that everything was viewed as new in the light of the gospel of Christ. The transformed mind is thus able to see the things that really matter (12:1-2; Phil. 1:10).

What does Paul have to teach us about cross-cultural ministry? He was bicultural and bilingual, moving freely between Judaism and the larger Greco-Roman context. He forged partnerships with those in the cultures he encountered. He strived to communicate Christ in ways that his listeners could understand. He sought to remove stumbling blocks to the gospel. He did all this while remaining faithful to the gospel message; he did not seek to dilute the gospel to accommodate culture.[8]

Do we as Adventists take seriously the necessity of nonconformity to our respective cultures? Are we willing to examine critically our sinful biases based on ethnocentrism? Are we also willing to give up cultural preferences for unity in the body of Christ? Do we really appreciate the fact that in Christ believers are part of a new humanity?

It is on the basis of nonconformity to the world, including human cultures, that Paul urges Roman believers to "be transformed by the renewing of your mind." Here, he uses language that means to "be changed" through the power of another. Paul's focus on the renewal or transformation of the mind is not accidental. In the Greco-Roman philosophical circles of Paul's time, mental illness or disease was thought to be based on ignorance. It resulted in guilt, fear, doubt, and worry; such thinking led to diseased actions, i.e., inappropriate living. Thus the necessity of philosophy as a corrective.[9] Paul's emphasis on the need for the renewal of the mind through transformation is understandable given this context. He follows the moral philosophers to a point, but his analysis is different. For Paul, diseased thinking and its result, sinful living, has its origin in the rejection of God.[10]

Paul's call to mind renewal is based on his belief that the human mind, in fact, the whole person, is fallen, captive to sin, incapable of pleasing God (1:28; 5:12-21; 7:7-23). Believers in Christ, however, have been rescued from the power of sin (6:1-23). Moreover, they have received God's Spirit (8:5). For Paul, the reception of the Spirit makes the renewal of the mind possible (cf. Tit. 3:5).

Paul is not dealing in abstractions. When he exhorts believers in Rome to receive a change in their thinking, he has a specific end in mind. His aim is exposed in a later exhortation to believers in Philippi.

> If then there is any encouragement in Christ, any consolation from love, any sharing in the Spirit, any compassion and sympathy, make my joy complete: be of the same mind, having the same love, being in full accord and of one mind. Do nothing from selfish ambition or conceit, but in humility regard others as better than yourselves. Let each of you look not to your own interests, but to the interests of others. *Let the same mind be in you that was in Christ Jesus* (Phil. 2:1-5).

In this passage, Paul calls believers to proper living. He emphasizes that believers ultimately must receive the mind of Christ, an attitude characterized by condescension: voluntary self-emptying, humility, and sacrifice for the sake of others (Phil 2:6-8).

In Romans, Paul puts the same necessity in different words. "For those whom [God] foreknew he also predestined *to be conformed to the image of his Son,* in order that he might be the firstborn within a large family (8:29). When Paul urges Roman believers to experience mind renewal, he is calling for the necessity of a radical shift in thinking, in worldview, made possible by the Holy Spirit.

Paul is actually commanding believers to reject Greco-Roman thought and to receive the mind of Christ. He explains to Gentiles and Jews in Rome that this shift in thinking has a specific purpose, "so that you may discern what is the will of God—what is good and acceptable and perfect" (12:2b). Paul uses a verb that means "test and approve" to assert the ongoing responsibility of believers to use the will of God as the litmus test for proper communal living.

Many Yet One

Paul develops the implications of community life lived in response to God's mercies in Christ by exhorting believers to proper self-estimation based on their spiritual endowment (12:3-8; cf. Eph. 4:1-16). He subtly appropriates the metaphor of one body to promote unity in diversity (cf. 1 Cor. 12:12-31). Paul uses another contrast to further develop his description of the renewed mind in practice. "For by the grace given to me I say to everyone among you not to think of yourself more highly than you ought to think, but to think with sober judgment, each according to the measure of faith that God has assigned" (12:3).

Using the words, "by the grace given to me," Paul appeals to the apostolic authority given to him by God to admonish all Roman believers to reject arrogance, i.e., "high self-thought" (1:5; cf. 15:15). Paul has just used similar language to chastise the Gentile majority for their conceited attitude towards Jews (11:20). Now, in this divided community, he warns each individual believer that inflated self-estimation is incompatible with the renewed mind and is a rejection of life in Christ. Rather, Paul enjoins sober judgment: to think sensibly in line with the measure of faith given by God.

It should be noted that Paul links sober thinking, the proper functioning of the renewed mind, with the expression "measure of faith." With this linkage, he makes a subtle, yet significant, point. Just as he is able to speak to Roman Christians based on *the gift of grace* given to him by God, believers are to think and act in community in keeping with *the gift of faith* also apportioned by God to every believer (1:5; cf. Eph. 4:7). As we have seen, faith is trusting God's comprehensive saving ability through Christ. It is the means by which God's righteousness in Christ is apprehended and received (1:17; 3:21-22; 9:30-31). Thus, Paul maintains that sober judgment and its resulting appropriate action is impossible without divine intervention. He seeks to establish faith in God's ability in Christ as the standard for spiritual thought and action. He later makes the radical assertion "Whatever is not of faith is sin" (14:23).

Paul draws an analogy between the human body and the believing community. "For just as each of us has one body with many members, and these members do not all have the same function, so in Christ we, though many, form one body, and each member belongs to all the others" (12:4-5 NIV). Using this analogy, Paul moves from metaphor to application. He observes that the human body is one entity, while having many different organs with unique functions (12:4a). Paul's use of *soma,* "body," as a metaphor for instruction was not original. His explanation of the relationship of believers to one another in community can only be understood against the backdrop of the Greek idea of the individual and the state.

The metaphor of the body, as used by Paul, may be traced to several influences. For example, the image of the state as a body consisting of interdependent members was common in the Stoic philosophy of the time. Seneca, for instance, addresses Nero as "the soul of the republic [which] is your body,"[11] and in another place he says, "We are limbs of a great body."[12] Paul may well have been aware of the position of Philo, a Hellenized Jew. In commenting on the purpose of the sacrifices by the high priest on behalf of the nation of Israel, Philo states, "that every age [group] and all the parts of the nation may be welded into one and the same family as though it were a single body."[13]

Yet, Paul's application of body imagery is culturally unprecedented. Paul's statement, "so in Christ we, though many, form one body, and each member belongs to all the others," has no parallel in first-century Greco-Roman thought, whether among Gentiles or Jews (12:5). With his application of the metaphor, Paul makes three discrete points.

He reiterates that "in Christ" is the common identity of all believers (6:11; 8:1). Believers' participation in the death and resurrection of Jesus Christ creates a new primary identity. They are not first and foremost defined by ethnicity. Therefore, he can later say to the Colossians, "You are being renewed in knowledge according to the image of your Creator. In Christ there is not Greek and Jew, circumcision and uncircumcision, barbarian, Scythian, slave and free; but Christ is all and in all" (3:10b-11; cf. Gal. 3:28). Believers are to think and act in keeping with their primary identity in Christ. They are to reject ethnicity as a primary determinant for living. Believers have rejected life lived according to the flesh, which is sin (8:9-10; 14:23; cf. 2 Cor. 5:16-17).

Further, Paul acknowledges that believers in Christ are many. They are diverse individuals. Yet, he stresses that in reality, believers together constitute one entity. Paul makes the same point in Ephesians where he argues for a new ontological oneness between believing Gentiles and Jews based on the death of Christ (Eph.

2:14-16). Against the Greco-Roman concept of the primacy of the individual or its insistence on a stratified body composed of superiors and inferiors based on birth, wealth, gender, and ethnicity, Paul envisions a new humanity, one entity that is the body of Christ, enriched by its diversity. He posits the new reality of unity in diversity in Christ.

Then Paul maintains that believers share a unique intimacy. Believers are "members each one of one another" (12:5b). With the use of the reciprocal pronoun, "one another," Paul exposes an additional ontological reality based on the death of Christ. Although they are individual members, those in Christ belong to one another. While addressing the division among believers in Corinth, Paul explains his basis for this fundamental belief. He says, "And you belong to Christ, and Christ belongs to God." The "you" here is plural and refers to all believers in Corinth. Paul describes a chain of relational belonging between believers, Christ, and God rooted in the cross (1 Cor. 3:23; cf. 1:13, 22; 2:2; 12:27).

In Romans, he articulates the implication of believers' divine belonging. Roman believers are members of one another. They are not to think of themselves as isolated individuals or groups, but as belonging to each other in Christ. Paul later uses this reality as the basis for a long list of exhortations encouraging reciprocal, loving care (12:10, 16; 14:13; 15:5, 7, 14; 16:16). Because Paul is writing to divided Gentile and Jewish believers—an actual, dysfunctional community—his use of the body image is not theoretical but practical. It describes a new way of viewing the other.

Paul develops his description of a properly functioning body, writing,

> We have different gifts, according to the grace given to each of us. If your gift is prophesying, then prophesy in accordance with your faith; if it is serving, then serve; if it is teaching, then teach; if it is to encourage, then give encouragement; if it is giving, then give generously; if it is to lead, do it diligently; if it is to show mercy, do it cheerfully (12:6-8 NIV).

With these words, Paul echoes the belief that endowments are given by God and are bestowed on individual believers (cf. 12:3). He lists seven gifts possessed by members of the believing community: prophecy, service, teaching, encouraging, giving, leading, and showing mercy (12:6a-8). He has already established what believers have in Christ based on their justification: peace or reconciliation, access, hope, God's love through the gift of the Holy Spirit (5:1-11). Here, he identifies different spiritual gifts, all in aid of making the essential claim that each believer is endowed with gifts from God for the benefit of those in Christ. All gifts are to be exercised appropriately for the common good (cf. 1 Cor. 12:4-11, 27-31; Eph. 4:4-16).

One can only speculate on why Paul's lists of gifts differ in his letters to the Corinthians, the Ephesians, and the Romans. It is possible that the lists differ because of the specific occasions. Given the situation among believers in Rome, it is telling that Paul grammatically emphasizes the need for a continuous application of some of the gifts: teaching, encouraging, giving, leading, and showing mercy. Moreover, he ends his list with the gift of leading, which is in dispute among the divided factions, and showing mercy, which seems to be in short supply.

Love in the Body of Christ

Paul continues his depiction of how believers are to treat one another in the body of Christ (12:9-21). He argues for the necessity of love as the proper response to God's mercies in Christ (cf. 13:8-14). Paul employs a stack of maxims, or pithy sayings, often used in his time to instruct devotees on proper conduct. Rhetorical skill, the ability to speak persuasively, was highly prized in Paul's Greco-Roman world. It was the pinnacle of the educational system of the time. Maxims—concise, stylized, memorable statements—were a basic feature of rhetoric. The content of maxims was largely drawn from conventional wisdom, providing principles and rules of conduct for everyday life. The maxim was "particularly valued for its persuasive power and for its character-building qualities."[14]

Although many of these maxims are general ethical sayings of Paul, several seem to be created or tweaked based on the actual situation among believers in Rome (cf. 1 Thess. 5:14-22). Paul describes how believers should relate to one another in the body with a foundational maxim that will inform the entire section. "Love must be without hypocrisy" (12:9a). Paul begins with a maxim stressing the necessity of *agapē*, "love,"—unconditional, selfless care of others—a term not commonly used in Roman culture (cf. 1 Cor. 13:1-8; Phil. 2:1-4). This is not the first time he has broached this theme. He has already established that justified believers have received God's love through the gift of the Spirit. In addition, he has argued that the love of God in Christ for believers is the source of their salvation (5:5-8).

Paul focuses on the need for believers in Rome to love one another, thus extending to others that which has been received from God through Jesus Christ (cf. 8:39). The subject of communal love is a common topic in the letters of Paul (cf. 1 Cor. 8:1; 13:1-8, 13; 14:1; Gal. 5:22-23; 1 Thess. 3:12; 5:8). In these examples, Paul uses positive language to exhort believers to mutual love. Conversely, in this passage, Paul's love maxim is stated negatively, literally, "the love unhypocritical." Based on this difference, the question may be raised: is Paul's opening maxim constructed specifically to address the schism between Gentile and Jewish believers in Rome?

It is significant that Paul uses the term translated "without hypocrisy, sincere"[15] (cf. 2 Cor. 6:6; 8:8), which is a cognate of the term "hypocrite." The word "hypocrite" was used in Greco-Roman culture to describe a play-actor, a pretender, a person wearing a mask to deceive. It meant having two faces, to be insincere[16] (cf. Mt. 23:13-33). It seems that from the outset, Paul wants to warn this divided community of the danger of pretense, of papering over divisive attitudes, issues, and practices that are real and toxic among them (e.g., 11:13-25; 14:1-23).

Paul wants Roman believers to extend to one another the genuine love that they have received from God in Christ: genuine love that is only possible through the enabling power of the Spirit (12:1-2; cf. 5:5, 6-8; 13:8-10; Gal. 5:22-25). To this end, Paul uses two contrasting maxims designed to describe sincere love and its antithesis, relational malevolence. He exhorts, "Abhorring evil, being joined to the good" (12:9b). Paul's contrast is important for understanding what follows. Throughout his stack of maxims, Paul exhorts believers in Rome to reject evil and to embrace good. In fact, later he sums up his admonitions on proper living in the body of Christ with the two-fold imperative, "do not be conquered by evil, but conquer evil with good" (12:21; cf. 2:9-10).

Paul establishes the negative pole of his contrast with the dictum "abhorring evil." Here, he uses the term "evil," meaning "socially or moral reprehensible"[17] It seems that Paul is not referring to evil in the abstract. He enjoins the Roman believers to continuously reject all things that are hurtful to others in the body. Considering the ethnic division in Rome, Paul no doubt has in mind evil that flows from ethnic enmity (cf. 16:19).

However, avoiding negative living is not enough. Paul establishes the opposite pole with the maxim "be joined to the good." He uses the idea of that which is intrinsically good in a passive construction to urge Roman believers to submit to the work of the Spirit by actively embracing the good: that which seeks what benefits the other in the believing community (cf. 1 Cor. 12:7; Phil. 2:1-4).

Finally, Paul provides additional sayings to describe what good and evil look like in the body of Christ (12:10-21). Although Paul's list of maxims in this section may be viewed as general exhortations used to instruct believers in his missionary enterprise, it appears that Paul has tailored his list of maxims to mitigate the problem of division in Rome.

Paul exhorts Roman believers to "love one another with mutual affection" (12:10a). He echoes his earlier claim that believers have been adopted into God's family. Thus, believers, in spite of differences of ethnicity, theology, or liturgy, are one family and are to share familial love and affection (8:14, 16-17; cf. 1 Thess. 4:9). With this saying, Paul stresses reciprocity and intimacy. He enjoins mutual selfless care one for the other.

Building on his admonition to love as family, Paul uses an adage that turns the central value in Greco-Roman culture on its head. He urges believers to "outdo one another in showing honor" (12:10b). Instead of conforming to Roman culture in the quest for personal honor, believers are to outstrip one another in bestowing appropriate honor on each other. Again, Paul's admonition is reciprocal (cf. 13:7; Phil. 2:3).

Next, Paul uses a series of sayings that seem to be designed to undercut halfhearted service to others. He exhorts, "Do not lack diligence; be fervent in spirit; serve the Lord" (12:11). Paul employs language like that related to the gift of leadership (12:8). Leaders are to serve the entire community with zeal. In the same way, all believers are called to fervent service to one another as unto the Lord.

With the words, "rejoice in hope, be patient in suffering, persevere in prayer" (12:12), Paul links the temporal to the eternal. He echoes aspects of his earlier description of what believers possess in Christ. Justified believers have present and eschatological hope, which makes it possible to endure affliction (5:2-5). He exhorts believers in the present to live out who they are in Christ by rejoicing in hope and being patient in spite of communal affliction (cf. 12:14). This is only possible through constant prayer (cf. 1 Thess. 5:16-18).

Using the related maxims, "share with the saints in their needs; pursue hospitality" (12:13), Paul anticipates two critical issues to be addressed later in the letter. He will appeal obliquely to Gentile believers in Rome to relieve the needs of beleaguered Jews in Jerusalem, arguing that believing Jews have shared their spiritual blessing with believing Gentiles. Thus, Gentiles are obliged, based on family love, to relieve the material needs of Jewish believers (15:25-27).

Paul later ends his argument with a summary exhortation to mutual hospitality (15:7). Presently, he is urging the continuous pursuit of persons treated as strangers, those who are not considered friends. Based on Greco-Roman social stratification, hospitality was only extended to persons of equal social rank. For Paul, the saving activity of Christ undercuts this cultural norm (15:7-13). Paul exhorts believers in Rome to "bless those who persecute you; bless and do not curse" (12:14). Although some would argue that Paul has in mind persecution from outsiders, the occasion for the letter suggests that he is more likely describing believers persecuting other believers in Rome (cf. 2:1-11; 11:13-24; 14:1-12).

Paul's own experience witnesses to the possibility of persecution from within the believing community. His ministry has been hounded, not just by unbelieving Jews, but also by Jewish believers, Judaizers, who seek to overturn his understanding of the gospel (cf. 2 Cor. 12:10; Gal. 14; Phil. 3:2). It seems that Paul echoes part of Jesus' formative discourse in the so-called Sermon on the Mount, "But I tell you, love your enemies and pray for those who persecute you" (Mt. 5:44; cf. Lk. 6:22, 27). Paul's admonition is straightforward. In spite of persecution from within the community or from without, believers are to bless rather than curse. Paul shortly after expands on this exhortation (12:17-21).

The maxim "rejoice with those who rejoice, weep with those who weep," seems to reiterate Paul's earlier emphasis on the need for familial love among believers (12:15; cf. 12:5, 10). He urges mutual empathy among Roman believers. Paul embeds related sayings that if followed would nullify the schism in Rome. "Live in harmony with one another; do not be haughty, but associate with the lowly; do not claim to be wiser than you are" (12:16). With these maxims, Paul makes two important moves. He exhorts all believers to have one mind. Later, he makes the same appeal and cryptically suggests that this act of oneness is Christ's command (15:5; cf. Phil. 2:2). Next, Paul's demand to reject haughtiness echoes his earlier direct chastisement of the Gentile majority for their arrogance and conceit towards Jews (11:20, 25, cf. 12:3). Given societal norms in first-century Rome, it seems likely that Paul is subtly encouraging believing Gentiles to associate with the lowly Jews. Additionally, he is calling on the entire community to reject arrogance as antithetical to life in Christ.

To conclude his list of maxims, Paul introduces the evil of vengeance in the body of Christ and then proposes how the good might be achieved (12:17-21). With the tensions between believing Gentiles and Jews in mind, it is likely that Paul's admonition against retaliation is real; it addresses actual behavior. With the maxim, "do not repay anyone evil for evil," Paul echoes the wisdom tradition of the Old Testament and the teachings of Jesus (12:17a; Pro. 20:22; 24:29; cf. Mt. 5:39). Paul's negative maxim is culturally relevant. His call to non-retaliation would have been viewed as nonsensical in the Roman Empire. Vengeance was an essential value in Rome society. In fact, Romans viewed non-retaliation as a sign of weakness. All acts of humility were to be rejected as foreign to the honorable male ethos. Violent retaliation was thought to be the appropriate response to real or perceived injury by those possessing honor.

By contrast, Paul exhorts believers to respond to evil with good in two ways (12:17b-18). He says, "Be careful to do what is right in the eyes of everyone." With this maxim, Paul enjoins honorable living on all believers in the Roman assemblies. Because appropriate treatment of the other could be viewed subjectively, he contends that the standard is communal rather than individual (cf. 1 Cor. 5:12-13; 6:3-4). This saying also negates group think, in this case, the notion that the good is determined by one's group. The action must be right in the eyes of everyone, not just the individual's group of reference, whether Jewish or Gentile.

Then Paul says, "If possible, on your part, live at peace with everyone" (12:18). Soon after, while addressing specific contentious issues among the weak and the strong in Rome, Paul says to the divided community "We must pursue what promotes peace and what builds up one another" (14:19). With the present exhortation, he acknowledges that peace can be elusive because it does not depend solely on the individual or on a group. Nevertheless, he urges the ideal. Believers, collectively and individually, are to make every effort to live at peace with everyone. Believers are not to be satisfied with harmony just among members of their own ethnic group. They are to extend to all the peace received from God in Christ (cf. 1:7; 5:1).

Paul again admonishes believers to reject personal vengeance (12:19a; cf. 12:17). This time however, he adds a new theological dimension. He exhorts believers literally to "give place to the wrath," that is, the wrath of God (cf. 1:18). He supports this exhortation against communal retaliation in light of God's vengeance with a quotation from Scripture. "For it is written: Vengeance belongs to Me; I will repay, says the Lord" (12:19b; Dt. 32:35).

Paul's theological addition to his discussion of love in Christ's body is critical. It seems that he wants to remind all believers that there is a day of accountability. All believers must stand before the judgment seat of Christ, either vindicated or condemned (2 Cor. 5:10; cf. 2:16; 8:1). Believers must be mindful that God's final wrath against sin is a certainty. While the thoughts and actions of believers are to be motivated by God's love in Christ, there will be a day of reckoning for all those who refuse to share the love of Christ with others (12:1; cf. 2 Cor. 5:14).

Instead of retaliation, Paul quotes from the Hebrew wisdom tradition to expose the proper response to insult and injury in Christ's body. "But If your enemy is hungry, feed him. If he is thirsty, give him something to drink. For in so doing you will be heaping fiery coals on his head" (12:20; Pro. 25:21-22; cf. Mt. 5:44).

Finally, Paul comes full circle. He ends his stack of maxims with a double imperative that maintains the contrast between good and evil. "Do not be conquered by evil, but conquer evil with good" (12:21; cf. 12:9). He closes his exhortations on how to live in the body of Christ using military language. Paul's exhortation to believers in Rome to conquer evil through the good echoes the indicative earlier stated, believers are "more than conquerors through Him who loved" them (8:39; cf. Eph. 6:10-13). Paul ends by depicting the triumph of the love of God in Christ for others: a triumph of the love in the believing community made possible through the Spirit.

Believers' Obligations to Authorities

Paul now moves from exhortations about proper living within the body of Christ to believers' responsibility to those outside of Christ. He has more to say about the necessity of communal love later in the letter (13:8-14). But for now, he describes how Gentile and Jewish believers are to relate to the governing authorities in view of God's mercies in Christ (13:1-7). Paul has already subtly rejected the Greco-Roman honor-shame ethos, making it clear that unbelieving Gentiles, in fact, the whole Roman culture, stand in opposition to God's self-revelation in nature; and therefore are exposed to God's present and future wrath. On the other hand, Paul has exhorted believers to reject the values and practices of the surrounding culture in favor of a renewal of the mind wrought by the Spirit of God. It is against this backdrop that Paul instructs believers to submit to Roman authority.

Paul states, "Let every person be subject to the governing authorities" (13:1a). He again uses an apostolic command to establish the necessity of submission of each believer to the Roman government (cf. Tit. 3:1-2). He uses the imperative mood to stress the responsibility of every soul to voluntarily submit to rulers (cf. Eph. 5:21). Paul follows his command with a clarifying compound indicative. "For there is no authority except from God, and those which exist are established by God" (13:1b NASB). Using these words, Paul makes two important claims. He assumes that God possesses absolute sovereign authority over all things (cf. 1:20). It is on this premise that he says that there is no authority except from God. In other words, human authority is authority derived from God. Therefore, from Paul's perspective, in a fallen world, temporal or human authority is from God, and therefore is accountable to God (cf. Col. 2:15-16).

In addition, Paul asserts that legitimate human authority has been appointed by God. Here, it seems that Paul may have appropriated a claim made in the book of Daniel. Although Daniel was a Jewish captive of the Babylonian government and subject to its authority, he maintained the belief that God "removes kings and establishes kings" (2:21; 4:17; cf. 1 Pet. 2:13-14). Yet, the belief that God has appointed temporal authority, asserted by Daniel and echoed by Paul, raises a question that is contextually relevant. Does God establish evil leaders? This question is important given the fact that as Paul pens his letter to the Romans, the infamous and malevolent Emperor Nero is the head of the Roman government.

The short answer is that Paul views all human authority against three overarching realities. God has vested absolute authority in Christ alone (cf. Mt. 28:16). Also, God has given judgment to the Son, therefore, all people, including every human leader, will stand before the judgment seat of Christ to give an account of his or her works (2 Cor. 5:10; cf. 2:16). Because God allows evil leaders to reign, i.e., God's permissive will, Paul makes clear that God will rain vengeance on all those with delegated authority who persist in evil (12:19). Additionally, Paul views all things related to believers through the foundational conviction that Christ died and was raised for them. Therefore, God finally works all things for the good of the elect. For Paul, nothing can separate believers from the triumphant love of Christ (8:28, 35-37; cf. 1 Cor. 10:13). When Paul provides this counsel to Roman believers while an insane despot rules the Roman Empire, he is not being naïve. He is practicing his own mantra: "the just shall live by faith" (1:17).

Building on the prior premise, "there is no authority except from God," Paul provides his logical inference. "So then, the one who resists the authority is opposing God's command, and those who oppose it will bring judgment on themselves" (13:2). Paul identifies two theological consequences of believers' rejection of human authority. Paul declares that believers who resist human authority are resisting God. This is true because God has set up the system of authority. Paul also warns that believers who resist human authority will incur judgment. It is important to observe that Paul does not here specify either the source of judgment, divine or human, or the time of its execution, present or future. He only asserts its certainty (cf. 2:16).

Paul employs the categories of good and evil to explain further his reasoning (cf. 12:9-21). He states, "For rulers are not a terror to good conduct, but to bad. Do you want to be unafraid of the authority? Do what is good, and you will have its approval. For government is God's servant for your good" (13:3-4a). Using an assertion, a rhetorical question, and a conclusion, Paul argues for good civil conduct among believers. He does this by making the claim that ruling authorities are not a threat to good conduct, but to bad. Then, through his rhetorical question, "Do you want to be unafraid of the authority?" he exhorts believers to good conduct, which will result in governmental approval. Paul concludes his point by asserting that the ruling authorities are God's servants, literally, "ministers," for the good of believers in a fallen world.

Paul describes the temporal consequences of bad behavior. He states, "But if you do wrong, be afraid, because it does not carry the sword for no reason. For government is God's servant, an avenger that brings wrath on the one who does wrong" (13:4b). Paul uses a hypothetical to make the point that human authority exists to punish wrong, or illegal, conduct. He again calls the ruling authorities God's servants and then argues that the authorities execute God's wrath, i.e., God's present judgment against wrong doers (cf. 1:18). Using the sword as a metaphor for capital punishment, Paul seems to merge divine and governmental retribution. However, he stresses that the scope of punishment is limited to those *"practicing wrong."* He does not sanction injustice.

In light of what has been said, Paul restates his opening admonition. "Therefore, you must submit, not only because of wrath, but also because of your conscience" (13:5). By introducing the subject of conscience, Paul clarifies what should be the underlying motivation for proper conduct by believers *vis-a-vis* Roman authority. Believers are not to submit just to avoid the consequences, whether human or divine; they are to submit as a matter of inner conviction (14:5b, 23; cf. 9:1; 1 Pet. 2:13, 19). Believers must act based on the renewed mind (12:1-2).

Finally, Paul identifies an example of how his exhortation to submission to Roman authority should be implemented. He writes, "For the same reason you also pay taxes, for the authorities are God's servants, busy with this very thing" (13:6). Here, Paul begins by focusing on the necessity to pay taxes. He argues that believers, as a matter of conscience, must pay taxes that are owed to the state (cf. Mt. 22:15-21). Shortly after, Paul reinforces this specific obligation (13:7). But why? Is there a reason for Paul's emphasis on taxation? Why does he focus on this duty? Does this obligation have contextual significance?

Paul was no doubt cognizant of the sensitivity among both Jews and Gentiles on the topic of taxation. Tacitus records that in 58 A.D. there were complaints against companies that farmed indirect taxes as well as against tax collectors themselves.[18] The crisis had been building for a number of years; people who would otherwise have had no contact with the civil authorities would have had to interact with government officials on issues of taxation. Jews were in an especially sensitive situation because of their unique privilege of sending the temple tax to Jerusalem instead of paying it to Rome. Tacitus complains that Jews "always kept sending tribute and contributions to Jerusalem, thereby increasing the wealth of the Jews"[19] This provision for Jews led to some antagonism among Gentiles.[20]

Paul ends his counsel on submission to the government by providing a list of practical obligations for believers. He states, "Pay to all what is due them—taxes to whom taxes are due, revenue to whom revenue is due, respect to whom respect is due, honor to whom honor is due" (13:7). Paul enumerates four civic obligations owed to the Roman authorities. He begins with an imperative to stress the necessity of meeting civic obligations. All believers are to give to the authorities what is due. Then, he uses two related couplets to make his point: the first material, the second social. As noted above, taxes and revenue were two types of income exacted by Rome from individuals, provinces, and client nations. Paul's reiteration of paying taxes suggests the importance of this issue.

Paul closes by urging appropriate respect, literally, fear and honor. These were common social obligations due those of higher social status. Paul is not suggesting that believers are to submit to human authority when it conflicts with the will of God (cf. Dan. 3:1-30; 6:10-24; Acts 4:19; 5:29). In fact, the Old Testament prophets held that Gentile nations were also finally accountable before God (cf. Ezek. 25:1 – 32:32; Jonah 1:1-2). Ultimately, believers "must obey God rather than men" and be willing to suffer the consequences, knowing that their lives are "hidden with Christ in God" (Acts 5:29; Col. 3:3).

At this point, given Paul's rather idealistic depiction of Roman authorities, several questions may be raised that bear directly on the occasion for Paul's letter to Rome. Can there be any doubt that believing Jews suffered ecclesiastically and socially because of the expulsion by Claudius (ca. 49-54 A.D.)? Why did Claudius expel an entire ethnic group from Rome? Why not just the wrongdoers? How are believing Jews to hear Paul's counsel? How should Gentile believers view the actions of governing authority in light of ethnic bias? Should the Gentile majority resist obvious bias on the part of the government?

Many Adventists are confused about their obligation to the state with relationship to civil disobedience. Ellen White's admonition on the Fugitive Slave Law is instructive. The Fugitive Slave Law, or Fugitive Slave Act of 1850, was passed by the United States Congress on September 18th of that year as part the Compromise of 1850 between Free-Soilers in the North and slaveholding interests in the South. The law was passed in recognition of the South's support for California's admission to the Union as a free state and the ending of slavery in the District of Columbia.

The Fugitive Slave Law "provided for the seizure and return of runaway slaves who escaped from one state into another or into a federal territory."[21] It mandated the creation of a force of federal commissioners who could pursue runaway slaves in any state or territory, capture them, and return them to their owners. Abolitionists nicknamed the law the "Bloodhound Law" in reference to the dogs that were used to track down the fugitives. Passage of the law led to widespread protest in the North.

Ellen White was among those who urged civil disobedience. She was taken in vision at the Conference at Roosevelt, New York, August 3, 1861, "when the brethren and sisters were assembled on the day set apart for humiliation, fasting, and prayer, the Spirit of the Lord rested upon us, and I was taken off in vision and shown the sin of slavery, which has so long been a curse to this nation."[22] She described the vision as follows:

> I was shown that perplexity and fear have seized all hearts. God is punishing this nation for their sins. The sin of slavery has long existed. It has been a curse to this nation. The cries and groans and agony of God's creatures, held in bondage, placed upon a level with brute creatures by their fellow men, have risen to heaven. The fugitive slave law that went forth was calculated to crush out of man every noble, generous feeling of sympathy that should arise in his heart for the oppressed and suffering slave. It was in direct opposition to the teachings of Christ. God's scourge is now upon the North, that they have so long submitted to suffer slavery to exist and their fellow man be held in hopeless slavery, tyrannized over and tortured just as passionate man chooses to act out the demon. If they murder their fellow man, no matter; he is considered no more than a brute by them. I saw that the inhabitants of earth have nearly filled their cup of iniquity.[23]
>
> I was shown that we have men placed over us for rulers, and laws to govern the people. Were it not for these laws, the world would be in a worse condition than it is now. Some of these laws are good, and some bad The bad have been increasing, and we are yet to be brought into straight places. But God will sustain his people in being firm, and living up to the principles of his word. *Where the laws of men conflict with God's word and law, we are to obey the word and law of God, whatever the consequences may be.* The laws of our land requiring us to deliver a slave to his master, we are not to obey, and we must abide the consequences of the violation of this law. This slave is not the property of any man. God is his rightful Master, and man has no right to take God's workmanship into his hands, and claim his as his own.[24]

The Obligation of Love

After listing the obligations due the state by all believers, Paul returns to obligations within the body of Christ and the theme of love (13:8-14). He now seeks to establish that God's love in Christ received and extended must be the central value that actuates the believing community as they anticipate the *parousia.*

Paul focuses his audience on the necessity of love among believers. "Owe no one anything, except to love one another" (13:8a). In the verse, Paul returns to a thread introduced earlier. He has already admonished Roman believers to sincere love (12:9). Now, with a double negative for emphasis, literally, "to no one, nothing owe," Paul exhorts them to *continuous love*. He uses an awkward construction, which builds on his previous exhortations to pay what is owed to the Roman state (cf. 13:6-7). He does this to emphasize that there is one obligation that cannot be paid, one exception. It is the obligation to continuous mutual love in the body of Christ. For the first-time, Paul uses the verb *agapaō*, "love," ethically, in the infinitive form, to describe how believers are to relate to one another continually. Believers are to extend the self-sacrificing and self-renouncing love of Jesus Christ revealed through His death (5:6-8; cf. Phil. 2:1-11; 1 Cor. 13:1-8a; Jn. 3:16).

Paul provides for his divided audience in Rome the *indicative* on which his *imperative* is based. He offers, especially to his Jewish audience, the reason for the necessity of mutual love for those in Christ. Paul makes the radical claim, literally, "For the one loving has fulfilled the law" (13:8b). In other words, the righteous requirements of the law are met through ongoing love for the other. With this assertion, Paul undercuts the edifice of first-century Pharisaic Judaism that propagated an individual righteousness devoid of relationship through obedience to rules. Paul indirectly rejects a religious system that taught that righteousness was secured by works of the law, with little regard for people (3:20; 7:7-13; 10:1-4). Conversely, he argues that the righteous requirements of God's law have been met when believers extend the sacrificial love of Christ, received through His death, to one another in community (cf. Jn. 13:34-35). Concretely put, believers are to "do nothing from selfish ambition or conceit, but in humility count others more significant than" themselves (Phil. 2:3 ESV).

Recognizing that this assertion will be difficult for some believers to understand or accept, Paul clarifies his argument. "The commandments, 'You shall not commit adultery; You shall not murder; You shall not steal; You shall not covet'; and any other commandment, are summed up in this word, 'Love your neighbor as yourself'" (13:9). Paul quotes four commandments from the moral law, rather than from either the ceremonial laws or oral traditions of Judaism (Ex. 20:13-17; Dt. 5:17-12). He seems to use these commands as representative of the six social commands in the moral law, which outline covenant obligations towards others in community. Paul's point is clear: all commands which refer to ones' obligation to other people are summed up in the command "love your neighbor as yourself" (Lev. 19:18). Paul uses a quotation from the Mosaic law and echoes a central teaching of Jesus to demonstrate that unconditional, sacrificial love for the other fulfills all relational obligations required by the law of God (cf. Gal. 5:14, 19-21; Mt. 19:17-19; 22:36-39; Jam. 2:8).

Using another maxim, Paul subtly applies his ecclesiological indicative. "Love does no wrong to a neighbor" (13:10a). Paul emphasizes that he is not engaged in generalizations or abstractions. These words are contextually relevant. He has demonstrated that believers, both Jews and Gentiles, are doing harm to one another through judgmentalism and arrogance (cf. 2:1-16; 11:13-24). Now, he wants Roman believers to understand once and for all that love born of the Spirit does no evil to those for whom Christ died, especially other believers in His body (cf. 5:5-8). Rightly understood, Paul's maxim, "love does no wrong to a neighbor," articulates a spiritual principle rejecting ethnocentric living (cf. Lk. 10:25-37). As if to drive his point home, Paul repeats his central indicative for life in community, "Love, therefore, is the fulfillment of the law" (13:10b).

Finally, Paul intensifies his admonition for mutual love in Rome by placing it within the scope of the *eschaton*, or final things (13:11-14). Employing end-time language, he writes, "Besides this, knowing the time, it is already the hour for you to wake up from sleep, for now our salvation is nearer than when we first believed." Based on Paul's words, there can be little doubt that he believes that the *parousia,* i.e., the second coming of Christ, is imminent (cf. 1 Cor. 7:29- 31; 10:6-12; 1 Thess. 4:13-18). It is on this basis that Paul admonishes believers to wake from their sleep. He uses this metaphor to underscore the nearness of Christ's appearing, and therefore the need for alertness.

Paul restates his same eschatological claim and then exposes the implications for the Roman community. "The night is nearly over, and the daylight is near, so let us discard the deeds of darkness and put on the armor of light. Let us walk with decency, as in the daylight" (13:12-13a HCSB). Given the reality of the nearness of the *parousia*, Paul exhorts believers with two contrasting imperatives using the metaphors of light and darkness. He begins by urging believers to cast off the works of darkness (cf. Col. 3:5-8; Eph. 5:11).

To what does he refer? Paul uses a vice list to provide examples of the work of darkness. He says, "Not in carousing and drunkenness; not in sexual impurity and promiscuity; not in quarreling and jealousy" (13:13b HCSB). Paul has used a vice list earlier in the letter to describe pagan Gentile depravity because of their rejection of God (cf. 1:26, 28-29; cf. 2:5, 21-22). He ends this list with the community-specific vices of quarreling and jealousy. He equates these acts in which Roman believers are presently engaged, with the vilest types of pagan sin: carousing and drunkenness, sexual impurity and promiscuity.

By way of contrast, Paul exhorts Roman believers to "put on the armor of light" (13:12b; cf. 6:11-12). He explains his military image. "But put on the Lord Jesus Christ, and make no plans to satisfy the fleshly desires" (13:14). Paul's concluding exhortation, put on Christ, is not esoteric (cf. Col. 3:12-14; Eph. 4:22-24). With these words, he simply uses a different metaphor to emphasize an earlier teaching. To put on Christ is to walk according to the Spirit. Paul has made it abundantly clear that those in Christ have been called to participate in the death and resurrection life of Jesus Christ through the power of the Spirit. For Paul, it is only this continual participation in Christ that nullifies the desires of the flesh, that is, living life according to the flesh. Without a doubt, as we will now see, Paul has Roman ethnocentrism squarely in mind.

The Disputed Matters

Building on his admonition to put on the Lord Jesus Christ and make no plans to satisfy the fleshly desires, Paul confronts specific issues growing out of the ethnic prejudice that divides Gentiles and Jews in Rome (14:1-23). Ultimately, as the antidote for divisiveness, Paul establishes Christ as the example to be imitated. Believers are to look to the example of Jesus Christ for how they are to welcome one another (15:1-13).

Using the explicit category of the weak and the implied category of the strong, Paul first admonishes the believing Gentile majority to receive their Jewish brothers and sisters who are in the minority. Yet, he urges Gentiles that their acceptance must not be characterized by conflict over disputed matters (14:1-4).

Paul begins to confront some of the specific issues on which Gentile and Jewish believers are divided with the exhortation, "Now accept the one who is weak in faith" (14:1a NASB). Again, using individual language to represent the group, Paul urges Gentiles to accept Jews, i.e., "those who are weak in faith" (cf. 1:17; 2:1-5; 5:12-21; 7:37-23). Here, Paul establishes one of the two categories that will inform his entire argument: "the weak in faith," which generally represent Jewish believers (15:1).

Paul uses this category, weak in faith, as a metaphor to highlight the fact that many Jewish believers are still attempting to reconcile the gospel of Christ with the old covenant, especially with the law of God. We should recall that first century Pharisaic Judaism and the Judaizers emphasized observance of the law, including the oral traditions, as the basis for righteousness before God. Because of this belief, even believing Jews like those in Rome had to sort out what changed and what remained in light of salvation through Christ.

Paul has already addressed Jewish confusion pertaining to the role of the law in salvation. Now, he deemphasizes the importance of some matters that were made essential based on Jewish oral traditions. It is in this sense that Paul uses the category, weak in faith, to refer to Jewish Christians in Rome. He holds that believing Jews must grow in their faith by understanding God's law through the gospel of Christ.

Conversely, Paul later uses the category, the strong, to refer to Gentiles, but only in a limited sense. He believes that Gentiles, without the baggage of Jewish traditions, are stronger when it comes to several disputed matters, e.g., dietary restrictions and special days. Yet, Paul has explained that believing Gentiles, like their Jewish brothers and sisters, must mature in their faith (cf. 1:11-12; 11:13-24).

Paul's categories are not ethnically rigid. As we will see, Paul, himself a Jew, identifies with the theological position of the Gentiles on unclean food (14:14). It is also possible that some former Gentile proselytes would embrace the more restrictive Jewish position. With this explanation, it becomes clear that Paul's opening exhortation enjoins Gentiles, the strong, to take the initiative in acceptance of Jews, those weak in faith.

Paul begins his admonition with the verb variously translated "welcome, accept, receive" that will be critical to the conclusion of his present argument (15:7-13; cf. 14:3). With this term, Paul, as the apostle to the Gentiles, commands the Gentile majority to begin the reconciliation process (1:6-7; 11:13; 15:15-16; cf. 5:1-11). On the authority of Christ, he admonishes Gentiles in Christ to receive believing Jews into their circle of friendship. Why does Paul place the onus on Gentiles? Two answers may be suggested. Paul later argues that the strong are obligated to bear burdens of the weak (15:1; cf. Gal. 6:1-2; 1 Thess. 5:14). If Gentile believers possess superior theological knowledge and social, material, or political advantage, then they are not to use their advantage to please themselves. Believers are to use their advantage for the good of others (14:14-18; 15:1b-2, 25-27; 1 Cor. 8:7-13; Phil. 2:3-4; cf. Lk. 12:48).

Additionally, while attempting to correct the thought and practice of socially stratified believers in Corinth, Paul maintains that the inferior parts of the body should be given additional honor. He states,

> The eye cannot say to the hand, "I have no need of you," nor again the head to the feet, "I have no need of you." On the contrary, the members of the body that seem to be weaker are indispensable, and those members of the body that we think less honorable we clothe with greater honor, and our less respectable members are treated with greater respect; whereas our more respectable members do not need this. But God has so arranged the body, giving the greater honor to the inferior member, that there may be no dissension within the body, but the members may have the same care for one another. If one member suffers, all suffer together with it; if one member is honored, all rejoice together with it. Now you are the body of Christ and individually members of it (1 Cor. 12:21-27).

Against the central value of bestowing honor on those with the highest status in Greco-Roman culture, Paul argues that in the body of Christ, honor is distributed based on need. Those who are considered socially inferior in the culture are to receive greater compensatory honor. Paul is articulating a value system that is not based on fallen human culture. His understanding rests solely on the incarnation of Christ (Phil. 2:5-11; 2 Cor. 5:21).

Paul adds an important qualification to his imperative for Gentile acceptance of Jews that serves to introduce the actual subject at hand. He writes, "But not for the purpose of quarreling over opinions" (14:1b, cf. 7-9). Paul is emphatic that "quarreling over disputable matters" should be stopped in Rome. To appreciate Paul's prohibition, historical background is needed.

Although Paul does not use the technical term, *adiaphora*, "matters of indifference," it is agreed that this passage falls within this description. So, it is important to address how this subject was regarded in the larger society and by Paul. Greco-Roman moralists, like the Stoics, divided all human concerns into three categories: good things, bad things, and indifferent things. Good things were the virtues, i.e., discernment, prudence, courage, and justice, and things related to virtue, i.e., joy, cheerfulness, and confidence. Bad things were the opposite of good things: vices and things related to vice. Everything else, things without moral content—neither good nor bad—were matters of indifference. Such things were neutral, not contributing to benefit or harm. The moral philosophers categorized matters of indifference to include sickness and health, and wealth and poverty.[25] Such things were at the whim of fate; the individual had little or no control in these areas. The ability to distinguish matters of indifference led to proper conduct. [26]

What Paul identifies as matters of indifference is in some cases similar to what the moralists held. For example, existential issues, life and death, and status. In Romans 14:1-23, Paul identifies food and drink and the observance of days as matters of indifference. These issues had the potential of highlighting ethnic differences between Gentiles and Jews in his audience. Instead, Paul defines the differences of opinion in these areas as based on believers' differing measures of faith. Pointing out that each person has a range of options in terms of these matters, Paul implies that believers can agree to disagree on certain issues.[27]

It is worth noting that in his letter to the Galatians, Paul contrasts the things that matter with those that do not. "For through the Spirit, by faith, we eagerly wait for the hope of righteousness. For in Christ Jesus neither circumcision nor uncircumcision counts for anything; the only thing that counts is faith working through love" (Gal. 5:5-6). For Paul, matters of indifference were the things that did not have ultimate moral significance, while things that mattered have ultimate significance for now and for eternity. In context, circumcision and uncircumcision were in reference to ethnicity, i.e., Jews and Gentiles. What Paul is saying here is that ethnicity is a matter of indifference; it has no eternal significance.

In another letter, Paul prays that the Philippians will be able to discern the things that really matter. "And this I pray: that your love may abound still more and more in recognition and insight, so that you may discern the things that really matter, so that you may be pure and giving no offense until the day of Christ" (Phil. 1:9-10).[28]

In Romans, Paul identifies the first disputed issue. He writes, "Some believe in eating anything, while the weak eat only vegetables" (14:2). Just now, Paul pinpoints a major fault line among believers. He exposes Gentile and Jewish convictions related to food as the central issue being disputed in Rome (cf. 14:3-4, 6b, 13-23). Employing the categories of weak and strong as an interpretive guide, Paul declares that the Gentile majority, the strong, have taken the position that believers can eat anything, while Jewish believers, the weak in faith, hold that believers are restricted to eating only vegetables. Given the fact that Jews in the first century were not generally vegetarians, how are we to understand Paul's description?

Before treating Paul's corrective related to food as a disputed issue, it is necessary to understand his first-century milieu. Paul's designation of one who is weak in the faith refers to the Jewish believer who has but a limited conception of the principles of righteousness by faith. This is a person who is eager for salvation and willing to do whatever is required. But because of immaturity or the way he or she has been taught, there is an attempt to secure salvation by following rules and regulations that may not actually be binding. Because this person believes in the absolute necessity of such rules, he or she becomes distressed and confused when other Christians do not obey them. "Paul's statements in Rom. 14 have been variously interpreted, and have been used by some: (1) to disparage a vegetarian diet, (2) to abolish the distinction between clean and unclean meats, and (3) to remove all distinction between days, thus abolishing the seventh-day Sabbath."[29] The fact that Paul is suggesting none of these things becomes apparent when his statements are considered in their first-century context.

In 1 Corinthians 8, Paul deals with the issue of eating foods offered to idols. Since 1 Corinthians 8 and Romans 14 were written within a year of each other, it is likely that both references address the issue raised by the pagan practice of selling animal sacrifices from pagan temples in the marketplace for public consumption. Paul instructs the believers in Corinth that since idols are nothing, there was no wrong in eating foods dedicated to them. However, since some believers, those weak in the faith, had scruples about eating such meat, those without scruples should abstain from eating lest they place a stumbling block in the path of the weaker believers. Paul's counsel is in harmony with the decision of the Jerusalem Council (Acts 15:1-21). Apparently, in order to avoid offending in this matter, some Christians had stopped eating meat altogether and had become vegetarians. It would be incorrect to conclude that Paul is suggesting that those strong in the faith could eat anything, regardless of its effect on their physical wellbeing. Paul is not making a case regarding food that is hygienically harmful. He has already established that the body of the believer is the temple of God and should be treated as such.

In addition, Paul's counsel illuminates a fact that many Jewish Christians were slow to perceive: the ceremonial law had met its fulfillment in Christ. No longer were the annual Jewish feasts and ceremonial rites binding. For example, the ceremonial law required that Jews observe seven annual sabbaths. Gentile believers would be familiar with the special days associated with pagan worship (cf. Gal. 4:8-11).

Paul does not teach or imply that the seventh-day Sabbath has been abolished; it was not part of the ceremonial law. The Sabbath was more ancient than Judaism itself, having been instituted as part of the moral order from creation. Jesus declared Himself "Lord of the Sabbath" (Mk. 2:28). It would be difficult to show that Paul included the seventh-day Sabbath with the Jewish festival days that vanished with the ceremonial law. Only the weaker Jewish Christians held that the mandate to observe such days was still in force (cf. Mt. 15:1-20; Mk. 7:2-5; Lk. 11:38).[30]

Paul moves from identification of the problem to his corrective. He uses two negative imperatives. "Those who eat must not despise those who abstain, and those who abstain must not pass judgment on those who eat" (14:3). When it comes to disputed matters where sin and grace are not at stake, Paul's admonitions are evenhanded. With his first negative imperative, Paul commands Gentiles who hold that believers can eat anything not to despise the Jews who refrain from eating.

Paul's use of the word translated as despise should not be overlooked. The English translation does not transmit the full animus of the term. In Paul's time to despise meant that a person or thing had no merit or worth (14:10b, 14-18; cf. 1 Cor. 1:28; Gal.4:14). In other words, Gentile believers were treating Jewish believers with contempt. Their attitude may suggest a sense of superiority based on ethnic theology. Paul has earlier warned Gentiles about their general posture of arrogance and conceit towards Jewish people (11:17-22). Here, he is more specific.

In the same way, Paul exhorts the Jews who forego eating not to judge Gentiles. There can be little doubt that Jewish judgmentalism is born of a rigidity grounded in their traditions (14:10a; cf. 1 Cor. 8:4-13; Col. 2:16; Mt. 15:1-9). Paul has mentioned Jewish judgment of Gentiles before. He earlier warned Jews that their judgmentalism would result in condemnation from God (2:1-16).

To bolster his commands, Paul provides the overriding theological indicative. For Paul, Gentiles' despising of Jews or Jews' judging of Gentiles are anathema in the body of Christ. Why? "Because God has accepted him [them]" (14:3b). Here, Paul establishes God's acceptance of all believers through the death of Christ as nonnegotiable. Through the blood of Christ, all believers have been welcomed. They have become members of God's family (3:21-26; 5:1-11; 8:14-17). It is because of this inclusion that such behaviors are to be rejected. Here and throughout his argument, Paul attempts to establish a theological rather than a cultural basis for thought and practice in Rome (cf. 15:7).

Paul uses a rhetorical question and a Christological statement to support further his indicative. "Who are you to criticize another's household slave? Before his own Lord he stands or falls. And he will stand. For the Lord is able to make him stand" (14:4 HCSB). It is possible that based on his continued use of judgment language, Paul views Jewish behavior as being more egregious. Nevertheless, his central point is that inappropriate judgment of others, especially over disputed issues, is disallowed, because believers not only have been received by God, they belong to the Lord Jesus Christ and they are finally accountable to Him (cf. 1:1, 6; 2:16; 6:22; 2 Cor. 5:10).

Paul momentarily shifts to a second disputed issue troubling the believers Rome. He writes, "Some judge one day to be better than another, while others judge all days to be alike" (14:5a). Because both paganism and Judaism had special days of the year, it is not clear to which observance day or days Paul refers. Nor does he clarify which group espouses which position related to the dispute over days. It is most likely that Gentiles took the more liberal position, "all days to be alike," while Jews embraced the more conservative view, "one day to be better than another."

Although it cannot be said with absolute certainty, Paul's argument seems to suggest that the dispute in Rome related to days is based on Jewish insistence on the ongoing significance of special days in the Jewish calendar for all believers—a position rooted in the ceremonial law and Jewish oral traditions (cf. Col. 2:16-17; Gal. 4:8-11). While there can be little certainty on the exact nature of the dispute between Gentiles and Jews over days, what is certain is that Paul, whose view of life in Christ is grounded in the Old Testament, would never view creation Sabbath or Sabbath enjoined in the moral law as a matter of indifference (Gen. 2:1-3; Ex. 20:8-11; cf. 7:12).

In any event, to correct the dispute regarding days, Paul emphasizes the role of conviction in spiritual decision-making, especially as it related to non-essentials. He states, "Let all be fully convinced in their own minds" (14:5b). Paul uses the verb convinced, literally, "be completely certain" to stress the need for personal deliberation and conviction on matters with no clear Scriptural injunction (cf. 4:17). For Paul, believers are to act in gray areas only when fully convicted by the Holy Spirit (8:14; 12:1-2). As we will see, doubt is the opposite of full conviction and signals that a believer should not move forward at that moment[31] (cf. 14:23).

Yet, Paul does not stop with this clarification. He combines the two issues to posit a more fundamental criterion for adjudicating disputed matters in the body of Christ. Paul states,

> Those who observe the day, observe it in honor of the Lord. Also, those who eat, eat in honor of the Lord, since they give thanks to God; while those who abstain, abstain in honor of the Lord and give thanks to God. We do not live to ourselves, and we do not die to ourselves. If we live, we live to the Lord, and if we die, we die to the Lord; so then, whether we live or whether we die, we are the Lord's. For to this end Christ died and lived again, so that he might be Lord of both the dead and the living (14:6-9).

In this passage, Paul makes three critical points. He argues that in the matters of both days and food, believers must each act with God the Son and God the Father in mind. In other words, believers ultimately should do all things for the glory of God (Col. 3:17; 1 Cor. 10:31). Neither personal nor group preferences are to be determinative. Paul then reiterates the related existential point that believers in both life and death belong to Christ as Lord (14:4). They must act to please Him (2 Cor. 5:14-15). Finally, Paul maintains that all matters should be understood and acted upon in light of the fact that Christ died and was raised to exercise absolute authority over the living and the dead.

At this point, it should be observed that these disputed issues are not the basis for division between Gentiles and Jews in Rome. These matters are proxies. They are grounded in ethnic preference and group pride rather than life in the Spirit (1:18-3:9; 8:3-30; 12:1-2). It is life lived based on the cultural desire for ethnic power and control in thought and practice rather than in response to God's saving activity in Christ. Paul wants believers in Rome to renounce cultural particularity in light of the Lordship of Jesus Christ.

Paul now raises two rhetorical questions designed to continue his chastisement of Roman believers for their conduct towards one another. He queries, "Why do you pass judgment on your brother or sister? Or you, why do you despise your brother or sister?" (14:10a). Paul directs his first question squarely at his Jewish audience. He had earlier subtly mentioned their criticism, that is, judgmental attitude, towards Gentiles. Now with a question, he demands that they reconsider their behavior (cf. 14:3a; 2:1-3).

With the same evenhandedness, Paul uses his second question to call the Gentiles to account for despising Jews. He has reprimanded them before (14:3b; 11:13-24). Now along with their Jewish brothers and sisters, Paul charges Gentiles with wrong conduct. Their behavior is contrary to their new life in Christ. It is noteworthy that familial language is embedded in both questions. It seems that Paul wants to remind believing Jews and Gentiles that they are harming members of their own family (cf. 13:10).

As if to emphasize the seriousness of the situation among believers in Rome, Paul again employs accountability language. "For we will all stand before the judgment seat of God" (14:10b). Paul continues to maintain the tension of love and justice in the nature of God (11:22; cf. 1:17-18). The believers in Rome are not to forget that they will be held accountable before God—Father, Son, and Spirit—for their actions in the body (2:6-8). Believers will stand before the judgment seat of Christ, either vindicated or condemned (2:16; 8:1; cf. 2 Cor. 5:10). Paul supports his eschatological claim with a quotation from Scripture and then restates the certainty of final accountability. "For it is written, 'As I live, says the Lord, every knee shall bow to me, and every tongue shall give praise to God.' So then, each of us will be accountable to God" (14:11-12; Is. 45:23; cf. Phil. 2:10-11). We should note the gravity that Paul attributes to Gentile-Jewish animosity. Just as he warned Gentile Christians earlier, he now warns both groups that their salvation is at stake (11:22b).

Paul uses an internal summary of the foregoing argument before his conclusion. "Therefore, let us no longer criticize one another" (14:13a). Then using language of contrast, Paul culminates this phase of his argument with counsel for the immediate future. In the days ahead, Paul wants Gentiles and Jews to end their mutual criticism. He explains that future life among believers requires a decision. He wants both groups to reject disparagement, "but resolve instead never to put a stumbling block or hindrance in the way of another" (14:13b). Paul seems to have in view the appropriate exercise of personal or group freedom in Christ (cf. 1 Cor. 8:1-13). He uses the metaphorical language, stumbling block, to prohibit any action that will cause other believers to fall (cf. 1 Cor. 8:9). Thus, Paul encourages the Roman believers to make the good of each other their priority (13:10).

Drawing his corrective to a close, Paul makes a complicated argument to demonstrate for Gentile believers in Rome the priority of people, especially their Jewish brothers and sisters, over their correct knowledge related to food (14:14-23). In so doing, he deconstructs their ethnocentric theology. Paul's argument has two parts: Gentiles are not to destroy their Jewish brothers and sisters (14:14-18); all believers are to pursue peace (14:19-23).

Paul introduces his discourse with a statement about his personal conviction. "I know and am persuaded in the Lord Jesus that nothing is unclean in itself" (14:14a). With the use of the term "unclean," literally, "common," Paul, for the first time, broaches the subject of food that is ceremonially unclean. But before treating Paul's discussion, background is needed.

Jonathan Klawans draws a distinction between ritual and moral impurity. He maintains that the defilement described in Leviticus 11-15 and Deuteronomy 19 refers to a contagious but generally impermanent condition that he calls "ritual impurity." He differentiates this from "moral impurity" that calls for a higher level of evaluation, although neither term appears in the biblical text. He uses the terms to indicate that "there are two kinds of impurity in ancient Israel, one of which is more associated with sin than the other."[32]

Ritual impurity affected the ritual status of persons so defiled; they were excluded from participation in some ceremonial acts and from certain sacred places. There is no instance where there was not a process of purification for ritual impurity. The use of sacrifices, sprinklings, bathing, etc., as well as the passage of time led to ritual purification. Although long-lasting in some cases, ritual impurity was always an impermanent status.

Ritual impurity could be acquired by contact with bodily processes, such as childbirth, and other natural functions, such as death or sex; the carcasses of dead animals; and various diseases and discharges. It was almost impossible not to become ritually impure at some point in life. While contracting ritual impurity was not a sin, it could lead to sin or serve as a punishment for sin.

There was another form of defilement, however, called "moral impurity." This was more serious than ritual defilement. Moral impurity was the result of immoral acts. This category of activities, so heinous that their commission was an abomination to God, included sexual sins, idolatry, and bloodshed. The moral defilement that these offenses caused tainted the people, the sanctuary, and even the land of Israel. Such defilement led to exclusion from the land.[33]

In his present discussion, Paul uses strong language, "I know and am persuaded," to underscore the depth of his belief on the issue of what is ceremonially unclean. Yet, more importantly for his purpose of instruction, he emphasizes that his conviction on the disputed matter of clean and unclean turns on the person and work of Christ. Paul argues that he has been fully persuaded in the Lord Jesus. In other words, for Paul, the death and resurrection of Christ, and his present standing in Him, have become the interpretive key for clarifying this controversial issue. It is this Christological clarity that Paul now recommends to the Gentiles in Rome.

Paul begins to establish the tension between conviction and doubt. He states, "But it is unclean for anyone who thinks it unclean" (14:14b). Based on the foregoing argument, there can be little doubt that when Paul says, "it is unclean for anyone who thinks it unclean," he is referring to most Jewish believers, the weak in faith (14:1; cf. 15:1). This time, however, Paul contends that despite his personal conviction on this disputed matter, other believers are never to violate their consciences. And as he shortly after affirms, Paul believes that Roman believers, especially Jews, are not to act on the disputed matter of ritually unclean food without full conviction (14:23).

Paul moves from theological principle to application. "If your brother or sister is being injured by what you eat, you are no longer walking in love" (14:15a). With these words, Paul posits a hypothetical to highlight the priority of other believers over knowledge. Specifically, he warns the Gentiles that if their Jewish brothers and sisters are being grieved by what Gentiles eat, they are no longer walking according to love. When Paul uses this corrective language, he is simply repeating an earlier imperative, "be led by the Spirit," and a relational indicative, "love does no wrong to a neighbor" (8:14; 13:10). Paul's point is critical. Gentile freedom based on *correct knowledge* should not trump their love for their Jewish brothers and sisters in Christ (cf. 1 Cor. 8:1, 7-9). He agrees with the correct theology of Gentiles, the strong, over and against the perspective of his Jewish kinsmen, those weak in faith (cf. 14:1-3; 15:1). Nevertheless, he maintains that love for others, especially when non-essentials are at stake, must be the priority.

Paul intensifies his point with two imperatives. "By what you eat, do not destroy the one for whom Christ died. So, do not let what you regard as good be spoken of as evil" (14:15b-16 ESV). Paul's first admonition serves as a Christological reminder. Gentile believers must remember that Jewish believers, although weak in faith on matters pertaining to food, nevertheless, possess ultimate worth because of Christ's sacrificial death. Gentile freedom in Christ is not more important than the ones for whom Christ died. Further, with the words, "so do not let what you regard as good be spoken of as evil," Paul reinforces his earlier point. He reminds Gentiles that correct theology about food is good, but if it is used to harm the Jews, it has become an evil (cf. 12:9, 21).

To these imperatives, Paul adds a clarifying indicative. He writes, "For the kingdom of God is not food and drink but righteousness and peace and joy in the Holy Spirit" (14:17). In context, Paul instructs Gentile believers that they should not give secondary issues primary status. On this point, he may be echoing a teaching of Jesus about the relative priority of some matters over others. Jesus had said to the Pharisees, "You tithe the mint, the dill, and the cumin, but you have neglected the more important matters of the law; justice, mercy and faithfulness. You should have practiced the latter, without neglecting the former" (Mt. 23:23 NIV).

In His day, Jesus accused Pharisees of emphasizing personal piety over relational matters that had eternal weight. In the present passage, Paul reminds Gentiles that God's kingdom, His present reign in the lives of those in Christ, does not emphasize correct theology about food. Rather, God's present reign through the Holy Spirit focuses on matters of eternal consequence: righteousness, peace, and joy.

Why these three qualities? Could it be that Paul uses these three attributes to describe the necessary progression in the life of believers, that is, their sanctification? In any event, for Paul, what ultimately matters is God's present rule that issues in holistic salvation through the power of Holy Spirit (cf. Gal. 5:22-23). This possible interpretation is supported by Paul's next assertion. "Whoever serves Christ in this way is acceptable to God and approved by men" (14:18). Again, using enslavement language, Paul clarifies, especially for the knowledgeable Gentiles, that life emphasizing what ultimately matters is serving Christ (1:1, 6; 6:15-23). It is this type of believer that is acceptable to God and approved by the believing community.

Finally, Paul repeats much of what has been said to his Roman audience (14:19-23). Yet, to expose the necessary implications of his argument, he now places an accent on the pursuit of harmony. Paul states, "Let us then pursue what makes for peace and for mutual upbuilding" (14:19). Rather than controversy that has the potential to destroy the one for whom Christ died (14:15), Paul uses the verb "pursue, follow in haste" with the grammatical sense of potential action not yet realized (cf. 1 Cor. 14:1; 1 Tim. 6:11). He recommends that Roman believers pursue a two-pronged future course: peace and mutual upbuilding.

As it relates to the pursuit of peace, unlike the Roman state, Paul viewed peace as a condition achieved not through violence or domination resulting in tranquility. Rather, peace has been secured for believers through God's saving act in Christ. Thus, Paul argues in a later letter that Christ is the peace reconciling Jewish and Gentile believers (Eph. 2:14). Already in his letter to the Romans, he has established that, based on the death of Christ, believers now experience peace with God (5:1).

Having been justified, all believers enjoy relational intimacy with God the Father through the Son. It is on this basis that he now encourages Roman believers to pursue horizontally what they already possess vertically. In short, all believers, including Paul himself, are to pursue communal peace continuously. Through the power of the Spirit, believers are to extend aggressively what they have received in Christ as a result of justification (5:1-5, 11). It seems clear that Paul urges this focus on peace in community as opposed to their current emphasis on controversy.

Along with relational peace, Paul employs a metaphor drawn from architecture to advocate that Roman believers pursue upbuilding. He uses a noun that can mean, "building, construction, edification," which carried the ideas of planning and intentionality. Paul uses this term in his correspondence with believers in Corinth. He challenges the socially fractured and individualistic Corinthians to prioritize the upbuilding of others in Christ's body over their personal pursuit of showy gifts (1 Cor. 14:12, 26; cf. 2 Cor. 10:8; 13:10). In the present passage, Paul encourages a future between Gentile and Jewish believers marked by mutual edification.

Building on his call to peace and mutual care, Paul turns back to the issue at hand. "Do not, for the sake of food, destroy the work of God" (14:20a). Speaking to both groups, but especially to Gentile believers, Paul exhorts them not to destroy God's work of sanctification, individual and communal, because of different opinions about food (cf. 14:15).

Restating his conviction related to food, "everything is indeed clean," Paul drives home his relational point: "but it is wrong for you to make others fall by what you eat" (14:20b). Notwithstanding his personal conviction about food, Paul emphasizes that the Gentile focus must be on the well-being of those weak in faith in the community. Their freedom in this matter must not be the downfall of others (cf. 14:13, 15).

In addition, Paul uses a double commendation to stress the same point. He states: "It is good not to eat meat or drink wine or do anything that makes your brother or sister stumble" (14:21). While he disagrees with their theology, Paul commends Jewish believers for their restrictive behavior. He views it as noble—as a matter of conscience (14:23). More important, Paul has repeatedly affirmed Gentiles' having correct knowledge on their side of the dispute over food. However, he wants both groups to recognize that it is also good to forego one's rights in order to keep others from falling. Paul makes the same argument in his letter to Corinth. He has set aside his right to eat meat that has been offered to idols for the sake of weaker brothers and sisters for whom eating such meat is a sin (1 Cor. 8:1, 7-9, 11, 13; cf. 10:23, 31-32). Paul's point in both cases is that freedom in Christ must be exercised responsibly, showing due consideration for others.

In closing his argument, Paul offers a practical way forward. "The faith which you have, have as your own conviction before God" (14:22a NASB). Paul now recommends that if believers have convictions on a non-essential issue, they should make it a private matter between God and themselves. It should not be used to disrupt peace in the community.

To emphasize his recommendation, Paul juxtaposes a blessed person with one who is condemned. "Blessed are those who have no reason to condemn themselves because of what they approve. But those who have doubts are condemned if they eat, because they do not act from faith" (14:22b-23a). Here, Paul seems to stress two claims. Gentiles must remember that God blesses a person if what he or she approves does not result in final condemnation, which would be the consequence of acting on knowledge without love. Also, Paul reminds believers, especially the weak in faith, that they are not to violate their consciences by eating without faith, i.e., conviction.

Finally, Paul articulates an overarching principle that should serve to guide believers in Rome. He writes, "For whatever does not proceed from faith is sin." Paul uses a maxim, an indicative, to highlight the importance of faith or full conviction in disputed matters. For Paul, individual convictions are not definitive in areas that are clearly prohibited by vice lists, or the obligation to love summarized in the commandments.[34] (cf. 1:28-32; 12:9; 13:10). A contemplated action that is a clear rejection of God's saving purpose in Christ is sin. With this indicative, "for whatever does not proceed from faith is sin," Paul echoes part of his thesis that began the letter, "For in it God's righteousness is revealed from faith to faith, just as it is written: The righteous will live by faith" (1:17). For Paul, faith is trusting God's saving work in Christ from beginning to end. Life that is not lived in response, in total submission, to God's graciousness in Jesus Christ, whether communal or individual, is sin, a rejection of the sovereign love of God (1:18 - 3:20; 5:6-8).

Paul's allusion to "ethnic theology" practiced by both Gentiles and Jews in Rome raises the question of the appropriateness of an exclusively Eurocentric theology in Adventism while not denying the many contributions of Western theological reflection. The following sermon outline illustrates its limitations. This sermon was preached in 1980 at the Seventh-day Adventist Theological Seminary, at Andrews University. The preacher was a seminary student at the time. His sermon outline was preserved.

> Sermon Title: *Visible Works*
>
> Introduction
>
> Fellow students, faculty members and administration, welcome to our chapel services today sponsored by the Black Student's Association of the Seminary. It is a rare occasion that we speak before the seminary body. I will center my remarks around the works of James the second chapter. I have specifically chosen this letter because it was considered a straw epistle by a mighty reformer. My conclusions are at variance with Luther's. If straw,

then the straw that breaks the camel's back of high-minded theologians, then straw it is.

Our studies in this place introduce us to many teachings, theologians, reflections, and interpretations. I actually enjoy the egghead life of study, reflection, argument, and debate. But, there seems to be a hole in my soul and an unfulfilled thirst lingering after the lectures and discussions are over.

I. James 2

My remarks today are bathed in the soapy waters of James 2. James addresses his audience as his "dear brothers." God is merciful and the royal law is our guide in relationships (love one another). I fail to understand Martin Luther's reluctance to fully embrace this precious work. Mercy triumphs over condemnation, and I am left uplifted and fortified . . . UNTIL . . .

Yes, there is a major "but" to my message today. What good is served, my brothers and sisters, if we claim to have faith but have nothing to show visibly for our profession of faith?

Have we ventured to this university to learn theory, write papers, graduate, and depart to our segmented realities governed by custom and taste?

II. Application

When I apply the teachings of James 2 to my seminary experience, the joy of the text disappears. I have a Hebrew professor who belittles American education regularly and his students daily. His insults are evidence of a compassionless soul with possible authoritarian issues. Half of the registered students have already dropped his class and those of us who remain are uninspired and are functioning below our grade level.

Make no mistake, I am not speaking of grades. This ordained minister, seminary professor, and representative of our carpenter rabbi bumped into me in the hallway. And when I said, "Hello," he frowned without speaking and pushed his way by me. My problem is that the man's works are evil and his faith is dead to me. My personal frustration mounts daily.

So I visited the man in his home. At the end of the conversation, outside of the classroom, and with no witnesses, I told the man his actions turn me off and I have no respect for him. I am too stubborn to quit so I do not expect much of a grade from the man. Something must change; we are believers not combatants.

Allow me to speak to another very recent experience. Yesterday I ate lunch with a white seminarian from the South (Alabama). He was born in the South and raised in an Adventist home. He felt free enough to share with me his disdain for Martin Luther King, Jr. and the Civil Rights Movement. This was my first conversation ever with a resident Dixiecrat. We have a class together. I was much calmer than I would have predicted for myself. I simply asked why he had so many problems with black people standing up for their constitutional rights?

He told me it was easy to accept racial equality with me, "because you know you are not ignorant, lazy and stupid. If I accept Negroes as equals socially, I am immediately burdened with who I am."

I asked him, "What does that mean?"

He told me his grandfather and grandmother taught him that "we are superior to you. They taught me that whites brought savages to America and civilized them. We, whites, are obligated to keep a social distance from a less-developed people or we weaken the race. My parents are good people. They never used the 'N word' in my presence. But we never had a Negro enter our front door my whole life. My pastor preached that God made the races, and we go against God when we mix what he made pure.

"If I go with this King thing, I call my family, my culture, my society, and my God a liar. I lose my identity and I am not ready to jump into that pool. I actually believed God blessed America and gave this land to Europeans fleeing persecution. I believed white missionaries civilized black savages. I saw nothing wrong with keeping Negroes in their place.

> If God made the races, who are we to improve on God?"
>
> He told me his head tells him one thing with his new exposure, but his heart leads in another direction. He said when he returns home a black man will never sit at his dinner table. This man finished his confessional remarks by saying, "It is not my job to make the Gospel a social statement."
>
> Something needs to change, according to James. He knew personally about social, family, and religious pressure not to follow the teachings of his brother. For too long, he himself was confronted with the contradiction of ignoring Jesus in order to be at peace with custom, family, and religious leaders.

> Conclusion and Appeal
>
> Something is terribly wrong when the biblical text does not inform our social practice. Something is wrong when we define ourselves as God's remnant, or the commandment-keeping people, while not addressing a glaring fact of life. We misrepresent the royal law of James while teaching rules and regulations that separate us from one another.
>
> Faith without works is dead. This is not a negation of mercy and grace unto salvation. It is the Lord's reality that the Gospel is a person and He was extremely social. My appeal is simple. I can do better and will do better. Will you join me?[35]

It is important to note that this sermon points up the limitations of what we are calling Eurocentric theology, which is based on an Aristotelian worldview. Since the second and third centuries after Christ, and formalized during the European Enlightenment, biblical interpretation and Christian theology have assumed three major tenets: philosophical dualism; the rejection of mystery; and the propositional, rather than the relational, nature of truth.

Dualism posits the mutual exclusivity between two polarized opposites, demanding an either/or. A dualistic perspective rejects the possibility of paradox, a both/and. The rejection of paradox presents many difficulties in comprehending a biblical text that is replete with paradoxes. For example, consider the many church councils and unresolved debates on the nature of Jesus Christ. Was He human or divine? Dualism demands an either/or, while paradox allows Him to be both.

The sense empiricism of Western thinking rejects the possibility of mystery. "Empiricism is the theory that the origin of all knowledge is sense experience. It emphasizes the role of experience and evidence, especially sensory perception, in the formation of ideas, and argues that the only knowledge humans can have is *a posteriori* (i.e. based on experience)."[36] From this point of view, God can be fully known given correct methods of investigation. Whatever is not open to empirical tests is rejected. It is on this basis that many Western theologians dismiss the miracles of Christ or attempt to explain them in rational terms.

Probably the most insidious tenet of Western theology is the propositional nature of truth. Truth, from this perspective, is a set of doctrines, it is impersonal. Why is this notion so insidious? It strikes at the ultimate reality that Truth is, in fact, a Person. While there are many true statements, they are only "truths." The Truth is Christ. He is personal and relational. He must be known by the believer in order to provide the freedom of salvation (Jn. 8:32, 36). Often, we as Adventists assume that a correct knowledge of doctrine and scriptural propositions will lead to eternal life. This is a dangerous deception that allows us to substitute doctrinal correctness for the personal relationship with Christ and the reconciling love for one another that God requires.

In the sermon we just read, the ethnocentric comments by the white fellow seminarian illustrate this problem. This aspiring pastor no doubt understood the doctrines of the church, but his attitudes and prejudices reveal a total failure to appreciate the relational nature of the gospel.

Finally, Paul reminds us that all human knowing is at best partial. "We know in part" (1 Cor. 13:9). Theology from any one ethnic perspective is tainted by subjectivity, both individual and cultural, and points to the need for a "communal theology" that is based on the diversity within the body of Christ.

Western theological reflection in general, and Seventh-day Adventist theology with its emphasis on systematic theology in particular, are limited by an isolated perspective. Paul's allusions to the situation in Rome, and in the sermon above, to "ethnic theology" address an issue rarely raised in the Adventist community: is our theological reflection ethnocentric? Do we look at God from only one ethnic perspective in the body of Christ? Does our theological reflection suffer from the limitations of Aristotelian thinking? Can we engage in correct theological reflection if it is done in isolation from others in the body of Christ?

The Example of Christ

Paul brings his discussion of disputed matters to a close. He offers to Roman believers the example of Christ as the final resolution for their divisiveness (15:1-6). Paul brings his argument to closure by describing an enduring obligation of Gentiles in Rome. "Now we who are strong have an obligation to bear the weaknesses of those without strength, and not to please ourselves" (15:1 HCSB). Again, employing the categories of the weak and the strong as metaphors for Gentiles and Jews, Paul suggests one additional action to be taken by the Gentile majority.

Paul continues to identify with the strong in the controversy related to food and days (14:14). Yet, he now emphasizes the relational duty of those with correct knowledge, including himself. Using obligation language, Paul subtly suggests that Gentile believers have two overriding duties to those who are weak in faith: one positive, the other negative (13:8; cf. 14:1).

Positively, Gentiles are to bear with the failings of those without strength. Here, Paul uses an infinitive verb. He seeks to emphasize that it is an ongoing obligation of Gentiles to carry their Jewish brothers and sisters in the resolution of the controversy. His language has the sense of continual burden bearing—of suffering for the sake of those who are weak (cf. Gal. 6:2). On the other hand, Gentiles are not to use their position of advantage in this matter to please themselves. Paul uses a verb meaning "please, accommodate" negatively to prohibit self-satisfaction. Rather, Gentile believers are to forego their advantage to help their Jewish brothers and sisters (cf. 1 Cor. 10:33). Thus, Paul argues, "Each of us must please our neighbor for the good purpose of building up the neighbor" (15:2). With this maxim, Paul simply restates the necessity of seeking the good of others in the community, of building them up (cf. 12:9).

Paul shifts the tenor of his discourse. He recommends to Gentiles the example of Christ. "For even Christ did not please Himself" (15:3a NASB). Using a succinct indicative, Paul makes an exemplary claim about the character of Christ. He argues that Christ as man completely rejected self-centeredness—self-gratification. He did not use His incalculable advantage for His own benefit. Paul makes the same claim about Christ more comprehensively in his appeal for unity in Philippi. Again, we quote this seminal description:

> Make your own attitude that of Christ Jesus, who, existing in the form of God, did not consider equality with God as something to be used for His own advantage. Instead *He emptied Himself* by assuming the form of a slave, taking on the likeness of men. And when He had come as a man in His external form, He humbled Himself by becoming obedient to the point of death—even to death on a cross. For this reason God highly exalted Him and gave Him the name that is above every name (Phil. 2:5-8 HCSB).

By way of contrast, Paul quotes the Old Testament to describe further Christ's example. He states, "But, as it is written, 'The insults of those who insult you have fallen on me'" (15:3b; Ps. 69:9). The point of the quotation is clear. Rather than self-gratification, Christ bore unjustified shame for the benefit of sinful humanity.

With this scriptural illumination of the sacrifice of Christ as his predicate, Paul subtly urges imitation in the Roman assemblies. "For whatever was written in the past was written for our instruction, so that we may have hope through endurance and through the encouragement from the Scriptures" (15:4 HCSB). With these words, Paul emphasizes the teaching function of Scripture in the believing community. He suggests that believers may obtain hope based on attributes provided by Scripture.

Paul uses the term that means "endurance, constancy" with the sense of patient waiting. Then he uses the word, "encouragement" or "comfort," in the sense of consolation or solace. Paul's point is opaque, yet important. To embrace the sacrificial example of Christ, just shared from Scripture, believers must rely on the endurance and encouragement that come from Scripture. It is through mimicking the example of Christ revealed in Scripture that believers may continue to have hope (cf. 5:1-5). Yet, as Paul later explains, imitation of Christ requires God's power (cf. Eph. 2:10).

Paul now moves beyond the disputed matters. He begins a direct appeal for unity among Roman believers. "Now may the God of endurance and encouragement grant you to be of the same mind with one another according to Christ Jesus" (15:5; cf. 16:25). Continuing the language of imitation through benediction, Paul makes two critical points.

He moves from the description of Christ's example set forth in Scripture to the necessity of God's power to make Christ's life a living reality (cf. Eph. 2:10; Phil. 1:6; 2:12-13). Paul prays for unity among believers in Rome. In his supplication, he identifies God the Father as the source of the needed endurance and encouragement revealed in Scripture. More important, with the phrase "God . . . grant you to be of the same mind with one another," *Paul implies that the Roman believers are incapable of producing unity in and of themselves*. Building on his earlier maxim, "be in agreement with one another," Paul now asserts that in order for Roman believers to live in harmony, literally, "to think the same with one another," God must give them the power (cf. 12:16; Phil. 2:1-4; 1 Thess. 5:23). In short, believers must continually submit to God's Spirit (1:4; 8:3-30; 12:1-2).

Then Paul says that the fact of Gentiles and Jews living in harmony with one another is in "accordance with Christ Jesus." What is Paul saying? Could it be that he is suggesting that oneness in the body is synonymous with Christ's person and work? What is only implicit in this passage, Paul makes explicit in Ephesians.

> For he is our peace; in his flesh *he has made both groups into one* and has broken down the dividing wall, that is, the hostility between us. He has abolished the law with its commandments and ordinances, *that he might create in himself one new humanity in place of the two,* thus making peace, and, thus putting to death that hostility through it (Eph. 2:14-16).

According to Paul, one of the primary goals of Christ's incarnation, humiliation, and death was to create unity in His body!

Paul identifies the purpose of unity among believers in Rome. He writes, "So that together you may with one voice glorify the God and Father of our Lord Jesus Christ" (15:6 ESV). Here, Paul's intent is explicit. Employing unity language, he states that only as one people will Roman believers be able to glorify God, the Father of the believers' Lord Jesus Christ. Is it possible that Paul is actually suggesting that only through oneness in Christ's body is the full splendor of God in Christ revealed? (cf. Jn. 13:34-35; 17:20-26).

Finally, Paul comes to the end of the body of his letter and exposes its rhetorical high point. As an apostle of Christ, he commands, "Therefore welcome one another" (15:7a; 1:1). With the conjunction, "therefore," literally, "for this reason," Paul brings forward his previous discussion on oneness among believers in Rome (15:5-6). More important, with the words, "welcome one another," Paul issues the final and summary command in his sustained argument (1:18 - 15:13). He exhorts the Gentile and Jewish believers in Rome to embrace intimate acceptance of one another based on the example of Christ (15:7-13). Believers are not to mimic the world in their relations one to another. *Their model is Jesus Christ* (cf. 12:1-2).

Paul again uses the verb "welcome," but this time with a different intent (14:1, 3). Earlier, as part of his discussion on disputed matters, Paul had exhorted Gentiles to welcome Jews who believe that dietary regulation and special days of Judaism still have religious significance. He grounds the necessity of acceptance in the fact that God has accepted those weak in faith (14:3).

In this passage, Paul uses the term "*welcome,*" in a slightly different sense. Grammatically, Paul uses the Greek present imperative. This construction is used when the speaker, in this case Paul, commands the recipients, Roman believers, to a continual or habitual attitude or action. Further, the use of the present imperative enjoins an ongoing commitment, a continual way of living.[37] Beyond the matters in dispute in Rome, Paul now uses this command, welcome, to exhort Gentiles and Jews to a change of lifestyle. He enjoins a new permanent mutual intimacy.

And yet, the radical nature of Paul's imperative, welcome one another, cannot be fully appreciated without understanding the social implications of the term "welcome" in first century Greco-Roman society. When the verb translated, "welcome, accept, receive," was used in Roman culture, it carried the sense of friendship or hospitality. Its range of meaning included "to extend table fellowship," "taking or receiving into one's home," "receive into one's society" with "the collateral idea of showing kindness."[38] Yet, the radical nature of Paul's summary exhortation to mutual hospitality can only be fully understood when viewed against the backdrop of the criteria for friendship and hospitality in first century Greco-Roman culture for both Romans and Pharisaic Jews.

We should recall that Roman society was highly stratified. Both friendship and hospitality were only extended to persons of equal status. For the upper strata of Roman society, which embodied the ideal, friendship and hospitality required areas of commonality for full acceptance, including *ethnicity*. Wealth was important; and education was valued as well, but in and of itself did not guarantee high status.

> The Romans evaluated a person's status based on whether the person was a citizen or a foreigner, patron or client, free or slave, *ethnic Roman/Latin or not*, voluntary ally or conquered enemy, male or female, and married or unmarried. These categories each had a specific value for Romans. For example, a well-educated, wealthy, noncitizen, former slave would have been thought lower in status than a poor, uneducated, freeborn citizen.[39]

It is within this cultural environment that Paul exhorts believing Gentiles and Jews to mutual acceptance. We should also remember that for conservative Pharisaic Jews table fellowship could not be extended to Gentiles because they were ritually unclean. Although moderate Pharisees sought converts, their primary target was not Gentiles. Instead, they attempted to convert ethnic Jews to the traditions of ritual purity that Pharisees espoused. Paul, Josephus, and the gospel writers paint the Pharisees as a popular contemporary Jewish movement that tried to win other Jews to conform to conservative traditions related to tithing and ritual purity through table fellowship, which was the principal strategy used by Pharisees to gain adherents.[40]

With the imperative, welcome one another, Paul exhorts the ethnically divided Romans to embrace one another not just as friends, but as more than friends. Why? Because Gentiles and Jews are now part of one family—the family of God. Therefore, believers are to host each other in view of the fact that in Christ they are part of the same family (8:12-17). Despite their ethnic difference and the challenges arising from their cultural location, believers are to move beyond hostility and even tolerance of differences. Through the power of God's Spirit, they are to begin to practice the love of their different neighbors. Gentile and Jewish believers are to engage in social relations as one family (13:9-10; 15:2).

In addition, there is another dimension to the imperative: welcome one another. Given that the assemblies in Rome met in private homes, i.e., house churches, to worship, Paul's exhortation goes beyond a call to social intercourse, hospitality, or table fellowship (16:3-16). His apostolic command enjoins a common worship on the believers in Rome.[41] In spite of their cultural preferences and sensibilities, Paul exhorts believers to reject ethnically exclusive worship. He admonishes Gentles and Jews to begin to worship across ethnic lines. His call to joint worship in the body of Christ anticipates the worship of "a great multitude that no one can number, from every nation, from all tribes and peoples, and languages" worshipping with the heavenly host in the presence of God the Father and the Lamb (Rev. 7:9-12 ESV). Paul has already established that believers are to worship with one voice, a worship that anticipates eternity (15:6). Through the power of God in Christ, Paul now encourages believers in Rome to experience the eternal future as a present reality.

In light of Paul's appeal for mutual acceptance among believers in Rome, the following experience from a Colombian student points to the need for the same kind of acceptance among Adventists today.

> Born in Colombia, I was in Argentina studying at the Universidad Adventista Del Plata (UAP). It was the year 2014, and the FIFA World Cup soccer competition was being hosted in Brazil. The World Cup is an international competition that is contested every four years by the leading men's national soccer teams from 32 nations.
>
> When the time for the final game arrived every national group at the school separated and found somewhere to watch the game together. Most South American Christians prefer to watch the game with those of their own nationality, so they can cheer for their national team. But there is another reason for the separation: Brazilian, Chilean, and Argentinian Christians dislike each other and cannot watch the game together, because of the animosity and strife among them.
>
> Furthermore, at UAP, whenever Argentina and Brazil compete against each other, Argentinian students must be separated from Brazilian students. The school encouraged this division by putting the Brazilian students in the old sanctuary to watch the game, while the Argentinian students watched in the auditorium. In the semi-final World Cup game in 2014, Germany beat Brazil 7-1, which in soccer is a huge blow-out. All the Brazilian students at UAP were ashamed and sad, and all the Argentinian students poked fun and prodded the Brazilian students for at least a week. The Argentinians did this by constantly making jokes and disparaging the Brazilian students, composing songs and creating videos to rub it in.
>
> It is crucial to note that the soccer game is used as the measuring rod to determine the paramount nation in South America. The rivalry at the school was heightened by the fact that Argentina and Brazil are the two most powerful nations in South America, with Brazil being perceived as the most powerful due to its superiority in finances, land, and military might. So the Argentinian students took this opportunity to express their superiority as a nation over the other students, because their team had won all their World Cup playoff games leading up to the final game.

> This racial/cultural division among Adventists in South America is exemplified by the following experience. One Sabbath during the worship service at the UAP church the pastor during his sermon brought up the result of the match between Germany and Brazil and made fun of the Brazilians. When he did this, all the Argentines in the congregation said "Wooooooo!!!!" The preacher sought to calm the church, "So the Spirit of Jesus can return." I left the church in disgust.[42]

As Adventists we must ask ourselves whether or not this experience is unique in our colleges and universities. While Paul enjoins a worship experience anchored the acceptance of Christ for the glory of God, how do we account for the fact that a Seventh-day Adventist pastor in Argentina used the worship service to promote cultural pride and the humiliation of vulnerable students? What lessons are millennials around the world learning from our lack of one voice in worshipping God? But the larger question confronts us: how will Adventists worship together in the presence of God throughout eternity when we reject common worship in the present?

As he writes his summary admonition to Roman believers, Paul seems to recognize the impossibility of his exhortation based simply on human nature and cultural reality. Therefore, he couples his imperative, "welcome one another," with his summary indicative, "just as Christ also has welcomed you, for the glory of God" (15:7b; cf. 12:1). With this indicative, Paul establishes that the motivation and power for mutual acceptance must be rooted in the person and work of Jesus Christ. Christ Himself must be the basis of a new united community. Through his summary indicative, Paul reveals to believers in Rome the dimensions of mutual life in Christ.

By using the comparative conjunction, "just as," Paul signals that the welcome of Christ must be the model for mutual acceptance in the believing community. The standard is Christological, not political or cultural. Believers are to extend to one another the same welcome they have received in Jesus Christ, an acceptance characterized by His love, humility, and sacrifice (5:6-8; Phil. 2:1-9).[43] In this sense, Paul echoes the new command of Jesus to His eleven disciples before His passion. "I give you a new commandment, that you love one another. *Just as I have loved you,* you also should love one another. By this everyone will know that you are my disciples, if you have love for one another" (Jn. 13:34-35; cf. Lev. 19:18).

Paul uses the indicative, "Christ has welcomed you," to reiterate that through the sacrificial death of Christ believers are now in right relation with God. Believers have been reconciled, received into the divine family (3:21-26; 5:1-11; 8:12-17). It is on this basis that horizontal reconciliation is predicated and maintained. Believers must extend to one another what they have received from God in Christ to maintain right relation with God (Mk. 11:26; 1 Jn. 4:20).

With this indicative, Paul affirms the reality of believers' intimacy with Christ, both as individuals and more importantly, as His body. Thus, the welcome of Christ supplies security for unilateral action, whether as an individual or as a group. On this point, clarity is critical. Although Paul exhorts believers in Rome to mutual acceptance, their reception of one another is not predicated on reciprocity: I will accept you, if you accept me. Instead, believers must initiate unilateral acceptance, with no concern for the response of others, based solely on the fact that Christ has received the believer or believers. Christ frees believers to love with no regard for an in-kind response, but because they are loved (5:5-8; 1 Cor. 9:1, 19; Jn. 8:36).

In Paul's assertion, "Christ has welcomed you," the pronoun "you" is plural, not singular. Here, for Paul Christ's welcome is not just individual, it is communal. In fact, some biblical translations use the inclusive pronoun "us."[44] With this indicative, Paul testifies to the fact that Christ has welcomed all believers as His body. Through His blood, He has created one new humanity, in the place of two (Eph. 2:11-22). It is on this basis that Paul exhorts believers to welcome one another.

Paul provides the ultimate goal for Christ's welcome of both Gentile and Jewish believers. It is "for the glory of God" (1 Cor. 31:31; Col. 3:17). Based on this supreme theological aim, Paul either negates or makes secondary all other competing considerations in the believing community, whether ethnic, cultural, financial, or political. As mentioned earlier, Paul implies that unity in the body of Christ announces God's splendor and mirrors life within the Godhead (15:6).

Thus, with his summary imperative and indicative, "Therefore welcome one another as Christ has welcomed you, for the glory of God," Paul exposes the goal of the entire letter: mutual acceptance among the Roman believers, based on the acceptance of Christ, for the glory of God.

Seemingly to add perspective, Paul places his exhortation, "welcome one another," and its basis, "Christ has welcomed you, for the glory of God," within the scope of salvation history (15:8-12). He shares with the Roman believers the extent of God's plan of salvation through Christ (cf. 11:25-36). Paul begins by asserting the historical priority of Israel in God's saving activity through Christ. Then, he links it to the salvation of Gentiles. "For I tell you that Christ has become a servant of the circumcised on behalf of the truth of God in order that he might confirm the promises given to the patriarchs, and in order that the Gentiles might glorify God for his mercy" (15:8-9a).

In this passage, Paul uses language possibly drawn from the "Servant Song" of Isaiah to depict Christ as a servant or minister to the circumcised, the Jews, in fulfillment of the promises made to the fathers, Abraham, Isaac, and Jacob (9:5, 7-8). Paul's description of Christ as servant should be understood in the sense of the suffering servant in Isaiah (Is. 53:1-12). In salvation history, Christ came first to offer deliverance to the people of Israel through His sacrificial death (1:16; 3:29-30; 11:28, 30-31; cf. Mt. 15:24; Acts 3:25). Paul ties Christ's incarnation in fulfillment to promises made to the fathers to the salvation of Gentiles. For Paul, the Old Testament announces that Christ came not only to deliver the elect in Israel but also that the Gentile elect too might glorify God for His mercy (9:1 – 11:36).

Paul turns to the Old Testament to buttress his claim of Gentile inclusion in God's saving purpose. He quotes four passages to demonstrate that from the onset, Gentiles were part of the saving intent of God in Christ.

> As it is written, "Therefore I will confess you among the Gentiles, and sing praises to your name"; and again he says, "Rejoice, O Gentiles, with his people"; and again, "Praise the Lord, all you Gentiles, and let all the peoples praise him"; and again Isaiah says, "The root of Jesse shall come, the one who rises to rule the Gentiles; in him the Gentiles shall hope" (15:9b-12; Ps. 18:49; Dt. 32:43; Ps. 117:1; Is. 11:10).

In light of Paul's use of Scripture to foster unity, several questions may be raised. What would be the rhetorical force of these biblical quotations for Gentiles and Jews in Rome? Considering God's unifying purpose in Christ, how can Roman believers not be caught up in God's plan? Are their reasons for division more important than God's historical intent?

Finally, Paul closes his formal argument. He uses the language of benediction to stress the fact that Christ is the only hope for both Jews and Gentiles (cf. 5:3-5; 8:31-39). "May the God of hope fill you with all joy and peace in believing, so that you may abound in hope by the power of the Holy Spirit" (15:13). Paul ends with a prayer for corporate sanctification through the power of the Spirit (cf. 8:3-30).

So What? The Memphis Miracle

The Memphis Miracle occurred on October 18, 1994. But before we describe it, a bit of history is necessary.

The modern Pentecostal movement began with a white man, Charles Fox Parham, a somewhat controversial figure, in 1901. But its international expansion was experienced under the leadership of William J. Seymour, a black disciple of Parham, at the Azusa Street Mission in Los Angeles, California, beginning in 1906. The Azusa Street Revival led to the phenomenal growth of Pentecostalism in the decades that followed. The revival was distinguished by the breaking down of racial barriers in the context of a racist society. An often-quoted statement was, "The blood has washed away the color line." Unfortunately, the interracial fellowship at Azusa Street lasted only three years. By 1909, the Azusa Street racial unity came under attack by the secular media. White Pentecostals found themselves unable to resist the pressures of a racist culture. The racial segregation imposed by Jim Crow came increasingly into Pentecostal churches so that by 1924, the racial unity of Azusa Street had disappeared.

When the Pentecostal Fellowship of North America (PFNA) was established in Des Moines, Iowa, in 1948, all the participating churches were white. Over the years, there were attempts to heal the division between white and black Pentecostal churches, but the divide was too deep for reconciliation. The PFNA board came to the conclusion that only dramatic action could bridge the racial chasm.

The opportunity to begin the process of closing the gap came when Bishop B. E. Underwood was elected chairman of the PFNA board in 1991. Purposing in his heart to end the racial division, Underwood's first meeting with the board in 1992 resulted in a unanimous vote to pursue reconciliation with black Pentecostals. Underwood, a white leader, and Bishop Ithiel Clemmons of the Church of God in Christ (COGIC), a black leader, were the architects of the reunion.

A series of four meetings between whites and blacks over the next two years led to a plan for the historic meeting in Memphis, Tennessee, October 17-19, 1994. The conference, dubbed Pentecostal Partners: A Reconciliation Strategy for 21st Century Ministry, drew an interracial audience of over 1000 leaders for the morning scholars' sessions and 3000 attendees for the evening worship sessions.

The process that was presented for the Reconciliation Dialogue is notable. The first step was an examination of the historical roots of racial unity and division in the Pentecostal Church, followed by consideration of the problem of racism and discrimination. Then they would look for the biblical pattern for unity among believers, and finally focus on a strategy for reconciliation. There was a commitment to action, not just to dialogue. There was a plan to dissolve the old structure in favor of a new one during the conference.

The climactic moment of the conference occurred during the morning meeting of October 18th. Bishop Blake, a black leader, had just ended an impassioned presentation on the power of love to bring reconciliation, when Donald Evans, a white Assemblies of God pastor, approached the platform carrying a basin and a towel. Tearfully, he explained that he had been directed by the Holy Spirit to wash the feet of Bishop Clemmons and beg forgiveness for the sins of white Pentecostals against their black brothers and sisters.

Immediately, Bishop Blake approached Thomas Trask, the white General Superintendent of the Assemblies of God, and washed his feet as a sign of repentance for any animosity blacks had harbored against whites. A wave of emotion swept the audience who were convinced that this experience was an indication of the seal of the Spirit's approval for the proceedings. The next day, Dr. Paul Walker of the Church of God called this event the Miracle in Memphis, a name that stuck and inspired headlines around the world.

That afternoon, members of the PFNA convened for its final session. A motion was carried to dissolve the old all-white organization in favor of a new interracial entity that would be established the next day. On October 19th, a new constitution was presented to the delegates for the new Pentecostal and Charismatic Churches of North America (PCCNA). The new group adopted unanimously a Racial Reconciliation Manifesto, drafted by an interracial committee, which pledged to oppose racism, declared racism to be a sin, and promised to seek partnerships that would lead to oneness. Officers were elected, with Clemmons, a black man, as chairman, Underwood, a white man, as vice chairman, and a racially balanced board. While acknowledging that the road to reconciliation would not be easy, the constituent churches promised to pursue the eradication of racism in the Pentecostal/Charismatic community. There has been a ripple effect of the Memphis Miracle among other denominations.[45]

It should be acknowledged that Seventh-day Adventists disagree with much of the theology of the Pentecostal/Charismatic Movement, especially the role of the Holy Spirit, yet the Miracle in Memphis raises several questions. What do we make of Pentecostalism's response to the biblical call for unity in Christ? How do we explain the fact that white leaders were willing to divest themselves of political power and position in order to achieve oneness? What do we as Adventists make of the fact that Pentecostal whites were willing to repent and confess on the one hand, while Pentecostal blacks were willing to forgive and accept on the other? Are we as Adventists willing to submit to a restructuring conceived by Christ and communicated by the Holy Spirit?

---

[1] Victor Paul Furnish. *Theology and Ethics in Paul.* Louisville, KY: Westminster John Knox Press, 2009.

[2] Kathryn Tanner. *Theories of Culture* Minneapolis, MN: Fortress Press, 1997, pp. 24-28, internal quotation from Melvin Herskovitz. *Man and His Works.* New York, NY: Alfred A. Knopf, 1948, p. 625.

[3] Tanner, p. 28, internal quotation from Edward Reuter. In R. E. Park (ed.). *Race and Culture,.* New York, NY: McGraw-Hill, 1939, p. 191.

[4] Paul O. Wendland. The Apostle Paul and Culture. *Wisconsin Lutheran Quarterly* 2008; 105(Summer):4.

[5] Ibid.

[6] Ibid.

[7] Ibid, p. 6.

[8] Ibid.

[9] A. J. Malherbe. *Paul and the Popular Philosophers.* Minneapolis: Fortress Press, 1989.

[10] Ibid.

[11] Seneca. *De Clementia.* 1.5.1.

[12] Seneca, *Epistulae Morales.* 95.52.

[13] Philo. De *Specialibus Legibus.* 3.131; see Gerald Hawthorne, Ralph P. Martin, and Daniel G. Reid (eds.). *Dictionary of Paul and His Letters.* Downers Grove, IL: InterVarsity Press, 1993, and C. F. D. Moule *The Origins of Christology.* Cambridge: Cambridge University Press, 1978.

[14] Rollin A. Ramsaran. Paul and Maxims. In J. Paul Sampley (ed.). *Paul in the Greco-Roman World: A Handbook.* Harrisburg, PA: Trinity Press International, 2003, p. 430.

[15] It is noteworthy that the Greek term translated, "without hypocrisy" was not used in secular sources. It is used only in the New Testament (Rom. 12:9; 1 Tim. 1:5; 2 Tim. 1:5; 1 Pet. 1:22; Jam. 3:17). See Geoffrey W. Bromley. *Theological Dictionary of the New Testament (Abridged – Little Kittel).* Grand Rapids, MI: Eerdmans, 1985.

[16] Ceslas Spicq. *Theological Lexicon of the New Testament.* Peabody, MA: Frederickson Publishing, 1995.

[17] Ibid.

[18] Tacitus. *Annals* 13.

[19] Tacitus. *Histories* 5.5.

[20] James D. G. Dunn. *Word Commentary, vol. 38b, Romans 9-16.* Dallas, TX: Word, 1998; see Cicero. *For Flaccus* 28.67; Tacitus. *Histories* 5.5.1.

[21] The Editors of *Encyclopædia Britannica.* Fugitive Slave Acts: United States (1793, 1850). *Encyclopaedia Britannica.* britannica.com.

[22] Ellen G. White. *Testimonies for the Church*, vol. 1. Washington, DC: Ellen G. White Estate, p. 264.

[23] _____. Letter 16, 1861, para. 26.

[24] _____. *Spiritual Gifts*, vol. 4b. Washington, DC: Review and Herald Publishing, 1999 [1864], p. 42.

[25] Deming, Will. Paul and Indifferent Things. In J. Paul Sampley (ed.). *Paul in the Greco-Roman World: A Handbook.* Harrisburg, PA: Trinity Press International, 2003.

[26] James L. Jacquette. *Discerning What Counts: The Function of the* Adiaphora Topos *in Paul's Letters.* Atlanta, GA: Scholar Press, 1995.

[27] Ibid.

[28] J. Paul Sampley. *Walking Between the Times: Paul's Moral Reasoning.* Minneapolis: Augsburg Press, 1991.

[29] F. D. Nichol. *The Seventh-day Adventist Bible Commentary: The Holy Bible with Exegetical and Expository Comment.* Washington, D.C.: Review and Herald Publishing Association, 1978, p. 635.
[30] Ibid.

[31] Sampley. *Walking Between the Times.*

[32] Jonathan Klawans. *Impurity and Sin in Ancient Judaism.* New York, NY: Oxford University Press, 2000, p. 22.

[33] Ibid.

[34] Sampley. *Walking Between the Times.*

[35] Elliott Osborne.

[36] Empiricism. *The Basics of Philosophy.* philosophybasics.com.

[37] See Daniel B. Wallace. *The Basics of New Testament Syntax.* Grand Rapids, MI: Zondervan Press, 2000.

[38] Frederick William Danker and Walter Bauer. *Greek-English Lexicon of the New Testament and Other Early Christian Writers* (3rd ed.). Chicago, IL: University of Chicago Press, 2001. See also Johan Lust, Erik Eynikel, and Katrin Hauspin (compilers). *Greek-English Lexicon of the Septuagint* (rev. ed.). Peabody, MA: Hendrickson Press, 2012.

[39] Jeffers, p. 182.

[40] Jonathan Brumberg-Kraus. Were the Pharisees a Conversionist Sect? Table Fellowship as a Strategy of Conversion. In A. J. Levine and R. Pervo (eds.). *Approaches to Ancient Judaism: Jewish Proselytism.* Atlanta, GA: Scholars Press for the Society of Biblical Literature, 2002.

[41] See Francis Watson. The Two Roman Congregations: Romans 14:1-15:13. In Karl P. Donfried (ed.). *The Romans Debate.* Grand Rapids, MI: Baker Academic, 1991.

[42] Verbatim account from Nichelle Livingston Ward.

[43] Gregory J. Allen. *Reconciliation in the Pauline Tradition: Its Occasions, Meanings, and Functions.* Doctoral Dissertation. Boston University, School of Theology, 1995.

[44] *New American Standard Bible.* "Therefore, accept one another, just as Christ also accepted us to the glory of God" (Rom. 15:7). Some early manuscripts used the pronoun "us" rather than the plural "you."

[45] Vinson Synon. History, Memphis 1994: Miracle and Mandate. *PCCNA: Demonstrating Unity in the Power of the Spirit,* 2017. pccna.org.; The Story Behind the Foot Washing at eh 1994 "Memphis Miracle." Flower Pentecostal Heritage Center, July 13, 2011; Bishop B. E. Underwood. The Memphis Miracle. http://pctii.org/arc/underwoo.html.; Excerpt from B. E. Underwood's focus statement to the Racial Reconciliation Dialogue. *Legacy,* Number 4, Summer 1997, p. 6; Racial Reconciliation Manifesto. *Legacy,* Number 4, Summer 1997.

CHAPTER SEVEN
The Victor

Romans 15:14 - 16:27

Having appealed for mutual acceptance based of the example of Christ, Paul now brings his letter to a close. He reminds believers in Rome of his desire to visit them soon and then shares his immediate travel plans—plans that will benefit both Jews and Gentiles in his missionary enterprise. Further, Paul urges the Gentile majority to contribute to the welfare of impoverished Jews in Jerusalem. He reasons that Gentiles have benefited from the spiritual contributions from the Jews; therefore, Gentiles should be willing to share their material resources with Jewish Christians. Paul exhorts Roman believers to join in communal prayer for the success of his work in Jerusalem. He hopes that a united Roman community will serve as a forward base for his anticipated mission to Gentiles in Spain. Finally, with a ring of eschatological certainty, Paul warns both Gentiles and Jews to watch out for those believers in Rome who would foster ethnic division. He echoes Genesis 3:15: Satan's head will be crushed. Believers are to participate in God's victory in Christ. Paul's benediction, couched in the language of corporate sanctification, celebrates the mystery of God's power to enable believers to live out the gospel revealed in Jesus Christ.

Paul's Encouragement

After a straightforward correction, Paul encourages Roman believers by sharing his personal conviction about the genuineness of their conversion (1:11-12). "I myself feel confident about you, my brothers and sisters, that you yourselves are full of goodness, filled with all knowledge, and able to instruct one another" (15:14). Continuing the use of familial language, "my brothers and sisters," Paul builds up the ethos of his audience that he began in the introduction of his letter. He has already declared that Roman Christians are called to belong to Christ, called to be saints, and loved of God. In addition, he has extolled their faith in the salvation provided by God—a faith acknowledged in the entire believing world (1:8; cf. 16:19).

Now, Paul reassures the Roman believers, especially the Gentile majority, by adding to his earlier description of three convictions about their character. First, he describes the Romans as "full of goodness." Paul does not use the term translated "good," that was sometimes used in antiquity to describe an innate quality of absolute goodness (cf. Mk. 10:18); instead, he employs a cognate term to describe believers that suggests "generosity or beneficence." In fact, Paul uses the same word "goodness" to describe one of the fruit of the Spirit (cf. Gal. 5:22; Eph. 5:9). Paul may be stressing the Spirit-produced generosity of believers in Rome, a virtue in short supply in the Greco-Roman world.

Next, Paul acknowledges that believing Romans are "filled with all knowledge." Most likely he believes that they have received from God the knowledge necessary for salvation. With these words, Paul affirms that the believers in Rome have embraced *the knowledge* of righteousness by faith in Christ prior to his letter. Paul commends them for possessing a renowned faith (1:8, 12). However, as he has amply demonstrated, knowledge is good, but it is not enough; righteousness by faith must become a lived experience through the power of the Spirit. Finally, Paul says that believers Rome possess the ability to instruct one another. He uses a verb that means, "warn, caution, or reprove." With this description, Paul simply acknowledges that prior to his communication, God's Spirit has been at work among them, providing the ability for mutual instruction. One wonders, given the ethnic fragmentation in Rome, whether this instruction crossed ethnic lines.

Yet, despite their positive qualities, Paul reminds the Roman believers that they have spiritual weaknesses. "Nevertheless on some points I have written to you rather boldly by way of reminder" (15:15a). Paul seems to maintain the tension between encouragement and correction as integral to pastoral care (2 Tim. 4:2). Having acknowledged their gifts from the Spirit, Paul reminds believers in Rome that he has had to address directly some of their spiritual weaknesses. For their sake, he has pointed out Gentile arrogance towards Jews and Jewish judgmentalism toward Gentiles, resulting in carnal animosity and division (cf. 1:19-3:9; 11:13-24; 14:1 - 15:13).

Paul clarifies the apostolic reasons for his boldness. He says, "Because of the grace given me by God to be a minister of Christ Jesus to the Gentiles in the priestly service of the gospel of God, so that the offering of the Gentiles may be acceptable, sanctified by the Holy Spirit" (15:15b-16). Paul provides reasons for his correction of the Roman believers, especially the Gentile majority.

He has corrected Gentile believers based on his appointment by Christ as an apostle to the Gentiles. Paul has maintained from the beginning of his letter that he was appointed by Christ as the apostle to the Gentile nations (cf. 1:5; 11:13). Although the Gentile believers in Rome are the majority and enjoy a greater degree of cultural acceptance, Paul has corrected them in his role as an instrument of Christ. Paul is compelled to share the gospel of Christ (1 Cor. 9:16-17). Yet, embedded in his words is Paul's acknowledgement that his own appointment was based on the grace of God. He is able to correct the shortcomings of Roman believers because he himself had been corrected by Christ (Acts 9:1-9).

Paul now proclaims that his willingness to confront Gentiles in Rome is motivated by a desire to promote their good. He speaks with boldness because of his desire to present them as an offering sanctified through the Spirit (cf. 12:1-2). Paul uses priestly language to underscore his responsibility to work for the sanctification of those in Christ. From the beginning of his letter, Paul has made the case that although Roman believers are God's people, they are in need of spiritual growth.

They are in Christ; nevertheless, they need both corporate and individual sanctification (1:11-13, 17; 8:1).

Paul identifies the source of the success of his ministry to the Gentiles. He writes,

> In Christ Jesus, then, I have reason to boast of my work for God. For I will not venture to speak of anything except what Christ has accomplished through me to win obedience from the Gentiles, by word and deed, by the power of signs and wonders, by the power of the Spirit of God (15:17-19a).

Paul boasts in Christ Jesus about his mission to Gentiles. He acknowledges that all he has done has been accomplished by Christ working through him (cf. 1 Cor. 1:30-31). Specifically, Paul claims that Gentile obedience to the gospel has been achieved, not through his personal gifts or abilities, but through proclamation, and example, and miracles. In short, Paul's success in his ministry to Gentiles has come through the power of the Spirit of God (1:5; 10:17; 6:4; 8:11). With this description of his ministry, Paul shares a paradox of ministerial success that characterizes his service to Christ. In correction of those who boasted in their giftedness in Corinth, Paul writes,

> And when I came to you, brethren, I did not come with superiority of speech or of wisdom, proclaiming to you the testimony of God. For I determined to know nothing among you except Jesus Christ, and Him crucified. I was with you in weakness and in fear and in much trembling, and my message and my preaching were not in persuasive words of wisdom, but in demonstration of the Spirit and of power, so that your faith would not rest on the wisdom of men, but on the power of God (1 Cor. 2:1-4 NASB).

Paul moves from the success of his ministry to the scope of his mission. "So from Jerusalem all the way around to Illyricum, I have fully proclaimed the gospel of Christ" (15:19b NIV). Paul recounts a ministry that has included Jews in Jerusalem and extended to the Gentiles far as Illyricum, a "Roman province in the northwestern Balkan peninsula, stretching along the eastern coasts of the Adriatic Sea from the borders of Italy to Macedonia and inland as far as the Danube."[1] Paul's missionary strategy has focused on major cities. Thus far, he has fully proclaimed the good news of Christ in the eastern part of the Roman Empire (cf. Acts 19:21; 20:1-3). Why this narration? Paul is attempting to highlight the inclusiveness of his mission. He has sought to win both Jews and Gentiles to Christ—the motivation for his mission and the content of his proclamation (cf. 1 Cor. 9:19-23).

Before disclosing his immediate travel plans, Paul shares what has been the goal of his evangelistic mission and then uses a quotation from Isaiah to underscore his belief that his mission to the Gentiles is in fulfillment of biblical prophecy. "My aim is to evangelize where Christ has not been named, so that I will not build on someone else's foundation, but, as it is written: Those who were not told about Him will see, and those who have not heard will understand" (15:20-21). Paul asserts that the goal of his prophetic ministry is to evangelize Gentiles where Christ had not been preached. He intends to go only to virgin Gentile regions.

Yet, Paul's aim raises questions. How does his stated intent to only evangelize where Christ has not been named align with his foray into the affairs of Roman believers? On what basis does Paul justify his desire to visit believers in Rome and the sending of this letter?

The answer becomes clear when we recall that in the beginning of the epistle, Paul says that he will seek a harvest among Gentiles in Rome (1:13b). His goal is not to evangelize in the traditional sense; rather, Paul hopes that with his letter and a visit, he will be able to foster growth in Christ, to promote corporate sanctification. Paul realizes that unity among believers in Rome is not only critical to life in the Spirit. Unity among Gentiles and Jews in the believing community is also crucial to Christ's saving mission to the unbelieving western world (cf. Jn. 17:20-26).

Paul's Travel Plans

Paul now shares his travel itinerary. He skillfully weaves his plans with an additional incentive for Gentile and Jewish unity in Christ (15:22-33). Outlining his intentions, he writes, "This is the reason that I have so often been hindered from coming to you. But now, with no further place for me in these regions, I desire, as I have for many years, to come to you when I go to Spain" (15:22-24a). Paul restates his desire to visit the believers in Rome and intimates that he has been delayed by his missionary activity in the eastern part of the Roman Empire (1:11-13; cf. 15:19a). But now, Paul shares his plan to visit Spain, in the western empire, by way of Rome. He has completed his work among Gentiles in the east; now he envisions work in the west.

To make his missional goal a reality, Paul expects help from all believers in Rome. "For I do hope to see you on my journey and to be sent on by you, once I have enjoyed your company for a little while" (15:24b). Paul's suggestive language deserves notice. He makes several subtle points. Paul hopes to see all believers in Rome when he arrives, both Gentiles and Jews. He will not be content with just visiting his kinsmen. His language assumes a joint response. Paul expects to be sent on his way to Spain by all the Roman believers. He uses a verb that is a euphemism for support or sponsorship (cf. 1 Cor. 16:6, 11; Tit. 3:13; Acts 20:18). In other words, Paul expects all the believers in Rome to collectively support his mission to Spain.

Paul anticipates that by spending time with all the Roman believers he will be "satisfied or filled." He uses the language of fellowship—of social enjoyment. Taken together, Paul indirectly signals that in response to his letter, he anticipates unity when he arrives in Rome, and that a united community will support his mission to Spain. One can only wonder how this divided community would have reacted to Paul's optimistic expectations. Yet, Paul is confident that the Spirit is at work among believing Romans (15:14-15, 19, 30).

With this additional appeal for unity, Paul shares his immediate itinerary. "At present, however, I am going to Jerusalem in a ministry to the saints" (15:25; 1:7). Prior to his visit to Rome, he must fulfill a commitment made to Jewish believers in Jerusalem. These Jewish saints need financial aid (15:31; cf. Gal. 2:9-10; 2 Cor. 8:4, 19-20; 9:1-5, 12-13).

In keeping with his formational intent to establish oneness between Christian Gentiles and Jews, Paul argues that despite ethnic differences, believers are obligated to help one another. He writes,

> For Macedonia and Achaia have been pleased to make some contribution for the poor among the saints at Jerusalem. For they were pleased to do it, and indeed they owe it to them. For if the Gentiles have come to share in their spiritual blessings, they ought also to be of service to them in material blessings (15:26-27 ESV).

Paul here argues for an inherent reciprocity between Gentile and Jewish believers. His argument is three-dimensional. He uses the example of Greek believers in Macedonia and Achaia to establish his premise. He tells Roman believers that these Gentile Christians were pleased to make a financial contribution to help poor Jewish believers, i.e., the saints in Jerusalem. He did not use either manipulation or coercion while soliciting aid for the Jews among Greek believers. These Gentiles literally took pleasure in helping their Jewish brothers and sisters (2 Cor. 9:1-2).

Then, employing the language of obligation, Paul argues that Gentile contributors are indebted to believing Jews (cf. 1:14; 13:7). And last, with a hypothetical argument, Paul explains the basis for his reasoning. It goes something like this. If believing Gentiles have been partners in the spiritual things of the Jews, things that possess eternal value, then Gentile believers ought to serve Jewish believers with their material things, which have only temporal worth.

What is the significance of this argument for the situation among believers in Rome? Paul's hypothetical assumes an innate connection between Gentiles and Jews. He has used the metaphor of an olive tree with grafted wild branches to make the same claim about the relationship between Jews and Gentiles (11:17-21). Believing Gentiles and Jews belong to God and to one another, they are members of the same family. Paul subtly reminds his audience, especially Gentiles, of the priority of the Jews in salvation (1:16; cf. Acts 13:14-52). Indeed, Gentile believers have benefited from the spiritual things of Israel.

Paul summarizes his travel plans with a statement of confidence. "When therefore I have completed this and have delivered to them what has been collected, I will leave for Spain by way of you. I know that when I come to you, I will come in the fullness of the blessing of Christ" (15:28-29 ESV). Paul reiterates his expectation of a new situation on the ground when he visits Rome. He invokes the theological language of fullness. As in Colossians where he argues against his opponents who teach that Christ alone is insufficient for the salvation of believers—the so-called "Jesus plus" heresy—Paul maintains that all the fullness of God dwells in Christ, in fact, believers are made full in Him (Col. 1:19; 2:10). Paul expects the fullness of Christ's blessing, that which issues from Him, to be visible among believers when Paul comes to Rome. We must remember that Roman Christians are highly visible in early Christianity. Paul has said that their faith is renowned worldwide (1:8). Is Paul subtly suggesting that his mission to Spain would be jeopardized by continued division in Rome? To what extent does ethnic, racial, tribal, and caste division among Adventists jeopardize our worldwide end-time mission?

Finally, Paul concludes with an entreaty and a prayer (15:30-33). He begins with the words, "I appeal to you, brothers and sisters, by our Lord Jesus Christ and by the love of the Spirit, to join me in earnest prayer to God on my behalf" (15:30). Again, using the language of family, Paul makes the second of three appeals in his letter. His first appeal was for Roman believers to live their lives in view of the mercies of God, to live in response to God's undeserved salvation in Christ (12:1). Paul's final appeal will be for the believers in Rome to reject the work of those who would divide the community (16:17-18).

Here he appeals for a common prayer. He knows that his mission to Jerusalem is dangerous because of his gospel (15:31). Therefore, Paul urges the whole community to petition God on his behalf. Paul first anchors his appeal in the reality that all believers have a common Lord, Jesus Christ, and are partakers of a common love, the love of God through the Spirit (5:5-8; cf. Eph. 4:4-6). Then, he uses his appeal for prayer to foster unity. The infinitive used by Paul translated "to join" can also mean "strive together, make common effort, contend alongside," and is found nowhere else in the New Testament.[2] Paul employs this language to urge the ethnically divided Romans to come together in prayer for the success of God's mission through him.

Paul closes his appeal by sharing his concern and hope. He states, "That I may be rescued from the unbelievers in Judea, and that my ministry to Jerusalem may be acceptable to the saints, so that by God's will I may come to you with joy and be refreshed in your company" (15:31-32). Paul wants believers in Rome to pray for three things. First, that he be rescued from unbelieving Jews and Judaizers in Judea. Although Paul shares the same ethnic identity with the Judeans in Jerusalem, his primary identity in Christ ties his fate to the prayer of his true brothers and sisters in Rome, both Gentiles and Jews.

Second, believers are to pray that the material gifts from Gentiles be acceptable to the Jewish saints in Jerusalem. Although Paul does not say it, it is possible that he fears Jewish prejudice and exclusivity that would argue for the continued separation of Gentiles and Jews.

Third, Gentiles and Jews are to pray that he might finally be able to visit believers in Rome and experience the refreshment of a united community. Paul ends his appeal with a prayer for Roman Christians. "The God of peace be with all of you. Amen" (15:33). He again places the emphasis on communal peace through God (cf. 5:1; 8:6; 14:19; 15:13; 16:20).

Paul's Closing Argument

Paul comes to the end of his letter to believers in Rome. With his purpose of reconciliation and unity still in mind, he moves from commendation to exhortation, from warning to doxology. Paul begins by commending a woman to the Roman assemblies. "I commend to you our sister Phoebe, who is a servant of the church in Cenchreae. So you should welcome her in the Lord in a manner worthy of the saints and assist her in whatever matter she may require your help. For indeed she has been a benefactor of many—and of me also" (16:1-2 HCSB). He commends Phoebe to the entire community, using a verb, variously translated "commend, recommend, give approval to."

Paul uses the term "commendation" negatively in his questions to believers in Corinth. He asks, "Are we beginning to commend ourselves again? Or do we need, as some, letters of recommendation to you or from you?" (2 Cor. 3:1). In context, Paul rejects self-commendation, which was tantamount to boasting based on one's own achievement. His purpose is to undercut the work of the so-called super-apostles who have entered Corinth through self-commendation, eloquent speech, and flattery. Paul condemns these men as "false apostles," accusing them of Satanic deceit (2 Cor. 10:12, 18; 11:1-15). He can also use commendation positively as here in the case of Phoebe, who he recommends to both Gentile and Jewish believers in Rome. Yet, Paul's commendation of Phoebe raises two questions. Who is she? On what basis does Paul commend her to the believers in Rome?

The name Phoebe is mentioned only in this passage in Scripture; therefore, a profile can be constructed based solely on the information provided here. In these verses, Paul provides several pieces of information about this woman. Paul uses the Greek name *Phoibē,* translated, "Phoebe," which means "bright, radiant." In antiquity, this name was associated with the moon goddess Artemis. Because her name was associated with idolatry and Greek mythology, Phoebe was most likely a Gentile convert.[3] Paul refers to Phoebe as "our sister." This appellation is consistent with his use of familial language throughout the letter to affirm the spiritual relationship among those in Christ.

Paul calls Phoebe a servant of the church in Cenchreae. The term "servant" had a wide range of meaning in antiquity that included waiter, deacon, servant, minister, and even courier.[4] Because of this range of meaning, Phoebe's precise role is unknown. What can be said with certainty is that she was a Christian worker, a servant of Christ, affiliated with an assembly of believers in Cenchreae, a port city in Corinth (Acts 18:18; cf. 12:7). Paul describes Phoebe as a patron or benefactor. He uses a technical term that means "patron(ess), assistant," only here in his letters[5] (cf. 12:8b, 13). In Greco-Roman culture, a patron engaged in acts of beneficence to gain honor.

The Greco-Roman society of Paul's time was a highly stratified structure of vertical relationships of dependency. With the Caesar, the ultimate benefactor, at the pinnacle of this patron-client system, everyone else was in a client relationship to his or her patron and in a patron relationship to one or more clients of lower status. Clients could be clubs, communities, and entire provinces, as well as individuals. The patron provided material resources, sponsorship, protection, legal services, and even public buildings to clients. Clients in return gave loyalty, political support, and public acclaim. The patron, a person of wealth and status, accrued the highly valued commodity of honor from this system.[6]

In the first two centuries of the Christian era, there was no such thing as church owned buildings. Congregations met for worship in the private homes of wealthy patrons. In the larger cities, there were too many members to meet in the home of one patron, so several "house churches" coexisted. Paul cites five house churches in Corinth and its satellite town of Cenchreae, including the group that met in the home of Phoebe.[7]

Paul depended on several patrons who supported his missionary activities, hosted him, and provided helpers. He mentions such people in his letters, but the only person he actually names as a patron is Phoebe. She apparently supported many Christian workers in addition to Paul. But in the case of her relationship with Paul, Phoebe is paradoxically both patron and client. Paul also terms her a sister and a servant, and calls on other Christians to provide her with hospitality when she travels. In this case, Paul acts as a patron in her behalf, writing her letters of commendation as a patron would do. The fact that the traditional patron-client relationship was dynamic in the early church, and that it could be reversed, speaks to the equality that existed among Christians.[8]

Thus, Phoebe was most likely a believer who possessed material wealth and supported or sponsored many believers, including Paul. While using the language of patronage, Paul subtly redefines its meaning in Christ. We should note that of the three terms used to describe Phoebe, our sister, servant, and patroness, Paul places the culturally significant descriptor, patron, last. In so doing, he undercuts another value in Roman culture (12:1-2). He prioritizes familial relationship in Christ and service for believers over patronage. In summary, although it cannot be definitively proven, based on her name and the city in which she resides, Phoebe is most likely a

Gentile convert of Greek origin. She is a servant leader of the church in Cenchreae. She clearly uses her wealth and the status her means afford her to benefit other believers in the prosecution of the gospel.

Next, the question, on what basis does Paul commend Phoebe to the believers in Rome? Before addressing this question, background information is needed.

> Commendation was an instrument of power in the Greco-Roman world. By means of commendation letters, powerful patrons endorsed clients and friends to their social peers throughout the Roman Empire, including Asia Minor and Greece, the heart of the Apostle Paul's missionary activities . . . . Paul also used commendation in his letters to endorse supporters in his churches.[9]

Typically, persons were commended based on high status and meritorious deeds. With this background, the reason for Paul's commendation of Phoebe to Roman believers becomes clear. He does not commend Phoebe based on her status, mirroring Greco-Roman hierarchy. Paul rejects the cultural norms of Roman society (12:1-2). He views such a use of commendation as carnal (2 Cor. 3:1; 10:12, 18; 11:1-15). Rather, Paul commends this conceivably Gentile believer because, as a sister in Christ, she serves His church and uses her resources to benefit His body, especially those engaged in spreading the gospel (cf. 12:8, 13; 15:27).

If, as the evidence suggests, Phoebe was a Gentile patroness who became a believer, then Paul provides an example of a wealthy Gentile woman of status who used her means to serve both Gentiles and Jews to further the gospel of Christ. Paul encourages the entire community to accept her in the Lord and to stand by her in whatever ways she needs help. Although it cannot be said with certainty, it is very likely that this kind of servant of Christ is the bearer of Paul's letter to Rome.

Paul moves from commending Phoebe to the Romans to exhorting all Roman believers to greet twenty-six believers among them. He states,

> Greet Prisca and Aquila, who work with me in Christ Jesus, and who risked their necks for my life, to whom not only I give thanks, but also all the churches of the Gentiles. Greet also the church in their house. Greet my beloved Epaenetus, who was the first convert in Asia for Christ. Greet Mary, who has worked very hard among you. Greet Andronicus and Junia, my relatives who were in prison with me; they are prominent among the apostles, and they were in Christ before I was. Greet Ampliatus, my beloved in the Lord. Greet Urbanus, our co-worker in Christ, and my beloved Stachys. Greet Apelles, who is approved in Christ. Greet those who belong to the family of Aristobulus. Greet my relative Herodion. Greet those in the Lord who belong to the family of Narcissus. Greet those workers in the Lord, Tryphaena and

> Tryphosa. Greet the beloved Persis, who has worked hard in the Lord. Greet Rufus, chosen in the Lord; and greet his mother—a mother to me also. Greet Asyncritus, Phlegon, Hermes, Patrobas, Hermas, and the brothers and sisters who are with them. Greet Philologus, Julia, Nereus and his sister, and Olympas, and all the saints who are with them. Greet one another with a holy kiss. All the churches of Christ greet you (16:3-16).

In analyzing Paul's greeting list, it is important to observe that throughout most of the list (16:3-15), Paul uses the imperative form of the verb translated "greet." This term also carries the idea of enfolding in the arms, welcome.[10] In these verses, Paul employs the term as a command seventeen times; sixteen times of specific persons, or of households, and a final time in commanding mutual greetings among Roman believers with a holy kiss (16:16). It is also important to note that this list, enjoining personal greeting, is unique in Paul's letters. He only uses the imperative mood five times in all his other letters combined, most often to urge mutual greeting among believers (2 Cor. 13:12; Phil. 4:21; 1 Thess. 5:26; cf. Col. 4:15; 2 Tim. 4:19).

Although Paul's list enjoining greeting of particular believers will not be treated in detail, three questions are critical to a possible understanding of how this list functioned. Why does Paul begin his command for the community to greet Prisca and Aquila? What can be known about the ethnic composition of the names on the list? Why does Paul employ this unique device, that is, how does the list function in his overall purpose?

Paul begins his list with an exhortation for all believers to greet Prisca and Aquila. "Greet Prisca and Aquila, who work with me in Christ Jesus, and who risked their necks for my life, to whom not only I give thanks, but also all the churches of the Gentiles. Greet also the church in their house" (16:3-5). Before analysis of his description of this couple, a sketch of what is known about Paul's relationship with Prisca and Aquila is in order.

Luke preserves a brief history in the book of Acts:

> After this, he left Athens and went to Corinth, where he found a Jewish man named Aquila, a native of Pontus, who had recently come from Italy with his wife Priscilla because Claudius had ordered all the Jews to leave Rome. Paul came to them, and being of the same occupation, stayed with them and worked, for they were tentmakers by trade . . . So Paul, having stayed on for many days, said good-bye to the brothers and sailed away to Syria. Priscilla and Aquila were with him. He shaved his head at Cenchreae because he had taken a vow. When they reached Ephesus he left them there, but he himself entered the synagogue

> and engaged in discussion with the Jews (Acts 18:1-3, 18-19 HCSB).

Based on Luke's description, important elements emerge. Paul meets Aquila and his wife Prisca (Priscilla), possibly for the first time in Corinth. Aquila was a Diaspora Jew born in Pontus, and most likely, Prisca was also of Jewish ancestry. Paul meets Aquila and Prisca sometime after 49 A.D., after their exile with other Jews from Rome. As mentioned in the introduction, Luke's reference to Prisca and Aquila provides biblical and historical evidence for the expulsion of Jews from Rome by Claudius. Paul, Aquila, and Prisca shared a common trade. They were leather workers. Aquila and Prisca assisted Paul in his missionary work, traveling with him to Syria and Ephesus.

Now in his letter to Rome, Paul singles out Prisca and Aquila for special consideration (1 Cor. 16:19; 2 Tim. 4:19). He provides reasons for this attention. He describes Prisca and Aquila as literally as "my fellow workers in Christ Jesus." This couple is to be recognized, because under exigent circumstances, they have assisted Paul in his mission to the Gentile world. Although the Roman authorities had treated them unjustly, forced them from their home in Rome because of their ethnicity, and heaped shame on them because of their banishment, Prisca and Aquila continued to serve the Lord and labor for the conversion of unbelieving Gentiles. Thus, for Paul, Prisca and Aquila provide an example of faithfulness to Christ despite ethnic injustice (cf. 2 Cor. 11-23-28).

By insisting that the whole Roman community greet Prisca and Aquila, especially the Gentiles, Paul undercuts their shame within the culture. He had already established the principle through metaphorical language in his letter to Corinth,

> The members of the body that seem to be weaker are indispensable, and those members of the body that we think less honorable we clothe with greater honor, and our less respectable members are treated with greater respect; whereas our more respectable members do not need this. But God has so arranged the body, giving the greater honor to the inferior member, that there may be no dissension within the body, but the members may have the same care for one another. If one member suffers, all suffer together with it; if one member is honored, all rejoice together with it (1 Cor. 12:22b-26).

The faithful Jews, Prisca and Aquila, shamed by Roman authorities, are to be given special recognition in the body of Christ.

For Paul, Prisca and Aquila are to be greeted by all believers because they "risked their necks for my life." Rightly understood, Paul's point is not just personal but missional. Christ has appointed Paul as the apostle to the Gentiles. Prisca and Aquila have assisted him to the point of death so that he could fulfill his mission to the Gentile world. This is most likely why he adds, "Not only do I thank them, but so do all the Gentile churches" (16:4b). Finally, Paul's exhortation for all believers to greet Prisca and Aquila is to be extended to the assembly, i.e., the church that meets in their home. Given the ethnic division in Rome, the church hosted by this Jewish couple is most likely Jewish. Therefore, Gentile assemblies are to greet, enfold in their arms, their Jewish brothers and sisters meeting in Prisca and Aquila's house (cf. 15:7).

Before addressing the question of how the greeting list functioned, a cursory analysis of the list reveals that Paul uses several descriptors within the list. He uses the language of coworker or worker to describe Prisca and Aquila, Mary, Urbanus, Tryphaena and Tryphosa. He makes either direct or indirect reference to five assemblies meeting in private homes: the assembly of Prisca and Aquila, the household of Aristobulus, the household of Narcissus, the brothers and sisters who are with Asyncritus, Phlegon, Hermes, Patrobas, Hermas, and finally all the saints who are with Philologus, Julia, Nereus and Olympas. Paul uses a term of endearment, "beloved," to refer to Epaenetus, Ampliatus, Stachys, and Persis. He refers to Apelles as "approved in Christ" and to Rufus as "chosen in the Lord." Paul employs language that suggests a shared Jewish heritage; he refers to Andronicus, Junia, and Herodion as relatives.[11]

Based on an analysis of first-century names, Peter Lampe has concluded that Jews were in the minority among the believers in Rome.[12] In light of this analysis, Paul's list may function in two ways. First, although Paul is not known to most believers in Rome, this list indicates that he is known to some. Thus, Paul would be aware of the situation among believers in Rome. He has Gentile and Jewish informants who are familiar with the issues among believers. Additionally, in anticipation of what he hopes is an imminent visit, Paul exhorts believers to begin the process of breaking down the barriers through a simple greeting. Gentiles and Jews are admonished to cross the ethnic divide in order to welcome faithful Gentiles and Jews known to the apostle Paul (cf. 15:7). Moreover, it is worth noting that Paul ends his greeting list by urging this divided community to show mutual affection, one to another. These believers are to physically, greet one another with a "holy kiss." A kiss made possible only through the Spirit of Christ!

Christ the Victor

Paul closes his letter with an appeal, an eschatological insight, further greetings, and a doxology (16:17-27). Here, he issues a third and final appeal to believing Romans (cf. 12:1; 15:30). "Now I appeal to you brothers and sisters to watch out for those who cause divisions and create obstacles contrary to the teachings which you have learned. Avoid them" (16:17). Again, using the language of family, Paul appeals to all Roman believers. Paul enjoins awareness, constant vigilance. He urges Roman Christians to continually watch out for certain believers, most likely from within the community (cf. Phil. 3:17-18). Paul identifies who they are by what they do. He argues that these are false teachers—those that cause divisions and create obstacles in opposition to the teachings the Romans have learned.

Paul uses critical language to describe the activities of these persons. He employs a term meaning "division, dissension, disunion." Paul uses this word only one other time in his letters as part of a vice list identifying activity contrary to life in Christ: an activity that disqualifies a person from salvation. His list reads,

> Now the works of the flesh are obvious: fornication, impurity, licentiousness, idolatry, sorcery, enmities, strife, jealousy, anger, quarrels, *dissensions*, factions, envy, drunkenness, carousing, and things like these. I am warning you, as I warned you before: those who do such things will not inherit the kingdom of God (Gal. 5:19-21).

In Greco-Roman usage, the term *dissensions* carried the sense of either "causing . . . two groups in place of one group," or "more frequently . . . in terms of attitudes . . . to cause people to be angry at one another or to cause people not to like one another or to cause people to think of one another as enemies."[13] In context, Paul accuses some members of the believing assemblies in Rome of promoting disunity and factionalism. Paul also uses the term, literally, "obstacle," or stumbling block, to describe the activities of these evil doers. He has used this language before when discussing disputed matters, urging believers to forego actions that would cause others to fall (14:13, 21). Now, he couples the word "obstacles" with "divisions" to refer to activity that is designed to undermine unity in Rome between ethnic groups.

Paul is not specific about the obstacles employed by these members. He has criticized Jewish judgmentalism and Gentile arrogance and any who use disputed issues to foster disunity. Yet, it is clear that Paul views these members as false teachers because, through their divisive activity, they seek to overturn the gospel and its implications for unity in Christ. This is the very gospel that Roman believers know and that Paul has painstakingly explained in his letter (16:25; cf. 1 Tim. 1:3; 6:3).

Paul intensifies his appeal with a terse apostolic command. He urges Roman believers to avoid them. Believers are not to associate with members of the assemblies who foster carnal disunity (cf. 1 Cor. 5:9-13). According to Scripture, the only legitimate cause for division is that which is created by humanity's response to the person and work of Jesus Christ (Mt. 10:34-39). Believers are not to fellowship with those who willfully attempt to create factionalism on any grounds, whether based on ethnicity, race, tribe, or caste.

However, Paul goes deeper. He discloses specifically why these persons are to be avoided. "For such people do not serve our Lord Christ, but their own appetites" (16:18a). With this invective, Paul supplies the motivation of the false teachers seeking to divide the Roman community. He uses rhetorical comparison to stress his point. On the one hand, Paul argues that these teachers do not serve the Lord. Literally, they are not slaves of Christ. From the beginning and throughout his letter, Paul has established voluntary enslavement to God in Christ as the very essence of sanctification (cf. 6:15-23; 8:3-11; 13:14).

For Paul to say that these false teachers do not serve the Lord is a grave indictment. It is tantamount to saying that they are enemies of the cross. They have rejected the Lordship of Christ and the Spirit's work of sanctification (6:19; Phil. 3:18 cf. Pro. 6:19). On the other hand, Paul says that these persons are motivated by their appetite. Paul uses a term that literally means, "belly, stomach," as a metaphor for that which pertains to carnal desire, to that which is earthy rather than spiritual.[14] In describing the Judaizers to the believers in Philippi, Paul uses similar language: "Their end is destruction; *their god is the belly;* and their glory is in their shame; their minds are set on earthly things" (Phil. 3:19).

With this contrasting metaphor, Paul depicts these false teachers as being motivated by carnality. They are slaves to self-interest, to culture, rather than to Christ. He accuses these teachers of idolatry, of placing their ethnocentric agendas over the person and work of Christ. In short, they advocate life according to the flesh. This figurative language may suggest that these teachers benefit personally from their divisive activity. They may use division for personal gain, whether theological—disputed matters—political, social, or economic (cf. 2 Pet. 2:3).

Moreover, Paul argues that these false teachers are to be avoided because they employ deceptive methods to achieve their divisive ends. He states, "by smooth talk and flattery they deceive the hearts of the simple-minded" (16:18b). Here, Paul identifies the ways these false teachers accomplish their goal. They use smooth talk. Paul uses this term that may be translated, "good words, plausible speech" only here in his letters. Culturally, this word carried the idea of eloquence, of "attractive speech involving pleasing rhetorical devices."[15] In context, Paul suggests that these teachers are using good words for nefarious ends (Col. 2:4; 2 Pet. 2:3).

Then Paul says, the false teachers employ flattery to accomplish their purpose. Paul uses a culturally explosive term with the sense of "excessive praise." As we have seen, rhetoric, or persuasive speech, was highly valued in Greco-Roman society. Speakers were idealized into diametrically opposed character types and professions. The most common positive examples included teachers, mothers, nurses, philosophers, friends, generals, and moral guides, among others. These were all people involved in persuading, guiding, supervising, and caring for others. They were viewed as reliable and trustworthy; there was perfect harmony between their words and their actions.

Negative examples were flatterers, demagogues, and related character types—people who were pretentious, charlatans, obsequious, and "the friends of many." These flatterers were hypocritical persons who had only their own advantage in mind; they spoke in order to please. Able to adapt in speech and behavior, flatterers were changeable as chameleons. Among their representative professions was prostitution[16] (cf. 1 Thess. 2:5-6).

Paul states that both uses of speech have one goal: to deceive the naïve in order to promote division. By using a verb meaning "deceive, beguile," Paul subtly connects the methods of the false teachers with those of Satan. This connection is made explicit in a letter to Corinth. "But I am afraid that as the serpent deceived Eve by his cunning, your thoughts will be led astray from a sincere and pure devotion to Christ" (2 Cor. 11:3; cf. 1 Tim. 2:13-14).

Shortly, using eschatological language, Paul makes the same explicit connection (16:20). In sum, Paul exposes the false teachers in Rome as those who use persuasive arguments and insincere praise calculated to deceive. He is unambiguous about their carnal purpose. They seek to foster division among the innocent in Rome. In so doing, these "leaders" are working against the peace of God that believers now have through Christ (1:7; 5:1; cf. Eph. 2:14).

The Satanic work of division in the church does not only characterize the first century, it is alive and well in contemporary times. Consider the following account.

The 1990 Southern California Conference Constituency Session[17]

> *In 1990, the Southern California Conference of Seventh-day Adventists took a radical change of direction in their historic approach to conference leadership. The conference structure had been based on ethnic division—Anglo, Black, Asian, and Hispanic. Each group had a coordinator who, together with an assigned board, oversaw the work among the churches of their own ethnicity. But in 1990 the conference decided to reorganize the territory based on geographic location rather than ethnic distinction.*
>
> *The plan was to divide the conference territory into four regions with each area being supervised by a vice president. The Area Vice Presidents were to be chosen from the four groups, one Anglo, one Asian, one Black, one Hispanic. They were to oversee the work in four geographic areas. They would serve as members of the Conference Executive Committee and the Administrative Committee, among others. But the plan would not to go through as smoothly as some hoped. There would be opposition. Even before the session took place, a deep divide between laity and clergy was revealed.*
>
> #### ***Pre-session***
>
> *In anticipation of the triennial session, some of the pastors stated their opposition. One ethnic group went so far as to lobby their prospective vice president to refuse the position and drop out of the process. They contacted him by phone and argued that the proposal was an affront to their right to self-determination. In their view, the structural change was deliberately meant to water down their authority. Though unstated, the pastor sensed an underlying fear of the loss of control over "their" constituency. He was offered the VP position and he accepted.*

During the session

As the proposal came to the session floor for discussion, the laypeople supported it in great numbers, while many of the clergy were dubious, if not openly opposed. The majority of the laypeople felt the change was long overdue. They lined up at the microphone to express their support and at one point the line stretched to the back of the auditorium. Some asked the question, "What took us so long?" The lay support for the plan crossed cultural lines, and in the end it was voted by a sizeable majority.

Post-session

After failing to stop the proposal from being voted, some members of the clergy continued their assault on it. Pastors pressured the conference president to return to the old format at the next triennial session. They made it clear that their support for his reelection was at stake. In 1993, the conference went back to the old structure.

Our informant states that conference laypersons expressed their opinion that unity was what God requires. That is why they were overwhelmingly in support of the restructuring along geographical rather than racial and ethnic lines. It was as if they were chastising conference leadership for taking so long to carry the church in this direction. We must ask ourselves if we as the "remnant church" are unwitting proxies for Satan in the Great Controversy when we implement and maintain ethnocentric and divisive church structures?

Paul continues to encourage Roman Christians and then provides a critical insight. "For while your obedience is known to all, so that I rejoice over you, I want you to be wise in what is good and guileless in what is evil. The God of peace will shortly crush Satan under your feet. The grace of our Lord Jesus Christ be with you" (16:19-20). Paul commends the obedience of the Roman believers with rejoicing (1:5; 15:14). Yet, he also continues to exhort them to appropriate discernment using the same rubric of good versus evil introduced earlier. Believers are to be wise in good, but innocent in evil (12:1-2, 9).

Paul again uses the phrase "the peace of God." His initial use of "peace" celebrates the new standing received by believers through the death of Christ that reconciled believers to God, along with the resulting necessity and power for reconciliation among believers. Paul has demonstrated that the death of Christ resulted in the union of believing Jews and Gentiles into one new humanity (1:7; 5:1-11; 15:13; 15:33; cf. Eph. 2:15-16).

In the present passage, with the phrase, "the peace of God," Paul again uses eschatological language. This time it is not related to human accountability (13:11-14). Paul uses God's peace as a metaphor for the certainty of the final defeat of Satan through Christ. The expression, "the peace of God," coupled with the phrase "will soon crush Satan under your feet," echoes the first promise in the Old Testament. The allusion is to the promise in Genesis,

> The Lord God said to the serpent, "Because you have done this, cursed are you among all animals and among all wild creatures; upon your belly you shall go, and dust you shall eat all the days of your life. I will put enmity between you and the woman, and between your offspring and hers; he will strike your head, and you will strike his heel" (3:14-15).

In the New Testament, these verses from Genesis were interpreted as a Messianic prophecy, a promise of Christ's final victory over Satan (cf. 1 Cor. 15:24-27; Heb. 2:14; Rev. 20:1-4). Thus, the interpretation, his heel refers to Christ, the offspring or seed of the woman, that would be bruised, prefiguring His sacrificial death. The head of the serpent refers to Satan, who will receive a fatal wound, predictive of the Messianic victory.

Therefore, with the expression, "the God of peace will soon crush Satan under your feet," Paul echoes the central claims of his earlier doxology. Although Satan, the adversary, may bring a charge against God's elect, Christ is victorious and believers are now more than conquerors in Him (8:33-39; Col. 2:14-15; cf. Lk. 10:18-19). With this language, Paul broadens the scope of his final appeal (16:17-18). Believers in Rome are to understand that the divisive activities of the false teachers fall within the scope of the Great Controversy, the cosmic conflict between good and evil, Christ and Satan.

Thus, in context, Paul identifies Satan as the malevolent power that stands behind the false teachers who promote ethnic division in Rome. These teachers are wittingly or unwittingly proxies for Satan. They are functioning in the controversy as the offspring of the serpent whose defeat is sure. Roman believers are to resist the demonic activity of the false teachers corporately and individually through the power of God (Eph. 6:12-12; cf. Jam. 4:7; 1 Pet. 5:6-11; 1 Jn. 3:8-10)

Paul ends his eschatological insight describing Satan's certain defeat with a Christological benediction invoking the power of grace for the assemblies: "The grace of our Lord Jesus be with you" (16:20b). Here, grace is Christ's power made available to defeat the adversary between the times (5:20; 8:37; cf. 2 Cor. 12:9). Writing to believing communities in Asia Minor, Paul put the same eschatological conclusion this way:

> In him we have redemption through his blood, the forgiveness of sins, in accordance with the riches of God's grace that he lavished on us. With all wisdom and understanding, he made known to us the mystery of his will according to his good pleasure, *which he purposed in Christ,* to be put into effect when the times reach their

> fulfillment—*to bring unity to all things in heaven and on earth under Christ* (Eph. 1:7-11 NIV).
>
> God put this power to work in Christ when he raised him from the dead and seated him at his right hand in the heavenly places, far above all rule and authority and power and dominion, and above every name that is named, not only in this age but also in the age to come. *And he has put all things under his feet and has made him the head over all things for the church, which is his body, the fullness of him who fills all in all* (Eph. 2:20-23).

Final Praise

Before his final doxology, Paul shares the greetings of seven believers with his Roman audience. While Tertius, his secretary, offers a personal greeting, Paul identifies seven men, Timothy, Lucius, Jason, Sosipater, Gaius, Erastus, and Quartus, who have either served with or facilitated his mission to the Gentiles in the eastern empire (16:21-23). In his list, Paul shares bits of information about those sending greetings to the house churches in Rome. For example, he describes Timothy as his co-worker. In several of his letters, Paul indicates that Timothy was a significant member of his missionary team and was considered a dear son (1 Tim. 1:1-2; 2 Tim. 1:1-2; Thess. 3:1-2). In addition, Luke's history indicates that Timothy was a product of mixed parentage, his father being Greek and his mother being Jewish (Acts 16:1-2). Timothy's background no doubt aided Paul's work among Gentiles.

Paul identifies Lucius, Jason, and Sosipater as his relatives or kinsmen, signaling their Jewish ethnicity (16:21). Next, he shares that Gaius is his host as he writes his letter from Corinth to Rome. If the Gaius mentioned here is the same person mentioned elsewhere in the New Testament, then he was possibly a Gentile convert living in Corinth, born in Derbe (1 Cor. 1:14; Acts 20:4). Paul describes Erastus as the administrator, or treasurer, of the city. While the city that he served is not mentioned, the fact that he held an administrative position in one of the municipalities of the Roman Empire suggests that he was most likely Gentile (cf. Acts 19:22). Finally, Paul shares the greeting of Quartus. He is only mentioned here in the New Testament, and Paul describes him simply as our brother, an appellation he uses for those in Christ.

Why this list of greeters? Although it cannot be stated with absolute certainty, the evidence suggests that Paul, the apostle to the Gentiles, chose a diverse evangelistic team composed of both Jews and Gentiles. It is also likely that Paul uses this list of greeters to model unity of purpose and mission without regard to ethnicity. If this reading is accurate, as we have noted earlier, then Paul rejects ethnically exclusive evangelism, the so-called "homogeneity principle," made popular in modern times based on church growth theory. The idea is that only persons of the same ethnic group can reach people of that ethnic group. As you will recall, this heresy contradicts Paul's evangelistic dictum made to those in Corinth (1 Cor. 9:19-23). Paul asserts that he follows the incarnational approach of God in Christ (2 Cor. 5:19-20; Mt. 1:23; Jn. 1:14). For Paul, ethnic sameness is not the key to missional success: it is extending the love of God through Jesus Christ.

Paul ends his letter with praise to God for God's saving plan in Christ. Paul's doxology picks up themes from his introduction and echoes his earlier doxology (cf. 1:1-17; 11:33-36). He states,

> Now to Him who has power to strengthen you according to my gospel and the proclamation about Jesus Christ, according to the revelation of the mystery kept silent for long ages but now revealed and made known through the prophetic Scriptures, according to the command of the eternal God to advance the obedience of faith among all nations—to the only wise God, through Jesus Christ—to Him be the glory forever! Amen (16:25-27 HCSB).

In this doxology, Paul restates claims made in his letter about God to remind the Roman believers of God's sovereign glory in Jesus Christ (cf. 2 Cor. 4:4-6). Paul reminds the believers that God alone has the power to strengthen them. He uses the language of sanctification that characterizes the letter's opening. Roman believers possess a renowned faith; nevertheless, they need spiritual growth. Believers need the very life of Christ as individuals and as a body (1:11-12, 16-17; 6:1-4; 12:1-2; cf. Col. 1:27).

God has set Paul apart for the proclamation of what he earlier called the gospel of God (1:1). Now in his doxology, he reminds believers of the importance of his gospel articulation and its implications for sanctification, communal and individual (Gal. 1:8; cf. 2 Cor. 11:4). Paul stresses that his gospel announces holistic righteousness through Jesus Christ alone (1:1-4, 16-17).

Paul uses the term "mystery" to underscore God's sovereign foreknowledge made known through the prophetic Scriptures (1:2; cf. 15:9-13). Unlike the Greek mystery cults of the first century that promoted the necessity of esoteric knowledge possessed only by the initiated, Paul uses mystery to refer to both the revelation of Jesus Christ and the union of believing Gentiles with believing Jews into the people of God (cf. 11:25, 33, 36; Eph. 3:3-5, 8-9; Col. 1:25-27).

Paul reminds Roman believers, especially the Gentile majority, that God has commanded him to bring about the obedience of faith among all nations. As in his introduction, Paul argues for an understanding of salvation based solely on trusting God's work in Christ, which expresses itself in complete submission (cf. 1:5; 15:15-19).

Finally, Paul praises the plan of God (cf. 11:31-36). In his earlier doxology, he extolled the depth of the riches and wisdom and knowledge of God (11:33). Paul closes his letter echoing the same praise. Because of God's wisdom mediated through the person and work of Christ, God is worthy to receive eternal glory. Amen.

So What? Reconciliation

This story begins within the context of the history of apartheid in South Africa and its impact on the Adventist church. As mentioned in the introduction, apartheid, "apartness," the racial policy of the South African government from 1948 to 1994, provided for the complete segregation of whites and blacks in every aspect of life: social, educational, residential, and economic. Whites held the franchise in all areas and blacks were severely discriminated against and disenfranchised. Many faith communities violated their central beliefs to accommodate apartheid, turning a blind eye to the violent state machine that brutalized black Africans. The Seventh-day Adventist Church was one of the faith communities that participated wholeheartedly. Support for apartheid was easy for Adventists, because a great deal of racial separation and discrimination against black Africans had long been the practice of the church.[18] As two authors note,

> the Adventist church was always far ahead of the government of the day in applying racial segregation in the church, and far behind when it comes to scrapping racially discriminatory measures. By the time apartheid was introduced in law after 1948, Adventists had been practicing it for twenty years or more.[19]

During the time of the Truth and Reconciliation Committee hearings (1995-1998), the Seventh-day Adventist Church in South Africa, in 1997, issued a statement confessing sins of omission and commission with regard to apartheid and asking for forgiveness from God and from its fellow citizens.[20]

The General Conference in 1997 began to mandate the restructuring of South African segregated church conferences and missions to bring Afrikaners, Africans, Coloureds, and Indians into interracial configurations. Unlike the South African government, the church did not engage in a truth and reconciliation process, nor was there any effort to educate the church through Bible study and prayer to prepare for the mergers.

Now to our story. It was 1997. We, along with our guide, an Afrikaner professor from Helderberg College, had driven the Garden Route from Johannesburg to Cape Town. Along the way we visited Adventist believers in their homes, in churches, and in several townships, including Soweto.

There was widespread resentment among the Afrikaner pastors we encountered as we taught along the Garden Route. They railed against the hypocrisy of the General

Conference in forcing them to unite racially while the races in North America were in divided church structures. Young pastors complained that they were leading large churches for which they were ill-prepared, because the more experienced pastors had fled to Canada, Australia, and New Zealand in the face of forced integration.

At the end of the trip, we were scheduled to meet with all the Adventist pastors in the Cape Town area: African, Afrikaner, English, Indian, and Coloured. This was to be the first such inclusive meeting of South African pastors since the end of apartheid in 1994.

It was in this historical and contemporary context that God commissioned us to share the message of reconciliation and unity from Paul's letter to the Romans with the pastors. On the night before the meeting, the Helderberg professor and a local Coloured church administrator questioned us about our presentation. When they discovered the proposed topic, both were vehement in their objections. They said that we should not broach this topic; we would only stir up trouble and then leave.

After we prayed together before retiring, we were led by the Spirit to hold to our original plan. The next day we shared Paul's message of reconciliation and unity with the pastors. The response was unforgettable. At the end of the presentation, one pastor, speaking for the group, said, "We do not have the vocabulary to understand what you are saying to us." In a real sense, the belief in and practice of apartheid in Adventism had nullified the gospel of Jesus Christ.

The pastors then expressed a desire for additional Bible study on this topic and indicated that they would need more support in the difficult journey toward unity. As we all studied Romans together that morning, Africans, Afrikaners, Coloured, Indian, English, and African Americans, the presence of the Spirit was evident.

In anticipation of the working of the Spirit, a communion service had been planned. We will never forget the scene during the ordinance of humility. Pastors set aside their ethnic divisions, and, like Jesus, picked up basins and towels to wash one another's feet across racial lines.

When we returned to the United States, a report was made to the General Conference.[21] Was there any follow-up? Unfortunately, not; we did not build on what the Holy Spirit had started that morning in Cape Town. Skeptics will say, "See, it did not last; it will never happen." But they are wrong. The good news for God's remnant is that Jesus' commandment for mutual love and His prayer for oneness will become a reality through the power of the Spirit. The question for us as individuals and as a church is whether we will be a part of what Jesus is doing.

---

[1] A. C. Myers. *The Eerdmans Bible Dictionary*. Grand Rapids, MI: Eerdmans, 1987, p. 515.

[2] Frederick William Danker and Walter Bauer. *Greek-English Lexicon of the New Testament and Other Early Christian Writers* (3rd ed.). Chicago, IL: University of Chicago Press, 2001; Horst Balz and Gerhard Schneider (eds.). *Exegetical Dictionary of the New Testament* (vol. 3). Grand Rapids, MI: Eerdmans, 2003.

[3] James D. G. Dunn. *Word Commentary, vol. 38b, Romans 9–16.* Dallas, TX: Word, 1998.

[4] Danker and Bauer. See also Johan Lust, Erik Eynikel, and Katrin Hauspin (compilers). *Greek-English Lexicon of the Septuagint* (rev. ed.). Peabody, MA: Hendrickson Press, 2012.

[5] Ibid.

[6] James S. Jeffers. *The Greco-Roman World of the New Testament Era: Exploring the Background of Early Christianity.* Downers Grove, IL: InterVarsity Press, 1999.

[7] Peter Lampe. Paul, Patrons, and Clients. In J. Paul Sampley (ed.). *Paul in the Greco-Roman World: A Handbook.* New York, NY: Trinity Press International, 2003.

[8] Ibid.

[9] Efrain Agosto. Paul and Commendation. In Sampley, p. 101.

[10] Geoffrey W. Bromley. *Theological Dictionary of the New Testament (Abridged – Little Kittel).* Grand Rapids, MI: Eerdmans, 1985.

[11] See Peter Lampe. The Romans Christians of 16. In Karl P. Donfried (ed.). *The Romans Debate.* Grand Rapids, MI: Baker Academic, 1991.

[12] Ibid.

[13] Johannes P. Louw and Eugene A. Nida. *Greek-English Lexicon of the New Testament: Based on Semantic Domains.* Stonehill Green, UK: United Bible Societies, 1999.

[14] Danker and Bauer.

[15] Louw and Nida.

[16] Clarence E. Glad. Paul and Adaptability. In Sampley.

[17] A verbatim perspective on the Southern California Conference of Seventh-day Adventists Constituency Meeting, April 29, 1990.

[18] Jeff Crocombe. *The Seventh-day Adventist Church in Southern Africa—Race Relations and Apartheid.* A paper presented at the Association of Seventh-day Adventist Historians meetings, April 19-22, 2007, at Oakwood College, Huntsville, Alabama.

[19] I. F. du Preez and Roy H. du Pre. *A Century of Good Hope: A History of the Good Hope Conference, its Educational Institutions and Early Workers, 1893-1993.* East London: Western Research Group/Southern History Association, 1994, p. 116.

[20] Quoted in Antonio Pantalone. A Missiological Evaluation of the Afrikaanse Konferensie (1968-1974) and its significance for the Seventh-day Adventist Church in South Africa. DTh, University of Durban-Westville, 1998, p. 307.

[21] At the time, Gregory, a co-author of this book, was employed at the Ellen G. White Estate.

Epilogue

What have we learned? In face of the unprecedented hatred and division in the global society that is mirrored in Christianity, even in Adventism, God's solution for ethnocentrism among believers, ancient and post-modern, *is Jesus Christ.* No doctrinal, political, or social justice solution will suffice. The theological idea that a believer can have a relationship with God while being indifferent to others for whom Christ died is fanciful. "The nearer we get to Christ, the more clearly we discern our unity with all who belong to him."[1]

What is needed today is a demonstration of eschatological unity that mirrors the oneness that is God, irrespective of ethnicity, race, tribe, and caste: a manifestation of God's love in Christ made available through the Spirit. Corporate sanctification, just as individual sanctification, is ultimately a spiritual matter. The Holy Spirit must be allowed to form our thinking, living, and serving. It is through the Spirit that Christ is experienced as the Risen Lord.

We close with Paul's prayer. "May the God of steadfastness and encouragement grant you to live in harmony with one another, in accordance with Christ Jesus, so that together you may with one voice glorify the God and Father of our Lord Jesus Christ. Welcome one another, therefore, just as Christ has welcomed you, for the glory of God." Amen.

---

[1] F. B. Meyer. *Joshua: And the Land of Promise.* Fort Washington, PA: CLC Publications, 2002, p. 190.

Made in the USA
Coppell, TX
23 June 2021